# DATE DUE

| NO 22 '96 | | | |
|-----------|---|---|---|
| FE 9'09 | | | |
| | | | |
| | | | |
| | | | |
| | | | |
| | | | |
| | | | |
| | | | |
| | | | |
| | | | |
| | | | |
| | | | |
| | | | |
| | | | |
| | | | |
| | | | |

DEMCO 38-296

# The Successor States to the USSR

# The Successor States to the USSR

John W. Blaney, editor

Congressional Quarterly Inc.
Washington, D.C.

Printed in the United States of America

Cover design: Tina Chovanec, Corvallis, Oregon

**Library of Congress Cataloging-in-Publication Data**

The successor states to the USSR / John W. Blaney, editor
        p.     cm.
    Includes bibliographical references and index.
    ISBN 0-87187-979-4.—ISBN 0-87187-978-6 (pbk.)
    1. Former Soviet republics — Politics and government. 2. Former Soviet republics — Foreign relations. I. Blaney, John W.
    DK293.S83      1994
    947.086 — dc20                                                        94-46162
                                                                              CIP

*For R. S-B., M. E. B., Marla, and Vanessa,
and to the memory of M. D.*

# Contents

# Foreword

Following the breakup of the Soviet Union into fifteen successor states, the Foreign Service Institute (FSI) was faced with a major challenge in preparing personnel for assignment to new embassies in new countries. Languages such as Ukrainian, Georgian, Latvian, Lithuanian, Estonian, Belorussian, East Armenian, Azerbaijani, Uzbek, Kazakh, Kyrgyz, Tajik, and Turkmen were added to the curriculum, bringing to sixty-three the number of languages taught at FSI. The Institute's School of Area Studies urgently needed course materials that reflected the dramatic changes in this vast area. Most of the literature in the field had been overtaken by events or failed to take sufficient account of burgeoning new issues and problems.

The materials in this collection will help meet the acute need for authoritative background materials for use in training the next generation of American diplomats in what many would agree is the most critical region for U.S. foreign policy today. It is hoped that the materials printed in this collection will have equal resonance and utility for U.S. businesses seeking to understand and penetrate untapped markets, as well as for academic specialists and others interested in emerging trends in what was once the Soviet Union.

FSI's new seventy-two-acre National Foreign Affairs Training Center (NFATC) in Arlington, Virginia, has adopted an "Agenda for Change" designed to provide innovative and cost-effective training to strengthen American diplomacy and leadership in a changing world. This volume forms part of the agenda for change in area studies. It was published through the good offices of the Association for Diplomatic Studies and Training (ADST), a private, nonprofit organization founded in 1986 to enhance U.S. government training in foreign affairs and to encourage the study of American diplomatic history. ADST, located with the Foreign Service Institute on the NFATC campus, seeks to strengthen contacts between the Foreign Service Institute and nongovernmental groups and individuals in the foreign affairs field. *The Successor States to the USSR* represents part of that effort. The book benefited from the personal attention and support of ADST's president, Ambassador Stephen Low.

We were particularly fortunate to have as editor John Blaney, FSI's 1992-1993 area studies course chair for the successor states. Mr. Blaney was ably assisted by Mary Louise Bothwell. Patrick Bernuth and Jeanne Ferris of CQ Books were a pleasure to work with and models of forbearance in responding to momentous changes within the successor states. The resulting work, drawing on the different perspectives of leading academics and foreign affairs practitioners, represents the personal, and sometimes conflicting, viewpoints of the authors rather than those of the U.S. government.

Richard L. Jackson
Dean, School of Area Studies
Foreign Service Institute

# Contributors

**John W. Blaney** is a senior member of the U.S. Foreign Service. He is currently serving as the U.S. deputy representative on the Economic and Social Council of the United Nations and as minister-counselor for economic and social affairs at the U.S. mission to the United Nations. He served as minister-counselor for economic affairs at the U.S. embassy in Moscow from 1988 to 1991. Subsequently, he was named chairperson for the successor states at the Foreign Service Institute. He also worked on nuclear arms control negotiations, including START and INF. He was the chief State Department negotiator of the U.S.-Soviet Nuclear Risk Reduction Center Agreement. Earlier, Mr. Blaney served in Congress as a legislative assistant on defense and arms control issues. He also worked in the U.S. Treasury Department, the Arms Control and Disarmament Agency, and in Africa. Mr. Blaney was an army officer and teacher at West Point. His degrees are from Syracuse University and Georgetown University.

**Murray Feshbach** is research professor of demography at Georgetown University. He is coauthor of *Ecocide in the USSR: Health and Nature Under Siege* (Basic Books, 1992). He holds a Ph.D. in economics from The American University and served as the first Sovietologist-in-residence at NATO headquarters, working under the secretary-general, Lord Carrington.

**Michael Gfoeller** is a foreign service officer assigned to the U.S. embassy in Moscow. From 1991 to 1993 he was a member of the U.S. mission to the European Economic Community. He served in the U.S. embassy in Moscow from 1989 to 1991.

**Paul A. Goble** is a senior associate at the Carnegie Endowment for International Peace. Before joining the endowment in 1992, he was special adviser for Soviet nationality problems and Baltic affairs at the U.S. Department of State. Author of numerous studies on ethnic conflict and nationality policy in the

USSR and the post-Soviet states, he is most recently coeditor of *International Relations in Russia and the CIS* (in Russian) (Moscow: ITS "AIRO-XX," 1994).

**John P. Hardt** is associate director and senior specialist in post-Soviet economics at the Congressional Research Service. He is also adjunct professor of economics at George Washington University. He holds a Ph.D. from Columbia University. He has edited, coordinated, and contributed to many volumes on the economies of the former Soviet Union, Eastern Europe, and the PRC for the U.S. Congress.

**Henry R. Huttenbach** is director of the Russian and East European Studies Program at the City College of New York and an associate of the Harriman Institute at Columbia University. He is editor in chief of *Nationalities Papers,* a semiannual publication of the Association for the Study of the Nationalities of CIS and Eastern Europe. Mr. Huttenbach received his Ph.D. from the Russian and Far Eastern Institute at the University of Washington.

**Richard L. Jackson** is dean of the School of Area Studies at the Foreign Service Institute. A senior foreign service officer with the rank of minister counselor, Mr. Jackson has served in Somalia, Libya, Greece, and Morocco, where he was deputy chief of mission and political counselor at the consulate general in Casablanca. He has also served as special assistant to the under secretary for political affairs in Washington and as political adviser at the U.S. mission to the United Nations.

**Phillip J. Kaiser** is a consultant at the Congressional Research Service of the Library of Congress specializing in economic and trade issues of the former Soviet Union and East-Central Europe.

**Robbin Frederick Laird** has published several studies of the nuclear posture of the Soviet Union and the new dynamics of security policy in the former Soviet Union. With his consulting firm, International Consulting Associates, he works with the Institute for Defense Analyses in Alexandria, Virginia, on strategic, political, and economic issues affecting Western Europe and the successor states to the USSR.

**Eugene K. Lawson** is president of the U.S.-Russia Business Council. He was vice chairman of the Export-Import Bank of the United States from 1989 to

1993 and deputy under secretary of labor for international affairs from 1988 to 1989. In the early 1980s he served as deputy assistant secretary of commerce, with responsibility first for East-West trade and subsequently for East Asia and the Pacific. He is the author of two books on China and has taught at Georgetown University.

**John W. R. Lepingwell** is assistant professor of political science at the University of Illinois at Urbana-Champaign. During 1992-1994, while on leave from the University of Illinois, Dr. Lepingwell was a senior research analyst at the Radio Free Europe/Radio Liberty Research Institute in Munich. He has published widely on Soviet and Russian civil-military relations and Russian and Ukrainian nuclear weapons policy and relations. He received his Ph.D. in political science from MIT in 1988.

**Steven E. Miller** is director of studies at the Center for Science and International Affairs in the John F. Kennedy School of Government at Harvard University. He is also editor of the quarterly *International Security*. Previously, Mr. Miller served as senior research fellow at the Stockholm International Peace Research Institute (SIPRI) and taught defense and arms control studies in the Department of Political Science at the Massachusetts Institute of Technology. He is editor or coeditor of numerous books, including *Cooperative Denuclearization: From Pledges to Deeds* (1993), *America's Strategy in a Changing World* (1992), and *Europe and Naval Arms Control in the Gorbachev Era* (1992).

**Martha Brill Olcott** is a professor of political science at Colgate University and senior fellow at the Foreign Policy Institute in Philadelphia. She received her Ph.D. from the University of Chicago. She has performed research supported by the Kennan Institute, the U.S. Department of State, Harvard University, the MacArthur Foundation, and the U.S. Institute of Peace. She is the author of numerous books and articles, including *Religion and Tradition in Islamic Central Asia*.

**Tönu Parming** is president of Estonian Publishing Company, Ltd., in Toronto. Earlier he was associate professor of sociology and codirector of the Russian Area Studies Program at the University of Maryland and director of Soviet and East European studies at the Foreign Service Institute, U.S. Department of State. He has been a visiting professor of sociology and professor of

Estonian studies at the University of Toronto and visiting professor of Estonian history at the University of Tartu.

**Ilya Prizel** is a professor at The Paul H. Nitze School of Advanced International Studies of The Johns Hopkins University in Washington, D.C.

**Thomas W. Robinson** is president of American Asian Research Enterprises. He teaches Chinese and Russian politics, Asian international relations, and Chinese foreign policy at Georgetown University and has been director of the China Studies Program at the American Enterprise Institute. He earned his Ph.D. in international relations from Columbia University and is the author of 9 books and more than 150 articles in diverse fields.

**S. Frederick Starr** is president of The Aspen Institute and the author of numerous books on Russian history, culture, and politics. In recent years he has focused on the historical roots of the emergence of private economic activity and civil society in Russia and other states carved from the former USSR.

**Angela E. Stent** is associate professor of government at Georgetown University and former director of Georgetown's Russian Area Studies Program. She has published widely on Soviet and Russian relations with Germany, on German foreign policy, and on East-West economic relations and technology transfer. Her publications include *From Embargo to Ostpolitik, Areas of Challenge for Soviet Foreign Policy in the 1980s, Technology Transfer to the Soviet Union: American and West German Perspectives, Soviet Energy and Western Europe,* "The One Germany," "Women in the Post-Communist World: The Politics of Ethnicity and Identity," and, most recently, "Ukraine's Fate."

**Orest Subtelny** is professor of history and political science at York University. He is the author of several books, including *Ukraine: A History,* which is now a standard history text in Ukraine.

**Roman Szporluk** is M. S. Hrushevskyi Professor of Ukrainian History at Harvard University. He is author of many publications on Ukrainian, East European, and Russian history and politics, including, most recently, "Reflections on Ukraine after 1994: The Dilemmas of Nationhood," *The Harriman Review* (March-May 1994): 1-10; and "After Empire: What?" *Daedalus* (Summer 1994): 21-39. He is the editor of *The Influence of National Identity,* volume 2, in

*The International Politics of Eurasia: Newly Independent States*, ed. Karen Dawisha and Bruce Parrott (Armonk, N.Y.: M. E. Sharpe, 1994).

**John E. Tedstrom** is a senior economist and associate director of the Center for International Security and Defense Policy at the RAND Corporation. He holds a Ph.D. in economics and Russian and East European studies from the University of Birmingham, England.

**J. Michael Waller** is vice president of the American Foreign Policy Council. He is also executive editor of *Demokratizatsiya: The Journal of Post-Soviet Democratization*. He received his Ph.D. in International Security Affairs from Boston University and is author of *Secret Empire: The KGB in Russia Today* (Boulder, Colo.: Westview, 1994).

# 1 Introduction

## John W. Blaney

The end of the Soviet Union was a superquake of history. Its many impacts and continuing aftershocks are difficult to measure but even harder to overestimate. Many bilateral, regional, and even global relationships based largely on the bipolar struggle of the Cold War era have been flattened or shaken badly. Since the end of Soviet history in late 1991, key institutions around the world have been struggling to adjust and reinforce their foundations in order to brace, not for the end of history, but rather for its complication and seeming fragmentation.

Even mighty NATO had no choice but to begin its search for a new identity following the demise of the Soviet empire and the Red Army. Controversial decisions on new missions, such as NATO's intervention in the war in Bosnia, have been agonizing. This and other aggravating questions, such as the composition of NATO's future membership, reflect understandable uncertainty within the alliance over some very basic issues. After all, without the Berlin Wall and the hammer and sickle over the Kremlin, who and where is the enemy?

NATO's introspection and adjustments are, however, still being guided by historical benchmarks. The threat of a massive Red Army invasion is gone, but NATO's other and, indeed, original mission and raison d'être, that of ensuring peace and security among the countries of Europe, is sadly still valid.

Other key European institutions hit by this tidal wave of history may not have such durable anchors. It is hardly a coincidence, for example, that the pace of Western European unification slowed markedly just as the Soviet Union's decline accelerated. The European Community's long-awaited event of 1992, billed as the great leap forward in European economic integration and

The views and opinions expressed here are the author's and do not necessarily represent those of the Department of State. The content of the other essays in this volume is the sole responsibility of their respective authors.

1

eventual unification, was tripped up by an even bigger jolt—the end of Soviet history. As exogenous, unifying pressures lifted, a general reassessment of interests and a reassertion of local identities naturally began in the European Community and throughout Europe. With the Czechoslovak Federation divorcing into two new states, the *Zeitgeist* of unity in Western Europe was dispelled and postponed, at a minimum.

Even outside Europe, the still-unfolding consequences of the Soviet collapse have been impressive. Important security relationships have unraveled or been altered on both sides of the old bipolar world. An extreme example is a still communist, but now very isolated Cuba. But profound change can be found on the "winning" side as well. The downsizing of the U.S. military and the withdrawal of U.S. forces from the Philippines would have been hard to envision had East-West competition persisted.

New rents have appeared in the security fabric of the world. Without East-West competition, the threshold for U.S. and Western military and political involvement has risen noticeably. Released after decades from the policy of containment, America and its allies no longer have to react reflexively and almost anywhere in response to the Soviet threat. Particularly in the Third World, however, the absence of competitive Eastern and Western security camps has created considerable uncertainty and anxiety. Frequently, these countries are unable to fill this void, whether by expanding their security relationships with the remaining American superpower or by strengthening other alliances.

Such new security concerns are often directed inwardly as much as outwardly. The cost-effectiveness of modern guerrilla warfare, combined with the realization that big-power intervention or deep involvement in the internal affairs of many countries is now less likely, has encouraged indigenous groups to attempt to seize heretofore unattainable objectives, including autonomy or even political independence. A global rise in ethnic pressures and violence is manifesting itself daily, often in unexpected places like Chiapas, Mexico. Since many of the world's twentieth-century boundaries were drawn by now-defunct colonial powers with very little regard for ethnic considerations, the potential threat to many countries is clear. This situation in turn has led to calls for international institutions to expand their operations and stitch together the emerging rents in the fabric of global security. Thus, the end of the Soviet Union both permitted and stimulated the expansion of multilateral peacekeeping efforts around the world.

Exacerbating the problem of ethnic conflict has been the worldwide proliferation of sophisticated conventional weapons at bargain basement prices due in large measure to manufacturing and inventory surpluses created by the end of the Cold War.

To these ramifications of Soviet collapse must be added an intensified and increasingly multipolar jockeying for power both regionally and globally. New balances of power have yet to be achieved, as is evident in ongoing negotiations to expand the membership of the United Nations Security Council, or in China's growing power in Asia, where it is no longer eclipsed by the Soviet state.

Meanwhile, the shock wave that was the end of the Soviet Union is playing itself out economically as well. The very serious economic declines and trade disruptions in Eastern Europe and the former Soviet Union (the old COMECON countries) have also strained Western Europe, the Nordic countries, and other economic partners. Elsewhere, developing countries worry about declining aid from the West now that the threat of world communism has faded. They are also concerned that economic assistance to the former Soviet Union and Eastern Europe will replace assistance to themselves. Even in the rarefied atmosphere of the world's most important economic institutions—the G-7, GATT, the International Monetary Fund and World Bank, and all the Wall Streets of the world—there is widespread recognition and concern that severe instability in the former Soviet Union represents not only a potential political threat, but also a weak and unstable component of the global economy.

## Still the Epicenter of Change

This discussion is meant to underline the importance of the passing of the Soviet Union, not to mourn its demise. The end of the Soviet Union presents an unparalleled opportunity to expand freedom and prosperity in the world, particularly in the fifteen new countries that comprise the successor states to the Soviet Union.

As long as the West no longer faces a hostile superpower, the United States and others should be able to shift resources and attention toward long-neglected domestic problems. Some regional disputes should become more manageable without Cold War polarization and the creation and support by both sides of antagonistic proxy forces. Pursuit of growing global ecological issues and efforts to improve the business climate for regional and global trade and investment are also quickening, as evidenced by follow-up to the Rio Summit and the conclusion of the NAFTA and GATT agreements. Furthermore, issues such as human rights can now take on a higher priority in the West.

Unfortunately, these and other benefits are still unsecured. The Soviet Union did not disintegrate into fifteen well-run, pluralistic, responsible members of the world community. Continuing economic decline and political instability throughout the successor states is unquestionably dangerous. Inside Russia, the hardliner revolt of October 1993 and the rise of Russian nationalism signal a continuing internal political struggle of immense importance to the United States and its allies. Outside Russia, the most serious security risk is that Ukraine, Belarus, or Kazakhstan might become an independent nuclear power, but the risks of nuclear proliferation do not end there. Conventional arms, meanwhile, are completely out of control. Ethnic violence and related irredentist pressures have already led to civil war in several spots. Corruption, crime, and the grasp of the mob are expanding virtually unchecked.

There is little doubt that all this upheaval in the successor states will continue to affect a wide range of national interests. Given such high stakes, it is essential that we improve our knowledge of this volatile region.

### The Objective of This Work

The difficulty of understanding the successor states should not be underestimated. Very few of the West's celebrated pundits managed to predict accurately the watershed events of the past several years, even in Russia where attention was greatest. This is unfortunately true for milestones such as the August 1991 anti-Gorbachev coup attempt; the disintegration of the Soviet Union; the October 1993 revolt in Moscow; and the December election success of Vladimir Zhirinovsky and the Russian ultranationalists.

Kremlinologists have had such problems because their focus on the Soviet Union and successor states was and is too narrow. What they concentrated on—the Communist party, leadership issues, the security and military apparatus, and related foreign policy matters—are all crucial factors, but they did not encompass enough or penetrate deeply enough into what constituted the overall societal and political dynamics of the Soviet Union in its final decade. Nationalities issues, economics, labor, and other not-very-flashy societal and political trends were seen incorrectly as tertiary concerns that might play only a small role in determining political events and outcomes.

What then is a better approach for understanding the disintegration of a country or the prospects for nation building? The death throes of the Soviet

Union were extremely messy and disjointed. Accordingly, any explanatory or predictive approach to the successor states must be complex and cover a spectrum of topics. It must eschew seductive claims that one or a few forces (for example, the party, the military, the security apparatus, summitry, nationalities, the economy, or the military-industrial complex) can explain enough in isolation from the rest.

Thus, the objective of this work is twofold. First, it aims to take stock broadly of the new states. Second, it attempts to construct, by presenting a carefully chosen and rich array of interrelated topics—addressed through analysis and opinion—a framework that can be used to better assess the individual topics discussed and to evaluate future issues.

## Design of the Book—The Two Legacies

To identify the best topics and include the right factors in such a dynamic framework, two different vintages of history must be tapped. The older one is the rich and unique blend of peoples, regional factors, trends, and relationships at work in each of the distinctly different successor states. The newer one is the common legacy they all share—the experience of being part of the former Soviet Union.

Regional security issues and questions are addressed in depth in Section 1. Many of these issues stem from the Soviet era or follow in large measure from that time. The changing dynamics of nuclear weapons in the region and the challenges presented head the list. Robbin Laird (Institute for Defense Analysis) looks at those strategic dynamics, while Steven Miller (Harvard) analyzes nuclear proliferation dangers. Michael Waller (International Freedom Foundation) peers into the realm of the KGB and answers questions about the activities of its successor organizations. John Lepingwell (RFE/RL Research Institute/University of Illinois) completes the treatment of security issues with essays on the militaries of the successor states and the pivotal question of the loyalty of the Russian military.

Economic, social, commercial, and environmental issues form the subject matter of Section 2. John Tedstrom (RAND Corporation) takes on the very difficult issue of converting military industries to civilian production, a key obstacle to reform. Eugene Lawson (U.S.-Russia Business Council) analyzes the tough but promising business climate in Russia and summarizes the prospects for trade and investment. Michael Gfoeller and I (U.S. Department of State) examine the often overlooked but important topic of the independent labor movement. Murray Feshbach (Georgetown University) reminds us of the terrible ecological legacy of the Soviet Union and the resulting ecocide in the successor states. Finally, John Hardt and Phillip Kaiser (Congressional Research Service, Library of Congress) distill the discussion into a policy agenda for Russian economic reform in the coming year.

Section 3 contains essays by leading authorities on the countries and regions constituting the successor states. Paul Goble (Carnegie Endowment for International Peace) provides a treatise on Russia and its peoples, struggles, and future. Three works are offered on Ukraine because of its growing problems, its strategic and regional importance, and its strained relationship with Russia. Ilya Prizel (Paul H. Nitze School of Advanced International Studies, Johns Hopkins University) writes on Ukraine's foreign policy. Roman Szporluk (Harvard University) and Orest Subtelny (York University) provide differing views and new insights on Ukraine's nation building and policies. Turning elsewhere, Martha Brill Olcott (Colgate) analyzes the tough realities of the new countries of Central Asia. Henry Huttenbach (City College, City University of New York) decodes the complex nature of the Caucasus. Finally, Tönu Parming (Toronto University) discusses and differentiates the situation in the Baltic countries.

How the successor states interact with the rest of the world will help define them. Three key relationships with the outside have been included in Section 4. Relations with the United States, Germany, and China were selected because they are likely to be the most important for the successor states in the foreseeable future. S. Frederick Starr (Aspen Institute) tackles the relationship of the United States with the successor states and makes recommendations for U.S. policy. Drawing on history, geography, politics and economics, Angela Stent (Georgetown University) provides convincing analysis on the central importance of Germany's role in the region. Lastly, Thomas Robinson (American-Asian Research Enterprises) provides intriguing perspectives on the Chinese view of the successor states and comments on possible Chinese foreign policy moves in the future. Northeast Asia (Japan and Korea) would have merited inclusion were it not for the continuing Russo-Japanese dispute over the Kurile Islands, which has served as a serious obstacle to development of deeper relationships.

Given the broad approach of this volume, certain decisions became unavoidable. Some ephemeral topics (such as leadership changes and struggles in Russia) were downplayed in favor of more lasting ones. In any case, such high visibility and constantly changing topics are often covered in the media. Furthermore, promoting particular U.S. policy recommendations is also not a central focus of this volume. Policy commentary by the contributing authors is often included, however, where it aids in understanding the issues or illustrates the thinking of authorities in the field. A fuller treatment of policy is undertaken in some instances in order to deal adequately with the subject matter. S. Frederick Starr's essay on the U.S. relationship with the successor states and John Hardt and Phillip Kaiser's work on economic reform in Russia represent two such cases.

Author expertise was sought out wherever it resided. The volume contains essays from representatives of think tanks, American business, and the U.S. government as well as from distinguished members of the academic community. Gathering insights from such a diversity of backgrounds and opinions was, in fact, an objective of the book.

## The Dynamics Exposed by the Soviet Collapse

There is considerable and even growing disagreement as to why the Soviet Union ended. Many of the more popular explanations revolve around various leadership struggles in the 1980s and early 1990s. Some scholars believe that Gorbachev's cardinal mistake was to allow Yeltsin to be elected president of Russia, while Gorbachev himself lacked such a mandate. Others assert that the weakening of the Communist party and its mechanisms of control was the principal reason the Soviet Union collapsed. Alternatively, the West's policy of containment of the Soviet Union is frequently cited as critical to the downfall. More recently, a number of observers highlight the events of summitry as key to the collapse. Still others point to even more specific episodes to explain this huge event, such as Gorbachev's attempt to conclude a last minute Union Treaty in 1991.[1]

There is little doubt that all of these events affected to some extent the timing of the end of Soviet history. But the roots of the downfall of the Soviet Union run much deeper. They were exposed most glaringly by the failure of perestroika, Gorbachev's attempt to reform and thereby preserve a Soviet federative state.

Perestroika became Gorbachev's centerpiece, not so much out of enlightenment as out of necessity. Well before Gorbachev came to power, most of the Soviet leadership recognized that their society and economy were stagnating and that reform of some kind was needed. They worried constantly about competing with the West but did not comprehend the perilousness of the foundations of the Soviet system, especially the degree of increasing economic rot.

This lack of comprehension was somewhat understandable, because the Soviet economy was not without achievements, although some of these have turned out to be Pyrrhic victories. The impressive and sustained growth in earlier decades had been achieved in large part through brutal direction of the economy towards industrialization and collectivization. Similarly, the vertically directed economy of the USSR attained conventional, strategic, and political superpower status because, as a centralized system, it was able to target and skew lavish resources toward meeting those objectives.

The astronomic yearly costs of producing these achievements drained the economy and badly distorted its structure. Despite this, even when the need to redirect resources away from defense and related activities was clear, the heavily vested Soviet military-industrial complex prevented meaningful corrective action. Nevertheless, these ephemeral successes masked the serious internal contradictions of the economic system and the issue of its long-run viability. Until the end of the Soviet Union, many Soviet leaders thought that the growing malaise of their economy could be cured by simple injections of western technology and modernization.

By Gorbachev's time, the command economy was already profoundly corroded and corrupted, as promised rises in production and living standards were repeatedly not met. Gorbachev adopted a series of cautious approaches to economic restructuring. From 1986 onward he tinkered with a series of modest moves to decentralize parts of the economy without disrupting the center's overall control. Later programs sought to create an oxymoronic "regulated market economy," which kept largely intact the infamous state-ordered system of production. Genuinely radical market-oriented economic moves were never attempted, and Gorbachev's reform programs only accelerated the decline of the economy and the Soviet Union. But why was reform so daunting?

### Control at Any Price

Most fundamentally, Soviet leaders failed in economic reform efforts because their economy was designed and constructed as an instrument of political control. As readers of Karl Marx and Friedrich Engels know, their writings, including the monumental Das Kapital, hold little in the way of concrete economic prescriptions. They are mostly critiques of nineteenth century capitalism, not blueprints for building an economic system. Nor did V.I. Lenin and his successors have a precise economic ideology. What Lenin clearly thought, however, was that only by controlling the economic system could the political situation be controlled. He knew that the Communist party must attack private property in order to deprive the citizenry of the ability to resist the centralized structure of power he was building. Lenin and his successors took bloodily, and held on tightly, to what Lenin called the "commanding heights" of the economy. In fact, it was the design of the Soviet economy that played the most important role in keeping the Communist party and elite in power for so long.

As time passed, the structure of the Soviet economy became increasingly bizarre. The quest for political control over the huge and ethnically diverse area of the Soviet Union was pursued without regard to costs. Whole cities were created to make steel where no iron ore existed, precisely to tie the economic well-being of localities to the centralized direction of the Moscow metropole.

Virtually all economic institutions and policies were manipulated to maximize political control. Prices were controlled by a state committee. Money was denied its normal resource-allocation role and became the domain of the Communist party and centralized state institutions. Business profits were confiscated. Development of normal market and financial institutions was prohibited. Horizontal communication was restricted because it was anathema to the Soviet system's first principle of centralized, vertical control. The economic system provided potent means to punish or reward citizens. The state and the Communist party largely determined where a citizen could live or travel, his employment, the food and medical care he received, his housing, and the schools his children attended.

The cumulative result of decades of nonmarket resource allocations was progressively greater systemic inefficiency. With resource allocations made a priori by party and state committees, and not by money, the system became characterized by massive corruption and a wide-ranging system of privileges for the party, government, and military-industrial elite. Thanks to Gorbachev's policy of glasnost, the average citizen became increasingly aware and resentful of these realities.

The average citizen also felt very strongly that the Soviet regime owed him a minimum (and even an improving) standard of living. Ironically, because the state had consciously stripped enterprises, institutions, groups, churches, family, and individuals of economic and political power, it became entirely responsible for living conditions—a kind of social contract. In tacit exchange for cradle-to-grave security, the people granted the revolutionary Communist regime a kind of legitimacy it could not claim historically. As the economy deteriorated, however, the state became unable to meet its end of the deal. Both independent labor and ethnic leaders used this failure of the center very effectively to rally followers, first against Moscow's inept economic leadership, and later in support of outright separatism.

### The House of Cards

The design of the Soviet economy ensured its fragility. To maintain political control, Moscow planned and constructed a gigantic monopoly system of production and supply. This meant that the Soviet economy was extremely vulnerable to any sort of shock whether caused by production shortfalls, bad weather, or strikes. Such shocks always struck more broadly and deeply than necessary due to the lack of alternative markets and suppliers, which act as shock absorbers in western economies. For example, the onset of the serious decline in Russian oil production can be traced to the failure of a single plant in Azerbaijan to deliver the planned number of compressors to Siberian oil fields in the early 1990s. The failure was due to labor and ethnic unrest, and to the Azeris' decision to use the plant for unauthorized military production. Subsequently, many hundreds of Siberian wells froze over and will remain out of production until they can be redrilled. Because the Soviet state owned the foreign exchange earned by its oil companies, those firms were not able to move quickly to import compressors from abroad to make up for the shortfall in domestic production.

Like a house of cards collapsing, this disaster is still expanding outwardly. Other industries and energy-dependent sectors have been hit by energy shortages in Russia. Moreover, oil is Russia's primary foreign exchange earner, and falling exports have necessitated cuts in badly needed imports in all sectors. There are many other examples of destructive cascade effects in the USSR's monopolized economy.

The severe weaknesses of the Soviet economy—especially its sectoral distortions, growing inefficiencies, brittle monopoly structure, entrenched elite interests, open-ended social contract, and lack of market institutions and modern horizontal communication—combined to make successful economic reform a Herculean task for Gorbachev or for anyone else. While Gorbachev's program of perestroika did start to tear down some of the mechanisms of the command economic system, it was unable to provide new market institutions to take the place of the system that was being removed. Old chains of command, which had given a kind of crude order to the system, became disrupted.

By 1990, a widespread disgust had developed in response to the bungling of reform, especially outside Moscow. Across the Soviet Union, local authorities and plant managers found themselves without clear instructions and without needed inputs. All of these shortfalls, exacerbated greatly by cascade effects, fed on one another. Local leaders even tried to seal off their districts and cities with trade barriers, imposed local rationing schemes, and withheld tax revenues from Moscow in hopes that economic autarky might protect them. As the centralized distribution system crumbled, living standards began a sharp downward spiral spurred on by hoarding, wage demands, strikes, and inflation. By 1991, the economy was compressing at double digit rates. Barter and the shadow economy expanded even faster, and the ruble lost its residual meaning.

Meanwhile, regional and ethnic leaders rose to challenge Moscow's economic sovereignty. The most important of those leaders was Boris Yeltsin, who launched the Russian Republic into market-oriented reform programs that were more extensive than those of the central government. A war of laws erupted between the Russian and Soviet governments, adding to the growing economic and political chaos.

Even before perestroika, the stage was set for the struggle between Moscow and the regions. As S. Frederick Starr points out, the Soviet government began to slip in its support of local needs by the mid-1970s. It responded to this problem by taking limited steps toward decentralization, steps which unintentionally began the process of the political devolution of power. In Starr's words:

The Soviet state's deepening failure to generate and designate resources for local needs during the 1970s set in motion a chain of unexpected consequences. Moscow's solution was to devolve authority to local officials in the hope that they could solve what the central government could not. The central government was unwilling to return tax money to the localities, however, and so everything from hospitals to road maintenance only got worse. Faced with such decay, and convinced that the "system" could not help them further, ordinary citizens took matters into their own hands. To some extent the government allowed this. . . . Many people went further, however, creating a vast illegal network of free trade, services, and even production. . . .

With the rise of independent economic activity and volunteerism, a true public sphere emerged, challenging the Party's monopoly over the guidance of society "from above." True, the scale of this public or civic sphere varied from republic to republic, with the greatest mobilization in the Baltic region and the lowest rates in Tajikistan and Kyrgyzstan. This effervescence was eventually manifest in the creation in ten of the republics of Popular Front organizations, all of which embodied the notion that concerns of the local society took priority over those of the Soviet state. Thus, the new social activism had a political edge, and its message was both nationalistic and democratic.

The rise of democratic currents correlated with the degree of independent economic life locally and the vigor of movements toward voluntarism. Thus, the Baltic republics, Russia, Armenia, and Georgia stood high on the list, while Tajikistan, Turkmenistan, and Uzbekistan ranked low. The pattern that emerged between 1980 and 1990 still sets the tone today.[2]

### The New Legacy of Wreckage

Although most events and factors cited in alternative explanations of the end of the Soviet Union undoubtedly affected the timing of that historic event, the collapse of the Soviet Union was first and foremost an internal systemic failure that would have been almost impossible to avoid. The core of this failure was the design and construction of an economic and social system fatally flawed by an obsession for political control at any cost. In short, the Soviet system contained the seeds of its own destruction.

The implications of this conclusion are profound for the successor states. Are the same corrosive forces still at work in the successor states? How will they affect prospects for creating viable economic and political systems in these countries? What can be done to ameliorate their effects?

The answer to the first question is painfully clear. There can be little doubt that the systemic legacy of the Soviet Union is still greatly impeding stability and the construction of viable economic and political systems in almost all of the new countries. Some may even cease to exist largely because of those dynamics.

By design, the regions of the old Soviet Union were largely unable to produce finished goods without Moscow's direction and inputs from other regions. The Ukrainians have a saying: "Nothing is produced in Ukraine." Moscow's policy of keeping Ukraine's production dependent on inputs from other parts of the USSR is a major reason why Ukraine—like other successor states—is in such dire economic straits today.

The old economic design continues to provide Russia with considerable leverage over the rest of the successor states. Russia's use of the "energy weapon" against Ukraine is only the most celebrated example of the many economic ties that still bind the successor states together, and to Moscow. This interdependence also occasionally reignites interest in the Commonwealth of Independent States, the limited security and economic umbrella organization comprising most of the successor states.

Certainly, it will take some time for all the successor states to move away from this rigid structure to more diversified market-determined production, trade, and investment patterns. Until they do so, however, the successor states must also endure the burden and risks of the old system's fragility, especially its susceptibility to shocks and cascade effects. In fact, the imperative of diversification must also be applied internally to create competition and privatize these economies, which still are characterized by their excessive state ownership and monopoly structures. But as agonizing as these residual economic problems are, an even tougher part of the Soviet legacy is psychological.

### Gorbachev's Dilemma Transferred

Gorbachev's understanding of market-oriented reform was limited, but it did improve with time. His advisers and others developed programs for accelerating reform, but Gorbachev refused to take that course. The main conundrum was always this: genuine economic liberalization and transition to a market economy would undermine the foundations of Communist party power. An expansion of private wealth and resource allocation based on money and profits would erode state control and eventually challenge the one-party system. Although needed for modernization, new institutions that would expand horizontal communication (for example, a real banking system and stock markets) would also directly challenge vertical control from the center.

Gorbachev's dilemma did not die with the Soviet Union. Leaders of many of the successor states are no less obsessed with retaining power. It is understandable, after decades of Communist rule, that they would be accustomed to centralized economic and political control as the means of governance. Continuing economic decline and social unrest is pressing such leaders to make the transition towards market economics and political pluralism. But how can the successor states, with few of the traditions and institutions of civil societies, become economically and politically freer without risking disintegration?

The legacy and dynamics of the old Soviet economic system unfortunately remain very strong in many other ways as well. Defense expenditures are still bloated in many of the successor states, and the vested interests of the military-industrial complex remain entrenched. Elite privilege, job security, and the reliability of the social safety net are swirling undertows throughout the region. The ecological legacy of the Soviet Union is an unending nightmare. Lastly, and undermining all progress, is the pervasive deficit of intellectual capital available to build new institutions and better address all of the foregoing problems. Unfortunately, this is even a problem among the elites of these states. After all, the communist system took its "best and brightest" and trained them as authoritarian leaders. It taught its average citizens to obey those leaders. Given the problems facing these new states, is it really surprising that their deeply troubled people sometimes turn to old leaders or are tempted by other brands of authoritarianism?

## Notes

1. Some of the themes and ideas for this section were taken from John Blaney and Michael Gfoeller, "Lessons from the Failure of Perestroika," *Political Science Quarterly* 108, 3 (Fall 1993): 481-496.

2. S. Frederick Starr, "United States Policy and National Development in the Post-Soviet States" (Paper presented to the Aspen Strategy Group, Aspen, Colorado, July 20, 1993). Dr. Starr's contribution to this volume is an edited version of the same paper.

# Part I   Security Issues

# 2 Proliferation Dangers in the Former Soviet Union

Steven E. Miller

The disintegration of the Soviet Union has raised unprecedented nonproliferation challenges. The USSR left behind a legacy of some thirty thousand nuclear weapons and an extensive and far-flung nuclear infrastructure for the production and maintenance of these weapons. The devolution of the Soviet Union into fifteen newly independent states left unsettled the destiny of this vast arsenal and its associated nuclear complex. The Soviet nuclear legacy could plausibly end up safely and securely consolidated in Russia. But this outcome is far from assured. And it is perhaps equally plausible that the disposition of the Soviet nuclear legacy will contribute to regional and global nuclear proliferation. This essay will describe and assess the proliferation risks associated with the demise of a nuclear superpower.[1]

The proliferation risks produced by the disintegration of the Soviet Union arise from four features of the post-Soviet landscape. First, the nuclear arsenal and nuclear infrastructure left behind by the USSR were widely distributed geographically. Indeed, until the last year or two of its existence the Soviet Union had weapons deployed in fourteen of its fifteen republics and on the territory of several of its East European allies. However, a substantial consolidation of the nuclear arsenal, which removed nuclear weapons from East Europe and from eleven of the Soviet republics, has already taken place.[2] But nuclear weapons remain in three Soviet successor states and, in addition, are widely distributed throughout Russia. Second, the nuclear custodial system charged with responsibility for the safety and security of the nuclear arsenal and infrastructure is functioning in conditions of political instability and socioeconomic distress. It appears to have performed well so far, but its effectiveness could erode if subjected to further dislocations. Third, almost unnoticed, the demise of the USSR has raised a traditional nonproliferation concern: a number of the newly independent states have inherited nuclear reactors that have heretofore been and are still completely outside the international safeguards system. Hence, the option of exploiting spent reactor fuel as a source of fissile material for use in nuclear weapons—which international safeguards are meant to prevent—is available to these states. Finally, the post-Soviet international order in Soviet Eurasia, already less than peaceful, could come to be marked by high levels of insecurity and conflict. This could create incentives for successor states to proliferate.

These four sources of potential trouble lead to three types of nuclear proliferation risks. One is the risk of successor state proliferation—the possibility that the collapse of the USSR could give rise to more than one nuclear-armed state. A second is the risk of nuclear terrorism or other illicit or unauthorized seizure or use of nuclear weapons. And third is the possibility of nuclear spillover: the risk the nuclear weapons or weapons-related items and materials will leak out of the former Soviet Union and contribute to the global spread of nuclear capability. I will discuss each of these risks in turn.

### Four Paths to Successor State Proliferation

One proliferation risk raised by the demise of the Soviet Union is the possibility that more than one successor state will opt to acquire a nuclear weapons capability. There are four ways in which this might come about.

*Gaining Custody of Soviet Nuclear Weapons Deployed Outside of Russia*

Three newly independent states, Belarus, Kazakhstan, and Ukraine, still have strategic nuclear forces deployed on their territory. Indeed, both Ukraine and Kazakhstan have in excess of one thousand nuclear weapons within their borders—enough to make them the third and fourth largest nuclear powers, respectively. One or more of these three states could decide to take custody of these weapons.

This could lead to a nuclear weapons capability in two ways. One, obviously, is that the existing warheads may be usable by whatever party gains physical custody of them. However, most of the nuclear weapons on the territory of these states are deployed on ICBMs targeted against the United States, and the weapons themselves may be safeguarded in a variety of ways. They may not be easily adaptable for use by a new owner. In addition, the present Russian custodians may be able to disable some or all of the weapons before relinquishing control of them. The "grab and use" scenario is thus less straightforward than is often assumed—although usable nuclear capability could be gained this way.

There is a second scenario, however. The weapons still deployed outside

Russia represent a large inventory of missile material. This material could be removed from existing weapons and refabricated into new weapons, probably of simpler design, that would be more suitable to the requirements of the state in question. This could plausibly be done in a matter of weeks or months.[3]

At present, this is not the explicit intention of any of the three governments in question. On the contrary, all three have repeatedly pledged to denuclearize their territories and to become members of the Nuclear Nonproliferation Treaty (NPT) as non-nuclear-weapon states. Further, in the May 1992 Lisbon Protocol to the START agreement, which made these three states party to the START treaty (joining with Russia and the United States), they reiterated these pledges in a formal and legally binding agreement with the United States; Ukraine reaffirmed that commitment in the January 1994 trilateral deal with the United States and Russia. With respect to the current declared policies of current governments, therefore, this path does not represent an immediate concern.

However, so long as nuclear weapons are stored or deployed within these states, the possibility remains that one or more of them could decide at some point in the future to take control of them. This possibility remains a source of concern because the timetables for denuclearization of these states stretch years into the future. Belarus has negotiated an agreement with Russia whereby all nuclear weapons will be withdrawn from its territory, but only another two years down the road. Ukraine and Kazakhstan have committed to denuclearize within the START implementation schedule, which is seven years from the entry into force of the treaty. Since START was not ratified by the end of 1993, the deadline accepted by Kiev and Alma Ata will arrive no sooner than the year 2001, and perhaps later if ratification is delayed. As the past several years have vividly demonstrated, a lot can change in two years, much less seven, including governments and their policies. In short, while current governments have promised denuclearization, neither current policies nor current governments will necessarily survive the two-to-seven year implementation timetable presently envisioned.

*Leakage from the Soviet Nuclear Arsenal or Complex to Newly Independent States*

Any of the Soviet successor states—including Belarus, Kazakhstan, or Ukraine after nuclear weapons are removed from their territories—could, by illicit means, acquire nuclear weapons from somewhere in the nuclear establishment left behind by the USSR. The custodial system responsible for the safety and security of the nuclear arsenal has so far continued to function remarkably well in difficult political and economic circumstances. But should political instability or economic distress intensify, the nuclear custodial system could erode or break down altogether. This could lead to much greater risk of leakage of weapons or weapons-related materials out of the system to parties seeking nuclear capability. While most analyses of this problem have focused on the question of nuclear spillover out of the former Soviet Union (about which more below), there is no reason why this means of nuclear spread could not take place within Soviet Eurasia.

At present, none of the Soviet successor states (other than Russia) seems strongly or clearly motivated to seek a nuclear weapons capability. But there can be no certainty that this will remain the case indefinitely for all the Soviet successor states. If, as seems quite possible given the instability and conflict evident so far, the post-Soviet regional order turns out to be malign and conflict-prone, some of these states could come to conclude that nuclear weapons are desirable or necessary to ensure their security. Indeed, Russia's newly independent neighbors will face two conditions that historically have been powerful motivations to acquire nuclear weapons: a potential nuclear adversary and an overwhelming conventional threat. If Russia turns menacing (or is perceived as such), these motivations to acquire nuclear weapons could become irresistible. Russia's increasingly assertive foreign policy towards its neighbors and the growing number of open Russian proponents of Russian dominance in the former Soviet Union is bound to be of great concern to the other newly independent states.[4]

In addition, the newly independent states may also confront other difficult security challenges, whether disputes with one another or rivalries with other relatively powerful states, such as China or Turkey. Thus, for example, Armenia fits the motivational profile of a potential proliferator: it is locked in a bitter conflict with Azerbaijan, has a long and bloody rivalry with its much more powerful southern neighbor, Turkey (including memories of genocide earlier in this century), and in general feels encircled by potential enemies: Armenia could be, it has been suggested, the Caucasian Israel. But while some may be more prone than others to seriously consider or to exercise the nuclear option, in theory all fourteen non-Russian successor states could do so and any among them might be able to amass at least a modest inventory of nuclear weapons by illicit means.

*Soviet Successor States Can Develop Indigenous Nuclear Weapons Programs*

The Soviet successor states will always have the same proliferation option that is available to any other non-nuclear state: they can develop indigenous nuclear weapons programs. As noted, in the coming years, some of these states could well find themselves in regional settings that provide considerable incentive to do so.

Starting from scratch will be longer, more difficult, and more costly than the proliferation paths described above. In this scenario, the nuclear shortcut provided by the Soviet nuclear legacy is foregone—or at least it is not the primary path to a nuclear weapons capability. And it will bring potential proliferators into collision with the international regime of export controls on nuclear commerce, which is intended to make it as difficult as possible for states to develop nuclear weapons capabilities. As the experiences of recent aspiring proliferators attests, this is not an easy path to nuclear weapons.

But there is no reason to suppose that it is beyond the capacities of all the Soviet successor states to adopt this strategy, should nuclear acquisitions be deemed necessary now or in the future. The larger and wealthier successor states, particularly Ukraine, will undoubtedly possess the financial and technical resources to move in this direction. It is hard to know what the lower threshold of capability would be, but suffice it to say that most of the Soviet successor states possess at least roughly the population of Israel and at least roughly the GNP and technological level of North Korea—to compare them to two states that are thought to have nuclear weapons programs.

Moreover, some of the Soviet successor states will not be starting from zero. They may, for example, inherit personnel from the Soviet complex who provide useful or necessary expertise. Further, nuclear research centers are located in Armenia, Belarus, Georgia, and Kazakhstan.[5] More importantly, five of the newly independent states—Armenia, Belarus, Kazakhstan, Lithuania, and Ukraine—have nuclear power reactors on their territory; and Belarus, Estonia, Georgia, Kazakhstan, Latvia, and Ukraine have research or training reactors within their borders.[6] To date, most of the newly independent states have moved slowly in terms of joining the NPT and signing safeguards agreements with the International Atomic Energy Agency (IAEA). In the context of the other proliferation worries associated with the former Soviet Union, this fact has attracted relatively little notice. But in any other setting, the existence of nearly twenty large, unsafeguarded nuclear power reactors, spread across at least five newly independent and not particularly stable states (some of which have plausible incentives for acquiring nuclear weapons), would be regarded as a crisis for the nonproliferation regime.

Unsafeguarded reactors provide potential access to fissile material because spent reactor fuel contains extractable plutonium. A notional 1 GWe reactor will produce about 200-300 kilograms per year of plutonium in spent fuel.[7] Ukraine—which has by far the largest nuclear power industry of these states—possesses reactors with a combined capacity of some 12-16 GWe: in other words, several thousand kilograms of plutonium in spent fuel are accumulating in Ukraine on an annual basis. This represents fissile material for some six hundred weapons per year. The same is true, at lower levels of capacity, for the other Soviet successor states with nuclear reactors. These states may already have substantial inventories of spent fuel accumulating in cooling pools at their facilities.[8]

Before it can be used to fabricate weapons, plutonium must be separated from spent fuel by reprocessing. This involves cutting the spent fuel rods into pieces, dissolving the contents of the rods in acid, and chemically separating the plutonium. Although handling radioactive and highly toxic materials is not easy, this process should not pose an insurmountable challenge to a determined Soviet successor state.[9]

One of the basic purposes of the IAEA safeguards system is to prevent the diversion to nuclear weapons programs of the fissile material produced by civilian nuclear power reactors. The strict materials accounting procedures and inspection requirements raise a risk of detection that is thought to inhibit or deter diversion. For the time being, and so long as safeguards are not applied to their nuclear power plants, the Soviet successor states do not face this constraint and can divert spent fuel to military purposes with no international accountability. Moreover, even if these states eventually do join the IAEA safeguards system, by the time they do so they will have had ample opportunity to accumulate inventories of spent fuel for use in a weapons program; any material that is not in the initial inventory reported to the IAEA is invisible to the safeguards system. Thus, these states have potential access to significant quantities of fissile material. Were it not for the fact that the other paths to nuclear acquisition for Soviet successor states seem more immediate and more attractive, this would be a preoccupying nonproliferation problem.

### The Disintegration of Russia as a Path to Nuclear Proliferation

Should Russia disintegrate, all three of the paths to successor state proliferation described above would come into play, perhaps in exacerbated form. Like the Soviet Union, Russia is a multinational state (albeit with a largely Russian population), and it is experiencing centrifugal tendencies. This does not mean that disintegration is inevitable. Indeed, the potential breakaway areas in Russia are for the most part remote, weak, sparsely populated, and lacking any historical memory of statehood; it will not be easy for them to escape Russia's grasp, nor is this the present objective of most of the regions in question. But Moscow's authority has clearly weakened, and many areas within Russia have already explicitly asserted their desire for autonomy or independence.[10] Disintegration may not be likely, but it could happen. Further, the effort to make it happen could produce civil strife and violence or even civil war.

All three paths to successor state proliferation could be replicated in the event that the Russian Federation breaks into two or more successor states:

- The collapse of Russia could lead directly to successor state proliferation due to the geographic distribution of weapons and facilities. These are scattered from one end of Russia to the other, including areas of political disturbance that could break from Moscow. One or more newly independent Russian successor states could end up with nuclear weapons on its territory—whether strategic missile fields, air defense units, or even tactical nuclear weapons associated with the army. Many of Russia's trouble spots are found along its vast southern frontier, an area in which large numbers of such bases and installations are found. Because most of the potential breakaway states are so weak relative to Russia, they could feel it imperative to retain a nuclear capability to have any hope of preserving their independence against Russian revanchism.[11] In this way, the splintering of Russia, like the demise of the USSR, has the potential to produce multiple nuclear states.

- The collapse of Russia could disrupt or dismember the nuclear custodial system. Depending on where the states seeking independence were located, pieces of this system could be lost. Transportation connections to some facilities or bases could be disturbed or interrupted. For example, a band of autonomous republics—including Mordovia, Chuvashia, Mari, Tatarstan, Udmurtia, and Bashkiria—stands between Moscow and Russian territory in the Urals and eastwards and stands astride almost all the east-west land lines of communication. All but two of the major facilities of the Russian nuclear complex lie east of this cluster of autonomous republics and parts of the complex lie near or in Mordovia. Obviously, political disturbance, civil violence, or attempted breakaway in these Russian republics has considerable potential to cause problems for the Russian nuclear establishment. Thus, even Russia—the one Soviet successor state that possesses a full nuclear infrastructure—could be left without a coherent nuclear complex or a fully functioning custodial system. This, in turn, could increase the risk of nuclear spread by illicit means—including, possibly, to successor states of Russia as well as to those of the Soviet Union. There are several reasons why the nuclear custodial system might erode or break down, and this could happen even if Russia remains fully intact. But the disintegration scenario is certainly one that could put enormous stress on the system, depending on the locations and extent of the secession. The breakup of Russia could cause the problem of illicit leakage to become acute.

- Some Russian successor states, like some Soviet successor states, could inherit unsafeguarded nuclear reactors—not to mention dedicated nuclear weapons production facilities. In fact, the largest number of Soviet nuclear reactors are located in Russia, and they are widely scattered. Thus, Russian successor states could have the same head start on an indigenous nuclear weapons program as do several Soviet successor states.

Many observers, both inside and outside of Russia, expect the Russian Federation to disintegrate. The current facts do not fully confirm that interpretation. But neither do they confidently disconfirm it. Accordingly, any comprehensive analysis of the proliferation risks in the former Soviet Union must take into account the possibility of the disintegration scenario.

In sum, there are four routes to nuclear multipolarity in the former Soviet Union. At present, the first of these—possible seizure by Belarus, Kazakhstan, or Ukraine of the nuclear weapons deployed on their territory—has attracted the most attention because it poses the most immediate and large-scale proliferation threat. But internal and regional instability are likely to be the hallmarks in the former Soviet Union for years to come, in which case the nuclear proliferation issue may well be a lingering concern. And even if all weapons are removed from Belarus, Kazakhstan, and Ukraine—no doubt a big and reassuring step—this closes off only one of the paths to nuclear capability for Soviet successor states and hence is not a definitive end to the threat of proliferation in the former Soviet Union.

Moreover, these paths are not mutually exclusive, but can be pursued in combination. A sensible approach, for example, would be to combine an indigenous program with as much illicit access to the Soviet arsenal and complex as possible; in this way, the paths can reinforce one another. They may also reinforce one another in the sense that proliferation by some successor states may increase the incentives of others to proliferate by whatever path is available to them. Thus, in the seven-year timetable for START implementation and for denuclearization of Kazakhstan and Ukraine, any of the four nuclear spread scenarios, or combinations thereof, could plausibly come into play.

### Nuclear Terrorism and Other Illicit Use

The erosion or breakdown of the nuclear custodial system in the former Soviet Union could provide opportunities for illicit access not only to states desirous of nuclear weapons, but also to nonstate actors.[12] Any number of nonstate actors could seek to grab and exploit nuclear weapons or nuclear materials. The temptation to do so could be especially strong if the deterioration of the system were so severe that nuclear weapons seemed to be there for the taking.[13] But even leakage on a smaller scale could be troublesome.

This problem could have several dimensions. One is the misuse of nuclear weapons by nonstate actors within Russia—whether disgruntled nationalists seeking independence from Russia, disillusioned Communists dismayed by their lapse from power, or rogue military units hungry for wealth or influence. In addition, nuclear weapons could get caught up in civil strife or civil war within Russia. This could involve Moscow in nuclear confrontations with breakaway groups or regions. Finally, international terrorists of whatever stripe could have keen appetites to acquire nuclear capabilities, should these become available on the international black market. Little imagination is required to envision the trouble that might ensue if the PLO, the Red Brigade, or other highly motivated political groups succeeded in obtaining nuclear weapons.

It seems reasonable to posit that the greater the erosion of the nuclear custodial system, the greater the risk of nuclear terrorism. However, some risk of leakage undoubtedly exists even now.

### Nuclear Spillover

If the Soviet nuclear legacy is not successfully consolidated and safely controlled, it may contribute to proliferation on a global scale. There is no guarantee that the proliferation effects associated with the demise of the USSR can be contained within the borders of the former Soviet Union.

There are two aspects to this problem.[14] The first is whether the Soviet successor states, including but not limited to Russia, will be willing and able to enforce nuclear export controls that accord with the rules governing international nuclear commerce. Several facts suggest that concern is warranted. For one thing, over the past several years, both before and after the disintegration of the USSR, Moscow made or considered a number of disturbing nuclear export deals, involving sales to non-NPT members and lax observance of the principle that safeguards should precede sales.[15] Another potential problem is that most of the Soviet successor states (notably excepting Russia, which inherited the USSR's legal status) are not participants in the international institutions and regimes that regulate international nuclear commerce. Their compliance with rules that they have never formally accepted should not be taken for granted—particularly in view of the desperate economic pressures to sell that may exist. Finally, it is unclear whether all of the Soviet successor states have in place legal frameworks for nuclear export controls. But even where such legal frameworks do clearly exist, as in Russia, there is reason to doubt that the governments in question have a true capacity to enforce them effectively, given the new, unsettled, and resource-constrained character of most of the successor states. In short, damage may be done to the international nuclear nonproliferation regime by nuclear deals undertaken outside the international frameworks for controlling such exports.

Second, and more important, if the nuclear custodial system begins to erode and substantial leakage starts to occur, any aspiring proliferator, whether inside Soviet Eurasia or out, may be able to gain access to weapons-related items and materials or to weapons themselves. The full range of the enormous and comprehensive Soviet nuclear legacy is probably saleable on the international black market: human expertise (the so-called brain drain problem), weapons design information, weapons components, fissile material, and nuclear weapons and delivery systems.

Moreover, the threat of leakage appears to be more than hypothetical. Persistent reports of low-grade leakage have appeared in the press. The most dramatic allegations—sales of nuclear weapons from Kazakhstan to Iran, for example—have been vigorously denied and are unsubstantiated. Nevertheless, the existing trickle of illicit exports from the Soviet nuclear establishment is distressing evidence that there are those willing to supply nuclear assets on the international market. Should the trickle become a torrent, the world would face a proliferation disaster.

### Conclusion

The collapse of the Soviet Union has produced a series of potential proliferation problems of major magnitude. Some aspects of the Soviet nuclear legacy—particularly nuclear weapons in Ukraine and the potential brain drain of nuclear scientists from Russia—have received considerable attention from policy makers and the media. Others have been somewhat overshadowed. However, all must be successfully handled if the Soviet nuclear arsenal is not to contribute to further nuclear proliferation and thereby undermine the international nonproliferation regime.

### Notes

1. This essay draws heavily on earlier work on this subject, in particular, Steven E. Miller, "The Former Soviet Union," in *Nuclear Proliferation after the Cold War*, ed. Robert Litwak and Mitchell Reiss (Baltimore: Johns Hopkins University Press, 1994), 89-128; and Steven E. Miller, "Alternative Nuclear Futures: What Fate for the Soviet Nuclear Arsenal?" in *Sicherheitsinteressen und Nationale Planung der Bundesrepublik* (Ebenhausen, Germany: Stiftung Wissenschaft und Politik, 1993), 65-110. Additional background on these problems and more extensive analyses can be found in Kurt Campbell, Ashton B. Carter, Steven E. Miller, and Charles A. Zraket, *Soviet Nuclear Fission: Control of the Nuclear Arsenal in a Disintegrating Soviet Union*, CSIA Studies in International Security no. 1 (Cambridge, Mass.: Center for Science and International Affairs, Harvard University, November 1991); and Graham Allison, Ashton B. Carter, Steven E. Miller, and Philip Zelikow, eds., *Cooperative Denuclearization: From Pledges to Deeds*, CSIA Studies in International Security no. 2 (Cambridge, Mass.: Center for Science and International Affairs, Harvard University, January 1993).

2. This resulted from the relocation of all Soviet tactical nuclear weapons back into Russia. On the tactical withdrawal and the diplomacy associated with it, see Steven E. Miller, "Western Diplomacy and the Soviet Nuclear Legacy," *Survival* 34, 3 (Autumn 1992): 3-27.

3. See, for example, Mason Willrich and Theodore Taylor, *Nuclear Theft: Risks and Safeguards* (Cambridge, Mass.: Ballinger, 1974), 20-21 and 226-227, on the feasibility of rapidly fabricating weapons once missile material is obtained.

4. Russia's neighbors are unlikely to be comforted, for example, by the position expressed by the Russian parliament's foreign affairs committee: "Russian foreign policy must be based on a doctrine that proclaims the entire geopolitical space of the former (Soviet) Union a sphere of vital interests. . . . Russia must secure . . . the role of political and military guarantor of stability on all the territory of the former USSR." Quoted in "Russia: Imperfect Peace," *The Economist*, November 14, 1992, 60. The growing emphasis on nuclear weapons in Russia's defense policy is also unlikely to discourage the nuclear appetites of its neighbors. See George Leopold and Neil Munro, "Russia Renews Nuclear Reliance," *Defense News*, December 21-27, 1992, 1. For a survey of the potential for conflict in the former Soviet Union, see "Flash Points," *Jane's Defense Weekly*, January 2, 1993, 13-15.

5. Most of the information in this paragraph is drawn from William C. Potter with Eve E. Cohen and Edward V. Kayukov, *Nuclear Profiles of the Soviet Successor States*, Program for Nonproliferation Studies, Monograph no. 1 (Monterey, Calif.: Monterey

Institute of International Studies, May 1993). The monograph is extremely useful.

6. For the location and number of reactors in the former Soviet Union, see Thomas Cochran, William Arkin, Robert Norris, and Jeffrey Sands, *Soviet Nuclear Weapons* (New York: Harper and Row, 1989), 84-85.

7. Ashton B. Carter and Owen Cote, "Disposition of Fissile Material," in *Cooperative Denuclearization: From Pledges to Deeds,* ed. Allison, Carter, Miller, and Zelikow, 132. Carter and Cote use the 200 kilogram number. "Fuel Reprocessing and Spent Fuel Management," in *Nuclear Proliferation Factbook*, Congressional Research Service, Joint Committee Print (Washington, D.C.: U.S. Government Printing Office, August 1985), 405. This latter publication suggests 300 kg.

8. Moreover, according to one source, spent reactor fuel in the former Soviet Union was normally stored at the reactor site for three to five years before being transported to central storage or preprocessing. See Oleg Bukharin, "The Threat of Nuclear Terrorism and the Physical Security of Nuclear Installations and Materials in the Former Soviet Union," Occasional Paper no. 2, Center for Russian and Eurasian Studies (Monterey, Calif.: Monterey Institute of International Studies, August 1992), 6. If true, this would imply that Ukraine is in possession of many thousands of kilograms of plutonium in spent fuel.

9. See, for example, "Routes to Nuclear Weapons," in *Nuclear Proliferation Factbook* 304, which describes chemical separation of plutonium as "only a minor obstacle" for states with unsafeguarded reactors. William Potter, *Nuclear Power and Non-Proliferation: An Interdisciplinary Perspective* (Cambridge, Mass.: Oelgeschlager, Dunn, and Hain, 1982), 78-79, makes the point that building a reprocessing capability would be affordable for most states and could be accomplished in less than a year. Ted Greenwood, George Rathjens, and Jack Ruina, *Nuclear Power and Weapons Proliferation*, Adelphi Paper no. 130 (London: IISS, Winter 1976), 18, conclude that "almost any state with a modest chemical industry could on its own build a reprocessing plant large enough to supply plutonium to a small explosives programme." See also Robert K. Mullen, "Nuclear Violence," in *Preventing Nuclear Terrorism*, ed. Paul Leventhal and Yonah Alexander (Lexington, Mass.: Lexington Books, 1987), 231-234, which provides a detailed description of the requirements for reprocessing.

10. On the prospects that Russia might disintegrate, see Jessica Stern, "Moscow Meltdown: Can Russia Survive?" *International Security* 18, 4 (Spring 1994): 40-65; and Bogdan Szajkowski, "Will Russia Disintegrate into Bantustans?" *The World Today* 49, 8-9 (August-September 1993): 172-175.

11. The nuclear assets available to some of these states might not be easily usable or suitable for their security needs—particularly if what they inherit are strategic nuclear weapons. But some might also gain custody of more usable tactical nuclear weapons. And uncertainty about what nuclear capability was in the hands of a newly independent state could have considerable deterrent effect.

12. This has to do, first and foremost, with the integrity of Russia's nuclear custodial system, since Russia inherited most of the Soviet nuclear arsenal and provides custodial arrangements for the rest under the CIS Joint Strategic Command. But should other Soviet successor states gain nuclear weapons capabilities, the reliability and effectiveness of their custodial systems would also be a concern.

13. Note, for example, Campbell, Carter, Miller, and Zraket, *Soviet Nuclear Fission*, 40, which comments that "a systemic disintegration of the nuclear command and control system—accompanied by a general loss of discipline or confusion of political loyal-

ties—would lay open virtually all of the 27,000 weapons to abuse."

14. In the following discussion, I draw on William Hartel and Steven E. Miller, "Controlling Borders and Nuclear Exports," in *Cooperative Denuclearization*, ed. Allison, Carter, Miller, and Zelikow, 198-215.

15. For examples, see William C. Potter, "The New Nuclear Suppliers," *Orbis*, 36, 2 (Spring 1992): 199-210.

# 3 Rethinking the Role of Nuclear Weapons: The Experience of the Former Soviet Union

Robbin Frederick Laird

The collapse of the Soviet Union has led to an unprecedented historical experience—the elimination of a state that controlled approximately forty thousand nuclear weapons. The state that had governed an empire and threatened others with its blandishments collapsed of its own weight, unable to meet the challenges of economic and cultural modernization in the evolving global system. But the weight of the Soviet nuclear weapons legacy remains.

Nuclear weapons were part of Soviet state power; they verified the country's superpower status. The USSR's parity with the United States, its ability to sit at the great power table, rested upon its military power and, above all, upon its substantial nuclear arsenal. This article examines the intersection of changes in the former Soviet Union (FSU), in the European security environment, and in the role of nuclear weapons around the world.

## Sustaining a Weak Custodian: The West's Dilemma

The global role of nuclear weapons has been substantially altered since 1990. In that time, the world has shifted from a single superpower competition and confrontation—rooted paradoxically in joint custodianship—to a pluralistic world of potential nuclear proliferation, a world in which counterproliferation and the use of nuclear weapons are important diplomatic coinage, not just in East-West relations but in global relations in general.

The collapse of the Soviet Union came more quickly than most would have thought. Although Mikhail Gorbachev did much as president of the Soviet Union to undermine the integrity of the Soviet empire, he struggled until the end of his rule to preserve some sort of union. Ultimately, the logic of nationalism overcame this effort. Within the Soviet Union diverse ethnic groups had coexisted with a dominant ethnic group—the Russians. Upon the collapse of the Soviet Union, however, a new Russia emerged; immediately the relationships among the successor states and particularly the relationship between Russia and the rest became the dominant question.

Faced with this new state of affairs, the Western states sought two contradictory objectives. On the one hand, Western states wished to ensure that nuclear weapons remained under the custodianship of a single center of control, and Russia was ready to assume the military and economic obligations of the Soviet Union. On the other hand, there was no desire to see an imperial Russia arising to take the place of its prime successor states. The logic of the first objective led to strengthening of a Russian state; the logic of the second led to a diversification of relations within the former Soviet empire. For the first time in history the logic of the nuclear arms race had reversed itself. Hitherto, the existence of nuclear weapons presupposed a strong centralized state. Now the need to exert control over nuclear weapons required the construction, or at any rate the maintenance, of a custodial state.

### The New European Security Environment

The end of the Cold War and the dissolution of the Soviet Union carried with them a shift in the global role of the western half of the European continent. An entire generation of Americans and their West European counterparts had grown up with maps colored blue on one side of the European divide and red on the other. The division of Europe into western and eastern parts seemed to the postwar generation to be part of the geography of the continent, a given, a natural component of inherited history.

With the breaching of the divide, a given of history has become a variable. The western part of the continent seems no longer certain of its place within the continent, while the Eastern part is dissolving into new regional subsystems.

West European political and economic systems in the postwar period were constructed around liberal democratic paradigms defined in part by the negation of their opposites: communist political and economic systems. With the collapse of the latter, the definition, indeed the validity, of these liberal democratic paradigms has come into question. Political coalitions are shifting in Western Europe; economic challenges associated with high unemployment and the need for structural change are once more coming to the fore of political debate.

The term "Eastern Europe" emerged during the Cold War. Previously, Poland, Ukraine, and Belarus had been part of Central Europe, a region dominated by various northern European neighbors. With the end of the Cold War, the nations of the region began to emerge anew. In some cases national identity reinforced existing state boundaries; in others, nationalist sentiments challenged the states that had emerged from the Cold War.

While the search for identity continues, the eastern part of the European continent is being pulled in three directions. The first direction is the economic space of Western Europe. The Central European states seek attachment to the European Union, and much of the investment by key West European states in Central Europe is oriented toward infrastructure development in preparation for a widening of Europe. The second pull is toward nationhood defined in ethnic terms. The conflict in the former Yugoslavia is an expression of this ethnic dynamic, which often takes ugly and exclusionary forms. The third direction is toward association with other regional entities—within the former Soviet Empire, in Turkey, in the Balkans, or within classic Central Europe (the Austro-Hungarian Empire).

During the Cold War, the Western alliance protected Western territory against Eastern expansion. The challenge was to contain the communist threat to a clearly defined Western territory. With the end of the East-West divide and with the definition of Western territory under reexamination, the alliance confronts three related prospects, each associated with one of the pulls on Eastern Europe described above.

In the first case—associated with the pull toward Europe—the alliance may have the opportunity to redefine its territorial base eastward. That is, "Europe" may become larger economically, politically, and ideologically.

In the second case—associated with the risk of ethnicity overwhelming states—the alliance's role as an entity is unclear. One expects that coalitions of states within the alliance will form to shape responses to ethnic tensions, but other frameworks and orientations are likely to become salient in the resolution of conflicts involving ethnicity. To the extent that ethnicity undercuts the nation-state as an entity, it may compromise interstate organizations designed to manage conflict based on the nation-state model of organization.

In the third case, new or redefined national entities in Central Europe and the Commonwealth of Independent States (CIS) may generate new regional groupings. Here the pull on the alliance to act at the subgroup level will be enormous. Regional diversification within the alliance has always posed a challenge to the definition of the common good. In the years ahead the challenge of diversification might well overwhelm the ability of the alliance to act.

The United States must try to act as the flywheel that balances interests within the alliance, a role the country has played throughout the history of the alliance.

## The Challenge to the West of the Nuclear Dynamics of the Former Soviet Union

The end of the Soviet Union eliminated the state that directly controlled more than forty thousand nuclear warheads (according to the Russian General Staff). Much of American diplomacy toward the newly independent states (NIS) over the past three years has been concerned with ensuring that those warheads remain in the custody of a responsible state. But dealing with the nuclear arsenal of the FSU also has become part of the West's general challenge in dealing with the successor states. The collapse of the Soviet Union ended the direct threat to the North Atlantic zone from a significant military superpower, a threat that had created and sustained a sense of immediate danger throughout the Cold War. As noted above, that sense of danger permitted Western leaders to define common interests in the trans-Atlantic zone. With the fragmentation of the Soviet Union a global trend toward the regionalization of security challenges has become much more visible. The "strategic space" of the Soviet Union has been replaced by four distinct zones of security dynamics within the former Soviet Union—the northern European zone, the southern European zone, the Caucasus and the Middle East, and the Far East. Less clear, however, is how the West will define its common interests in the face of the new, regionally dispersed nuclear threats.

In many ways, the major challenge facing NATO remains that of dealing with Russia. For the United States, too, developing a relationship with Russia and trying to manage the dynamics of transition in Russia is the overarching challenge. Among the successor states Russia is the most significant player in European security. But the Russian state is not a single entity, and the question of whether Moscow will continue to govern the entire Russian Federation remains an open one. Russia's volatility necessarily shapes Western and Asian thinking in security matters. At the same time, the actions of the new states— notably Ukraine and Kazakhstan—have begun to affect perceptions of security in the European and Middle Eastern security zones.

The bargaining between the West and the so-called nuclear republics— Belarus, Ukraine, and Kazakhstan—has underscored the diplomatic utility of being a nuclear state. Having inherited the nuclear weapons installed on their territory, these states have been taken more seriously in the West than other states of the FSU. But nuclear weapons are coins of a very special diplomatic realm, and although they have proven useful instruments of persuasion in negotiations with the West, it is not clear that they would have been useful (at least in this period) as instruments of intimidation. Nor is it clear that the mere presence of nuclear weapons on one's territory—without the ability to control those weapons or to sustain a national nuclear program—will confer lasting diplomatic benefits.

Beyond the question of the disposition of nuclear assets on the territories of the three non-Russian NIS states, the core question remains the role and significance of nuclear weapons within Russia itself. That problem is multifaceted.

One might first focus upon the inability of the Russians to replace the Soviet state with a viable Russian one. While regionalism develops by design and default on the territory of the Russian republic, Moscow has sought to use its international role to augment its domestic significance. Nowhere is this more true than in the case of nuclear weapons. As the custodian of the Soviet nuclear arsenal, the Russian state is empowered by the international community to continue to act as a broker for Russian interests. It may be, however, that the Western interest in nuclear custodianship is coming at the expense of an equally compelling Western interest in political reform and change. Nuclear custodianship requires centralized control; political and economic reform may well require the breakup of the Russian state.

A second focus is the terrorist threat associated with the theft by non-state forces of fissile material. Several undocumented cases of the theft of Russian fissile material have been reported; recently, the Germans have documented a certain case of theft. The movement of Russian material and know-how in the nuclear domain into regions of instability and into the hands of rogue or terrorist states is a great fear of many analysts. Unfortunately, the threat of proliferation of nuclear material and know-how from the FSU is not easily grasped using deterrence theory. Indeed, it is not clear that classic assessments of nuclear weapons as instruments of state power provide much help in understanding the threat of non-state actors acquiring and using a nuclear threat to advance their goals.

Third, one can focus upon the attempt to develop a cooperative security regime with the Russians by reducing nuclear stockpiles and managing a "cooperative" transition to a world in which the significance of nuclear weapons is radically reduced. The challenges to carrying out such a policy are legion, but the organizational tasks are notably significant.

The immense task of the Russians is to rebuild government so that nuclear drawdowns become reality and to shift from a militarized economy with a significant nuclear sector to a privatized economy within which the nuclear sector is reduced dramatically in significance. This must be done while maintaining control over fissile materials under chaotic political and social conditions. It will be necessary, as part of the conversion process, to change Russian organizational systems so that modern management of the nuclear sector can emerge. The Russian tradition of centralized control of information and isolation of middle managers from one another and from top management must be modified to allow cooperation with Western organizations to work effectively.

For the United States, the challenge is equally daunting. Can the United States government reorganize itself in the ways necessary to induce and influence Russian participation in a new cooperative security system? Can the United States develop a realistic and effective aid mechanism? Can the United States reform its public sector to play a more effective role in cooperative security management?

Fourth, there is the question of the role of the Russians and the other recognized nuclear powers in the nonproliferation regime. This issue is associated with, but distinct from, the challenge of bilateral security management. Here the question is less one of cooperating to draw down nuclear forces than of intervening cooperatively to reduce the threat from the proliferation of nuclear weapons. How should the United States work with the Russians (and other nuclear states) in providing the guarantees and security assurances required under the Nuclear Nonproliferation Treaty? Russian and American interests in Europe and Asia are hardly the same—how will these interests be coordinated in dealing with proliferant threats to the South?

Fifth, one may ask how the Russians will use their remaining nuclear weapons as part of their military force structure. Will the new military doctrine actually become an expression of real state policy? Will the Russians pursue a first-use strategy in Asia and Europe? Will they rely on nuclear weapons to compensate for conventional weaknesses? If so, how will the military and political components of the Russian state build a realistic nuclear intervention instrument? Or is the mere presence of large numbers of nuclear weapons enough to create a threat of use?

## Conclusion

It is only with respect to this fifth dimension of the nuclear dynamic within Russia that classic deterrence theory developed during the Cold War is of direct relevance. In all other cases, fragments of thinking from the past forty years may be useful, but the situation is so different as to suggest the irrelevance of much our post-World War II experience. That is not to say that nuclear weapons themselves have become irrelevant, but it does reflect the fact that they have become important in new ways. Rather than as instruments of a national deterrent strategy alone, nuclear weapons are variously:

- Diplomatic entrées to the Western institutional club
- Instruments to assure Western support for the continued existence of a centralized Russian state
- Elements of a global terrorism problem, the solutions to which are not easily pursued on a state-to-state basis
- Part of a new organizational restructuring of the Russian-American relationship, a restructuring that could lead to a new Russian-American global bargain
- Potential instruments to sanction proliferant states within the context of a more effective global nonproliferation regime.

The nuclear situation in the former Soviet Union is a major part of the international challenge now confronting the West. The United States and the European Community are rightly investing significant resources in trying to manage the circulation of enriched uranium, weapons systems, and nuclear know-how, yet the West has not yet devised a comprehensive system to deal with this new version of an old nuclear threat.

But the challenge of the successor states is not simply a residuum of the military challenge. It is a moral one as well. On one level, the West's task must be to provide effective material assistance and to reorganize aid efforts to intervene effectively in the domestic political, economic, and cultural life of these states. On another level, there remains the question of whether the West, and particularly the United States, can participate creatively in the invention of democracy. It is unlikely that Western liberal democratic regimes will emerge any time soon in the FSU, but is it too much to hope that new democratic forms or systems could be invented that the West could accept and that Slavic publics could authenticate as their own?

The past five years have seen a revolution in the making in Europe and the

FSU. The collapse of the communist regimes in the East have been met by upheaval in the West. In response to the dramatic changes in the East, the West European and American states have radically restructured the role of military power within the Western systems.

The emergence of the newly independent states has already altered the map of Europe. Indeed, the concept of Western Europe as we have known it has begun to recede, an artifact of the Cold War. Will a new concept of Europe emerge in the wake of the dissolution of the Soviet Union and the collapse of communism in Central Europe? What will replace the Atlantic alliance that existed to contain communism? If the Soviet Union has disappeared and Europe is in mutation, will the Atlantic alliance remain viable?

# 4 Commonwealth of Chekists: The Former KGB Is Alive and Well in Post-Soviet Society

J. Michael Waller

Political and economic reforms that are sweeping much of the former Soviet Union have created the impression that the vast apparatus once known as the Committee for State Security (KGB) has been transformed to a shadow of its former self since the collapse of Communist party rule. Following the failed coup of August 1991, the Soviet government announced with much fanfare that the KGB had been "abolished" and its bureaucracy dismembered, and that completely new security services had been created in its place. However, examination of the KGB's successors reveals more continuity than change.

The KGB was the only major Soviet institution to have been untouched by glasnost and perestroika. Its structures in 1991 were little different from a decade earlier when Leonid Brezhnev ruled the country. Although freedoms had been expanded dramatically under Mikhail Gorbachev, the KGB maintained its active networks of informants and agents at home, and worked aggressively against the West abroad. After the Soviet collapse a large portion of the Soviet public reported in a major poll that they felt the KGB invaded their personal lives. One in three former Soviet citizens said that they or their relatives had suffered at the hands of the KGB or its predecessors. One in four said the KGB watched them as individuals. Six years of glasnost made little difference in this regard. Almost as many young people who came of age during the Gorbachev era reported that their activities, too, had been monitored or compromised by the KGB. Among the most educated and politically active population, including scientists and artists, the number was even greater. Thirty-five percent of those with some higher education and more than half with advanced degrees said that they had been spied upon by the KGB. Skeptics were hard-pressed to dismiss the results, since the poll was commissioned not by KGB opponents but by the state security organs themselves.[1]

A reasonable person might expect that a society truly attempting to rid itself of its totalitarian past would logically take measures to do away with such an abusive machine. However, reason and logic are seldom the rule in the former Soviet Union. To resolve the question of who would seize and wield power, the leaders of most republics of the Commonwealth of Independent States (CIS) chose not to undo the KGB structures they inherited, but to maintain them.

## The Chekist Legacy

Although state security organs have undergone some reorganization since the Soviet collapse, they have not shed their KGB legacy, either in terms of their basic structures and missions, their leadership and personnel, their training and bureaucratic culture, or their behavior. Despite abandonment of an official political ideology, the successors to the KGB maintain a political and bureaucratic continuity with the original secret service of the early Soviet state: the All-Russian Extraordinary Commission for Combating Counterrevolution and Sabotage, known as the VChK or Cheka.

The role of the Cheka was inherently political: to wipe out all opposition to the Communist party. In the process of carrying out its mandate, the Cheka utilized what founder Feliks Dzerzhinsky approvingly called "mass terror" against the opposition, liquidating as many as five hundred thousand people in the first five years of Bolshevik rule.[2] Over the years the security service underwent a series of name changes, finally becoming the KGB in 1954. Bureaucratic modifications and personnel purges—many of them bloody during the Stalin years—failed to cleanse the security organs of their original essence. Their officers still call themselves "chekists." Even in the 1990s, chekists maintain a world view that places them in what the KGB's final chairman, Vadim Bakatin, called a "constant search for an enemy." [3] The Dzerzhinsky personality cult survives to this day, and Chekism's elitist culture permeates every level of the security services.

Yet in addition to maintaining the chekist abodes and personnel, the security organs maintained the more esoteric images of chekism for internal consumption. The initiative after the putsch to tear down Feliks Dzerzhinsky's massive statue from the traffic circle in front of KGB headquarters and to erase his name from the square and rename it Lubyanka was made not by the chekists but by protesters and sympathetic members of the Moscow city government. On the main building itself, aside from the unceremonious removal of a plaque honoring former KGB chairman Yuri Andropov, nothing has changed. The outer dark gray stone and yellow brick walls continue to sport the outward symbolism of the KGB, with cast metal chekist hammer-and-sickle on sword-and-shield crests festooning the building's perimeter. Busts of Lenin and Dzerzhinsky remain on display within, and a portrait of the Cheka chief hangs religiously in seemingly every office. A great red marble wall with the names in bronze of chekists killed on duty remains in a main lobby, illuminated from below by a red eternal flame. Dzerzhinsky iconography still hangs in the notorious Lefortovo Prison. In the foreign intelligence service, too, Dzerzhinsky survives as a revered figure. A huge bust carved in stone remains at foreign intelligence headquarters in Yasenevo outside Moscow.[4]

## Breakup of the Soviet KGB

On the heels of the August 1991 coup attempt, the KGB was dismembered along functional and regional lines under the direction of Vadim Bakatin, a reform communist who had been Soviet minister of internal affairs between 1988 and 1990. Working with a special USSR state commission dominated by Russian Federation figures, Bakatin split the KGB into five major bodies at the Union level: counterintelligence and internal security, foreign intelligence, communications and electronic intelligence, presidential security, and border guards. KGB organs on the republic level were placed under the control of the governments of each republic, with the exception of the three Baltic states, where the formal KGB structures were transitioned into the Russian government, leaving clandestine agent networks behind. All of the KGB's structures on Russian territory were transferred to the Russian Federation.

Orderly partition of the KGB in this fashion was not quite a move toward curbing abuses, although this is what Bakatin ultimately had in mind.[5] The net result of the changes was to maintain an extremely strong apparatus, albeit decentralized. The dying Soviet government attempted to coordinate the republic KGBs loosely from the center and to administer foreign intelligence and the border guards. Bakatin soon backed away from promises of large-scale firings, thanks to resistance within, and to desires of the Russian Federation to absorb all remaining Soviet security structures for itself.

## Russian State Security Today

The state security and intelligence services of the Russian Federation have gone to great lengths to show the public that they are radically different from the KGB, and that they are configured and staffed to meet the country's needs as it develops market and democratic reforms. In reality, however, the Russian special services have more in common with the KGB than they have differences.[6] Five major state security organs emerged from the former KGB: the Federal Counterintelligence Service, the Federal Agency for Government Communications and Information, the Main Guard Administration, the Federal Border Service, and the External Intelligence Service.

### Federal Counterintelligence Service

The internal security structure of the KGB was preserved almost intact in the Russian Federation and renamed the Ministry of Security (*Ministerstvo bezopasnosti*) in January 1992. Renamed the Federal Counterintelligence Service (*Federalnaya sluzhba kontrrazvedki*, FSK), it retains most of the KGB's internal structures and functions, including counterintelligence; border guards; military and police counterintelligence; physical security of subways, highways, railroads, and the Aeroflot airline fleet; economic and industrial security; organized-crime prevention and counter-narcotics; security of bomb shelters and certain government buildings; analysis; military construction; technical laboratories; surveillance; mail interception; wiretapping; archives; investigations; and training. The FSK also maintains the networks and archives of secret informers.[7]

FSK personnel are almost all holdovers from the KGB. The service's first director, Nikolai Golushko, had spent most of his thirty-year career in the dissident-hunting Fifth Chief Directorate. Golushko was soon replaced by Sergei Stepashin, a veteran of the Ministry of Internal Affairs who seemed to hold out promises of real reform. Stepashin proved a real disappointment. His deputies include Valery Timofeyev, former KGB chief of Gorky (now Nizhny Novgorod); Aleksandr Strelkov, who until 1992 was head of a department responsible for the gulag system; Viktor Cherkesov, formerly of the Fifth Chief Directorate; and another veteran of the Fifth, Igor Mezhakov, now responsible for personnel.[8]

### Federal Agency for Government Communications and Information

The Federal Agency for Government Communications and Information (*Federalnoye agentsvo pravitelstvennoy sviazi i informatsiy*, FAPSI), which likes to compare itself to the U.S. National Security Agency (NSA), was formed from the KGB Eighth Chief Directorate responsible for communications security and cryptography, the Sixteenth Directorate for communications intelligence (COMINT) and signals intelligence (SIGINT), and the KGB communications troops.[9]

FAPSI controls Russia's government telephone lines and high-frequency communications, as well as the large signals-intelligence-gathering facility in Lourdes, Cuba. FAPSI chief Aleksandr V. Starovoytov, a former KGB lieutenant general, deplored the proliferation of free channels of information and launched an initiative to increase "state control . . . over the information and communications sector" in both government and private hands, a move denounced by one leading newspaper as a plan "to bring all flows of information back to 'former KGB channels.' " [10] Starovoytov also persuaded President Yeltsin to turn over his own independent information administration to FAPSI control.[11]

## Main Guard Administration

Responsible for the physical protection of Russian political leaders and foreign dignitaries, the Main Guard Administration (*Glavnoye upravelniye okhrany*, GUO) consists of the KGB Ninth (Guards) Directorate, the Alfa Group of the KGB Seventh (Surveillance) Directorate, and the former Russian MVD parliamentary guards unit.[12] Alfa is frequently cited as an "antiterrorist" force, but it is also a unit of shock troops trained to storm public buildings. It won fame and appreciation from President Yeltsin for not having attacked the Russian Supreme Soviet building during the 1991 putsch but was used to take over the same facility during the crushing of parliament two years later. However, its most prolific combat experience was the attack on the television tower in Vilnius, Lithuania, in January 1991.

## Federal Border Service

The Federal Border Service is comprised of most of the KGB Border Guards Chief Directorate not only on the territory of the Russian Federation, but also in the Caucasus and parts of Central Asia—including Tajikistan, which has no common border with Russia. Command and discipline broke down after the Soviet collapse, and plans for a CIS border force failed to materialize after Ukraine established its own independent border service to secure its frontier independently of Moscow. The Federal Border Service, with between 120,000 and 180,000 troops, became an independent organization in January 1994, with an army general placed in charge. Instead of being brought under Ministry of Defense control as many had speculated, the service leadership became embroiled in a bitter battle with defense minister Pavel Grachev, and a serious command and control crisis developed.[13]

*External Intelligence Service*

The External Intelligence Service (*Sluzhba vneshnei razvedki,* SVR) is the former KGB First Chief Directorate. The SVR was established by decree on December 20, 1991, the seventy-first anniversary of the founding of the first Soviet foreign intelligence service, and the seventy-fourth anniversary of the Cheka. Although the SVR publicly takes pains to distance itself from the KGB, especially among intellectual and political elites in the West, it internally underscores its chekist roots within the ranks. On December 20, 1992, the SVR quietly celebrated not its first birthday, but its seventy-second.[14] Thus the "new" intelligence service represents not a symbolic break with the past, but a continuum.

## Russian Foreign Intelligence Today

The SVR apparently plays less of a role in the Russian decision making process than did the KGB First Chief Directorate. Boris Yeltsin has given foreign intelligence relatively low bureaucratic status. While elevating the former KGB's internal security functions to cabinet level as the Ministry of Security, he created the SVR as an autonomous "service," ranking in the fourth echelon of bureaucracy after ministries, state committees, and committees. The SVR chief reports directly to the president, but unlike ministers and state committee chiefs, he is not an ex officio member of the government. He does, however, sit on a special Interdepartmental Foreign Policy Commission within the presidential Security Council, which formulates foreign policy and instructs the foreign minister, who also sits on the commission.[15] Most SVR activities are conducted abroad, although the service contains the former KGB Territorial Directorate for recruitment of foreigners inside the Russian Federation and possibly other CIS countries. The SVR officially does not operate in other CIS republics (presumably this is left to the Federal Counterintelligence Service which maintains archives and networks throughout former Soviet territory), but it does officially operate against Estonia, Latvia, and Lithuania, where the KGB bureaucracies were pulled out.[16]

As with the Federal Counterintelligence Service, little desovietization has taken place in the foreign intelligence service. The SVR has seen no dismantling of the old Soviet intelligence systems and structures, no significant removal of old-thinking personnel (in fact, by 1994 they remained at the top echelons of the SVR), and no noticeable infusion of new, more forward-thinking personnel. No Russian diplomats who spied for the KGB were relieved of their duties, in contrast to the situation in Bulgaria, where 10 percent of the diplomatic corps was cashiered for having served as communist spies.[17] No more than a token few documents were released to the public concerning Soviet international abuses. Some of the most poisonous elements of the old KGB remain in the SVR. A top SVR official confirmed the continued existence of Directorate S, which handles "illegals," or deep-cover agents living abroad under assumed identities. Directorate S likely still includes Department Eight, once known as Department V, for "wet affairs," or terrorism and political assassinations.[18]

Like the rest of the Soviet and Russian bureaucracy, the foreign intelligence service was bloated and needed to be reduced and reorganized if it was to remain effective. It no longer had to serve a political party as it did when, as the KGB First Chief Directorate (PGU), it spent most of its resources to satisfy what Bakatin called its "main consultant and client," the International Department of the Communist party (CPSU). Much of its presence abroad was completely unnecessary for the needs of the state. Bakatin commented,

The secret service was able to "yawn" at some of the most important events of international politics, but made up for it by regularly reporting to the center the reaction in various countries to the recurrent speech of the Soviet leader or about the squabbles in the diminutive Communist Party of some African country. . . . The disproportionately inflated staffs of the embassy secret agencies in no way corresponded with the actual results of the work.[19]

Nevertheless the KGB maintained world-class espionage networks, operations, and officers. These human and technical resources had to be preserved, and their effectiveness maximized, for the postcommunist government. Increased defections forced some reorganization.[20] Far-flung outposts in small Third World countries with little strategic value were an unnecessary strain on resources. SVR leaders make a point of saying that between thirty and forty intelligence posts were closed down in minor Third World countries as a cost-cutting measure, but they decline to name which countries, ostensibly so as not to risk offending local leaders by implying that they are not important enough to merit Moscow's continued attention.[21] Reductions were also made in major posts such as Washington, where the SVR presence was said by U.S. counterintelligence in early 1993 to be about 25 percent lower than in December 1991, totaling about forty agents.[22] This was not at the expense of espionage potential. It is safer and cheaper for the SVR to handle its American agents on Russian instead of U.S. soil. The publicly stated staff-reductions goal, almost certainly for propaganda purposes, was 50 percent, though the Russian parliament has not been able to determine exact figures.[23]

### SVR Leadership

One factor to indicate continuity in the SVR is leadership. The SVR is not using staff reductions to rid itself of old-thinking personnel. Unlike the economic team of former Prime Minister Yegor Gaidar—reformers with an instinctive trust and sympathy toward the West and its institutions—Russia's civilian and military intelligence services contain no proven progressives among their leaders. Indeed, Russia's only top-level holdover from the pre-putsch Soviet government is SVR director Yevgeny Primakov.[24] A member of Gorbachev's inner circle who was appointed chairman of the KGB First Chief Directorate in September 1991, Primakov was chief of its short-lived transitional successor and was retained by Yeltsin. The fluent speaker of English and Arabic who earned credentials as an academic, journalist, and policy maker was no newcomer to the KGB. He denies published reports that he began informing for the intelligence services in the late 1950s, but admits to having assisted the KGB as a newspaper correspondent in the Middle East.[25] He wrote, inter alia, the CPSU's most authoritative ideological rationale for the invasion of Afghanistan in 1979 and later spoke and wrote supportively of the Soviet occupation of that country. In 1990, prior to Operation Desert Storm, Primakov was the Kremlin's point man to try to prevent the U.S.-led coalition from driving the Iraqi military from Kuwait.[26] Primakov's deputies in the SVR show no signs of liberalism either.

The chief of the old chekists surrounding Primakov as his consultants group is retired Lt. Gen. Vadim Kirpichenko, whose career dates to the Stalin period. Kirpichenko served five years as deputy head of the KGB First Chief Directorate and twelve years as first deputy head under Vladimir Kryuchkov, who became KGB chairman. Kirpichenko was also in charge of Directorate S (Illegals) while deputy head of the First Chief Directorate.[27] Given the intense Soviet involvement in supporting Middle Eastern terrorist groups, and the reported role of Department Eight in carrying out political assassinations and training terrorists, it appears that Gen. Kirpichenko was not uninvolved in attacks on American, Israeli, and other Western targets.[28]

### Conduct of the Russian External Intelligence Service

Conduct is another indicator of continuity of the Russian intelligence service and its chiefs with the past. The SVR is maintaining KGB agent networks from surrogate services in Eastern Europe for political influence and espionage. It continues aggressive espionage operations in Western Europe, North America, and elsewhere. In addition to all the KGB First Chief Directorate archives and many CPSU international department documents, state security retains immense files from the internal informant and agent networks of the Communist parties of the former Warsaw Pact states. German investigators learned of a massive database in Moscow of informant and agent files for all Warsaw Pact member states. Joachim Gauck, chief of the German government's commission to preserve, catalogue, and process the archives of the defunct Stasi, reported that the internal security services of Soviet bloc governments

formed a single system, which operated under the name SOUD, Interlinked System for Recognizing Enemies. Its headquarters were in Moscow. Information concerning anything that qualified as a threat to the system was sent there and investigated. Particular cases were analyzed and appropriate tactics were devised for them. It was enough for someone to be considered—only potentially—an opponent of the system, and the appropriate actions were initiated: he was put under surveillance and information was collected on him . . . and his case would end up in headquarters in Moscow.[29]

Yet the SVR has indicated that it will not cooperate with former Warsaw Pact countries to help uncover the old Soviet networks. Nor has it turned over the files to the Russian State Commission for the Transfer-Reception of Archives or to relevant parliamentary security committees or commissions. In response to a journalist's question about this issue, Primakov responded, "The intelligence service does not intend to provide former socialist countries with lists of its agents who worked there." [30] Thus one may conclude that Moscow has opted to keep the old Soviet agent systems intact and therefore operational. These networks are not simply for traditional espionage, but represent political dangers to the new democratic governments. Those in possession of the networks and archives have the potential to undermine democratic gains in Central and Eastern Europe, to blackmail or otherwise manipulate present and future democratic governments there, to exact financial and business concessions, and to renew regional espionage and political and economic influence networks for operation in third countries, including the industrialized democracies.

The SVR and its military counterpart, known as the GRU, have been taking advantage of the networks left behind by the former East German Stasi throughout all of Germany. Bonn's interior minister, Rudolf Seiters, issued a report in April 1992 by the Federal Office for the Protection of the Constitution (BfV) which found that intelligence work by the KGB's successor services in Germany "continued unabated," and that the Russians maintained much of the Stasi framework in the former German Democratic Republic to carry out intelligence work and set up new, effective "networks of sources" in the medium term.[31] German counterintelligence found that Russian operations in the country were actually on the increase. Chief prosecutor Alexander von Stahl noted that Russian intelligence was in the process of "widening" its German network and "reactivating" an estimated four hundred former East German Stasi officers and agents. The SVR is also reported to have recruited "a large number" of former members of the defunct East German *Hauptverwaltung Aufklarung,* or foreign intelligence service.[32] Many of the increased espionage activities were staged from former Soviet military installations in the eastern part of the country that were served by troop trains operated directly from Russia. In accordance with bilateral agreements for Soviet troop withdrawal, the trains, which were guarded by the Ministry of Security/FSK, were not subject to inspections by German authorities. Chancellor Helmut Kohl reportedly sent an emissary to Moscow to complain that "The former Soviet intelligence agencies continue their spying activities unabated against military, political, and economic targets in unified Germany." [33]

*Espionage, 1992-1994*

Intelligence and counterintelligence officials from the United States, the European Community, and elsewhere have indicated that Russian espionage operations continued into 1994 roughly at the same levels as in the Soviet period. The targets, however, have shifted. SVR operations are reported to have declined, while GRU operations sharply increased, but the net total has also increased.[34] Moscow's emphasis on stealing economic and technological proprietary information, which began in earnest in the mid-1980s, has moved with increasing intensity now that military tensions between the superpowers have eased. In addition to Germany and the United States, countries that have reported continued Russian economic and industrial spying include Belgium, Denmark, France, Norway, Portugal, and Sweden. Several of them expelled Russian agents, as did Finland and the Netherlands. Spain deported Cuban technological spies who apparently continued to work as Moscow surrogates.[35]

Businessmen and private companies remain prime espionage targets at home and inside Russia. Many have opened themselves up by retaining former

KGB officers as partners, advisers, and due diligence investigators who report back to the FSK and SVR as members of the "active reserve" or in other capacities. The SVR maintains the old Territorial Directorate of the KGB First Chief Directorate, which assesses and recruits foreigners, particularly businessmen, within Russia and possibly in Ukraine. Joint ventures with Russian firms, particularly in the technological, communications, and financial spheres, may hold short-term profits for western companies, but present long-term dangers. A spate of defections in 1991 and 1992 exposed large Soviet/Russian economic and technological espionage rings, resulting in their disruption or destruction and forcing the SVR and GRU to reorganize their operations.[36]

Russian intelligence officials on occasion acknowledged their new emphasis on theft of technological and economic secrets. One senior SVR officer said that Russia is so dependent on economic and industrial espionage that it even improves its bread industry by combing the world for quality strains of yeast.[37] At the same time, the spy services give the Russian public a new excuse to justify their need to remain well-funded in a time of severe economic hardship.

Of course, the SVR's increased emphasis on economic and industrial espionage does not mean that more classic security and counterespionage targets have been forgotten, nor have the agents involved been abandoned. The Aldrich Ames spy affair attests to the continued determination of the SVR to protect its classic espionage assets.

Even though German and American intelligence services are cooperating with the SVR on certain very limited matters, German intelligence coordinator Bernd Schmidbauer cautioned that with respect to economic and industrial espionage, "Counterintelligence must remain wide awake, despite all the steps that we are taking now. Whoever is now succumbing to euphoria and does not see things realistically cannot be helped." [38]

In other developments, Russia forged new intelligence agreements with the People's Republic of China and Cuba. Intelligence ties with Beijing that had been severed in 1959 were secretly reestablished in September 1992, when an agreement was made for the SVR and GRU to share information and cooperate with the Military Intelligence Department of the People's Liberation Army. A major American concern is that the SVR and GRU are joining forces with Chinese espionage to steal Western weapons technology.[39] On the heels of signing the agreement with China came an accord with Fidel Castro's government in Cuba to continue use of the giant electronic intelligence facility near Lourdes.[40] The pact was signed by Deputy Prime Minister for Foreign Economic Affairs Aleksandr Shokhin, an indication that Moscow will use the site for commercial and economic espionage against the United States and Russia's expanding trading partners in Latin America. At the same time, Russian intelligence has tried to portray itself as a normal, Western-style intelligence service completely different from the KGB.

### Civil Controls and Oversight

Civil controls over the security and intelligence services are uncertain. The chain of command to the president is unclear. A presidential security council has not proven to be an effective means of management or control and has been neutralized by a combination of political rivalry between reformers and nonreformers, President Yeltsin's lack of interest in security matters, and a power struggle between the presidential apparat and the parliament.

Russia's parliament has taken steps to exert a degree of control over the security organs, but these controls are negligible. No oversight exists in the Western sense of the word. Parliament has not ascertained the security and intelligence budgets and has no ability to approve or prohibit expenditures in these areas. The Supreme Soviet of 1990-1993 almost willfully legislated itself out of a position to have meaningful, intrusive, and comprehensive oversight of the organs. Indeed, the key legislation concerning security and intelligence matters was authored by the affected chekist organs themselves. Far from being parliamentary impositions on the former KGB, the laws are the former KGB's impositions on parliament.[41] The new Federal Assembly, elected in December 1993 to replace the Supreme Soviet, is considerably weakened by new constitutional constraints and is practically ignored by the executive branch. There is no independent judiciary.

Russia has insulated the security and intelligence services from public criticism by enacting laws which criminalize revelations and certain criticisms published in the news media. One law provides for criminal sanctions against individuals who "insult . . . [the] honor and dignity" of internal security personnel. Another specifically states that journalists should present their intelligence-related materials and articles to the SVR prior to publication for official authorization. Publication without SVR authorization, especially if the published material inflicts "moral or material damages on foreign intelligence agencies and their personnel," is now a crime.[42] Thus the security and intelligence organs have wide latitude in legally restricting undesirable revelations and criticisms.

## Commonwealth of Chekists

The situation is similar or worse in the rest of the CIS, where few republics have truly defined their national interests in a post-Soviet context, and even fewer have chosen to make the break from chekism. Following the August 1991 putsch, Moscow tried to accommodate the nationalist aspirations of the newly independent states by decentralizing the Second Chief Directorate of the KGB, which was responsible for counterintelligence and most other internal security duties, and by transferring to local control the republican units of other KGB directorates aside from foreign intelligence and border guards. All government communications equipment, including codes, was to belong to the republic on whose territory it was based.[43]

Thenceforth, each republic—except Estonia, Latvia, and Lithuania, where official state security structures were withdrawn to Russia—would officially control its own KGB. This move, made by the center in part to minimize the potential for future putschists to seize control of the entire Soviet Union, acknowledged at the same time that the union was disintegrating. All CIS countries with the exception of Belarus renamed their KGBs, while only Armenia made a serious attempt to purge its services. Only in the four former Soviet republics outside the CIS did meaningful reforms occur. With the exception of the Baltic states, where the official KGB structures made an orderly withdrawal, and Georgia, where the republican KGB was purged twice and its headquarters incinerated in heavy fighting, the chekist organs did anything but disintegrate. (Even in the Baltic states and Georgia, clandestine networks were left behind.) Speaking in the third person about most of the former USSR, Bakatin said in an interview:

Everyone keeps saying that Bakatin has torn down the KGB structure. For goodness' sake, this is not so. If you come to Kazakhstan, not a single hair has fallen from the head of any official in Kazakhstan. Or to Kyrgyzstan—I just got back from there, everything is still as it was there. The situation is the same in the Moscow department, and in the Kemerovo one. That is, all the capillaries at the bottom and the structures have remained the same.[44]

Most CIS countries went through the motions of making it look like the KGB was gone by renaming their security services. Only Belarus preserved the name "KGB." However, as in Russia, reforms were minimal, if any were undertaken at all. The regime in Uzbekistan systematically persecutes political opponents. Kazakhstan, despite a rather reformist image in the West, continues to resort to brute force to silence critics. In one celebrated case, Kazakh state security agents severely beat an American representative of the International Republican Institute, breaking bones in his face, after he was warned that his prodemocracy work was interfering in the country's internal affairs.[45]

Professional officer networks link chekists from one republic to another. Several countries—Armenia, Belarus, Moldova, Ukraine, and Uzbekistan—began to set up their own foreign intelligence services in late 1991 with Russian assistance.[46] Russian services continue to provide training, technical support, codes and ciphers, information, and other forms of assistance to their CIS counterparts.[47] All CIS members agreed in 1992 to cooperate on counterintelligence matters and not to run intelligence operations against one another. In the words of an SVR spokesman, they would work not "against one another, but for one another." [48] As was the practice of the Soviet Union with its Warsaw Pact allies, Russia has signed individual bilateral intelligence, counterintelligence, and law-enforcement agreements with other CIS republics. When Georgia was pressured to join the CIS in 1993, it soon signed similar accords with Moscow. Some non-Russian republics also signed similar agreements with one another.[49] Thus the security organs of the CIS member states are "defending" their countries against the West, and not against the imperial center of the old Soviet Union. Indeed, as more mutual cooperation agreements among the commonwealth chekists were signed in 1994, Russian intelligence chief Primakov issued a provocative public report that underscored Moscow's strategic plans for security hegemony over the CIS despite the West's concerns.[50]

## Can the Security Services Be Reformed?

Individuals who dare challenge the Russian security services by suggesting comprehensive reforms and civil controls have been roundly attacked in official and semi-official statements. Critics' motives are impugned, the implication—or direct allegation—being that they are working for foreign intelligence services. American nongovernmental organizations that provide Russian reformers with ideas for comprehensive civil controls and oversight mechanisms over the special services have been singled out by the FSK and SVR, which have branded them as CIA and FBI fronts.[51] The apparent objective is to stigmatize U.S. groups as well as the Russian reformers who work with them. Another objective may be to create a political backdrop to planned criminal prosecutions of pro-Western reformers by branding their political beliefs or foreign affiliations as threats to state security.

While technicians and certain specialists may be able to provide positive contributions to democratic society, many if not most chekist personnel are unreformable. Bakatin in late 1991 called for a "very robust shake-up," citing "very great stagnation in the cadres." [52] A Russian parliamentary investigator who interviewed numerous KGB officers of various ranks after the August 1991 putsch found, "They have no understanding in their minds that they are serving the constitution or the law, they have no reverence for the rule of law and citizens' rights. They unquestioningly and consistently fulfilled only the orders of their superiors; this for them was the main value, even though there may have been declarations of the 'we serve the people and the motherland' type." [53]

A real housecleaning never took place. A Russian parliamentary commission found that of thirty-two pro-putsch KGB leaders due to have been dismissed, only one—Kryuchkov—was forced out in public disgrace. Six were retired, and the other twenty-five were allowed to remain in state security; none was publicly identified. The situation was similar in the Ministry of Internal Affairs and the armed forces, according to the commission. [54]

Even President Yeltsin admitted that the chekist services were "unreformable." In a remarkable December 1993 decree to revamp the internal security apparatus he stated,

The attempts at reorganization that have been made in recent years were basically superficial and cosmetic. Up to the present moment the Russian Ministry of Security lacks a strategic concept of ensuring Russia's security. Counterintelligence work has deteriorated. The system of political investigation has been mothballed and could easily be recreated. [55]

Yet the chekists managed to preserve themselves despite the presidential decree, limiting damage to a mere name change (from Ministry of Security to FSK). Although Yeltsin has gone further than any other sitting leader in the CIS, he has been unwilling to challenge the Soviet state security legacy. Cognizant of his own limitations—and his dependency on the chekists for lack of other stable institutions—Yeltsin has chosen to coexist with them. Nor is there much political sentiment anywhere in the CIS to do away with the most noxious elements of the old KGB, which is now a mainstay of all of the pseudo-democratic regimes there. Western encouragement has been almost nil. Chekism is ingrained in most of post-Soviet society.

So what is the prognosis for the old KGB? Bakatin summed it up best. Reflecting on his 107 days as KGB chairman, he commented, "No one will ever turn the KGB upside-down, at least not at present. ... I am sure that in the future, society will gradually rid itself of the chekist ideology, but that requires that it become a really democratic, civil society."

## Notes

1. Olga Kryshtanovskaya, "Advocates and Antagonists of the KGB," *Nezavisimaya gazeta*, international edition in English, August 1993, 3.

2. Merle Fainsod, *How Russia Is Ruled* (Cambridge, Mass.: Harvard University Press, 1967), 426, 663-664n; Robert Conquest, "The Human Cost of Soviet Communism," Report for the Senate Committee on the Judiciary, 1971, 11.

3. Vadim Bakatin, *Izvestiya*, January 2, 1992, morning edition, 6, trans. Foreign Broadcast Information Service *Daily Report-Central Eurasia* (hereafter referenced as FBIS-SOV) 92-002, January 3, 1992, 4-5.

4. Descriptions of KGB headquarters derived from author's personal observations and from conversations with current and former state security officers, who also described Yasenevo. Description of Lefortovo prison is from interviews with dissident scientist Vil Mirzayanov in 1994.

5. Vadim Bakatin, interviews with author, September 1992. Also see his memoirs of his KGB chairmanship, *Isbavleniye ot KGB* (Moscow: Novosti, 1992).

6. See Yevgenia Albats, *A State within a State* (New York: Farrar, Strauss and Giroux, 1994), and J. Michael Waller, *Secret Empire: The KGB in Russia Today* (Boulder, Colo.: Westview Press, 1994).

7. Yevgeniya Albats, "KGB-MSB-MBVD: Substantive Changes?" *Moscow News*, no. 2, January 13, 1992, 5; and Victor Yasmann, "Where Has the KGB Gone?" Radio Free Europe/Radio Liberty (hereafter referenced as RFE/RL) *Research Report* 2, 2, January 8, 1993.

8. Natalya Gevorkyan, "Appointments," *Moscow News*, no. 13, April 1994, English-language electronic mail version; and Alexander Rahr, "Old Leaders at Head of Counterintelligence," *RFE/RL Daily Report*, no. 25, February 7, 1994, 2.

9. *Rossiiskaya gazeta*, December 28, 1991, first edition, 2, trans. in FBIS-SOV-92-001, January 2, 1992, 57; and *Krasnaya zvezda*, February 18, 1993, 2, trans. in FBIS-SOV-93-032, February 19, 1993, 21-22.

10. Vera Selivanova, "All Information to Have One Color: KGB Will Determine Which One," *Segodnya*, no. 38, July 30, 1993, 2, trans. in FBIS-SOV-93-147, August 3, 1993, 10-11.

11. *Kommersant-Daily*, February 23, 1994, 2, trans. in FBIS-SOV-94-037, February 24, 1994, 29-30.

12. *Komsomolskaya pravda*, September 20, 1991, 2, trans. in FBIS-SOV-91-187, September 26, 1992, 22; and Igor Nikulin, member, Russian Federation Supreme Soviet Committee on Defense and Security, *Komsomolskaya pravda*, October 20, 1992, 1-2, trans. in FBIS-SOV-92-204, October 21, 1992, 21-23.

13. Bill Gertz, "Moscow Losing Control of Army; Strategic Exercise Lacked Central OK," *Washington Times*, September 30, 1994, 1, 15.

14. Kirpichenko, discussion with author and U.S. legal experts, American Bar Assn. Standing Comm. on Law and National Security, Washington, D.C., January 13, 1993.

15. Presidential Decree no. 1147, "On the System of Central Organs of Federal Executive Power," September 30, 1992, trans. in FBIS-SOV-92-195, October 7, 1992, 11-12; and *Rossiiskaya gazeta*, February 3, 1993, first edition, 7, trans. in FBIS-SOV-93-025, February 9, 1993, 17.

16. Lt. Gen. Vadim Kirpichenko, presentation at Kennan Institute for Advanced Russian Studies, Woodrow Wilson Center, Smithsonian Institution, Washington, D.C., January 12, 1993.

17. "Bulgaria to Sack Diplomats Who Spied for Communists," Reuters Library Report, March 4, 1992. Bulgarian Telegraph Agency (BTA) in English, 1501 GMT, December 17, 1991, in British Broadcasting Corporation Summary of World Broadcasts (hereafter referenced as BBCSWB), December 19, 1991, EE/1259/B/1; and BTA in English, 1415 GMT, December 18, 1991, in BBCSWB, December 23, 1991, EE/1262/B/1.

18. Kirpichenko, conversation with author at Kennan Institute, January 12, 1993. While in the KGB First Chief Directorate, Kirpichenko was responsible for Directorate S. For references to the purpose of Department Eight, see John J. Dziak, *Chekisty: A History of the KGB* (Lexington, Mass.: Lexington Books, 1988), 162-163. Kirpichenko later told the *Washington Post*, "We think that 'illegal intelligence' is one of the legitimate forms of intelligence gathering. But we no longer have goals of a subversive character." Michael Dobbs and R. Jeffrey Smith, "From Inside the KGB: A Tale of Incompetence," *Washington Post*, February 21, 1993, A26.

19. Vadim Bakatin, *Izbavleniye ot KGB* (Moscow: Novosti, 1992), 39.

20. KGB First Chief Directorate First Deputy Director Vyacheslav Trubinkov, on Teleradiokompaniya Ostankino Television First Program Network, 1100 GMT, September 9, 1992, trans. in FBIS-SOV-92-176, September 10, 1992, 21.

21. SVR consultants group chief Lt. Gen. Vadim Kirpichenko, and SVR press and public affairs chief Yuri Kobaladze, presentation at the Kennan Institute, January 12, 1993.

22. Dobbs and Smith, "From Inside the KGB," A26.

23. Igor Nikulin, member, Supreme Soviet Committee on Questions of Legality, Law, Order, and Combatting Crime, in Radio Rossii, 1300 GMT, January 24, 1992, trans. in FBIS-SOV-92-019, January 29, 1992, 48. Members of the new parliament elected in 1993 who sit on the committees that are supposed to oversee the SVR confirmed in 1994 interviews with the author their inability to perform their duties.

24. Primakov was a top adviser to Gorbachev and was chairman of the Council of the Union of the USSR Supreme Soviet in 1989. He was on Gorbachev's presidential council until late 1991.

25. According to former KGB foreign counterintelligence chief Oleg Kalugin, Primakov was a KGB asset as early as 1957, with the cryptonym "Maxim." Albats, "KGB-MSB-MBVD," 5.

26. Avigdor Haselkorn and Christopher Coker, "The Spies Who Stayed in the Cold," *European Security Analyst*, no. 20, Institute for European Defence and Strategic Studies, London, August 1992, 2.

27. Kirpichenko, conversation with author, January 12, 1993; and in *Patriot* (Moscow), no. 34, in *RFE/RL Daily Report*, no. 169, September 3, 1992, 2. See also, "Russian Foreign Intelligence Service Delegation Biographies," Center for Democracy, Washington, January 1993.

28. See Jillian Becker, *The PLO: The Rise and Fall of the Palestine Liberation Organization* (New York: St. Martin's Press, 1984); Roberta Goren, *The Soviet Union and*

*Terrorism* (London: George Allen & Unwin, 1984), 106-141; Michael Ledeen, "Intelligence, Training, and Support Components," in *Hydra of Carnage: The International Linkages of Terrorism—The Witnesses Speak,* ed. Uri Ra'anan, et al., (Lexington, Mass.: Lexington Books, 1986), 155-168; Ra'anan, et al., "Surrogate Actors in the Middle East," in *Hydra of Carnage,* 519-527, 544-547; and Richard H. Shultz, Jr., *The Soviet Union and Revolutionary Warfare: Principles, Practices, and Regional Comparisons* (Stanford, Calif.: Hoover Institution, 1988), 76-114.

29. Jozef Darski, "Police Agents in the Transition Period," *Uncaptive Minds* 4, 4 (Winter 1991-1992): 15-16.

30. *Izvestiya,* November 29, 1991, union edition, 1, 6, trans. in FBIS-SOV-91-232, December 3, 1991, 36-37.

31. *Handelsblatt* (Düsseldorf), August 14-15, 1992, 5, trans. in FBIS-WEU-92-160, August 18, 1992, 11.

32. Haselkorn and Coker, "Spies Who Stayed in the Cold," 1.

33. *Der Spiegel* (Hamburg), August 31, 1992, 16-17, trans. in FBIS-WEU-92-170, September 1, 1992, 4.

34. James Sherr, "Change and Continuity in the Former KGB," *Jane's Intelligence Review,* March 1993, 112.

35. For examples, see Waller, *Secret Empire,* 144-148.

36. Erich Inciyan, "Russian Spies at the Heart of Nuclear Secrets," *Le Monde,* Paris, November 3, 1992, 14, trans. in FBIS-WEU-92-216, November 6, 1992, 25. First Chief Directorate first deputy director Vyacheslav Trubinkov, reported by Natalya Gorodetskaya and Yelena Tregubova, *Nezavisimaya gazeta,* September 10, 1992, 1-2, trans. in FBIS-SOV-92-180, September 16, 1992, 19-20.

37. "I Have the Honor . . . Intelligence Service," Teleradiokompaniya Ostankino Television First Program Network, 1850 GMT, August 13, 1992, trans. in FBIS-SOV-92-160, August 18, 1992, 33-34. Ellipses in original.

38. *Focus,* Munich, Feb. 22, 1993, 12, trans. in FBIS-WEU-93-034, Feb. 23, 1993.

39. Bill Gertz, "Russia, China Sign Pact Restoring Intelligence Ties," *Washington Times,* October 21, 1992, A7.

40. *Izvestiya,* November 5, 1992, morning edition, 5, trans. in FBIS-SOV-92-215, November 5, 1992, 16; and Pascal Fletcher, "Moscow, Havana Ink Pact," Reuters, November 4, 1992

41. The main laws are the Law on Security, the Law on Federal Agencies of State Security, the Law on Intelligence, and the Law on State Secrets, passed by the Supreme Soviet in 1992. The Federal Assembly was considering draft legislation in late 1994 to replace these laws, but the drafts showed little improvement over current law.

42. Section IV, Article 15, clause 1, Law on Federal Organs of State Security, *Rossiiskaya gazeta,* August 12, 1992, 1, 4, trans. in FBIS-USSR-92-121, September 24, 1992, 25; Section 9, Law on Foreign Intelligence, *Rossiiskaya gazeta,* August 11, 1992, 4, trans. in FBIS-USSR-92-110, September 1, 1992, 23.

43. Bakatin, *Izbavleniye ot KGB,* 83-84.

44. Albats, "KGB-MSB-MBVD," 5.

45. For a survey of the former KGB in the CIS, see J. Michael Waller, "Commonwealth of Chekists: State Security and Intelligence Services in the Commonwealth of Independent States Today" (Paper presented at the annual conference of the International Studies Association, Washington, D.C., March 31, 1994. The Kazakh case was reported to the author by the victim, Eric Rudenshiold, in an interview.

46. *Handelsblatt* (Düsseldorf), citing 1991 constitutional protection report, August 14-15, 1992, 5, trans. in FBIS-WEU-92-160, August 18, 1992, 11.

47. Tatyana Samolis, press secretary to the SVR director general, *Nezavisimaya gazeta*, January 20, 1992, 1, trans. in FBIS-SOV-92-035, February 21, 1992, 45; and Kirpichenko, presentation at Kennan Institute, January 12, 1993.

48. Tatyana Samolis, ITAR-TASS, March 25, 1992, cited in "CIS Intelligence Services Agree to Cooperate," *RFE/RL Research Report*, April 10, 1992, 56; Samolis, in *Izvestiya*, March 27, 1992, morning edition, 6, trans. in FBIS-SOV-92-064, April 2, 1992, 29; and Samolis, in ITAR-TASS World Service in Russian, 1255 GMT, April 6, 1992, trans. in BBCSWB, April 11, 1992, SU/1353/B/1.

49. For ties with Belarus, see ITAR-TASS world service in Russian, 1700 GMT, May 13, 1992, trans. BBCSWB, May 20, 1992, SU/1385/B/1. For Ukraine, see Victor Yasmann, "Russian-Ukrainian Intelligence Agreement," *RFE/RL Daily Report*, no. 137, July 21, 1992, 1. Belarus and Ukraine signed a bilateral accord similar to the ones they each signed with Russia. See Ukrinform for ITAR-TASS world service in Russian, 1550 GMT, July 31, 1992, trans. in FBIS-SOV-92- 150, August 4, 1992, 64. Belarus, Russia, and Ukraine signed similar bilateral agreements with Kazakhstan. See Alexander Lukashuk, "Belarus's KGB: In Search of an Identity," *RFE/RL Research Report* 1, 47, November 27, 1992, 20.

50. Primakov's report was published in *Rossiyskaya gazeta*, Sept. 22, 1994, 1, 6.

51. Gen. Andrei Chernenko, chief of public relations, Ministry of Security, *Pravda*, September 30, 1992, 2, trans. in FBIS-SOV- 930, 2-195, October 7, 1992, 32-33; Interfax, 1745 GMT, October 29, 1992, in FBIS-SOV-92-211, October 1992, 9; and Andrew Higgins, "New KGB Lashes Out at 'Foreign Meddling,' " *The Independent* (London), January 28, 1993. The International Freedom Foundation, where the author directed a program to promote Russian discussion of U.S. security and intelligence oversight theory and practice, was denounced by the Ministry of Security in the *Independent* article. Also see *Nezavisimaya gazeta*, August 24, 1994.

52. Russian Television Network, 2108 GMT, September 19, 1991, trans. in FBIS-SOV-91-184, September 23, 1991, 25-26.

53. RSFSR People's Deputy Nikolai Ryabov, Deputy Chairman of the State Commission to Investigate the Activity of the State Security Organs, *Rossiiskaya gazeta*, September 18, 1991, 1, trans. in FBIS-SOV-91-181, September 18, 1991, 25.

54. Lev Ponomarev, chairman of the Russian parliamentary Committee to Investigate the Causes and Circumstances of the August Putsch, on All-Union Radio Mayak Network, Moscow, 1540 GMT, December 25, 1991, trans. in FBIS-SOV-91-248, December 26, 1991, 42. Aleksei Surkov, a member of the Ponomarev Commission, told Radio Mayak that the commission found that *militsiya* leaders who supported the putsch were subsequently appointed to "major leading posts" in the Soviet MVD. Another commission member, Deputy Lyushenkov, said that army commanders supportive of the putsch "are still occupying high-level posts and are being promoted." In 1993, a state security spokesman confirmed the approximate number. Lt. Col. Aleksei Petrovich Kandaurov, deputy chief of public affairs of the Ministry of Security, said that the total numbers of officers removed in relation to the putsch was thirty. Kandaurov, presentation at "KGB: Yesterday, Today and Tomorrow," conference sponsored by the Glasnost Foundation, Moscow, February 19, 1993.

55. ITAR-TASS World Service, in Russian, 1704 GMT, December 21, 1993, trans. in FBIS-SOV-93-244, December 22, 1993, 35.

# 5 New States and Old Soldiers: Civil-Military Relations in the Former Soviet Union

John W. R. Lepingwell

When the Soviet Union collapsed it left behind a vast array of arms and troops scattered throughout the successor states. This military legacy has complicated both the development of relations between the newly independent states (NIS) and the creation of stable civil-military relations within them.[1] These states face the challenge of creating a military that can safeguard their newfound independence without threatening their freedoms and civilian government. A number of tasks must be accomplished before this goal can be met: creating a loyal officer corps and recruiting troops; removing undesired foreign troops from their territory; and establishing a system of civilian oversight and control. Many different approaches to solving these problems have been taken, with outcomes ranging from coups and civil war to relative stability. This survey of civil-military relations in the region suggests that the military legacy of the Soviet Union will continue to plague the area for years, and even decades, to come, possibly triggering larger conflicts within and between the states of the former USSR.

This chapter examines the collapse of the Soviet military and the emergence of new military forces in the former Soviet republics. In highlighting the strategies the new states have used to create new national militaries and secure their loyalty, the survey reveals wide variance in the development of civil-military relations in the region and provides a basis for conjectures on their future stability.

## The Collapse of the USSR and the Unraveling of the CIS

The Soviet military numbered approximately three million when the USSR disintegrated in late 1991. Indeed, the Soviet military played a major role in the dissolution of the Soviet Union and the creation of the Commonwealth of Independent States (CIS). The military had been weakened politically and morally by its ambiguous role in the August 1991 coup attempt, and the new military high command under Marshal Yevgeny Shaposhnikov was confronted in December 1991 with a difficult choice: support a greatly weakened Mikhail Gorbachev in his attempt to hold together a rapidly disintegrating Soviet Union or throw its weight behind Russian president Boris Yeltsin and the nascent CIS. In the end, the military supported Yeltsin and thereby materially acquiesced, and even assisted, in the collapse of the USSR.

The military's decision to back the CIS was motivated less by an altruistic desire to see the republics free and independent than by a recognition that only force could keep the USSR together, and only then with the potential of precipitating a massive civil war. Furthermore, in December 1991 the CIS appeared a means by which the centrifugal tendencies in the Soviet Union could be accommodated while maintaining a unified, or at least a jointly commanded, CIS military. Of particular concern was preventing Ukraine from breaking completely from the former Soviet military, political, and economic structure.

The military's hopes that the CIS would be a functioning confederation with some form of joint military were quickly dispelled. Ukraine was clearly determined to move ahead rapidly to establish its own, independent armed forces, and in doing so it triggered a number of disputes with the CIS Joint Command. Russia, trying to emphasize the primacy of the CIS command, delayed creating its own ministry of defense for several months, until May 1992. The creation of the Russian defense ministry substantially weakened the role of the CIS Joint Command, for most of the Soviet military organization was transferred to Russian subordination, leaving the CIS command a rather hollow organization with only strategic nuclear weapons formally under its control. The final acknowledgment of the CIS command's powerlessness came a year later, when Marshal Shaposhnikov resigned his position and briefly joined the Russian government as secretary of the Security Council.[2]

The creation of the Russian military established Russia as the preeminent military successor to the Soviet Union. Russia gained control over former Soviet forces in Cuba, Germany, Mongolia, Poland, Armenia, Azerbaijan, Estonia, Georgia, Latvia, Lithuania, part of Moldova, Tajikistan, and Turkmenistan.[3] Although some of these forces have subsequently been withdrawn or reassigned, their assumption by Russia served to awaken fears of new Russian influence in the "near abroad" and it has complicated the rebuilding of the Russian military.

The crumbling of the CIS military command was driven by the competing dynamics of state-building and collective security. The concept of a joint CIS military presupposed a collective security system in which the CIS states had shared security concerns and believed that a joint security force was the best means of ensuring the security of individual states. Collective security required that adherents surrender a degree of sovereignty upon entering into defensive pacts and collaborating in joint military commands. However, this collective-security approach collided in many cases with the imperatives of state-building. In Ukraine, in particular, the primary security concern was Russia, and participation in a collective security system created and dominated by Russia was viewed as a direct threat to Ukraine's sovereignty. This view was shared to some extent by Georgia, Moldova, and Azerbaijan. Conversely, the Central Asian states and Belarus viewed Russia as a potential guarantor of security and endeavored to develop good relations. Nevertheless, the diversity of views and interests within the states of the CIS doomed the CIS military structure and resulted in the emergence of a dozen new military forces.

### State-Building: New Armies, Old Soldiers

While most of the NIS found themselves with large numbers of troops and arms on their territory, they were far from possessing reliable combat-ready forces. They faced the task of dismantling the remnants of the Soviet military while building an indigenous military.

Two fundamentally different approaches to the problem of dissolving the old Soviet military and forming new militaries may be discerned. On the one hand, some states have started with an almost clean slate, creating their military force from scratch in terms of both personnel and equipment. On the other hand, in some cases personnel and equipment have simply been nationalized, with subsequent moves to change the internal structure and loyalty of the resulting force.

The Baltic States have adopted perhaps the most radical approach by creating new military forces utilizing a minimum of former Soviet personnel and equipment. This decision was motivated by their view that the former Soviet, and now Russian, forces located on their territories constituted an army of occupation. Hence, a claim to ownership or inheritance of even a part of the Soviet military could be construed as a de facto acceptance of the legality of Soviet rule.[4] Yet without access to the substantial caches of arms located in the area, the Baltic states have had to turn to other suppliers of both materiel and training, including the Nordic countries and Israel. The preference for Western arms is in part motivated by the long-term aspiration of these states to join

NATO, and they are attempting to achieve technical interoperability with NATO forces rather than with Russian.[5] Given the small size and the ongoing economic difficulties of the Baltic states, however, the process of building military forces will undoubtedly be a slow and difficult one.

But the Baltic states appear to be an exception to the rule in the former Soviet Union. Most other former Soviet republics have employed a rather different approach and have "nationalized" the Soviet personnel and equipment on their territory. At the forefront of this process was Ukraine, which in early 1992 laid claim to all former Soviet forces (except strategic nuclear forces) on its territory and required that military personnel take an oath of allegiance to Ukraine.[6] Similar moves followed in Belarus, Kazakhstan, Moldova, and the Central Asian states.[7]

In several cases a mixed approach was adopted. In Turkmenistan a joint Russian-Turkmen command was created, whereas Georgia and Azerbaijan sought the immediate withdrawal of Russian troops, but not their materiel. Russian forces did pull out of Azerbaijan with remarkable haste, completing their withdrawal in May 1992, but in Georgia they prolonged their stay. In Moldova, the former Soviet forces were split; troops on the right bank of the Dniester River became subordinate to the Moldovan government while Russia claimed those on the left bank. In Armenia a new military force was created with arms from the former Soviet units, but some units were taken over by Russia and have remained in Armenia, with the Armenian government's consent.

Thus, the military forces of the NIS have been pieced together from the remnants of the Soviet military, but in many cases they remain closely intertwined with Russian forces. While the new states have taken very different paths towards the creation of their military forces, they have a number of problems in common. Housing and pay problems have been perhaps the most pressing and immediate in many states, and in Russia especially, accommodations for troops are inadequate. Because of the fiscal and currency problems of most of these states, salaries have often been paid irregularly. Budget constraints and shortages have also limited the flow of fuel, parts, and equipment to the troops, resulting in a further decline in training and readiness. These problems, present to a greater or lesser extent in most of the militaries of the NIS, have had a corrosive effect on both morale and military capability.

The most pressing problems for the NIS militaries, however, lie on the personnel front. These concern the creation of a loyal officer corps and finding sufficient enlisted personnel.

*The Officer Corps*

The Soviet officer corps was both numerous and dominated by officers of Slavic descent.[8] Furthermore, officers were distributed on the basis of need, not with a view to having them serve in their native republic. When the Soviet military fragmented, those states which laid claim to the forces and personnel on their territory therefore inherited a predominantly Russian officer corps. Almost overnight, military personnel had to change their allegiance from the Soviet Union to the newly sovereign state in which they found themselves. This sudden change of allegiance has led to doubts in many of the new states concerning the reliability and loyalty of the military. All of the states thus face a common problem: how to create an officer corps that is loyal to the state, and preferably one that is composed of officers indigenous to the state. Several approaches to solving this problem have been tried, both singly and in combination.

First, attempts have been made to encourage former Soviet officers to return to their native states. For example, both Ukraine and Belarus have issued appeals calling for former Soviet officers of their respective nationalities to return to serve in the new national armies. This approach is limited, though, for there is a disproportionately low number of non-Russians, and especially Central Asians, in the former Soviet officer corps. Important specialties and experience at higher ranks may be underrepresented even in those cases where there are sufficient officers available.

A second approach is through "attestation." Most states inherited militaries far larger than they require, and the officer corps must therefore be reduced. While the attestation process is usually portrayed as one of eliminating less skilled officers, it also lends itself to eliminating noncitizens, or potentially disloyal officers. There have been claims that attestation is being used in Ukraine to eliminate officers suspected of Russian sympathies. While the Ukrainian defense ministry protests that it is not discriminating against Russian officers, the problem of creating a loyal officer corps is clearly of utmost concern and the former Ukrainian defense minister has expressed doubts over the motives and allegiance of much of the current officer corps.[9]

The third approach is to train a new officer corps to replace the old one. This is, however, a lengthy process, and it requires access to military training institutions. Since many of the NIS do not have their own educational facilities, they are for the most part dependent upon Russian military academies, or limited (and possibly expensive) slots in Western military training programs.[10] This approach is usually combined with the other two approaches and may also require measures to ensure the loyalty of the officer corps during the transition period.

The process of creating a new officer corps might be smoothest in the Baltic states, because their new military forces are small and require only a small pool of qualified officer candidates. Furthermore, the Baltic diaspora has provided a source of some advisers and officers while the Nordic countries are assisting in training officers. Even so, the Baltic states have not been able to avoid completely the problems associated with the Soviet legacy. Almost all of their new officers were trained in the Soviet military and have inherited its organizational culture, thus hindering the development of a new, more efficient military.[11] For many of the other states, the various approaches to "nativizing" the officer corps have potential pitfalls. They threaten to split the military along ethnic lines, as non-native officers see their career prospects and even their current positions threatened by an influx of native officers and the attestation process. For example, out of approximately one hundred thousand officers in the former Soviet forces stationed in Ukraine, some ten thousand refused the Ukrainian oath and left for Russia, but some forty thousand ethnic Ukrainian officers have returned to join the forces.[12] Similarly, more than thirteen thousand servicemen applied to join the Belorussian military, but only seven thousand were accepted.[13] Although in both cases this has helped the ethnic balance, it may also generate increased tension. The surplus of officers in Ukraine means that many will have to be discharged, with the ethnic Russian officers likely to go first. This may accentuate the loyalty problem and undermine stability in the short term.

Loyalty is not the only desirable attribute of an officer corps—so are competence and skill. If national origin rather than merit is the primary selection criterion in the attestation process it is likely that many talented officers will be dismissed. Thus, one potential benefit of the attestation process, the opportunity to eliminate less competent officers, may be foregone in exchange for ethnic balance. Rather than a smaller but more competent military the result may be simply a smaller military.

A rather different approach is to concede that there is little prospect of forming an indigenous officer corps in the short run and to maintain the existing Russian-dominated corps. This path is being taken by some of the Central Asian states where the number of qualified native officers is very small. Such a decision carries with it both advantages and disadvantages. On the one hand, the officer corps may resemble a mercenary formation, with questionable loyalty, and a large gulf may develop between officers and native enlisted personnel. In Turkmenistan, for example, tensions between Russian officers and Turkmen conscripts have been growing, while relations with the Turkmen government have been soured by disputes over financing and the rights of officers serving there.[14] Given the disparities in officers' wages and living conditions throughout the CIS, as well as opportunities for mercenary work, many Russian officers in the Central Asian states are resigning, creating the possibility of a shortage of both indigenous and nonindigenous officers.[15] While these tensions may not be sufficient to produce a revolt or massive exodus on the part of the officers, the situation is unlikely to produce a combat-ready force.

Conversely, however, the existence of an officer corps that does not have local ties may serve to insulate it from local political intrigues and reduce the probability of intervention in domestic affairs. Such a condition would appear to depend, however, on Moscow's support for the existing regime in the state. Under certain circumstances the dual loyalty of the officer corps could become an instrument in Moscow's attempts to maintain friendly regimes in the Central Asian states and prevent the rise to power of unfriendly regimes. Indeed, this approach is rather reminiscent of that taken by many former colonial powers in the formation of the militaries of their colonies, where former colonial small military forces or training units can play a significant role in maintaining security ties.

The process of securing the full allegiance of the officer corps may therefore take at least a decade in most of these states as force reductions and officer training take place. During this transition period the potential for unrest within the military may be at its greatest as large numbers of officers conclude that they are being discriminated against during the process of state-building. The reductions may have other destabilizing effects as large numbers of officers are discharged into an unsettled economic and political situation. Even if only a small proportion of discharged officers become mercenaries or criminals, they could produce a further destabilization of the situation in their home states, throughout the former Soviet Union, and in other potential conflict zones.

### Enlisted Ranks: Too Few Good Men?

In its last years the Soviet military began to experience increasing draft shortfalls as the authoritarian system crumbled and the threat of punishment for draft dodging dwindled. Furthermore, many of the republics began to endorse calls for conscripts to serve only within their native regions. Even after independence the problem of ensuring adequate numbers of conscripts has persisted, with draft dodging and exemptions increasing despite the establishment of national armies. Although this phenomenon has been best documented in Russia, it is also causing significant problems in Ukraine and Kazakhstan.[16] In the Caucasian states the draft shortfall problem may be even worse than in Russia.[17] In Azerbaijan "press gangs" roam the streets, rounding up youths and taking them off for rudimentary training before they are sent into battle in the Nagorno-Karabakh region.[18]

The conscription problem may be partly alleviated by planned reductions in force size. In Ukraine, for example, where the total force size is to decline by more than 30 percent, a reduced conscript intake may be sufficient to meet the military's needs.[19] Even in such a case, however, fundamental issues concerning enforcing conscription and the merits of volunteer service will need to be addressed.

So far, only Russia has decided to address the personnel problem by planning a fairly rapid and large-scale transition to a mixed system of conscripts and volunteers. Even so, it is expected that volunteers will not make up half the force until the end of the decade.[20] Ukraine and Belarus are also considering mixed forces; however, the increased costs associated with a mixed or all-volunteer force in Russia, and presumably in the other states as well, would appear to be a significant problem for most of the NIS states.

While the creation of an all-volunteer force would eliminate personnel shortages and increase combat capability, it could affect civil-military relations. An all-volunteer force would likely be drawn from a more narrow and conservative socioeconomic base than a conscript military and might therefore be more inclined to intervene in civilian politics. A conscript military does not necessarily solve this problem, however, for although it can draw personnel from a wider socioeconomic and political background, this advantage may be lost if exemptions and draft dodging favor the upper classes. A military that fails to conscript from a wide base in society may find that its quality levels are dropping while internal disciplinary problems grow. Greater support for conservative policies may also play a role, especially in Russia, in determining whether enlisted personnel would participate in coup attempts led by senior officers, or whether they might balk at orders to intervene.

Even if quantitative conscription targets can be met, the quality of enlisted personnel must also be taken into consideration. The ability of these states to retain a modern military capability will directly depend on enlisting personnel from the most educated and urbanized groups, particularly in the comparatively rural Central Asian states. Since these are also the most privileged groups and those which are most able to avoid service, a substantial toughening of draft laws, and their enforcement, might be necessary to achieve high education and performance levels. Such an outcome appears unlikely, however, and the capability of the Central Asian military forces is unlikely to match that of the Soviet forces formerly stationed there, even though they may field the same equipment.

Throughout the NIS the problem of obtaining sufficient enlisted personnel will remain a difficult one over the short term. Even if conscription requirements fall, a significant tightening of draft laws and enforcement may be necessary to maintain military staffing levels. It is likely that militaries in many of these states will therefore continue to press for action in this area, despite the unpopularity of such moves within the populace as a whole. The widespread introduction of volunteer service appears unlikely given the financial constraints imposed upon most of the militaries. If personnel levels remain low or drop, the combat capability and morale of these militaries is likely to decline still further and could exacerbate civil-military tensions.

### Dealing with the Soviet Legacy

In many states the process of establishing stable civil-military relations is hampered by the presence of Russian troops. Although many Russian troops were transferred back to Russia in 1992-93, in late 1994 Russian troops were still present in Armenia, Belarus, Kazakhstan, Georgia, and Tajikistan.[21] The role and impact of these forces has also varied widely. In Belarus and Kazakhstan Russian forces maintaining nuclear weapons have kept a low profile. However, in Georgia and Moldova Russian troops have been covertly supporting separatist forces in armed insurrections. Conversely, in Tajikistan Russian troops have played important roles in propping up the government and protecting its borders. The last Russian troops departed Latvia and Estonia in August 1994, ending a highly contentious dispute in which the Kremlin used its forces as bargaining chips in an attempt to force concessions on the status of Russians living in the Baltic states. The role of these military formations is thus a major component of the study of civil-military relations within the NIS and limits the sovereignty of some of these states as well.

In Moldova, the Russian Fourteenth Army has played a decisive role in the creation and maintenance of the breakaway "Dniester Republic," while the army's commander, General Major Aleksandr Lebed, has become a key political actor in the "republic." In many respects the Fourteenth Army has become the army of the Dniester Republic, poised to defend its interests and putative independence.[22] Indeed, this unit is also reportedly beginning to recruit and even draft personnel from the Dniester region, further blurring the line between its Russian and Dniester allegiance. An agreement calling for the withdrawal of all Russian troops from Moldova within three years was signed on October 21, 1994, but General Lebed commented afterwards that many of his troops might stay; he would leave "with the army's flag and seal." The troop withdrawal also is contingent on an agreement being reached between the Moldovan government and leaders of the Dniester Republic on a form of autonomy for the region. The presence of Russian troops in Moldova has thus limited the sovereignty of the Moldovan government by bolstering the Dniester leaders and making Russian withdrawal dependent upon Moldova revising its system of regional government.[23]

Russian forces have played a more convoluted role in Georgia. In 1992 Georgia demanded that Russian troops be withdrawn, but Russia left the forces in place while negotiations over withdrawal dragged on. While Russia officially asserted that its forces in the Abkhazia region of Georgia were neutral, reports consistently indicated that they were providing support and training to Abkhazian separatist forces and that Russian personnel and even whole units may have fought for the Abkhaz side.[24] When the Russian-mediated ceasefire in the region collapsed in September 1993 after Abkhazian forces launched a major assault on Sukhumi, the Russian military refused to intervene to assist Georgian forces. Only after the battle for Sukhumi was won by Abkhazian forces and the Georgian leadership signed a number of agreements ceding basing and other military rights to Russia were Russian troops deployed to bolster the Georgian government forces.[25]

In Tajikistan the Russian 201st Motorized Rifle Division (MRD) declared its neutrality when civil war broke out in 1992. However, Western press reports and other sources suggested that the 201st MRD may have participated in armed actions against both sides at different times during the civil war.[26] The establishment of a relatively conservative, pro-Russian government, with at least some Russian military assistance, has solidified the division's position. Subsequently, the 201st MRD has taken over the training of the new Tajik army as well as supporting Russian border guards on the Tajik-Afghan border, where they have been interdicting opposition forces attempting to infiltrate into Tajikistan.[27] As long as Russia continues to support the current regime, the 201st MRD acts as a form of guarantee against both external threats and possible insurrections within Tajikistan.

The Russian forces in Armenia also reflect both Russian and Armenian security concerns. Bordered by its historical enemies, Turkey and Azerbaijan, the Armenian government has chosen to maintain close ties to Russia and to allow Russian forces to remain in place.[28] By doing so, the Russian troops act not only as a southern outpost defending Russian interests, but also as a "trip-wire" force that might act as a deterrent to any attack against Armenia. Russian troops may be pursuing an active policy in Armenia and are reportedly providing support and training, and possibly participating in combat actions in Azerbaijan, where Armenian-backed forces have scored a series of military victories in the Nagorno-Karabakh region.[29]

Russian troops in the Baltic states did not intervene as directly in political processes, but they did represent an implicit Russian threat to use force to support the rights of Russian minorities. Despite repeated Russian threats to halt promised withdrawals, however, all Russian troops departed Lithuania in August 1993; they left Latvia and Estonia a year later.

The presence of Russian troops thus proves to be a double-edged sword. In several cases they are actively engaged in undoing the state-building efforts of the new governments, while in others (Tajikistan, Turkmenistan, Armenia) they are implicitly or explicitly supporting them. In the latter case the states in question have chosen to trade some sovereignty for security in the form of Russian troops. In Georgia, Russian pressure on the Georgian government in the wake of military setbacks in Abkhazia has resulted in the extraction of a series of concessions concerning the stationing of Russian troops in Georgia, as well as prompting its decision to join the CIS. In all cases, however, the presence of Russian forces represents a clear Russian foreign-policy interest in maintaining its sphere of influence. In many of the NIS states, then, civil-military relations are not a simple "two-body problem" but a far more complex "multiple-body" problem involving a range of interactions between state military formations, Russian forces, and militias. If stability is often difficult to ensure with only a regular military establishment, this more complex system cannot help but have a significant destabilizing impact on the development of civil-military relations.

### Stability in NIS Civil-Military Relations

The political role of the militaries in the former Soviet Union has been rather mixed: since 1991, military forces have been used in political struggles in Georgia, Azerbaijan, Moldova, Tajikistan, and Russia. Yet in other states, such intervention has not, at least yet, been forthcoming. The question immediately arises: what might explain this wide variation in outcomes? By adopting an inductive approach and looking at similarities and differences in outcomes, some broad patterns and tentative hypotheses concerning civil-military relations in the region emerge.

*The Caucasus: Patterns of Instability*

The most striking pattern is the instability in the Caucasus. The region has seen several coups and civil wars and persistent ethnic conflicts over the past few years. What are the underlying causes of this instability, and why are they present in the Caucasus?

In both Georgia and Azerbaijan the creation of a new military has been complicated, and in part driven, by ongoing civil conflicts that have undermined the government's credibility and legitimacy. Indeed, in these states the "military" is more a group of militias that are under tenuous central control and that have closer ties to regional political leaders than to the ministry of defense.

In Georgia, the military evolved from early pre-independence attempts to create a national guard and from militias associated with political movements and figures. The result has been an extreme politicization of the military and a very low level of professionalism. The militias and the national guard played a major role in the overthrow of Georgian leader Zviad Gamsakhurdia in late 1991, demonstrating their loyalty to their militia leaders rather than to the head of state. Eduard Shevardnadze, who took power after the coup at the behest of its leaders, has only limited control over the militias and the official military forces. The former defense minister, Tengiz Kitovani, who was replaced in May 1993 by General Giorgy Karkarashvili, was a powerful political figure who was on several occasions rumored to be plotting to overthrow Shevardnadze. Indeed, Kitovani's power base in one of the militias made him an influential and independent actor.[30] Because the military and militias were involved both in starting and in prosecuting the war in Abkhazia as well as destroying rebels supporting Gamsakhurdia, their political importance has tended to increase rather than diminish over time. The militias have also reportedly established strong links to organized crime and profit from gun running and drug smuggling. They therefore have strong incentives to maintain an unstable situation and continue low-level ethnic conflicts. This, in turn, makes the reestablishment of a stable government, still less the creation of a reliable system of civilian control, exceptionally difficult.

The situation in Azerbaijan is similar in many respects. Hastily departing Russian troops left behind a large armory, yet the availability of equipment was not matched by the supply of trained personnel, particularly in the officer corps. The level of training and professionalism in the Azerbaijani military is thus very low, resembling that of a militia more than a modern military.[31] These facts, which contributed to the continuing, humiliating Azerbaijani losses in Nagorno-Karabakh, have in turn seriously undermined Azerbaijani civil-military relations. As a consequence, the military has been extensively politicized and has played a direct role in domestic politics, including the June 1993 overthrow of President Elchibey.[32]

The situation in Armenia is somewhat different from that in the other Caucasus states—there do not appear to be any substantial militias within Armenia. This may be due to the fact that the fight for Nagorno-Karabakh is taking place beyond Armenia's borders. Furthermore, the Armenian-backed Nagorno-Karabakh Self-Defense Committee has been strikingly successful in the fighting inside Azerbaijan. Perhaps as a result of these successes and the relatively benign presence of the Russian military, the Armenian military does not appear to have intervened in domestic politics, nor have militias entrenched themselves. Yet this may change if there are persistent and substantial setbacks on the battlefield.

Why have militias played such a prominent role in the Caucasus states? To a large extent this prominence may have been determined by the process of transition from Soviet rule, which was in turn driven by existing ethnic rivalries and geopolitical disputes and perhaps by the underlying political culture. In all three of the Caucasus states, armed conflicts, or at least ethnic tensions, started before 1992 as long-suppressed territorial and ethnic disputes emerged. Moscow-directed attempts to stem the fighting in Nagorno-Karabakh failed, while in Georgia the independence movement organized rapidly after the deaths of peaceful pro-independence demonstrators in 1989. Coupled with the availability of arms from Soviet weapons caches, militias found fertile ground for growth. These features, together with a tradition of armed rebellion against Russian rule and conflicting territorial claims, set the stage for instability and violence.

Military structures were thus largely based upon, or complemented by, the existing militias. The result was a hasty and haphazard arming of forces that are now under tenuous control at best. Even the formal military forces that exist have little professional training or discipline and resemble militias more than a modern military force. The civil wars in the region have also increased reliance upon the military, and thereby their influence, while battlefield setbacks have created the impetus for moving against civilian leaders who are viewed as inept and to blame for the losses. Finally, the rather ambiguous role of Russian forces in providing arms, whether in an organized or informal capacity, and Russian support for competing forces have further inflamed the situation.

In the Caucasus then, the prior existence of militias or the deterioration of the military into an unprofessional organization appears to have had a primary role in undermining stability. Civil-military relations in the region promise continued instability, for creating a strong, professional and apolitical military out of the existing forces, particularly during a time of ongoing civil and ethnic conflicts, may require a degree of political consensus and civilian control that does not exist in any of these states.

### Explaining Stability in Civil-Military Relations

What is perhaps more surprising is that other regions of the former Soviet Union have not followed a similar path. There are other cases of instability, such as the civil war in Tajikistan, as well as the ethnic conflicts in the Caucasus region of Russia, but many regions appear to be clusters of stability rather than instability. Once again, this may be due to different transition processes within the regions, and in particular the relative absence of ongoing ethnic conflicts. In the Baltic states, for example, the leadership of the independence movement emphasized the use of peaceful means, rather than encouraging the formation of militias. Even so, militias and volunteer forces were formed, and although they harassed Soviet forces, they did not achieve political prominence.[33] These militias have continued to play a role even after independence. Yet, a small-scale rebellion by volunteer militia forces in Lithuania served more to illustrate the political weakness of such forces rather than to threaten the government. Efforts are also being made to subordinate these units and bring them under tighter government control.[34]

In the Central Asian states civil-military relations appear comparatively stable, with the notable exception of Tajikistan. This stability may reflect the fact that government controls on political activity remain relatively tight in these countries, in part because the transition from Soviet rule to post-Soviet independence took place with little or no turnover in the top political leadership. Dissent, both prior to independence and subsequently, has been suppressed quite effectively. With the exception of Tajikistan, local ethnic conflicts and border disputes have also been relatively quickly suppressed. Within the military the presence of the predominately Russian officer corps may be a stabilizing factor. The comparatively close ties of these post-Soviet governments to Russia has also reduced Moscow's interest in using Russian forces to foment conflict within or between the Central Asian states.

Strong leadership in the Central Asian states, if it develops in an authoritarian direction, may be better able to impose civilian control over the military. Such strong regimes might also continue to prevent the emergence of militias and other challenges to the uniformed army. Paradoxically, then, the prospects for civil-military stability might be best in those states where the prospects for democracy are the worst.

In comparison to the states of the Caucasus, the Slavic states appear to be comparatively stable. This is perhaps the most surprising in the case of Ukraine, which has moved rapidly to nationalize the former Soviet forces on its territory, and which implicitly considers Russia its potential foe. Given that a large proportion of the officer corps remains Russian by origin and faces large-scale reductions during downsizing, the prospects for stability would appear to be relatively poor. So far, however, there have been surprisingly few signs of civil-military strain or grassroots actions by junior officers, apart from the disturbances in the Black Sea fleet. Whether this comparative stability will be sustained as force reductions and financial hardships imperil the position of the officers remains an open question.[35] Indeed, there are already indications that some officers are reconsidering their decision to swear allegiance to Ukraine, particularly since they have seen a significant drop in their wages compared to their Russian counterparts since 1993.[36] The summer 1993 election of President Leonid Kuchma may provide an opportunity to further stabilize Ukrainian civil-military relations. Kuchma's program of improving Ukrainian-Russian relations, together with his commitment to reforming the Ukrainian economy, may reduce some of the potential strains and splits within the Ukrainian military. The difficult task of the Ukrainian civilian and military leadership is to prevent this mixture from reaching the point of explosion.

In Belarus, such tensions are also visible beneath a relatively stable facade, but overall they may be less explosive than those in Ukraine.[37] Ties with Russia are much closer and nationalist sentiment rather more muted than in Ukraine, thereby reducing tension between Belorussian and Russian personnel. Even so, a proportionally much larger force reduction is scheduled to take place in Belarus, which will result in the discharge of a large number of officers, most of whom are likely to be of Russian origin. For both these states, therefore, a key element of civil-military stability will be their ability to manage the force reductions and provide an adequate standard of living for officers discharged from the military.

### The Role of Elite Units and Paramilitary Forces

One aspect of civil-military relations that stands out in this survey is the important role of militia and national guard formations. While militias have been most influential in the Caucasus, they have also played a role in the Baltic states, Moldova, and Tajikistan. In Ukraine, the Ukrainian National Assembly (a right-wing political organization) and its paramilitary affiliate, the Ukrainian People's Self-Defense organization, were banned by parliament in October 1992, due to an alarming increase in their activities and visibility. Nevertheless, the latter has continued to operate, albeit with lower visibility; the Ukrainian National Assembly won only three seats in the summer 1994 parliamentary elections.[38]

One reaction to potential instability in civil-military relations is the creation of elite units directly subordinate to the head of state. This trend is most visible within the Central Asian states where national guards or presidential guard units have been created, apparently consisting of troops chosen for their loyalty.[39] In Ukraine a national guard exists which is considered more nationalist than the military, while in Russia there have been attempts by both the old, now-defunct parliament and the president to create special security and guard units.[40] These units are oriented towards internal rather than external threats and may serve as a counterbalance to the military as well as a means of suppressing civil disorders or threats to the government. The very existence of such units underlines the concern with which the leaders of these new states view both potential military and civilian challenges. Whether such formations provide much additional security for the leadership, however, is open to question: "palace coups" carried out by the presidential guard are not unknown in other states.

## The Challenge: Exerting Civilian Control over Military Structures

Finally, even where new militaries are being created, many defense structures and decision-making processes are holdovers from the Soviet period. To ensure civilian control over the military, new structures and processes must be created. However the pace of institutional change within and around the military is very slow. Most of these states inherited or created defense ministries run by military officers. Very few civilians were, or are, involved in the decision-making process. Furthermore, most parliamentarians lack both experience and staff support in the area of military affairs. Ensuring civilian oversight of the military entails creating expertise and institutions in both the executive and legislative branches that can scrutinize and control the operation of the military. In particular, civilian components in the ministries of defense will be needed, as will parliamentary committees with knowledgeable staffs. The development of such a system will require substantial levels of civilian knowledge of military affairs as well as a willingness on the part of the military to grant civilians access to these areas of policy.[41] This will test the openness of the decision-making process and could temporarily strain civil-military relations. In the long term, however, it holds out the promise of strengthening those relations.

The prospects for stable civil-military relations in the newly independent states are mixed: instability fueled by ethnic conflict is likely to continue in the Caucasus, while a form of stability may emerge in Central Asia under semi-authoritarian regimes. Perhaps the greatest prospect for stability lies in the Baltic states, where a nonviolent transition to independence, together with a lack of violent ethnic conflicts and a strong Western orientation (in both military and political terms) have quelled some of the sources of instability in other states. In both Ukraine and Belarus, civil-military relations have been almost surprisingly stable in light of the major transformations that are to take place within their respective militaries. However, the full impact of this restructuring has yet to be felt within the officer corps. It is conceivable, and even likely, that more signs of instability will appear as the restructuring begins to affect the officer corps directly. At the very least it will take a decade or more for most of the NIS militaries to shed the negative aspects of their Soviet heritage and to develop stable and loyal militaries able to support national goals and policies.

## Notes

1. The term NIS is used here in preference to the Commonwealth of Independent States because it includes the Baltic states, which are not members of the CIS.

2. *Krasnaya zvezda*, June 15, 1993, 1. Shaposhnikov failed to win parliamentary confirmation for his position and apparently did not find it a particularly attractive job. He resigned in August. See *Izvestia*, August 12, 1993, 1. In December 1993 the CIS Joint Command was formally replaced by a smaller CIS Joint Staff with reduced responsibil-

ities. ITAR-TASS, December 21, 1993.

3. For a detailed examination of the "nationalization" and current status of former Soviet forces see Roy Allison, "Military Forces in the Successor States," *Adelphi Paper 280*, International Institute for Strategic Studies (London: Brassey's, 1993), 20.

4. The Baltic states have claimed compensation for their losses and equipment seized in 1940, and this claim has been a major point of disagreement in the withdrawal negotiations with Russia, which disavows responsibility for Soviet actions in this regard. For an overview of troop withdrawal negotiations in the Baltic states see Dzintra Bungs, "Progress on Withdrawal from the Baltic States,"*RFE/RL Research Report*, 2, 5, June 18, 1993, 50-59.

5. Estonia is buying some arms from Israel. See *Krasnaya zvezda*, July 13, 1993, 2; Baltfax, September 13 and October 30, 1993. Lithuania reportedly plans to use some former Soviet military equipment and maintain supply links with Russia. See Interfax, May 21, 1993. On NATO standards see Interfax, September 14 and November 30, 1993. Lithuania applied for NATO membership in January 1994. See Interfax, January 5, 1994. Questions concerning the method of approving the Israeli arms deal contributed to the fall of the government headed by Prime Minister Mart Laar. See *Financial Times*, October 3, 1994, 2.

6. For a discussion of the process of "nationalization" in the Ukrainian military see Stephen Foye, "The Ukrainian Armed Forces: Prospects and Problems," *RFE/RL Research Report* 1, 16, June 26, 1992, 55-60, and Stephen Foye, "Civilian-Military Tensions in Ukraine," *RFE/RL Research Report* 2, 25, June 18, 1993, 60-66.

7. Allison, "Military Forces in the Soviet Successor States."

8. See Ellen Jones, *Red Army and Society: A Sociology of the Soviet Military* (Boston: Allen and Unwin, 1985), Chap. 4.

9. See, for example, Reuters, January 25, 1993; Ukrinform-TASS, April 11, 1993.

10. Even Russian facilities may not be cheap. Russia is reportedly charging Belarus a thousand dollars per year in tuition for each officer candidate. See Interfax, April 8, 1993.

11. Estonia, for example, has taken the unusual step of recruiting a former U.S. Army officer of Estonian descent to act as commander of its ground forces. See Interfax, May 20, 1993, and *New York Times*, December 2, 1993. On training see Baltic News Service, May 17, 1993, December 15, 1993. Latvia has appointed a retired U.S. Army officer and former Radio Free Europe/Radio Liberty employee to the position of minister of defense. *RFE/RL Daily Report*, September 16, 1994. For a discussion of some of the difficulties the Baltic states are encountering in setting up their militaries see Marybeth Peterson Ulrich, "When East Meets West: The U.S. Military's Efforts to Assist the Post-Communist States of the Former Eastern Bloc" (Manuscript prepared for the Institute of National Security Studies, October 11, 1994); *Financial Times*, October 10, 1994.

12. *New York Times*, December 2, 1993.

13. Interfax, November 4, 1993.

14. *Armiya*, no. 15, 1993, pp. 10-14. Some of these problems may have been resolved by a Russia-Turkmenistan agreement signed in December 1993. See Interfax, December 27, 1993.

15. See, for example, *Panorama*, no. 46, December 18, 1993, 5.

16. The Ukrainian government temporarily extended the service period from eighteen months to two years because of a personnel shortage, but it did so after many

conscripts had been discharged. There are apparently only some 1,600 contract soldiers in the Ukrainian military. See *Krasnaya zvezda*, November 25, 1993, 3; *Narodnaya armiya*, December 14, 1993, 1. On Kazakhstan see Interfax, October 21, 1993.

17. In Georgia, only 20 percent of those called up actually enlisted in the military. The recruitment rate for the militias is unknown. See Interfax, September 12, 1993.

18. For a description of Azerbaijan's conscript and training problems see *Washington Post*, September 13, 1993. The press gangs were condemned by the new Azerbaijani leader, Geidar Aliev. See Interfax, November 2, 1993. If seized by the press gangs freedom may apparently be had—for a price. See *Komsomolskaya pravda*, November 4, 1993, 1.

19. Interfax, October 22, 1993.

20. For a more detailed discussion of the personnel problems in the Russian military see John W. R. Lepingwell, "Is the Military Disintegrating from Within?" *RFE/RL Research Report* 2, 25, June 18, 1993, 9-16.

21. The forces in Belarus and Kazakhstan are Strategic Rocket Forces troops responsible for the nuclear arsenal. In addition, there are Russian servicemen in the Black Sea Fleet, although the fleet is under dual Russian-Ukrainian command.

22. See Vladimir Socor, "The Fourteenth Army in Moldova," *RFE/RL Research Report* 2, 25, June 18, 1993, 42-49. A small contingent of Russian troops in Belarus were caught in transit from Germany when the Soviet Union collapsed; they are to be transferred to Russia. See Reuters, January 20, 1994. Russia's security interests vary widely across the former Soviet republics; thus the status of Russia's troops varies as well. For a more detailed discussion of Russian security policy and the role of Russian troops in the "near abroad" see John W. R. Lepingwell, "The Russian Military and Security Policy in the 'Near Abroad,' " *Survival* (Autumn 1994): 70-92.

23. For accounts of the signing and Lebed's reaction, see Interfax, October 21-22, 1994.

24. See, for example, Interfax, September 24, 1993, and Reuters, July 11, 1993. For an overview of Russia's role in the Abkhazian conflict see Catherine Dale, "Turmoil in Abkhazia: Russian Responses," *RFE/RL Research Report* 2, 34, August 17, 1993, 48-57.

25. See Grachev's comments on the situation, as reported in Interfax, September 18, 1993. The agreements were reported by ITAR-TASS, October 9, 1993. There have been reports of Russian troops operating armor and other equipment on the Georgian side in the subsequent battles with the militias of former president Zviad Gamsakhurdia. See *Washington Post*, October 27, 1993. On the deployment of troops to protect the naval base at Poti and the railroad lines from it see *Washington Post*, October 21, 1993. For more discussion of the Russian military's role in Georgia, see Lepingwell, "The Russian Military and Security Policy in the 'Near Abroad,' " 75-77.

26. In November the 201st appeared to be supporting Akhbarshah Iskandrov's reformist forces, but subsequently it backed the forces of the conservative former president, Rakhmon Nabiev. On support for Iskandrov see *Washington Post*, November 3, 1993; Reuters, October 27, 1993; ITAR-TASS, October 27, 1993; Agence France Presse, October 25, 1993. The Russian military commander in Tajikistan was briefly a member of the governing council, but resigned on November 4, citing a conflict with his role as a professional soldier. See Interfax, November 10, 1992. On subsequent support for Nabiev and allegations that Iskandrov's forces were provoking the Russians, see Interfax, December 6, 1992, and Reuters, December 6, 1992.

27. On training and support see *Krasnaya zvezda*, April 27, 1993, 2. Formally, the

forces on the border are under CIS control. See *Krasnaya zvezda*, November 9, 1993, 1-2.

28. The size of the Russian force in Armenia is unclear, but it probably consists of at least two regiments and possibly a full division. See Interfax, February 18, 1993, September 14, 1993, and Allison, "Military Forces," 64-65.

29. Interfax, February 25 and May 25, 1993.

30. The discussion here draws heavily on the material presented in Elizabeth Fuller, "Paramilitary Forces Dominate Fighting in Transcaucasus," *RFE/RL Research Report* 2, 25, June 18, 1993, 74-82. See also *Izvestia*, April 21, 1993; Elizabeth Fuller, "Shevardnadze's Via Dolorosa," *RFE/RL Research Report* 2, 43, October 29, 1993, 17-23.

31. In late 1993 there were reports that both Russian and U.S. former servicemen were training Azerbaijani troops. The U.S. connection is unofficial, but there are indications that the Russian presence is officially authorized. On the Russian troops see Interfax, September 22, 1993, and *Boston Globe*, November 22, 1993; concerning the U.S. advisers see *The Observer*, November 28, 1993, 19.

32. See Fuller, "Paramilitary Forces" and Elizabeth Fuller, "Azerbaijan's June Revolution," *RFE/RL Research Report* 2, 32, August 13, 1993, 24-29. It has been suggested that Russia played an indirect but significant role in ousting Elchibey in an attempt to install a leader more sympathetic to Russian interests in the region. See, for example, Elizabeth Fuller, "Russia, Turkey, Iran, and the Karabakh Mediation Process," *RFE/RL Research Report* 3, 8, February 25, 1994, 31-36.

33. See, for example, *Krasnaya zvezda*, July 25, 1990, November 28, 1990, March 16, 1991.

34. Saulius Girnius, "Problems in the Lithuanian Military," *RFE/RL Research Report* 2, 42, October 22, 1993, 44-47; *New York Times*, December 2, 1993.

35. At least one case has been reported of former Soviet officers who have sworn allegiance to Ukraine subsequently requesting to return to Russia to join the Russian military. See ITAR-TASS, November 27, 1993. A detailed description of the development of Ukrainian civil-military relations may be found in John Jaworsky, "The Military-Strategic Significance of Recent Developments in Ukraine," Project Report no. 645, Directorate of Strategic Analysis, Department of National Defense, Ottawa, August 1993.

36. ITAR-TASS, May 27, 1993, November 27, 1993.

37. For an excellent discussion of Belarus see David R. Marples, "Belarus: The Illusion of Stability," *Post-Soviet Affairs*, 9, 3, 253-277.

38. Jaworsky, "Military-Strategic Significance," 102-104, and Bohdan Nahaylo, "Ukraine," *RFE/RL Research Report* 3, 16, April 22, 1994, 42-49.

39. The Kazakhstani national guard, for example, has both Kazakh and Slavic personnel, but approximately 68 percent of the officers are Kazakh, an unusually high proportion. See Interfax, October 19, 1993, March 16, 1993.

40. On the Russian parliamentary guard see Interfax, April 1, 1993.

41. There are several Western programs intended to facilitate this process by providing training for both civilian and military personnel. The largest of these is based at the George C. Marshall Center in Germany and funded by the U.S., German, and other NATO governments.

# 6 The Loyalty of the Russian Military

John W. R. Lepingwell

When tanks opened fire on Yeltsin's opponents in the White House on the morning of October 4, 1993, it appeared that the question of whom the Russian military would support in the constitutional crisis had been answered. The event also underscored the importance of the military in Russian politics. Yet although the October crisis resolved some questions concerning the Russian military and its political role, it has raised even more.

The Russian military views itself as the direct heir of the Soviet military, having inherited the bulk of its personnel and manpower. Because of this direct line of descent, the Russian military does not face all of the state-building problems of the other former Soviet Republics: it already has an indigenous officer corps and a large network of defense industries. By the same token, though, it has inherited many of the problems of the Soviet military: poor living conditions, declining morale, increasing personnel shortages, dwindling budgets, and increasing corruption.[1] And like many of the other new states, it must reduce and reconfigure its forces while simultaneously managing the transition from the old Soviet system of civil-military relations to a new democratic system. This process is taxing the skills and capabilities of military and civilian leaders alike.

### Political Legitimacy and the Legitimate Use of Military Power

By most measures the Russian military has experienced a remarkable decline in the last few years. Manpower levels have plunged as draft exemptions and draft dodging have increased. By some estimates the military may be receiving only half the number of conscripts it requires, while some observers suggest that if the trend continues officers will soon outnumber the enlisted personnel.[2] Training has suffered, as both personnel and material resources are scarce. There have even been cash shortages, with the result that in many areas servicemen have gone without pay for months.[3] Adding to this material decline has been the loss of prestige of military service, together with a loss of orientation that has accompanied the collapse of the Soviet Union and the end of the cold war. The result is a military that has suffered a dramatic defeat without having fired a shot.

Given these poor conditions, why did the military choose to side with President Yeltsin? Why did troops storm the White House in October 1993 when they would not do so in August 1991? The answer to these questions lies in the military's organizational interests, its professionalism, and the legitimacy of Yeltsin's leadership.

The old system of Soviet civil-military relations succeeded in maintaining civilian dominance of the military. To a large extent this was due to shared values between the civilian and military elites, security surveillance, and membership by many officers in the Communist party, but it also rested on a strong background of military professionalism and a tradition of military noninterference in politics. By 1991, however, an increasing rift had emerged between the civilian and military leaderships, as Gorbachev's reforms threatened many of the military's privileges as well as, ultimately, the existence of the Soviet Union. During the August 1991 putsch, the military's position was ambivalent—the Minister of Defense supported the putschists, as did the commander of the Ground Forces. But the putsch revealed deep rifts within the military, as many officers broke with the military leadership to support Yeltsin and Gorbachev.[4]

One key factor in the military's decision to withdraw its support from the putschists was Yeltsin's claim to legitimate authority: only two months earlier, Yeltsin had been elected president by a majority in the first free nationwide elections to such a post in Russian history. Any attempt to seize Yeltsin could have resulted in widespread bloodshed and precipitated a split within the military.

A second reason for the military's decision was that it was reluctant to undertake actions that were far from their professional purpose. Previous attempts to use force against civilian populations—in Tbilisi, Baku, and Vilnius—had produced strong backlashes, both within the general population and within the military. This aversion to the use of the military for political ends was certainly not shared by all officers or specialized units, but it appears to have been especially strong amongst the airborne forces, which had borne the brunt of both the Afghan war and the "internal security" missions of the late 1980s. Indeed, in 1991 the commander of the airborne forces, Pavel Grachev, was one of the strongest opponents of the use of force against Yeltsin and his supporters in the White House.[5]

Taken together, these factors seem sufficient to explain the military's decision to withdraw support from the putschists—an attack on the White House might have caused extensive casualties, defection of some units, and possibly civil war. Furthermore, the military was not sure how the governments of the Soviet republics might react—an armed assault could have caused the very disintegration of the USSR that the military leadership was seeking to avert.

### From Soviet to Russian Civil-Military Relations

After the disintegration of the Soviet Union and the introduction of extensive economic reforms in Russia in 1992, there was much reason to be apprehensive about the prospects for Russian civil-military relations. The reforms caused massive drops in industrial output accompanied by rapid inflation; consequently the Russian military saw its purchasing power and privileged position disappear. The military's problems were compounded by the return to Russia in 1992-93 of some two hundred thousand Russian troops from Eastern Europe and the CIS states. These developments, coupled with the growing confrontation between President Yeltsin and the parliament, raised the possibility of the military siding with conservative elements in an attempt to oust Yeltsin. Reasons to fear such a development were plentiful, not least because Yeltsin's mutinous vice-president, Aleksandr Rutskoi, a general and Afghan war hero, was an appealing figure to the officer corps. Although many top commanders had been replaced after the August events, conservative officers and sentiments were still evident within the military. Surveys indicated that Rutskoi was held in higher esteem than Yeltsin within the military, and Rutskoi made several attempts to court military support. At the same time, there were persistent reports that Yeltsin's defense minister, Pavel Grachev, was unpopular within the military.[6]

The first confrontation between Yeltsin and the Russian parliament took place in March 1993, when Yeltsin announced that he would rule by decree; at that time Yeltsin did not move to dissolve parliament. Amid widespread speculation as to which side the military would choose, it announced its "neutrality." Yet this neutrality was a form of implicit support for Yeltsin, and Grachev made his continued political support for Yeltsin clear, while arguing that troops should not be used to resolve the crisis.[7] Without any means of resolving the crisis by force, a compromise was reached, although it proved short-lived.

The October crisis initially followed a similar script, although Yeltsin went further and dissolved the parliament. The military again declared its neutrality, although Grachev again implicitly signaled his support for Yeltsin, while emphasizing the need for a peaceful resolution of the crisis.

### The Military Takes Action

Why did the military shift from a position of neutrality to an assault on the White House? Clearly, the riots and assault on the Ostankino television studios on October 3 constituted a direct challenge to Yeltsin's rule and forced the military to make a decision. Accounts of the decision-making process suggest that a number of factors played a role.[8]

First, the fact that violence had been initiated by the parliament's supporters lowered the threshold for choosing violence as a response. Had the military simply been ordered to storm the White House without prior provocation it would likely have refused.[9] After the unprecedented disorder and violence on the streets of Moscow, however, many in the military feared chaos and believed that decisive action was necessary to prevent a protracted battle for power within Moscow that could have imperiled the stability and even unity of the country. Indeed, military commentaries after the events stressed that the actions had been aimed at averting a civil war.[10]

A second consideration, as in August 1991, was the military's concern that meddling in politics could threaten military unity. There is little doubt that Grachev was very reluctant to commit the military to an attack on the White House. This may have reflected a real desire to maintain neutrality and to prevent forcing units within the military to take sides. While there are only scattered reports of individual officers defecting to the parliament's side, there are consistent reports suggesting that some senior officers sympathized with the parliamentary leaders. Indeed, Yeltsin devoted a substantial amount of his time on the evening of October 3 to calling military commanders and enlisting their support before he traveled to the Ministry of Defense, where he attended the collegium meeting that finally committed the military to action.[11]

Finally, Yeltsin's victory at the polls stood him in good stead in October 1993, just as it had in August 1991. Although Yeltsin's political fortunes have varied since his election, he remained a relatively popular figure, as indicated by his majority of support (albeit by a small margin) in the April 1993 referendum. Only Rutskoi appears to have challenged Yeltsin in popularity. But Rutskoi overplayed his hand before the April 1993 referendum, when he made sweeping charges of corruption against Yeltsin's administration, and particularly against the military leadership.[12] The allegations against the military leadership, while possibly based in fact, certainly did not incline Grachev or his immediate subordinates to support Rutskoi in October. Furthermore, Rutskoi's charges failed to win him wider support in the population as a whole—mud-slinging may weaken a political opponent, but it rarely increases the popularity of the slinger.

The other opposition leaders were in even weaker positions. Ruslan Khasbulatov, the parliament's speaker, had never been a popular figure and was viewed with suspicion within the military. Khasbulatov is an ethnic Chechen, a nationality that many Russians have come to associate with dishonesty, crime, and corruption. The parliament itself had gradually become discredited as an institution, in no small part due to Yeltsin's continuing attacks on it. It was readily portrayed as irrelevant at best, and obstructionist or destructive at worst. Thus, few good alternatives to supporting Yeltsin remained when the disturbances started.

As a result, many of the same factors that had been at work in August 1991 were at work in October 1993, although the direction of their effect was changed. Whereas Yeltsin's legitimacy and the military's fear of a split worked against intervention in 1991, in 1993 they worked in favor of intervention. The ferocity of the battle for the White House shocked most observers, and immediately raised the question of whether the Russian military would now play a significantly greater role in Russian politics.

## The Military After the October Crisis

If the Russian military became a decisive element in the political struggle in October 1993, its new political role and influence were far from decisive in 1994. Instead, Grachev's influence waned, as the military suffered defeats on personnel policy and the defense budget, and dissension within the ranks grew. By the end of the year, the military appeared weaker than ever before, both materially and politically, while it had become entangled in a brutal and demoralizing conflict in Chechnya.

This turn of events was not anticipated in the wake of the October storming of the White House. After that event, many commentators suggested that Yeltsin owed the military a favor; many expected that favor to take the form of an increased budget and concessions on several issues of interest to the military. In the last months of 1993 Yeltsin indeed made some concessions to military interests, but these proved to be short-lived. The long-delayed new military doctrine was approved only a month after the assault on the White House.[13] That doctrine included a very ambiguous clause that allowed use of the military for internal security tasks, especially separatist movements and "attempts to overthrow the constitutional system by force or to disrupt the functioning of organs of state power and administration."[14] These clauses were clearly intended as a retroactive legitimization for the military's actions on October 4. Passage of the doctrine after the dissolution of the Supreme Soviet also avoided a potentially lengthy and politically damaging debate over Russia's foreign and security policies in the parliament.

There were other, albeit somewhat ambiguous, indications of growing military influence. A long-standing dispute between the defense ministry and finance ministry over payment for arms procurement was finally resolved in favor of the former, although actual payment of debts was subsequently delayed.[15] There was a noticeable toughening of Russia's foreign policy stance towards East European membership in NATO, and towards the near abroad as well.

Apparently trying to capitalize on the momentum built by the approval of the doctrine, Grachev announced that by 1995 the military would be reduced to 2.1 million troops, rather than to 1.5 million as mandated by the Law on Defense promulgated by the defunct Supreme Soviet.[16] On this issue, as on many others, however, it proved easier for Grachev to call for changes than to push them through.

While these developments suggest that military influence increased somewhat in the wake of the October crisis, that increase should not be exaggerated, nor should the developments be attributed solely to the military. First, the changes were limited to military and security areas, where one would expect the military to exert its influence. Second, in the case of the tougher foreign policy and defense-industry payments, strong civilian lobbies were at work; these became even more influential in the wake of the December elections.

In any case, the increase in military influence was quickly limited. Indeed, rather than praise Grachev for his support, Yeltsin and members of his administration went out of their way to criticize his performance during the crisis. By mid-November 1993 rumors abounded of Grachev's imminent dismissal.[17] Although Yeltsin affirmed his continued confidence in Grachev, some of the president's comments seemed deliberately calculated to remind Grachev that he served at Yeltsin's discretion. The comments and rumors invited comparison with Khrushchev's decision to dismiss Marshal Zhukov only a few months after Zhukov backed Khrushchev in a crucial leadership struggle in 1957. In that case the personal debt to the minister of defense was great, but the latter proved readily replaceable.[18] While the rumors of Grachev's dismissal eventually faded, they had done their damage by weakening the defense minister's standing and prestige.

### How Little Is Enough? The Defense Budget Debate

Further indications of the military's limited influence became evident in early 1994 as the military suffered setbacks on several important issues, most notably the defense budget and the size of the military. In both these cases, military lobbying of both the newly elected Federal Assembly and the Chernomyrdin government proved surprisingly ineffective.

While the military doctrine received the most attention in November 1993, the defense budget was being drawn up at the same time, and it was at least as important to the military as was the doctrine. Surprisingly, the draft Russian defense budget called for no budget increase for 1994 over 1993 levels, with weapons procurement remaining stable or even declining slightly.[19] This was clearly not the reward the military expected. In early 1994 Grachev warned that the defense budget met only half the military's needs; First Deputy Defense Minister Andrei Kokoshin claimed that the budget was "politically dangerous" and would "ruin the country's defense capability." [20] Grachev lobbied Prime Minister Viktor Chernomyrdin, as well as Yeltsin, for an increase in the budget from thirty-seven trillion rubles to fifty-five trillion rubles. The military's request was supported by members of the State Duma's Committee on Defense, but surprisingly, it received relatively little support in the Duma as a whole. Despite their campaign calls for greater defense spending and subsidies for defense industries the large Communist and Liberal-Democratic factions in the Duma did not support more defense spending. In the Federation Council, which represents the interests of Russia's regions, support for the higher budget figure was greater, and a resolution increasing the defense budget was passed.[21] However, despite the lobbying efforts of the defense ministry, and the less visible efforts of the defense industry, the final budget passed by the Duma and Federation Council contained only a small increase to forty-one trillion rubles.[22]

Perhaps the most unusual aspect of the budget debacle was the manner in which Yeltsin held himself aloof. While there were reports that Yeltsin had endorsed the increase to fifty-five trillion rubles, he never came out publicly in favor of an increase. On the contrary, while the Duma and Federation Council were working out their compromise draft, Yeltsin turned on the military, accusing it of being slow to reform and of not economizing. While he spoke vaguely of finding off-budget means of financing any shortfall, Yeltsin was anything but supportive of the organization that had rescued him some nine months earlier.[23]

The result of the defense budget wrangle was a budget that Grachev criticized vociferously.[24] Nonetheless, it forced the military to cut its forces even more rapidly and led him to argue that in order to economize, all quasi-military forces, including the border guards, be placed under the Ministry of Defense.[25] Grachev also ordered more rapid cuts in military personnel, acknowledging that the military would be reduced to some 1.9 million troops by the end of 1994. He was also forced to back down on his suggestion that the force size be increased to 2.1 million after Yeltsin publicly affirmed that the military would eventually be reduced to 1.5 million troops.[26]

If this defeat were not sufficient, further humiliations were in store for Grachev and the defense ministry. In August it appeared that the controversial general, Aleksandr Lebed, commander of the Fourteenth Army located in the self-proclaimed Dniester Republic (a part of Moldova), would be removed from his position. The move may have been partly in response to increasingly political and provocative comments by Lebed, most notably a newspaper interview in which he made favorable comments about the Pinochet model of development and criticized both Yeltsin and the form of Russian democracy.[27] A senior defense ministry official traveled to the Dniester Republic while Lebed was on vacation, reportedly carrying orders dissolving the Fourteenth Army and reorganizing it into a division, with the implication that Lebed's position as commander would be eliminated.[28] A frenzy of media speculation greeted the report. Articles claimed that the army's officers had refused to serve under a different commander and had petitioned Yeltsin to retain Lebed.[29] The move came at a sensitive time, for negotiators from Russia and Moldova were close to reaching an agreement over the withdrawal of the Fourteenth Army.[30] Yeltsin was silent for approximately ten days after the story broke. Then, in an interview with the Interfax news agency, he praised Lebed's work with the Fourteenth Army and seemed to rule out removing him from his position or dismissing him from the military.[31] At almost the same time, the defense ministry announced that the command structure of the Fourteenth Army would be changed but that the issue of reassigning Lebed had not been discussed.[32]

The result was yet another setback for Grachev. Most of the evidence (and all of the rumors) suggested that Grachev had considered the proposed reorganization an opportunity to remove Lebed from his prominent position and power base. The need to do so was increasingly obvious—multiple opinion polls had shown that Lebed was far more popular in the military than Grachev, while newspaper commentators and others were continually mentioning Lebed as being likely to replace Grachev, or even to run against Yeltsin in the next presidential elections.[33] Yeltsin's decision to retain, and even praise, Lebed represented an implicit demonstration of his lack of confidence in Grachev, as well as a desire not to alienate the vast majority of the military.[34]

Personnel decisions again weakened Grachev's standing in the months following the confusion over Lebed. In late August Grachev appointed General Matvei Burlakov, then commander of the Western Group of Forces (WGF) in Germany, to the position of deputy defense minister with special responsibility for the support of Russian troops withdrawn from Germany and other states. The move immediately met with criticism from the press and politicians, who claimed that Burlakov had been implicated in allegations of corruption in the WGF. While Grachev strongly defended Burlakov, public unease and distrust peaked when Dmitry Kholodov, a reporter for the popular newspaper *Moskovsky komsomolets*, was killed by a bomb on October 17. Kholodov had been researching the charges of corruption against the WGF, and persons in or close to the WGF were immediately accused by the press of having murdered Kholodov. Indeed, the editor of the paper went so far as to accuse Grachev of direct involvement in the murder.[35] Given the severity of the charges being raised against Burlakov and the outcry following the murder, Yeltsin issued on November 1 a decree dismissing Burlakov from his position, once again dealing a major blow to Grachev's stature both within and outside the military.[36] Nevertheless, Grachev continued to defend Burlakov and stated that he would reappoint him once investigations proved his innocence; simultaneously, he criticized Lebed for having called for Burlakov's removal, stating that "if [Burlakov] is proven innocent, the most serious punishment will be given out to General Lebed for discrediting a top defense ministry official." [37]

Yeltsin's move to oust Burlakov also weakened Grachev's support within pro-Yeltsin factions in the State Duma. The head of the Duma's Committee on Security, Sergei Yushenkov, a member of the pro-Yeltsin Russia's Choice faction, called for Grachev's resignation.[38] Grachev managed to avoid a direct vote of no-confidence by the State Duma in a hearing during which he pleaded for more funding and depicted an increasingly impoverished, and restless, military.[39]

These rather Byzantine intrigues suggest that civil-military relations in Russia have become increasingly personalized, and perhaps less predictable, during 1994. The struggle between Lebed and Grachev is increasingly polarizing the military, even though the likelihood of Lebed jumping from the position of commander of a small army group to defense minister seems unlikely. Lebed's popularity within the military is clearly a warning, however, not only to Grachev, but to Yeltsin as well. Lebed stands for a more authoritarian form of rule, with greater support for the military and a tougher policy towards the near abroad. Yeltsin's (and Grachev's) strategy appears to be to ensure that Lebed stays sufficiently far away from Moscow that he cannot mount a direct threat to the regime in the event of a new constitutional crisis.

The net result of the foregoing personnel problems was to weaken severely Grachev's standing within the military and in the government. Although this may have limited his influence, it also has had the effect of exacerbating the demoralizing impact of the deterioration in military funding and effectiveness.

### The Military outside Moscow

The political battles in Moscow are only one aspect of Russian civil-military relations. By creating a strong central government to pull Russia together, the new constitution addresses one of the military's ongoing concerns. But although tensions between the federal government and the regions have dropped overall, there remains the possibility of a devolution of political power from the center to the regions. This trend is less pronounced in the military than in other spheres, but it is perhaps even more troubling, for devolution of authority from the central command to regional commanders may increase the opportunities for corruption and politicization.

Several processes are at work within the Russian military that may weaken central control. The system of personnel rotation has broken down, and corruption is creating new links between local commanders, politicians, and organized crime. Chaotic economic conditions, combined with plunging morale and financial difficulties, have opened new opportunities for military corruption. Russian officers are increasingly using the resources at their disposal for money-making activities. Although such entrepreneurism may have some economic benefits, it also has a corrosive effect on military discipline and readiness. A decaying military that is losing its military professionalism and suffers low morale may well be more susceptible to political intrigues.

The creation of corrupt links between regional military commanders and local organized crime structures and politicians could, over time, strengthen the centrifugal forces that are already growing within the Russian federation. A collapse similar to that of the USSR may be unlikely, but the weakening of central control that regionalization could cause would greatly complicate control of the Russian military. In such a scenario the interests of local commanders and the central military leadership would gradually diverge: whereas the central leadership requires a strong central power in order to maintain a unified military, regional commanders may develop strong allegiances to their regions based on their pecuniary interests. The potential thus emerges for a split along geographical and hierarchical lines, with military leaders in Moscow supporting the centralization of power, and regional commanders in some cases opposing it. Such a development, coupled with increasing demands for autonomy or sovereignty on the part of the regions, could produce an even more dangerous confrontation.[40]

In addition to the deterioration of the Russian military, the creation of new regional militias or armies is also possible. While no significant nationwide paramilitary organizations have yet formed in Russia, militias have played an important role in the North Caucasus. In Chechnya, which has proclaimed its independence from Russia, a small but effective military force was created; in North Ossetia and Ingushetia militias have played a key role in ethnic conflicts.[41]

So far, separatist movements in other Russian regions and republics have not gained much support, nor have they been as radical in their claims of sovereignty and independence as has Chechnya. As a result, the threat of Russia's disintegration appears to be waning. Nevertheless, unless strong, top-down command is reimposed, the process of devolution of authority within the military will prove to be an ongoing problem.

### The Assault on Chechnya

The most striking case of the military's involvement in regional affairs was the December 1994 assault on Chechnya. Initially the Russian government attempted to undermine and overthrow the government of Chechen president Dzhokar Dudayev through covert means, including support for an opposition-led "provisional government." Russian support extended to the provision of weaponry, air support, and the recruitment of Russian soldiers to serve in the opposition's anti-Dudayev drive. However, the extent of the Ministry of Defense's involvement in these early attempts to overthrow Dudayev remains somewhat unclear, as the operation was run by the Federal Counterintelligence Service (FCS), one of the KGB's successor organizations.

In late November 1994 a botched storming of Grozny by opposition forces led to the capture of more than twenty Russian soldiers recruited from the military by the FCS. Soon thereafter, the commander of the division from which they had been recruited resigned in protest at not having been consulted in the matter. One of Grachev's apparent rivals within the military leadership, Deputy Defense Minister Boris Gromov, also denounced the subterfuge and claimed that the military was not officially involved.[42] Despite these denials, however, it seems clear that the FCS must have coordinated its moves with Grachev and other Ministry of Defense officials, even if some leaders were left "out of the loop."

The moment of decision for the military came, however, when Yeltsin ordered a full-scale assault on Chechnya to disarm Dudayev's supporters and reimpose Moscow's control over the republic.[43] While Grachev had earlier boasted that "one paratroop regiment might have solved all questions [in Grozny] in two hours," a combined force of army and interior ministry troops was stalled by stiff resistance, both violent and nonviolent.[44] The commander of one of the three armored columns advancing on Grozny halted his troops well before they had reached their goal, declaring the assault unconstitutional and refusing to follow his orders.[45] This act of insubordination, combined with repeated reports of poor troop performance and morale, as well as atrocities committed by both sides, contributed to a rising view that the combat in Chechnya could become a second Afghanistan, or more appropriately, a second Caucasian War. Further reports of dissent within the military surfaced as the ferocity of the fighting grew and as the Russian air force carried out air attacks on civilian targets in Grozny.[46] Grachev, greatly weakened by his poor performance during 1994, began to look more vulnerable and more dispensable as the operation continued. Indeed, if nothing else, the Chechen operation demonstrated the depths of the deterioration of the Russian military, while it threatened to open yet more splits within the ranks of the democratic movement and to imperil Yeltsin's hopes of winning future presidential elections.

### Prospects for Russian Civil-Military Relations

What are the prospects for the development of Russian civil-military relations and military policy? The events of 1994 do not bode well for the creation of a new basis for civil-military relations in Russia. The old bases of stability in Soviet civil-military relations were shared values between the military and political elites, relatively generous funding of the military, a tradition of professionalism, and as a last resort a system of indoctrination and monitoring (via the KGB) that was effective in identifying potential disloyalty. Almost all of these bases have crumbled in the past few years as budgets have dwindled, missions have been redefined, and professionalism has been eroded. At the same time, new democratic institutions and instruments of control have not been firmly established.

Indeed, the path of events in 1994 points to a potentially dangerous trend—the concentration of power in the president's office and within Yeltsin's personal entourage. Rather than institutionalizing civilian control over the military within new democratic institutions power has become more personalized, as the Yeltsin-Grachev nexus has become the focus for civil-military relations. Yeltsin has clearly had to rely upon Grachev in his efforts to contain and control the military. At the same time, however, Yeltsin has moved to weaken Grachev so that he does not gain substantial influence over government policy. The result is that Grachev is dependent upon Yeltsin for his position (and is continually reminded of it), but that dependence is beginning to erode Grachev's ability to control and reform the military.

The other dismaying trend in Russian civil-military relations, one that was evident in 1993 but accelerated in 1994, is the growing distrust of Grachev within the military. Not only are lower-level field officers increasingly estranged from their leadership, but there are continual reports that even the General Staff is increasingly contemptuous of Grachev. That split has been greatly exacerbated by internal disputes within the military over its role in the assault on Chechnya.

Thus, Yeltsin's strategy may be self-defeating. Instead of appointing a strong, reform-oriented military leader who may be able to win a greater portion of available resources—as well as respect within the ranks—Yeltsin has maintained an unpopular and unsuccessful leader.[47] Furthermore, disarray in the military reflects poorly on the Yeltsin administration as a whole. Indeed, the pattern of decisions made and then retracted points to a general loss of direction on the part of the Yeltsin administration in its dealings with military matters. The tendency to centralize and concentrate control of the military in the executive branch, and especially within the office of the president, also provides a weak basis for effective civilian oversight. As the military correspondent for *Segodnya*, Pavel Felgengauer, has argued, the intense bureaucratic and factional in-fighting within the Russian government has seriously hampered the development and implementation of a coherent military policy. Those policies that have been developed are often implemented haphazardly, if at all.

The other problematic area in Russian civil-military relations is institution building. At present the military decision-making process and most of the necessary information is still largely controlled by the uniformed military within the Ministry of Defense. Almost no progress has been made in creating civilian structures within the ministry that could counterbalance military analyses. Furthermore, the concentration of power within the president's office tends to limit the influence of the wider political elite on military policy. Other institutions have largely been shut out of the defense decision-making process. The Duma's Committee on Defense reportedly has little access to essential information concerning the defense budget and the state of the military, and no control over top military appointments.[48] While it might be argued that over the short term this could contribute to stability, as it removes the military from the highly politicized arena of the Duma, over the longer term it hinders the development of effective civilian control.

In fact, this concentration of power may prove to be exceptionally dangerous in the long run. While President Yeltsin has often been accused of authoritarian tendencies, it is quite conceivable that his successor may have more pronounced tendencies in this direction. In such a case the concentration of power would provide the president with tremendous opportunities to employ the military and other "power ministries" for political or personal purposes.

Despite the many negative trends, there are some potentially positive trends. This is due less to developments within the military sphere than to more general trends towards stabilization in the economic and political spheres. The intense confrontation between the executive and legislative branches of 1993 has been resolved, at least temporarily, and the Duma appears to be functioning relatively smoothly. Similarly, while the Russian economy is still far from positive growth, there are signs of increasing stability as inflation rates have been lowered, and increased investment now seems feasible on the part of both Western and Russian concerns. The threat of regionalism and separatism, considered a serious danger to the territorial integrity of Russia, has receded since the October 1993 events and the signing of a treaty between the Russian government and Tatarstan. These developments lessen the likelihood of a confrontation between the centers of power within Russia, a confrontation that could again thrust the military into the position of having to choose sides in a political struggle. Unfortunately, even these modest achievements have been threatened by the Russian action in Chechnya, which threatens to destabilize Russian politics. Absent such a confrontation, the likelihood of the military intervening on its own accord appears relatively low.

Over the longer term the prospects for civil-military relations are not very encouraging. There is a substantial degree of uncertainty as to whether current positive trends in politics and the economy will be sustained. The opening skirmishes over the 1995 budget suggest that the imposition of a relatively harsh, austere budget such as that proposed by the Chernomyrdin government will prove politically very divisive. If an austere budget is passed, and if hard budget constraints are imposed on enterprises, the result could be a rise in social tensions that could again destabilize the political system. Coming in tandem with a debate over the date of both presidential and parliamentary elections, a new crisis could well emerge. Similarly, the assault on Chechnya has had a disruptive effect on Russian politics, splintering the ranks of the democrats in Moscow and dealing a possibly decisive blow to the prestige of both Yeltsin and Grachev. This, in turn, could jeopardize Yeltsin's already waning chances for victory in presidential elections scheduled to be held in 1996. Thus, the prospects for civil-military stability in Russia are highly scenario-dependent and unpredictable. Progress towards building a firm new foundation for democratic civil-military relations has been minimal, and in many respects what little progress was made in 1992 and 1993 has been eroded in 1994 by confused leadership and the failure to fully develop democratic institutions of civilian control.

## Notes

1. See John W. R. Lepingwell, "Is the Military Disintegrating from Within?" *RFE/RL Research Report* 2, 25, June 18, 1993, 9-16; Lepingwell, "Restructuring the Russian Military," *RFE/RL Research Report* 2, 25, June 18, 1993, 17-24; Stephen Foye, "Rebuilding the Russian Armed Forces: Rhetoric and Realities," *RFE/RL Research Report* 2, 30, July 23, 1993, 49-57; Foye, "Russia's Defense Establishment in Disarray," *RFE/RL Research Report* 2, 36, September 10, 1993, 49-54.

2. Foye, "Rebuilding the Russian Armed Forces," 52-53. By the end of 1993, the draft intake amounted to some 60 percent of what was required and some 123,000 volunteers had enlisted. See *Krasnaya zvezda*, December 31, 1993, 1.

3. *Krasnaya zvezda*, July 24, 1993, 1.

4. This argument and the analysis of the August 1991 events draws on the theoretical framework presented in John W. R. Lepingwell, "The Soviet Military and the August Coup," *World Politics* 44, 4 (July 1992): 539-572.

5. Conversely, however, the former commander of the Airborne Forces, General Vladislav Achalov, was one of the planners of the putsch. In a striking reversal of roles,

Achalov supported the parliament and was one of the planners of the defense of the White House in October. For an account of Achalov's activities see Serge Schmemann, "The Man in the Middle: A Trusted Military Aide," *New York Times*, October 6, 1993.

6. See *RFE/RL Daily Report*, April 3 and May 5, 1992.

7. ITAR-TASS, March 2, 1993.

8. For an overview of the crisis and the military's role, see Stephen Foye, "Confrontation in Moscow: The Army Backs Yeltsin, for Now," *RFE/RL Research Report* 2, 42, October 22, 1993, 10-15.

9. For Yeltsin's account of the military's reluctance to take action even after violence had broken out in Moscow, see Boris Yeltsin, *The Struggle for Russia* (New York: Times Books, 1994), 274-283. The actual storming of the building was carried out by the special Alfa and Vympel antiterrorist groups, which do not belong to the regular military. Concerning their reluctance to act, see Yeltsin, *Struggle for Russia*, 11-14.

10. See, for example, *Krasnaya zvezda*, October 9, 1993, 1-2.

11. One first-hand account of the decision-making process is that given by presidential adviser Dmitrii Volkogonov on Russian television's "Itogi" program on October 18, 1993. See also Yeltsin, *Struggle for Russia, passim*; and *Sovetskaya rossiya*, December 18, 1993, 4; *Krasnaya zvezda*, October 6, 1993; Reuters, October 18, 1993; *New York Times*, October 7, 1993; *Boston Globe*, October 7, 1993; *Komsomolskaya pravda*, October 7, 1993; *Washington Post*, October 8, 1993.

12. The text of Rutskoi's speech to the Supreme Soviet alleging widespread corruption may be found in *Pravda*, April 17, 1993, 1-3.

13. See Foye, "Updating Russian Civil-Military Relations," 44-50. The doctrine was apparently finished just before Yeltsin's decree dissolving the parliament. See *Kommersant*, September 18, 1993, 5.

14. *Rossiskiye vesti*, November 18, 1993, 1-2.

15. ITAR-TASS, December 24, 1993; Reuters, February 8, 1994.

16. To implement this decision, parliament will have to amend the Law on Defense, which sets limits on military force size in 1995. See ITAR-TASS, December 29, 1993.

17. See Yeltsin's interview with *Stern* magazine, as carried by ITAR-TASS on November 3, 1993, and especially his interview broadcast on the German ARD television network on November 12, 1993, and on Ostankino television on November 16, 1993. For a summary of the rumors see *Novaya ezhednevnaya gazeta*, November 13, 1993, 2. See also Yeltsin's very critical discussion of Grachev's performance during the crisis in Yeltsin, *Struggle for Russia*, 274-283.

18. For a discussion of this incident see Timothy Colton, *Commissars, Commanders, and Civilian Authority: The Structure of Soviet Military Politics* (Cambridge, Mass.: Harvard University Press, 1979), 175-195.

19. ITAR-TASS, November 25, 1993; Reuters, November 25, 1993.

20. Reuters, February 8, 1994; ITAR-TASS, March 3, 1994.

21. Even this proposed increase fell short of the military's preferred level of funding. See *Krasnaya zvezda*, March 17, 1994. Other key reports on the debate include ITAR-TASS, March 17, 1994; AFP, May 6, 1994; Interfax, May 10, 1994; Interfax, May 11, 1994; NTV, May 22, 1994; Interfax, June 2, 1994.

22. Reuters, June 24, 1994.

23. Russian television, June 10, 1994.

24. ITAR-TASS, July 8, 1994.

25. ITAR-TASS, July 11, 1994. Grachev specified that the railroad troops, commu-

nications troops, and construction troops all be included. These quasi-military units are vestiges of the Soviet system.

26. AFP, June 15, 1994. Subsequently, Yeltsin has mentioned a figure of 1.7 million as a possible final target. See Interfax, November 14, 1994.

27. *Izvestia*, July 20, 1994, 1, 4.

28. *Izvestia*, August 5, 1994, 1-2; *Krasnaya zvezda*, August 5, 1994, 1.

29. See, for example, AP and AFP, August 5, 1994; Reuters, ITAR-TASS, August 8, 1994.

30. Agreement was reached a few days later. See Reuters, August 10, 1994.

31. Interfax, August 15, 1994.

32. ITAR-TASS, August 15, 1994.

33. *Moskovsky komsomolets*, August 4, 1994; Reuters, August 9, 1994.

34. For an insightful analysis of the Lebed incident and the general disarray in Russian defense-policy decision making, see Pavel Felgengauer, "The Theory and Practice of Reaching a 'Consensus' in Moscow" (Paper prepared for the conference on National Security Decision-Making in Russia, Monterey, California, November 15-16, 1994).

35. Interfax, October 18 and October 20, 1994.

36. Reuters, November 1, 1994.

37. NTV, November 6, 1994.

38. Interfax, Reuters, November 2, 1994.

39. Interfax, November 2, 1994; Ostankino television, November 18, 1994.

40. Such a process of regionalization could be similar to that which occurred in Brazil in the 1960s. See Alfred Stepan, *The Military in Politics: Changing Patterns in Brazil* (Princeton, N.J.: Princeton University Press, 1971), 9-20.

41. For a discussion of regionalism see Ann Sheehy, "Russia's Republics: A Threat to Its Territorial Integrity?" *RFE/RL Research Report*, 2, 20, May 14, 1993, 34-40.

42. NTV, December 4, 1994; Reuters, December 7, 1994.

43. Reuters, December 9, 1994.

44. AP, November 28, 1994.

45. Reuters, December 16, 1994.

46. ITAR-TASS reported on December 22, 1994, that up to six military leaders involved in the assault, including a deputy commander of the army, had either resigned or been replaced because of their opposition to the handling of the affair. While this report was denied by the defense ministry, it was confirmed that General Colonel Vorobyev had refused to take command of the operation and tendered his resignation to the commander of Russian ground forces, who refused to accept it. See *Izvestia*, December 24, 1994, 1, 4.

47. See Felgenhauer, "Theory and Practice." In all fairness to Grachev, it should be noted that reforming the Russian military is an immense task, one that would tax the resources and resolve of the most energetic and dedicated reformer. Furthermore, Grachev's plans have met with substantial resistance from "old thinkers" schooled in the old Soviet system with its emphasis on large-scale warfare and the dominance of armor. Grachev's reform plan may be basically sound and may even be proceeding, but this progress is evidently too slow for most military personnel.

48. This point is emphasized in Alexander A. Belkin, "Civil-Military Relations and National Security Decisionmaking" (Paper prepared for the conference on National Security Decision-Making in Russia, Monterey, California, November 15-16, 1994).

# Part II   Economic and Related Issues

# 7 Defense Conversion, Demilitarization, and Privatization in Russia

John E. Tedstrom

The successful demilitarization of Russia's society and economy will be among the most important of all the reforms undertaken in the transitioning former Soviet Union. Efforts toward these goals have proven to be as daunting as they are consequential, both for future developments in Russia and for the future of East-West relations and global security. Because of the high stakes involved and Russia's inability to undertake the reforms alone, converting Russia's defense industries also remains a serious policy objective for the West.

In the years since Soviet president Mikhail Gorbachev announced his country's intentions to convert defense industries to civilian production, Russian reformers have made little progress toward that goal.[1] Not only has industrial conversion been impeded by many of the obstacles that have slowed economic reform and restructuring in Russia generally, but also it faces special problems stemming from the place and role of the defense industries in the Soviet, and now the Russian, economy and society.

Initial Western reaction to Gorbachev's statement on demilitarizing the USSR's economy was cautious but optimistic. On the one hand, the new policies represented an unprecedented opportunity to slow the arms race and promote democratization and free market reforms in the USSR. On the other hand, the West knew very little about the true size and shape of the Soviet defense budget, the political environment of the new policy, or the nature and influence of the Soviet defense industrial complex and its leadership.

Despite these and other uncertainties, the United States and other Western nations quickly grasped the potential importance of Gorbachev's speech and began to devise ways to support and even accelerate the Soviet efforts. Attention was focused on demobilizing Soviet troops, especially those in East-Cen-

The views expressed here are the author's own and should not be taken to reflect those of the RAND Corporation or its sponsors.

tral Europe; dismantling the Soviet military arsenal, especially nuclear weapons and their delivery systems; and converting the Soviet defense industries from military to civilian production.[2]

## Halting First Steps

Early efforts by Soviet reformers and their would-be collaborators in the West were largely stymied by an entrenched, conservative bureaucracy in Moscow, growing ethnic and regional tensions within the Soviet Union, and a resilient and resistant defense industry *nomenklatura* that bargained and pressured for continued financial support if not continued procurement orders.

Another problem was the failure on the part of the central government to reach consensus on a reform program and then move from the planning stage to implementation. A succession of reform programs were proposed and rejected from 1989 through 1991. Some, including the well-known "500 days" program of economist Stanislav Shatalin, included plans for industrial conversion. Yet because Gorbachev could not build a political consensus on reform, circumstances forced him to rule by executive order. His decrees were disjointed and uninspired, however, and ultimately they were largely ignored.

Most important, through 1991 the economic crisis that had been building steam for over a decade in the USSR had gathered enough pressure to prevent any effort at the federal level to effect serious, systemic, economic reform, including measures targeted toward industrial conversion. The Soviet budget deficit exceeded 25 percent of GDP by 1991[3] and "interenterprise debt" (a new phenomenon in the partially liberalized Soviet economy) soared to more than a trillion rubles, adding to already severe inflationary pressures. By the end of 1991, inflation emerged as the most prominent sign of the deepening economic crisis. Other social and economic problems—such as increased homelessness and crime, a breakdown of the already wobbly Soviet trading and distribution systems, a rise in the frequency and intensity of labor strikes, and, ultimately, the constitutional crisis that pulled the Soviet Union apart— all diverted attention from the plans to convert the Soviet defense industries. These factors, together with growing economic difficulties in the West, hindered efforts to put financial muscle behind the Soviet industrial conversion effort. The economic problems, coupled with the president's failure to push through a reform program, gave Gorbachev's opponents, including many in the military and the defense industries, the motive and the platform they needed to mount an increasingly serious campaign against privatization and market economics. In the end, of course, this campaign took the form of the short-lived coup of August 19-21, 1991, and eventually contributed to the demise of the USSR.

If these problems sound familiar, it is because they continue, in one way or another, to affect the progress of conversion and Western assistance for conversion in post-Soviet Russia. Since the formal dissolution of the USSR in December 1991, slow progress toward demilitarization and conversion continues to be a serious problem for the Soviet successor states, especially those with large shares of the former Soviet defense industry: Russia, Ukraine, Belarus, and Kazakhstan. Output, employment, and wages have all fallen, some of the former Soviet Union's most productive talent has moved abroad, and some arms producers have chosen to turn their attention away from the civilian market to foreign arms markets.

However, the record of demilitarization in Russia is not all negative. The large degree to which the former super-secret Soviet defense industries have opened their doors to Western scholars, policy analysts, and, in some cases, potential foreign investors is one of the most encouraging developments in the last five years.[4] These new relationships have proven invaluable to many in the former Soviet Union and have increased Western understanding of the problems of transition from socialism. Continued interaction between former Soviet defense industrialists and their Western interlocutors should be a top priority for those concerned with promoting the demobilization of Russia's defense sector. Other positive trends, such as the continued progress on privatization and the growing understanding of market economics in Russia are also cause for optimism.

The goals of this chapter are to examine the status of conversion of the Russian defense industrial base, analyze the underlying factors affecting the process of conversion, and suggest some policy alternatives for the Russians and the West. The focus on Russia is motivated by the following factors. First, of all the Soviet successor states, Russia has by far the largest defense industrial complex. Second, by virtue of Russia's relatively large economy, economic performance in Russia continues to influence economic performance elsewhere in the former Soviet Union. Finally, by its size and relatively progressive attitude toward reform, Russia is bound to serve as a model, at least to some degree, for the other former republics as they undertake their own conversion programs.

**Table 7-1** Production Index and Index of Employment in Russia's Defense Sector

|  | 1991 as share of 1990 | 1992 as share of 1990 |
|---|---|---|
| Total output | 86% | 70% |
| military | 74 | 50 |
| civilian | 96 | 90 |
| Industrial production personnel | 96 | 85 |
| military production | 86 | 50 |
| civilian production | 104 | 120 |

SOURCE: *Russia-1992: Economic Situation,* Center for Economic Forecasting, Moscow, 1992.

## Conversion in Post-Soviet Russia:
## A Mixed Record, and Massive Problems

The record on industrial conversion in Russia is mixed. Although the share of civilian output in defense plants has increased substantially, that growth has come from a very small base and results from cuts in military-related output, not increases in civilian production. Most restructuring thus far has come in the form of "diversification," that is, simply increasing production of civilian products without actually converting any production facilities from military activities. Table 7-1 shows how two measures of conversion activity compare.

Table 7-1 shows that although the share of civilian production in the defense sector has grown recently, in absolute terms it fell by some 10 percent from 1990 through 1992. (The output of military equipment fell faster.) In terms of selected consumer durables, 1993 production as a percentage of 1991 production was: radio receivers, 53 percent; televisions, 83 percent; refrigerators and freezers, 89 percent.[5] Likewise, while employment of industrial workers in the civilian operations of the defense sector has grown, the decrease in employment in the military factories has fallen even faster. Traditionally, at least as many people were involved in military production as in civilian production in Russia's defense sector. This means that overall employment in this sector has shrunk considerably.[6] These trends, coupled with falling wages and the threat of brain drain from the defense sector (especially in R&D and engineering) do little to generate faith in or support for the government's conversion policies.

Four main obstacles hinder conversion of the defense industries in Russia today. The first is a general macroeconomic disequilibrium and depression that shows few signs of improving significantly in the medium term, although there are indications that Russia may now be approaching the trough of her economic downturn. The second is lackluster progress on privatization of large industrial enterprises, though here, too, Russia may be at a turning point. The third obstacle is the growing pressure for economic and political disintegration within Russia. While the future of the Russian Federation is far from certain, decentralization is not a totally negative phenomenon; there is indeed good cause to believe that Russia can benefit from some degree of decentralization if managed properly. Finally, the fourth roadblock is the unsettled state of the CIS security arrangement, in terms of unclear security concepts (those that address the needs and interests of the former republics that have expressed a desire in seeing some type of regional security arrangement prevail), in terms of a competition between the CIS military establishment and those of the newly independent states, including Russia, and in terms of the security tensions that remain between East and West, tensions most clearly reflected in the divergence of opinion on the expansion of NATO.

## The Economic Crisis

The depression that has gripped Russia for the past several years continues to represent the single most important threat to political stability and economic reform, including conversion. Nevertheless, important positive developments are slowing the decline of welfare and living standards and will, ultimately, produce economic growth. Time is the critical factor here and, to his credit, Russian president Boris Yeltsin seems remarkably adept at buying more of it in the face of strong opposition.

After significant drops in national income and industrial production since the mid-1980s, Russian GDP fell by about 20 percent in 1992 according to official Russian statistics and perhaps another 12 percent in 1993. Final figures for 1994 are likely to show a further 10-percent decline. Figure 7-1 shows how the most recent independent estimates (by Russian economists) diverge from the official statistics. Most observers of the Russian economy believe that official figures understate the decline in 1985-1990 and overstate it in 1991 and 1992. In the figure, this trend is seen in the somewhat flatter curve of the independent estimates in 1991 and 1992.

There are many reasons to believe that the Russian statistical survey now fails to capture all of the economic activity that takes place; Russian business-

**Figure 7-1** Official and Independent Estimates of Trends in Russia's National Income, in constant prices

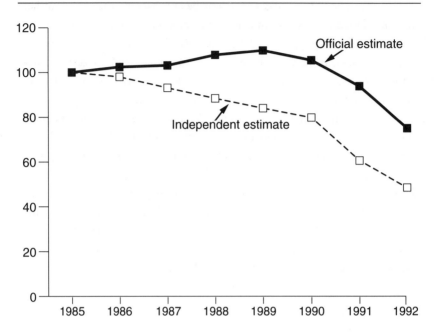

SOURCE: *Ekonomika i zhizn'*, No. 1, 1993.

men have many reasons, including high tax rates, to hide their operations from the authorities. The extent to which official data diverge from reality remains unknown, but if the official estimates in Figure 7-1 are anywhere near correct (they show a drop in national income of about 20 percent from 1990 through 1992), the decline they reveal would constitute a tremendous shock to any economy. Another 12-percent compression in 1993, although less than the drop in 1992, represents another strong jolt.

Some observers predicted a widespread famine in Russia. So far, this "food crisis" has been avoided. In 1992, gross agricultural output was down only 8 percent from 1991. However, the outlook for agriculture in 1994 and 1995 is moderate at best. Agriculture is hurt by slow privatization and low investment rates as well as by the rising costs of inputs. Performance in agriculture is critically important now that most other consumer basics are either unavailable or too costly for all but the wealthiest Russians. Unfortunately, until investment in agriculture increases and a land reform that really privatizes the large state farms is in place, agriculture's output is bound to flag. As a political force, Russian farmers are conservative; they are ambivalent at best on the question of private land and reluctant to exert their influence. Yet once provoked past a certain threshold, they could yet prove to be some of the reformers' most troubling problems.

Another problem for the longer term is the negative trend in investment rates in the economy—in both the private and the public sectors. In 1991 through 1994, capital investment declined with damaging consequences. Much of the investment was devoted to the consumer goods, rather than producer goods, industries. The focus on consumer goods was part of a well-intentioned plan to increase supplies in hopes of keeping prices low and consumer satisfaction with the reforms high, thereby boosting labor productivity. Unfortunately, the social, political, and economic crises in the former USSR have outweighed any positive effect on labor productivity that might have occurred as a result of this strategy. Meanwhile, investment in the capital goods sector has suffered, resulting in zero growth for capital productivity.

Significantly, those defense enterprises that were undergoing conversion or otherwise increasing output of civilian goods were beneficiaries of the investment program, at least through 1990. Since then, however, the constraints on investment have been so tight that even these industries are suffering. The result is that all Russian industry is hurting from a slowdown in what was already a very slow retirement rate of capital. Stories abound of idle plants, farms, and even hard-currency-producing oil wells, because of a lack of investment.[7]

The precise investment budget is unknown, but many Russian and Western officials seem to have landed on a figure of some $130 billion from 1993-1998; how the government intends to dispose of those funds is still somewhat of a mystery. With the Russian budget deficit in recent years running between 25 percent and 26 percent of GDP, it is clear that investment resources from both the public and the private sectors are extremely scarce.

Although some of the causes of Russia's economic crisis carry over from the Soviet period and were mentioned above, others are peculiar to post-Soviet Russia. The chief culprits are (1) continued deficit spending at the federal, regional, and local levels, especially on the large, loss-making industrial dinosaurs of the Soviet past; (2) the failure to establish new, market-oriented macroeconomic institutions (and related laws) such as an independent central bank to replace the now defunct Soviet versions; (3) the absence of a credible social safety net, which forces enterprises to continue to serve as life-long welfare providers; and (4) the shrinking domestic market for consumer durables.[8]

The first three weaknesses impede general economic reform and industrial restructuring—not just conversion of the defense sector. It is important to remember that conversion does not take place in a vacuum. To the contrary, efforts to undertake industrial conversion benefit from healthy markets for capital and labor, established market institutions and policies such as sound fiscal and monetary systems, and regulations on commercial activity including bankruptcy law. Finally, because conversion implies a significant restructuring of industry in general, an effective social safety net to accommodate the tens of thousands that will inevitably be displaced is critical.[9]

The domestic market for consumer durables—which make up a fairly large share of the civilian output of converted military factories—has become smaller due to shrinking real disposable incomes and rising prices for food and other consumer basics. The market has also become more competitive as a result of the influx of foreign products. Unfortunately for the conversion effort, raw materials and military equipment seem to remain the only Russian products that can compete effectively abroad in any consistent way; therefore, foreign sales stand little chance of offsetting the decline in domestic demand for consumer durables, at least for the time being.

### Moving Slowly Toward Privatization

To date the most promising results of the Russian privatization experience have been in the service sector. Privatizing small service firms requires less capital and less red tape. Often, the object of privatization in the service sector is less burdened by aging capital stock and difficult labor unions. Some forty-six thousand small firms were privatized in Russia in 1992, and the pace has increased through 1994. The development of new businesses—again, mostly small firms in the service sector—is also moving ahead fairly rapidly, another encouraging sign.

The privatization of larger enterprises is another story entirely. First, the privatization regulations that are now on the books in Russia make it much more difficult for would-be entrepreneurs to get permission to privatize large firms that are considered federal property and not subject to local and regional regulations. Second, the scarcity of investment capital and the tremendous risk involved in many of these ventures tend to put off both foreign and domestic

**Table 7-2** Size and Structure of Employment in Russia's Defense Sector, 1992

| | Number of employees | | | | | |
|---|---|---|---|---|---|---|
| | Up to 200 | 201-500 | 501-1000 | 1001-5000 | 5001-10,000 | More than 10,000 |
| All enterprises | 66.2% | 16.2% | 8.2% | 7.7% | 1.1% | 0.6% |
| Defense enterprises | 0.3 | 1.6 | 3.9 | 49.8 | 28.3 | 16.1 |

SOURCE: *Russia-1992: Economic Situation,* Center for Economic Forecasting, Moscow, 1992.

investors.

These problems aside, privatizing the defense sector remains taboo in Russia. The latest version of the Russian privatization program forbids the privatization of many defense enterprises and makes the privatization of others dependent on special executive waivers.[10] The privatization of enterprises in the numerous "one company towns" in Russia (many of which were for many years closed towns associated with defense-related industries) is particularly controversial for all of the social implications that privatization of the sole employer (especially one with few prospects for growth) carries for the community. Of course, because defense plants tend to be large relative to other enterprises in Russia, they will remain among the most difficult to privatize, even after the necessary legislation is in place. Table 7-2 shows that nearly half of Russia's defense firms employ between one thousand and five thousand workers, whereas only 7.7 percent of all firms have a work force of that size.

Of some six thousand (mostly non-defense) large enterprises scheduled for privatization in Russia by the end of 1993, nearly 200 had been technically privatized by spring. These successes, coupled with the successful privatization of thousands of smaller firms, are bound to spur privatization generally throughout the economy and should be key targets for Western support. However, the problems of privatizing large enterprises take on a special intensity when the private capital is coming from a foreign investor. A good deal of skepticism and even "economic xenophobia" persists in Russia generally, and among influential elements in Moscow in particular, concerning foreign investment and ownership of property. The special place accorded the defense industries in Russia means that foreign investment there will be doubly problematic.

A potentially large contribution from the West could be made by assisting in the development of laws that will facilitate foreign investment in converting defense enterprises. These laws will be complicated and will necessitate the restructuring of existing enterprises, for example, by spinning off the civilian operations into independent corporations. Further, Western support for businesses in the form of leveraged investments and insurance for private investors would be a welcome addition to the overall aid package.

In the face of strong resistance to, and slow progress on, conversion of the defense industries, it is not surprising that many Russian defense industrialists have turned to foreign arms markets to replace lost orders from Moscow. Some of these efforts are undertaken quietly and outside the boundaries of current Russian regulations. Others, however, have at least the tacit support of senior officials in Moscow who see this approach as one of the few ways of keeping the defense industries afloat.

This approach is worrisome from a Western perspective. It is not inconceivable that U.S. concerns over Russian (and other republics') arms sales could become a serious stumbling block to deliveries of financial and technical assistance, not to mention foreign investment. Russia's arms sales abroad raise three main concerns.

First, the United States has little influence over who purchases the Russian equipment, especially if the sales are done outside the normal channels. In all likelihood, moreover, those countries who are the most promising customers will be those whose roles in the international security regime tend not to promote stability and security.

Second, by shifting from producing arms for domestic procurement to satisfying foreign demand, Russian defense industries do nothing to demilitarize the economy. The plant and equipment, human capital, and financial resources used to satisfy foreign arms orders would clearly be better devoted to civilian production that would raise the welfare of the Russian people and reduce the threat of armed conflict. Some might argue that markets ought to give Russian defense industrialists these signals, but efficient markets have yet to emerge in Russia. This is why conversion's success in Russia is so closely linked to the fate of other reforms.

Third, most observers agree that the world's demand for Russian weaponry—even at bargain-basement prices—is not enough to sustain the Russian defense industrial complex for long. Instead, many of the defense enterprises that opt for arms sales over conversion in the short and medium terms will face bankruptcy in the longer term, exacerbating the social and economic dislocation in this sector.

These arguments are not meant to imply that there is no place for Russia in the world's arms markets. Indeed, some have argued that the West should guarantee Russia a certain share of world arms sales.[11] While that might help ease the transition in the short run, in the long run Russian arms manufacturers ought to compete on an even playing field with the rest of the world. In short, the United States must make it clear to the Russians why it is in their own interest to choose conversion over foreign arms sales now, before we are forced to restrict aid and investment or otherwise penalize them in the future.

### Russia: Cracks in the Federation

Although a wholesale splitting of Russia along ethnic or regional lines is very unlikely, cracks in the federation structure have emerged that impede the development and execution of reform policy; they have also interfered with efficient trade among and between Russia's numerous regional and local economies. Although calculations are somewhat speculative, some Russian economists estimate that as much as 30 percent of the fall in former Soviet GDP in 1992-1993 is due to the political barriers to trade that have developed in the former Soviet Union. This holds for the ties that used to bind together the former Soviet defense enterprises. Many Russian and Ukrainian defense plant managers, for example, note that the trade between them that survived the dissolution of the Union did so despite the political and economic barriers that were erected after December 1991.

As unlikely as a full breakup of the Russian Federation is, the current arrangement is probably just as unsustainable. Already an impressive amount of power and authority has shifted from the center (Moscow) to the periphery. Some of this has been by design. Yeltsin believes that the old system was too centralized and realizes that he must keep his local constituencies satisfied, so he has taken specific steps to delegate authority to them. These trends toward decentralization, however, transcend Yeltsin's ability to allocate power and authority. As early as 1987, with the adoption of the Law on State Enterprises, key components of economic power were transferred to enterprise and plant managers on the local level. As the transition from socialism became increasingly complex, many local political and economic authorities created opportunities to usurp even more power. Indeed, local economic and political leaders were the ones who stonewalled attempts to "save the Union" in 1990 and 1991 by preventing the adoption of the Union Treaty and other unifying documents.

The same phenomenon is reoccurring now in Russia (and to a lesser degree in Ukraine). In most cases the separatist sentiments in Russia are not as deeply or profoundly held as they were in the former Soviet republics. Yet, we have seen serious efforts—for example in Nizhny Novgorod—to accelerate the reform process beyond what Moscow has prescribed, including reforms of the defense industrial complex. Other regions are proceeding much more slowly. Still others seem bent, simply, on gaining ownership of the natural wealth within their territory.

Table 7-3 shows that some regions in Russia have particularly high concentrations of defense industries. These regions are all particularly vulnerable to economic and social dislocation and are all pursuing their own brands of reform and conversion. Too little is known in the West about these local- and regional-level programs and about the restructuring of specific enterprises. This is an important area for further research because technical assistance could be especially productive at the regional and local levels, and at the level of the enterprise.

The "regional issue" was a major point of contention in the negotiation of the new constitution. It is still not entirely clear, however, how this issue will play itself out. In one likely scenario increased autonomy at the local level will be embodied in law. Another would offer gradations of autonomy ranging from full subordination to federation laws and regulations to status as a free economic zone that determined its own trade policies and set local taxes and budgets independently of Moscow.

It would be a mistake to view this trend as having only negative consequences for Russia. To the contrary, regionalization, if managed properly, will be an advantage and will promote the demilitarization of Russian society and its economy. Those regions, such as Nizhny Novgorod, that have adopted more aggressive reform policies stand as relative success stories in Russia. Their positive examples will promote reform and restructuring in other parts of the country, one of the most effective ways of encouraging change.[12]

### The CIS Security Arrangement

The fourth key obstacle to successful conversion in Russia is the competition for military power and authority among the republics and between some of the republics and the armed forces of the Commonwealth of Independent States (CIS). Years after the formation of the CIS, the role and place of its defense establishment vis-à-vis those of Russia and the other Soviet successor

**Table 7-3** Areas with High Degrees of Defense Industrial Employment (percent of defense industrial employment in total industrial employment)

| Region | Share of defense industrial employment |
|---|---|
| Northwest | 32.6% |
| Novgorod oblast | 39.2 |
| St. Petersburg city | 34.4 |
| Urals | 31.2 |
| Udmurtiya | 57.0 |
| Perm' oblast | 37.8 |
| Sverdlovsk oblast | 32.5 |
| Volga-Vyatka | 29.9 |
| Mari ASSR | 45.7 |
| Kirov oblast | 31.4 |
| Volga | 29.5 |
| Kuibyshev oblast | 34.2 |
| Saratov oblast | 32.3 |
| Tatarstan | 30.1 |
| Central | 23.8 |
| Kaluga oblast | 46.9 |
| Vladimir | 37.0 |
| Tula oblast | 33.3 |
| Other | |
| Nikolaev oblast | 50.0 |
| N. Kazakhstan oblast | 45.6 |
| Omsk oblast | 42.5 |

SOURCE: Derived from unpublished Goskomstat data for 1985, *Trud v SSSR,* Moscow, *Financy i statistika,* 1988, *Narodnoe khozyaistvo RSFSR v 1989 godu,* Moscow, *Financy i statistika,* 1990.

states is still unclear.

The successor states have been remarkably slow at defining their own security concepts and doctrines. Russia aside, a key example of this problem is Ukraine, which has yet to find its place in the post-Soviet security system. The most important question concerning Ukrainian security is the fate of its longer-range nuclear weapons, but other weighty matters await resolution as well: the size of Ukraine's army, the role of conventional weapons in its force structure, and the articulation of its national interests and security priorities all are yet to be determined.

The outcome of that exercise will, of course, have important ramifications for conversion programs in each of the Soviet successor states because only after these doctrines are articulated can each state evaluate its demand for arms, its ability to satisfy that demand domestically, its need to purchase abroad, and the prospects for restructuring its domestic industrial base in the longer term.

### Thoughts on the Future

Conversion in Russia, as well as in the other Soviet successor states, is bound to be a long and painful process. The West has a vital interest in assisting the process, although it has not yet adopted a coherent or focused plan for doing so. In part this is the result of constantly aiming at a moving target in the former Soviet Union, where the politics of reform create a new crisis almost every day. Still, there are some underlying factors that can give direction to our thoughts on these problems.

The Russian defense sector is already crippled by several years of falling procurement orders and a shortage of investment. Factories are closed or are operating at a fraction of their total capacity and wages in the sector have fallen dramatically. This contributes to the social and economic crisis in Russia that could yet derail the economic reforms in some parts of the country. Western aid programs should be particularly aware of this potential problem.

Likewise, only after economic welfare begins to rise in Russia can we be more certain that democracy has gained a solid footing. The economic crisis stands as the single largest and most important threat to democracy and stability in Russia.

Industrial conversion is part of a bigger process of economic and political reform. Efforts to convert Russian defense plants hinge on successful transformation of other parts of the Russian economy, and the development of vibrant markets for capital, goods, and labor. Already, most of the old system has fallen away, but, as mentioned above, key elements of the new system have yet to be put in place. Privatization is the most important long-term reform goal in this regard.

Russian defense industrialists must be convinced of the need to pursue conversion instead of other activities such as selling arms in foreign markets. The most persuasive lever available is economic self-interest. Success of the reforms, either in terms of sectoral or institutional restructuring or in terms of regional economic development, will serve as important examples and should be supported. One area to watch closely is the development of conversion programs in various regions. They are smaller and easier to manage and their experiments with conversion may be worthy of special assistance if they show exceptional promise and applicability to other regions.

Privatizing the Russian defense sector as it now exists is unlikely to happen anytime soon. One alternative for the Russians is to cut the ties between the military-producing operations of the enterprise from the civilian operations, the latter of which could indeed be truly privatized. By proceeding resolutely on restructuring of the defense enterprises and privatizing the plant and equipment that is devoted to civilian production, the Russians will achieve more conversion at a faster pace. (In the meantime, the only viable option of supporting defense industrial workers is through continued state subsidies of their enterprises. That must remain a temporary policy, however, and not anything that conservatives in the system can perpetuate.)

These suggestions point to the complexities of the problem that conversion poses to policy makers in the West as well as in Russia. Rendering assistance to Russia's reforms will not be easy or cheap. The alternatives to successful reform in Russia, however, will present problems that are even more difficult and costly.

## Notes

1. See Gorbachev's speech to the United Nations, *Pravda*, December 8, 1988.

2. Decommissioning and dismantling nuclear weapons and converting nuclear and chemical entails environmental clean-up efforts that cannot be ignored.

3. International Monetary Fund, "The Economy of the Former Soviet Union in 1991" (Washington, D.C.: IMF, 1992).

4. Among the many successful ventures of this sort are the programs of the Berghof Institute for Conflict Studies in Berlin and of the Stanford University Center for International Security and Arms Control.

5. *Delovoi mir*, March 11, 1993, 11-14.

6. In 1988, after a significant, though gradual, slowdown in defense spending growth, civilian employment in Russia's defense sectors was split about evenly between civilian and military production. By 1992, the ratio was 25 percent military production and 75 percent civilian production.

7. Performance in the energy sector, a critical sector for any economy, is down significantly in Russia. Oil output, for example, is down roughly 30 percent from the 1988 level, and coal is down by about the same amount.

8. Part of Russia's economic problem is depression in other Soviet successor states. Russia and the successor states remain relatively interdependent economically, and several of the successor states are suffering drops in national income more drastic than that seen in Russia.

9. The importance of an effective social safety net in Russia as a prerequisite to fundamental, systemic reforms cannot be overstated. In fact, observers of the Russian scene will know when to expect radical reform in Russia's economy when the government establishes a comprehensive and functioning welfare system.

10. See *Rossiiskie vesti*, February 4, 1993, 2-6, for the draft privatization program.

11. Within limits. See the article by Charles Wolf, Jr., *Wall Street Journal*, April 16, 1993, A10.

12. Eugene B. Rumer and John Tedstrom, "Where the Action Is in Russia," *Christian Science Monitor*, December 16, 1992, 22.

# 8 U.S. Trade and Investment in Russia: Risks and Opportunities

Eugene K. Lawson

Russia today is a vast underserved consumer market containing 150 million potential customers for quality goods and services. As Daniel Yergin and Thane Gustafson, authors of *Russia 2010*, point out, "Russia is an industrial giant, if a misshapen one." It has some extraordinary advantages, however, that make it unique among developing economies:

- Immense untapped resources or, put another way, an excess capacity of many raw and semi-processed materials
- A large, low-wage, skilled work force (Russia graduates relatively more high-school level workers than the United States)
- Huge available capacity in many industrial plants, pipelines, and railroads, some of which is relatively new and efficient
- Enormous pent-up consumer demand for virtually every conceivable kind of consumer goods and services, which will be released as personal income rises
- Unexploited managerial energy and talent.[1]

## The Business Environment

Significant risks accompany the enormous promise of American business engagement in Russia. The top three, according to surveys of business experience conducted by the U.S. Commerce Department, are: arbitrary changes in tax laws and business regulations, uncertainty of ownership and authority over resources, and the rise of corruption and criminality.[2]

American business people have found that such basic matters as establishing title to property or determining who has authority to approve transactions can be maddeningly elusive. Taxes likewise can be raised or regulations altered after a deal has been negotiated and approved, thereby changing a venture

This paper was completed in the spring of 1994.

from profitable to unprofitable overnight. None of the protections provided in the United States against such occurrences is available in Russia, which can detract from the sanctity of a contract.[3]

Corruption and business-related crime also are a plague upon the conduct of transactions in contemporary Russia. Permits are accompanied by solicitations for bribes, and theft of business property is rampant. A new mafia preys on outside traders and investors for sustenance in a hard-hit economy. Corruption and criminality run like a red thread through the anecdotal reports of the more than 225 members of the U.S.-Russia Business Council. Most distressingly perhaps, there is currently no reliable avenue of redress against these depredations.[4]

This is in keeping with the generally inaccessible character of the legal system in Russia at the present time. Laws and regulations are frequently unpublished or unenforced. Even when they are openly declared, there is great doubt about their validity and meaning. This unfortunate reality has been exacerbated still further by the "war of laws" across Russia—pitting institutions and levels of government against each other in a struggle to determine who controls the future of the country and, more immediately, who stands to collect the rents and taxes from outside business transactions. This has been a very big barrier to American investors, who can scarcely justify committing their shareholders' money to negotiated ventures that can be readily overthrown by successive laws or administrations.

An underlying problem is that Western companies are often viewed in Russia as cash cows or Santa Claus visitors able to dish out any benefit desired. There is little idea in many quarters of such constraints as return on investment. This lack of market understanding can create tensions for American businessmen with venture partners, customers, creditors, employees, and governing authorities. It unquestionably enters into arbitrary and after-the-fact tax and regulatory decisions.

Along with all this, the facilities for conducting business in Russia are often rudimentary to nonexistent. Business information is hard to come by, as are reliable official statistics. Office space in the major cities is scarce and expensive, and telecommunications connections are weak. Banking and credit are inadequate for anything but spot loans. Given all these impediments, it is not surprising that foreign investment is still low and that Western commercial banks are not eager to underwrite it. For the next several years, outside investors will have to look to the U.S. government and multilateral institutions—the U.S. Export-Import Bank and Overseas Private Investment Corporation, the World Bank, the International Finance Corporation, and the European Bank for Reconstruction and Development—to shoulder the major risks. The lack of commercial financing is certainly one of the most severe constraints to expanded trade and investment.

Current Russian attitudes toward foreign investment are, on key points, often at cross-purposes with the aims of American investors. The two groups may use the same language but mean different things. This is not too surprising as a short-term phenomenon. As Yergin and Gustafson have pointed out, "It is difficult for foreign businessmen not to appear to Russian eyes as carpetbaggers descending on a defeated country." [5] Russian feelings need to be understood and addressed with tact and sensitivity if the conflict is to be surmounted.

At present the goals of the two sides diverge markedly. American companies want to gain access to raw materials and to the domestic Russian market; Russian policy by contrast is to move away from dependence on raw materials and to seek foreign markets for their own manufactured goods. The Russians want to get hold of foreign technology and capital and to preserve operational control over enterprises on Russian soil; Americans seek to limit capital and technology sharing and to acquire operational control.

To a fair degree these differences reflect a natural wariness, or lack of confidence, on the part of both Russians and Americans. Where that can be overcome, a working partnership will evolve. In the aircraft industry, for example, where Russian manufacturers look with appetite on their prospects in world markets, joint ventures have been welcomed with enthusiasm.

As further experience develops, and successes in energy, aerospace, and other areas are registered, it should become increasingly possible to locate a workable middle ground.

### The Ideal Environment

Business finds a home where conditions are congenial. American investors and traders would like an environment in Russia with the following features:[6]

*A Stable Financial Climate*
Budget and monetary policies would be tightened so as to curb inflation and to bring trade and payment imbalances down to manageable size. Tax and income policies would be structured so as to increase productivity by encouraging a movement to smaller labor forces and wage payments.

*Liberalized Markets.* Prices would be freed, currency swings constrained, and interest rates decontrolled. Barriers would be lifted on market entry and exit, and goods and services would move freely across national borders—as would capital and technology.

*Privatized Business.* Large state enterprises, including obsolete defense plants, would be rapidly liquidated or converted into private holdings with independent shareholders and boards of directors. Laws defining and protecting ownership and management prerogatives, and defending them against arbitrary encroachment, would be adopted and enforced.

*A Supportive Framework.* Reforms for these purposes would be introduced into national and regional laws and constitutions. Allocations of authority among the political bodies and levels of government would be settled with finality. An independent, fair, and reliable judicial system would be installed. Fiscal and banking systems, capital and equity markets, and dependable information networks all would be established on a sound and functioning basis.

This sounds ideal, but it is also unrealistic. The measures indicated could not be adopted suddenly without visiting on the Russian people the most severe pain and dislocation. Many of these improvements must depend for their realization on political and cultural evolutions that are still a long way from completion. Others will take time—and a learning curve—to become achievable.

That is why experienced American business people accept that the work of developing a supportive business climate in Russia will be a matter of patient and persistent engagement over several decades and perhaps generations. It will not be accomplished by any sudden or instant transformation. It will have to be done collaboratively with their Russian counterparts.[7]

### The Good News

Some constructive strides are being made in public policy. The CIA's economic survey of Russia for 1992 reported significant advances in freeing prices, cutting defense spending, unifying foreign exchange rates, and promoting privatization.[8] Although much remains to be done, and mistakes will be inevitable, there is reason to take heart.

Industrial output in 1992 reportedly fell by about one-fifth, but the actual decline in some industrial sectors was almost certainly less steep. Russian enterprises have a strong incentive, as well as ample opportunity, to understate production so as to minimize taxes. Official statistics, moreover, are unlikely to have caught up as yet with the achievements of the private sector, whose size and output are growing rapidly. The compression of the economy slowed in 1993, perhaps to around 12 percent.

There are now more than seventy thousand small shops in private hands in Russia, or fully one-half of all such shops, according to the 1993 testimony of Under Secretary of the Treasury Lawrence Summers.[9] Larger firms have been slower to privatize and to admit foreign partners, but as of summer 1993 there were significant converts, including such giant firms as Zil (automobiles) and Kalashnikov (firearms). By the end of the year, Mr. Summers projected, a third of the larger firms would be privatized.

To help things along, Russia in 1993 adopted its first bankruptcy law since the 1917 Revolution and actually moved the first bankruptcy papers through the competent court. To gain management experience, the Russians sent more than a thousand individuals to the United States for training in business-related disciplines such as banking, energy, and agribusiness.[10]

On the financial side, 1993 witnessed a substantial rescheduling of Russia's external debt by the Group of Seven industrial democracies. This stretched out over a period of ten years, starting in 1994, the repayment of some $15 billion dollars in principal and interest that would otherwise have fallen immediately due. There will be a continuing need for the Paris Club (the official creditors) to continue reschedulings, and more importantly, to provide for a future, phased *reduction* of Russian debt.

At the U.S.-Russia Summit in Vancouver in April 1993, and later at the G-7 meeting in Tokyo, American and Western leaders provided significant additional support for Russian efforts. This included quick disbursement aid for nonprofit groups working for reform within Russia, and also a Russian-American Enterprise Fund aimed at boosting Russia's privatization program.

By the end of the year, political developments had swung the pendulum of authority dramatically in the direction of centralized executive control, with parliamentary elections and a constitutional referendum slated. Businessmen and others followed these developments closely, as they have a major and continuing impact on the environment for trade and investment. Although a reform-minded parliament did not result from December's elections, a new constitution was achieved which could help gradually to ameliorate important obstacles such as the "war of laws."

## Monitoring Points

Nothing definitive is likely to take place soon. Instead there will be zigs and zags, advances and retreats, toward what ultimately will become a congenial climate. Along the way, businessmen have found, there are certain standards or guideposts that can be used to assess progress.

*Hyperinflation.* A deadly economic affliction, hyperinflation provokes capital flight and saps consumer confidence. The good news in 1993 was that, in the midst of its severe political tremors, the Russian government was able to take steps to curb the disease. The rate of inflation was reduced from 30 percent a month in January to what Under Secretary Summers calculated as a sustainable rate of 15 to 20 percent a month by September, compared to an annual rate of 2,270 percent.[11] That same progress continued into 1994, with the monthly figure dropping to single digits in several months.

*Unemployment.* The official unemployment rate has been too low for a healthy economy. Output dropped steadily from 1990 through 1992, yet unemployment remained constant at only 3 to 4 percent of Russia's 74-million-person labor force, although the International Labor Organization claims that unemployment rose to around 10 percent by early 1994.[12] Many of those recorded as on the job are severely underemployed and others have nothing to do at all. When farm and industrial work places are restructured on a leaner and more competitive basis, one initial result will be sharply higher unemployment. This will serve as a signal to outside investors to move in and begin to take up the employment slack. If the Russian economic path follows the Czech, Hungarian, and Polish models, Western investors will know that true and very painful industrial restructuring has begun when unemployment soars into the 15 to 20 percent range.

*Privatization.* Privatization has been an area of striking success for Russia. By the end of 1992, the portion of its population working in the private sector had reached nearly one-fifth.[13] The impulse to privatize, moreover, was coming not from the top down but upwards from a burgeoning class of entrepreneurs all over the country. To get a full impression of what is happening, one needs to get out of Moscow and spend some time in the regions.[14]

*Defense Conversion.* Developments here have not been so positive. What is needed, over time, is a sustained movement out of heavy industry and into a consumer-based economy. This is both practically and philosophically an up-heaval, however, and thus far only small progress has been recorded. The evolution is one that will have to be played out, and watched, well into the twenty-first century. John E. Tedstrom offers a detailed treatment of this topic in Chapter 7 of this volume.

*Political Stability.* The shots fired by the Russian Army at the parliament building in October 1993 may result in the removal of some of the barriers to real political reform. Yet the elections of December 1993, especially the strong showing of the ultranationalists, muddied the waters. The subsequent dismissal of Yegor Gaidar and other reformers also caused deep concern. Nevertheless, if Yeltsin and Prime Minister Viktor Chernomyrdin are able to move toward needed legal and political reforms that are properly drafted and approved, such reforms could establish an effective working relationship between the center and the regions, as well as among the competing organs of the central government. Given the centrifugal and often chaotic forces on display recently, American businessmen can only hope that the occasion will be taken to harmonize the operations of government and to solidify the system of laws.

*Corruption and Criminality.* One set of problems that will have to be addressed by a reformed and strengthened legal system is the imposition on business of what might be called the curse of the seeking hand. Crime and corruption in Russia are heavy burdens on, and deterrents to, American investment. The conventional wisdom is that the end is not in sight.

*Xenophobia.* Virulent Russian nationalism, extending sometimes to overt anti-Americanism, is also something that American businessmen encounter directly. It is, as we have observed, an understandable first-order reaction to the abrupt change of Russia's fortunes. It also has much deeper roots in Russian history. In order to defuse this issue, Americans must let themselves be understood not as some kind of alien predators but as helpful partners for the necessary change that must occur. This will take time and a great deal of patience, plus an accumulation of small successes that can be documented and shared.

## Market Strategies

American business is being invited today to introduce into Russia a way of doing things that works but that is largely unfamiliar to those who receive it. Market principles have not been understood or even taught in Russian universities until very recently. The cardinal attributes of a market system—pricing freedom, ease of entry, freedom to fail, and capital markets—were simply missing. Russia now is being obliged in large measure to reinvent itself in the face of deeply engraved antithetical values and practices. Plainly that is not something that is easy to do.

There are cultural bases for resistance dating back not just to the seventy years of the communist period but to the whole thousand-year span of Russia's existence as an organized society. That society was spared the transforming effects of the Renaissance, the Reformation, and the Enlightenment. It never acquired the conviction, shared by John Locke and Thomas Jefferson, that private ownership of property nurtures the spirit of liberty.

So a prudent outside investor is, of necessity, constrained to take the medium to long view.

The outside investor is well advised to start small. It should first find a Russian partner or partners in whom it can place confidence. Those partners should be allowed to take the lead in identifying and opening the doors of the official and business communities. The investor should find ways to establish itself as a good citizen, through acts of appropriate outreach and connection. It should work first with its Russian partners to shape the venture, and then go to local and regional and national authorities for the necessary approvals. When there is doubt or dispute about the location of authority, the venture should try to bring the various officials together to examine how a positive decision could benefit all parties.

### A Case History: Oil and Gas

The divergence of cultures and expectations, along with the overriding need for collaborative partnership, is nowhere more evident than in the oil and gas industry.

Russia, and more particularly western Siberia, is a major oil empire. It has vast unexplored reserves and was until 1989 the world's largest producer. Then production collapsed, from 11.5 million barrels a day in 1988 down to an estimated 6.5 million barrels a day in November 1993, a reduction equal in volume to 60 percent of all U.S. production. Here was a calamity, and an opportunity for the American oil, gas, and petrochemical industries.

But there were reservations. At the official level, there was some concern that foreign oil companies would become too dominant in a vital and strategic industry. At the enterprise level, the attitude was more enthusiastic, but the Siberian managers wanted to be in charge. And here as elsewhere there were differences of business perspective, between Americans who wanted everything spelled out in writing and Russians accustomed to operating on good faith.[15]

In the end, necessity, seasoned with mutual consideration, prevailed over the reservations. The steep decline in Russian production was, it appeared, the result of faulty oil field practices, which could be repaired; of outdated technology, which could be replaced; and of the drying up of investment flows within the former Soviet Union, for which there could be a substitution.

There was no way, however, that the Russian oil and gas industry could make these major adjustments without Western partners. And a turnaround was urgently needed. Nearly one in five Russian wells was idle simply for want of spare parts. Estimates are that a dollar invested in the rehabilitation of such wells will generate eighty cents in foreign exchange earnings within a year—plainly an opportunity of huge importance to the struggling Russian economy.[16]

So the Export-Import Bank of the United States (Exim) stepped forward, in partnership with elements of the Russian government, to underwrite at least $2 billion in loans and loan guarantees for the sale of American oil, gas, and petrochemical equipment and services. This will revitalize production, distribution, and processing from existing fields. Russia needs to improve its export capability in the meantime by repairing its pipelines, enlarging its storage and refinery capacity, and increasing its port capability. The Exim credits can be used for these downstream activities.[17]

The Exim credits are, however, only for existing production, and are far short of what is needed to restore Russia's past levels of production. Giant new credits will be needed in Russia's energy sector to aid in the exploration and production of Russia's proven and new reserves.

### Opportunities for Growth

There is a basis for confidence that business opportunities in the new Russian market will expand and that patience now will pay off in the future. If American business people cautiously choose small areas for investment, they can be optimistic that over longer term, as the confusion clears, they will be prepared to capitalize on areas of real growth.

Already American business is the number one source of outside private investment in Russia (in what is still admittedly a rather small pool). But the American share is solid and is positioned to grow along with the Russian economy, as is the American share of external Russian trade, which has long been held back by outdated Cold War restrictions. Becoming Russia's overall number one economic partner is an appropriate goal for American business to pursue.[18] Some of the obstacles now faced by American business will naturally wither with the achievement of Russian economic prosperity and self-confidence. Corruption and crime, for example, fall in this category.

What attitude should the United States adopt toward Russia in trade and investment? Is the glass half empty or half full? Whatever the answer, we can all agree it is a very large glass indeed. It is possible to reflect on the vast opportunities in Russia without becoming a mindless romantic. The Pacific Basin, for example, is the fastest growing region of the world. Some of its richest resources are to be found in eastern Russia. Getting those resources to market will be a prodigious undertaking, for which existing Russian infrastructure—roads, towns, railroads—provide only a bare beginning. At some point the Russian government is going to perceive the benefit of opening up this region to major collaborative development, which will require enormous infusions of wealth and technology—on the scale, we might say, of the Alaskan pipeline and the Trans-Siberian Railway.

A realistic dream, then, might be a long-term troika consisting of (1) an internally reconciled set of Russian authorities and entrepreneurs; (2) Asian partners from China, Japan, Korea, and other countries; and (3) a Western consortium ideally headed by American bankers and business people.

## Notes

1. Daniel Yergin and Thane Gustafson, *Russia 2010* (New York: Random House, 1993), 160.

2. U.S. Department of Commerce, International Trade Administration, "Obstacles to Trade and Investment in the New Republics of the Former Soviet Union" (Washington, D.C.: U.S. Government Printing Office, 1992), 4.

3. Yergin and Gustafson, *Russia 2010*, 104-105.

4. Evidence compiled by the U.S.-Russia Business Council, January to November, 1993.

5. Yergin and Gustafson, *Russia 2010*.

6. I am indebted for what follows to Shafiquil Islam, "Russia's Rough Road to

Capitalism," *Foreign Affairs* (Spring 1993). A shorthand list of factors would include secure property rights, stable money, and a government that shapes but does not interfere. See Yergin and Gustafson, *Russia 2010*, 160ff.

7. One reason why the transition to a market economy will not be swift is the need for attitudes and culture to change. Allan Greenspan, chairman of the Federal Reserve system, put it best:

The presumption that if you eliminate the infrastructure of central planning and free prices, wages, capital movements, etc., [then] a free market will automatically develop overnight is dubious. Scrapping the central planning system is obviously a necessary condition of the evolving of a market system. But unless there are rudimentary institutions that can be rapidly converted to effective market-based structures that can facilitate production and distribution, the transition will be significantly stretched out.

Even more deep-seated than the specific market institutions, the law of contracts, bankruptcy law, property rights, the disciplines of accounting, auditing, and marketing, are the attitudes of people: in the most profound sense, the culture. Differing attitudes and views are carried from generation to generation through family value and education systems [so] the process of full transition will obviously be slow.

National Foreign Policy Conference, U.S. State Department, Washington, D.C., October 20, 1993.

8. Central Intelligence Agency, "Economic Survey of Russia, 1992" (Langley, Va.: Central Intelligence Agency, 1993), 4.

9. Hon. Lawrence H. Summers, Testimony before the House Committee on Foreign Affairs, September 21, 1993, 5. In 1993, the Treasury Department estimated that Russia had privatized five thousand large industrial enterprises through a voucher-based giveaway scheme. Also in November 1993 a presidential decree provided for the private ownership and transfer of land. This decree may have begun a slow but important privatization of land. David Lipton, Deputy Assistant Secretary of Treasury, Testimony before the House Subcommittee on Commerce, Consumer, and Monetary Affairs, November 5, 1993.

10. Malcolm Butler, Director, NIS Task Force, U.S. Agency for International Development, Testimony before the House Foreign Affairs Committee, September 21, 1993, 3.

11. Summers, Testimony before the House Committee on Foreign Affairs, 8.

12. Central Intelligence Agency, "Economic Survey," 5. See also Eugene K. Lawson, president, U.S.-Russia Business Council, Testimony before the House Committee on Foreign Affairs, February 24, 1993.

13. Ibid.

14. For a somewhat contrary view, see Roman Sheiain, "Privatization: A Status Report," *Crossroads*, September 15, 1993.

15. Yergin and Gustafson, *Russia 2010*.

16. Summers, Testimony before the House Committee on Foreign Affairs, 6.

17. Export-Import Bank of the United States, "Eximbank Signs Historic U.S.-Russia Oil and Gas Agreement," press release dated July 6, 1993.

18. The number of U.S. firms that have officers in Moscow has increased from about forty in the late 1980s to more than 400 today. About seventy-five U.S. firms have already located in St. Petersburg. Franklin J. Vargo, Acting Assistant Secretary of Commerce, Testimony before the House Subcommittee on Commerce, Consumer, and Monetary Affairs, November 5, 1993.

# 9 Freedom from Below: The Independent Labor Movement in the Soviet Union

Michael Gfoeller and John W. Blaney

Western analysts and observers have devoted oceans of ink over the last several years to studying the continuing political and economic revolution in Russia and the other lands that once made up the Soviet Union. Understandably, their focus has been on the statements and actions of the old Soviet elite—high-ranking functionaries of the Soviet state and Communist Party—and leading post-Communist political figures such as Boris Yeltsin of Russia and Nursultan Nazarbayev of Kazakhstan. Due to this emphasis on the political elite, Western academics and experts have largely passed over and greatly undervalued the contributions to change in the former Soviet empire made by more ordinary people. This is especially true with regard to a force that will likely be of great importance to Russia and the other successor states of the old USSR—the independent, democratic labor movement.

Western observers have long known about the critical role played in Poland by the Solidarity trade union movement. Much less attention has been paid to its Soviet counterpart. Yet without the efforts and contributions of hundreds and thousands of coal miners, metallurgical workers, railway workers, auto workers, and others involved in the Soviet free trade union movement, the democratic revolution in Russia would very likely not have succeeded. Moreover, unless the architects of future economic and political reforms in Russia and other key republics of the old USSR take the workers' movement into account, the chances for success will be greatly diminished.

## From Beneath the Ground: The 1989 Miners' Strike

The origin of the independent labor movement in the Soviet Union is a tale of courage and daring. Because the Soviet state claimed for itself the exclusive

---

The authors' views are their own, and must not be taken to represent the views of the U.S. Department of State or the U.S. government. Their knowledge of the subject was gained first hand, as they were present at many of the events described herein.

right to represent the interests of the working class, it showed little tolerance for any group of workers acting independently. Punishment for labor unrest (defined under Soviet law as an "economic crime") was swift and often brutal. To further ensure control of the workers, a vast system of state-sponsored and controlled trade unions was established. These state appendages were never legitimate unions, having about the same kind of function and odor as did the Vichy government in World War II France. Indeed, democratic labor activists in the former USSR have often referred to the old official unions as a "transmission belt" connecting the Soviet elite to the carefully controlled working class.

Although small independent workers' organizations had existed and tried to organize for years in the Soviet republics of Russia, Kazakhstan, Ukraine, and Belarus, their actions had never amounted to much, and Soviet authorities were able to crush them without difficulty. The situation changed definitively in the summer of 1989.

Long considered the elite of the labor force, Soviet coal miners had by 1989 reached the limit of their patience and endurance in trying to eke out a decent life under intolerable and deteriorating conditions. Wages were low, living quarters were often filthy, and medical care was highly inadequate. Supplies of food and other necessities became more erratic in the late 1980s. Opportunity and education for miners' children were very poor.

The miners were also becoming more concerned over increasingly dangerous working conditions. One in ten miners could expect to be killed or crippled in work-related accidents. Miners were often sent into unsupported tunnels to drill out coal from overhead seams. Being buried alive from quick caveins was not uncommon. Teams of men specialized in quick extraction techniques, which were not always successful. Even a lucky miner would suffer daily cuts and bruises from tunnel work as the rocks and coal showered down upon him. Moreover, black lung was so common that Soviet miners often joked that theirs was the healthiest pension fund in the entire USSR, because no one ever survived long enough to retire and collect his share.

The huge strike in the summer of 1989 began spontaneously. Strike committees were formed at hundreds of coal mines in Ukraine, Russia, Kazakhstan, and Belarus. The strike leaders were mostly men cut from simple but tough cloth, chosen by the rank-and-file.

Most of the early leaders of the miners' movement would lose out in leadership struggles later on. Their honesty and courage, however, were inspirational. Asked why the workers went on strike, a gold- and steel-toothed, iron-jawed young strike committee leader replied with one stunning sentence: "Because we do not want to be slaves anymore."

## A Test of Perestroika in a Smoke-Filled Room

Even before Mikhail Gorbachev came to power in 1985, the elite of the Communist party and government *apparat* had generally accepted two ground rules of governance. First, there were to be no new Stalin-like waves of terror. Second, some sort of reform effort had to take place, because the Soviet economy was beginning to suffer from its severe structural defects. Finally, throughout his stewardship of the USSR, Gorbachev publicly aligned political change with economic reform. He believed that successful, market-oriented economic reform required some degree of political liberalization.

The August 1989 coal strike was, therefore, a political nightmare for Gorbachev and the rest of the Soviet political elite. More important than its damaging economic impact, the strike was a highly charged political dilemma and challenge. Crushing it would be bloody, making a lie out of perestroika, and would represent a dangerous contradiction for many members of the younger ruling elite who had ridden to power by repeatedly denouncing Stalin's violence. Much important domestic and international political support for the regime won by glasnost and perestroika would also vanish if force were used to crush the miners.

Seeking to avoid confrontation, Gorbachev deployed Prime Minister Nikolai Ryzhkov and Deputy Prime Minister Lev Ryabev to negotiate with the miners and serve as political heat shields. Ryabev was given front-line responsibility for the talks. Using classic divide-and-rule tactics, he traversed the USSR, negotiating separate settlement packages with the regional strike committees in order to defuse the crisis and fragment the miners' movement.

After many charged negotiating sessions, agreement was reached on complex settlement packages that addressed many of the miners' concerns over living and working conditions, wages, and benefits. Deadlines were set for the implementation of these agreements by the Soviet government and its ministries. The settlement included sharp pay increases (from an average of about 300 rubles a month to 500) and many other expensive government concessions. For example, miners were now paid for all the hours they spent in the mines, instead of merely for the time spent at the coal face. Health, safety, and pension improvements were promised as well. Ryzhkov signed many of these agreements himself. Thereafter, the miners held him politically accountable for their implementation.

The initial outcome of the August 1989 strike was a startling victory for the embryonic miners' movement. Workers outside the coal industry were inspired by it and accelerated or began labor-organizing activities outside the control of the official unions.

## Symptoms of Disintegration

The government's near-capitulation at the negotiating table was also a sign of its increasing incapacity. In a manner reminiscent of its bungled relief efforts for victims of the Armenian earthquake only months earlier, the Soviet government displayed an incredible lack of coherency in its attempts to deal with the strikers. After making concessions that it could not afford financially, Moscow temporized and eventually failed to fulfill many of its obligations to the workers under the strike settlements.

What the workers saw as the Ryzhkov regime's failure to keep its promises soon led to deep disillusionment with the government and, eventually, with Gorbachev himself. As a result, many emerging leaders in the worker's movement, who were often men and women of impressive intelligence and enormous "street smarts," began to look seriously at the alternative political and economic strategies offered by nascent opposition figures. It must also be said that the Soviet economy's accelerating economic crisis undermined the basis for any lasting settlement between independent labor and the government. By late 1989, the ruble was losing purchasing power quickly and many goods were routinely swept into the black market and given tremendous markups. In such a situation, even considerable wage concessions by the government did little to ameliorate the miners' economic plight.

Faced with recurrent deficits of promised goods, the miners grew increasingly angry in 1990. In response, they improved their organizational efforts. More sophisticated ties developed between a welter of local and regional strike committees. Eventually, nationwide organizations emerged linking coal miners from the Polish frontier to Sakhalin Island and from Vorkuta in the Arctic north to Karaganda in Kazakhstan. This is particularly noteworthy because at this time, on all other levels of governance and societal interaction in USSR, precisely the opposite was happening. In other words, the independent labor movement was the only social institution to grow in power and coherence, across virtually the entire Soviet Union, at a time of accelerating social, political, and economic disintegration. The independent miners' movement was the vanguard, but free labor movements in other industries began to follow their example.

This growth did not occur smoothly, however. Both the national and local leaderships of the miners' union turned over at a mind-boggling rate in the first years of the union's existence, a phenomenon partly due to inexperience. Fortunately, the miners established some very important links with Western free trade unions, including the AFL-CIO and Poland's Solidarity, from which they quickly learned much about the art of organizing a labor movement.

Soviet labor activists had long admired the AFL-CIO for its steadfast opposition to communism. They respected the late George Meany and current AFL-CIO president Lane Kirkland. Their linkage with the AFL-CIO provided needed expertise from the American labor movement. In addition, Kirkland's several visits to the Soviet Union served as rallying points and needed morale-boosters for the miners and other independent union activists.

## The Movement Goes Political

As the miners' frustration with the government grew, their goals and demands inevitably became more political in nature. The coal miners of Vorkuta, a former prison colony and coal mining center in the far-northern Komi Autonomous Republic of the Russian Federation, led the way with a bitter six-week walkout in October and November of 1989. For the first time, thousands of striking Soviet workers raised radical political demands such as the resignation of the Ryzhkov government and the eventual end of Communist party rule in the USSR. Fervent admirers of Alexandr Solzhenitsyn, the Vorkuta miners adopted as their emblem a banned Russian nationalist symbol: the flag of St. Andrew.

The miners' strike committees gradually reached out to form ties with workers organizing nascent democratic structures in other branches of industry, such as air traffic controllers, Aeroflot pilots, railway workers, metallurgical workers, and auto workers. In addition, the miners worked intensively to organize themselves within the confines of their own industry. The result was the emergence during 1990 of two crucial nationwide workers' federations with increasingly anticommunist political platforms: the Confederation of Labor (COL) and the Independent Miners' Union (IMU).

Led by worker-activists Mikhail Sobol of Belarus and Vyacheslav Golikov and Yuri Gerold of the Western Siberian Kuzbass region, the COL had its main power base in the rich coal mines of western Siberia, though it also included groups from Moscow and other major cities in the Russian Republic, Belarus, and Ukraine. It represented a major attempt on the part of workers from a variety of Soviet industries to link up with the growing miners' movement in a loose confederation based on shared opposition to Communist rule. Significantly, the COL injected itself immediately into the politically charged debate surrounding free-market economic reform in the USSR by offering early support for the "500 Days" program of radical economic reform championed by the still fledgling Russian Republic government of Boris N. Yeltsin.

The IMU was the result of the miners' effort to develop a more formal nationwide structure. Forged during two stormy congresses of Soviet coal miners held in Donetsk, Ukraine, in July and October 1990, the new union represented a major maturation of the independent workers' movement. Despite certain organizational weaknesses, by its very existence the IMU challenged the existing power structure inside the USSR and showed the official Soviet coal miner's union for what it really was: a "transmission belt" tying miners and other workers to the ruling Communist party apparatus.

These new worker organizations, formed spontaneously "from below" instead of by decree "from above," were a major blow to the power monopoly of the Communist party. By aligning themselves with Yeltsin and his supporters in Russia, and with other opposition groups such as the Belorussian National Front, the new workers' organizations gave the democratic opposition in the Soviet Union something it had never had before: foot soldiers who could do more to influence the actions of the central government than merely gather in Red Square for a few hours to chant slogans and wave signs.

### Yeltsin's Strike Weapon

The accelerating decline of the Soviet economy brought matters to a head by the beginning of 1991. Gorbachev by then had turned to the right in an effort to shore up his sagging support among Soviet conservatives. Armed attacks in January against unarmed civilian crowds by special forces in Vilnius, Lithuania, angered the leadership of the IMU and COL. The appointment of the Pavlov government further infuriated the workers, who were outraged by such economic blunders as Pavlov's 300 percent food-price increases, monetary confiscation, and policy of hostility to free trade unions. Convinced that no other course was open to them, coal miners in the Donetsk Basin began what was to become a nationwide labor protest on March 1, 1991.

The IMU and COL leadership decided to champion a set of radical political demands: resignation of the Pavlov government, dissolution of the Soviet parliament (the Supreme Soviet), transfer of political power to the republic governments, and creation of a "coalition government of national trust." Their reasoning was that only a democratic, noncommunist, and popular government could carry through the tough economic reforms the workers themselves admitted were necessary while observing basic workers' rights and interests. The leaders of the workers made no secret of their support for Boris Yeltsin and the democratic opposition, while insisting that the democrats, too, would have to meet basic standards on workers' rights and take workers' interests into account in carrying out economic reform.

At first, participation in the strike was limited to a few mines in eastern Ukraine, but as the tough miners of the Donbass held on through weeks of pressure, their colleagues in western Ukraine, Vorkuta, the Moscow region, western Siberia, Sakhalin, and the salt mines of Belarus joined the effort. They were joined by auto workers in the Moscow region, who organized prominent demonstrations, and by legions of industrial workers in heretofore quiescent Belarus, who demonstrated by the tens of thousands in Minsk and briefly cut the crucial rail link with the West running through the city of Orsha. After initially participating in the strike, the coal miners of Karaganda, in Kazakhstan, gave way to severe pressure from the republic's government and returned to work. As it ebbed and flowed through March and April 1991, the strike became a highly important symbolic political challenge to Gorbachev, the Soviet government, and the Communist *apparat*. By mid-April, as many as two million workers may have taken part in the strike at different times.

Stunned by the organizational skill, discipline, and grit shown by the workers' movement, the Pavlov government tried for a negotiated solution. The government offered the miners significant economic concessions while refusing to discuss their political demands. The IMU's negotiators refused these offers. The Pavlov government was severely weakened and publicly humiliated by the strikers' tenacity. A kind of moral high point was reached when Kuzbass miner and labor leader Anatoly Malikhin, on a hunger strike for two weeks, addressed the USSR Supreme Soviet at the strike's midpoint and, in remarks rebroadcast on national television, told the Soviet Solons in blunt terms that they had failed and should resign *en masse*.

By the first week of May 1991, the miners and their allies were running out of funds and tiring from the long effort. Russian leader Boris Yeltsin stepped in and negotiated an end to the two-month-old strike with the leaders of the

IMU. Under the terms of the agreement, all coal mines on Russian territory would be transferred from the control of the USSR Ministry of Coal Industry to the jurisdiction of the Russian Republic, which granted them broad economic freedoms. The leaders of the IMU accepted this moral and economic victory and ordered an end to the strike.

## The New Unions and the Failed Coup of August 1991

The 1991 strike's effect on the political and economic situation in the Soviet Union was major. Yeltsin himself stated publicly several times after the strike that the workers' action had halted the slide toward renewed totalitarianism in the USSR that had begun with the violent events of January 1991 in the Baltics. By throwing their support to Yeltsin and the democrats, the miners and their allies added desperately needed rank-and-file support to the reformers at a critical phase of their long struggle with Soviet conservatives and the Communist party.

Above all else, the 1991 strike exposed and exacerbated the weaknesses of the old power structure in the USSR, helping to set it up for removal by the democratic forces in the aftermath of the abortive August 1991 coup. During the crucial days of the attempted putsch, Yeltsin once again called on his supporters in the workers' movement, who responded with immediate strike calls, demonstrations, and declarations of opposition to the hard-line State Committee for the State of Emergency. The victory of the democratic forces in August 1991 was due in large measure to the quick and massive reaction of the democratic workers' movement.

Following the coup attempt, the leaders of the democratic labor movement in the Russian Federation continued their support for Yeltsin and his reforms, despite the political risk involved. In a remarkable display of political intelligence and courage, the leaders of the IMU, in particular, spoke to the rank-and-file frankly about the severe economic changes that would inevitably accompany market-oriented economic reform. The miners' movement adopted a policy of improving its own organizational basis, in expectation of its future role as an advocate of workers' interests in a free-market economy, while steadfastly supporting the Yeltsin government's often confused steps toward reform. Most importantly of all, Russian miners and other independent trade unionists adopted a de facto strike moratorium, in order to give the new government time to implement economic and political reforms.

## Adapting to the Division of the Soviet Union:
## New Challenges to the Labor Movement

The gradual fragmentation of the USSR following the August 1991 coup attempt influenced the independent labor movement profoundly. As the Soviet Union broke apart into independent states, the workers' movement was strained and tested. To a certain extent, it became the victim of its own success. Whereas once the movement had been united in a common struggle against Moscow, after August 1991 independent trade union leaders in Russia, Kazakhstan, Ukraine, and Belarus faced new and very different circumstances. Instead of working together against the central government in Moscow, the activists had to come to terms with the governments of the newly independent states. Although democratic worker activists in the former republics did not entirely lose contact with each other, they found coordinating their efforts to be far more difficult than before.

Organizational changes took place in the movement. In the case of the IMU, the union was reorganized into a loose confederation of nationally based miners' unions in Russia, Kazakhstan, Belarus, and Ukraine. Conditions for the independent trade unions in the post-Soviet states began to differ considerably from republic to republic. In the Russian Federation, independent trade unionists enjoyed nearly total freedom of action and considerable access to and influence over the Yeltsin government; in republics such as Kazakhstan and Ukraine the environment was far less congenial for independent labor organizing.

### Competing with the Official Unions in Russia

Paradoxically, the IMU and other independent unions linked to the Yeltsin government in a de facto alliance for reform found themselves at a disadvantage vis-à-vis the surviving remnants of the old official unions because of this very commitment. Whereas in the months after the coup the independent unionists adhered to a self-imposed labor peace, the surviving "transmission belt" unions used strike calls and hyperbolic rhetoric in an attempt to build up support among their remaining members and save themselves as institutions. Throughout 1992, the so-called Federation of Independent Trade Unions of Russia, an umbrella organization of old-school Russian unions, applied this tactic vigorously and with some success, much to the chagrin of the democratic unionists who had fought to overturn the old communist system.

## The Future

Despite the difficulties mentioned above, the workers' movement in the successor states will probably continue to play a key role in the evolution of these newly independent countries, especially in Russia and Ukraine, where it has shown the greatest and most consistent strength. Now that democratic government has put down very tender roots in Russia and some of the successor states, the free labor movement can be expected to give greater emphasis to economic issues in its agenda, while continuing to demand that the governments of these two newly independent states not backslide on civil and trade union rights.

One of the movement's primary areas of focus naturally enough appears to be protecting workers' rights during the painful transition to a market economy. In their dialogue and occasional disputes with the new authorities in Russia, democratic labor leaders stress such key issues as job retraining, occupational health and safety, and adequate minimum wages. In addition, they are attempting to have an impact on the strategy and tactics of the ongoing economic reform. Finally, Russian free trade unionists offered overt support to the Yeltsin government during the political crises associated with the April and December 1992 sessions of the Congress of People's Deputies. In each case, delegations of miners and other democratic worker activists showed up at the Congress to make known their continued support for Yeltsin and his reforms. More recently, the free trade unionists have been battered by continuing economic decline and the turmoil of events in late 1993. Some defections have occurred to the ultranationalists, whose large organizations (including the United Workers' Front) also court the workers. Generally, however, most remain key supporters of Yeltsin and reform.

The bottom line on free trade unions in Russia and other successor states is this: apart from a few political parties of intellectuals and former dissidents, the independent labor movement is really the only force for grassroots democracy. Moreover, the movement is the only institution still attempting to transcend ethnic divisions and interrepublic boundaries. Therefore, it is a potentially powerful source of stability and integration at a time of societal disintegration in the former Soviet lands.

# 10 Environmental and Health Crises in the Former Soviet Union

Murray Feshbach

## Introduction

Whether it be reports on population developments, health, or environmental trends, the basic thrust on the Russian scene is negative. New information appears almost every week or month indicating that the situation is much worse than hinted at in previous research by Russian/Soviet sources, or as discussed in my book (with Alfred Friendly, Jr.) *Ecocide in the USSR.*[1] The new incremental information on radioactivity, secret cities, chemicals, heavy metals, toxic wastes, and health in affected regions would seem to indicate that the environment has been subjected to much more devastation than has been understood previously.

Health indicators have fallen markedly, especially in the last two years. While not all drops are directly related to the environment, they could well have been exacerbated by environmental conditions. This is true now, and will be even more true in the future because the health status of the population is affected adversely as the effects of environmental hazards accumulate in human genetic structures and in the immune system.

Major declines in births, in part due to reproductive health problems but more often a consequence of conscious family planning choices to restrict the number of children given the current and expected disarray in society and in the economy, are accompanied by major shifts upward in a number of negative indicators. Thus, maternal mortality, infant mortality, deaths among prime working age males, and specific causes of death and illness such as accidents, suicides, poisoning, murders, and "normal" heart and cancer rates, add to this negative pattern.

In addition, infectious diseases have increased in terms of morbidity (illness rates) as well as mortality, and that trend is likely to continue until the public-health sector in Russia is restored to a reasonable state. As a consequence of all these and other factors, male life expectancy at birth is currently two-and-one-half years below the previous low point of 61.5 years (1980-1981). In sum, the long-term trends of these demographic and health indicators, when combined with the environmental factors noted above and discussed below, do not bode well for the future of Russia.

### More Evidence of Deepening Crises?

The assertions above are somber and harsh. But could it be that these negative trends are turning around? Perhaps the end of communism has brought rapid improvement? Unfortunately, recent findings indicate otherwise, and this new evidence merits a closer look.

If we were to stipulate that conditions could not be as bad as described by journalists, by nongovernmental organizations, and by Western commentators such as myself, then why is life expectancy decreasing to a point for males below that of their legal pension age? Reports for the year 1993 indicate that average life expectancy at birth for Russian males is now fifty-nine years. Unprecedented, even not believable if it were not from an impeccable source—the former presidential adviser on environment and health, Aleksei Yablokov. A drop of three years in life expectancy in the course of one year is five times higher a differential than has ever occurred in the United States—that of 0.6 once, and 0.3 twice in the entire post Second World War period.

What could have brought about this extraordinary decline? A number of nonenvironmental partial explanations can be given. They include accidents, traumas, murders as crime increased dramatically, suicides among the elderly at triple the rate of several years ago, increased drug abuse, and more venereal disease derived from increased prostitution. These factors may be necessary to cite, but they are not sufficient to explain all of the deaths. For this we need to turn to environmental conditions, particularly new information about the hazards to life.

### Radiation

Much more territory than originally reported from the Soviet government at the time of the Chernobyl accident has now been reported as being contaminated by radiation. The current information is that cesium-137 still affects eighteen oblasts (an oblast is equivalent roughly to a U.S. state) and one republic in Russia, ten in Ukraine, and six in Belarus, instead of one oblast in Russia, two in Ukraine, and two in Belarus. More radioactivity was released than previously reported as well. Not fifty million curies, but eighty million, or 60 percent more, is now reported by the competent authorities. A new estimate made by a Western observer for the amount of radioactivity released is as much as four to five times the original report.

But Chernobyl is no longer thought to be the worst radioactive area—Chelyabinsk, in the Urals, may be 100 to 120 times worse than the original estimate (measured in total curies released). Uncontained dumping into the Techa River in the late 1940s and early 1950s, accidents in 1957 and 1967, an unreported accident in 1991, and a reported (small) accident in 1993 all contributed to the problem. Perhaps 400,000 persons have been affected.

Even Chelyabinsk may not have been as devastating to the population as the consequences of open-air atomic-weapon testing between 1949 and 1962 in the Semipalatinsk region of Kazakhstan. Very recent information about the Trotsky Regiment illustrates the mortal impact of such testing. In August of 1954, some 44,000 young soldiers and their officers were ordered to move almost immediately into the region below the explosion of an atomic weapon only some 1,200 feet above the area. Many of these 44,000 men should still be alive (in their fifties and sixties), but by 1993 only one thousand had survived.

This low survival rate is far beneath the already poor survival rates for the population as a whole. In 1965 perhaps 72 percent of males sixteen years old survived to age sixty according to one survey. By 1980, the share of survivals declined to 68 percent, and by 1992, 62 percent. In the United States, the current rate of survival is about 80 percent.

### Chemical and Air Pollution

But again, it is not only radioactivity that is becoming even more clearly a danger to the population. Perhaps the next most crucial issue relates to chemicals—military- and civilian-related. It is sometimes hard to distinguish between their applications or dual use. They become potentially very hazardous with only a very slight change during the chemical process. Hazardous chemicals permeate the air in cities due to improper burning of fossil fuels in thermal power plants. American practice calls for burning coal at 1,600 degrees; the Russians consume this fuel at 800 degrees. As a consequence, benzo(a)pyrene and dioxin are produced as by-products of cost-saving procedures in place. Benzo(a)pyrene is a known carcinogen. Of the 350 cities monitored in Russia, 160 record benzo(a)pyrene at improper levels, 92 at hazardous levels. Dioxin is also a cause of high respiratory illness rates.

A former minister of health of Russia, A. Potapov, once stated: "To live longer, breathe less!" Not very helpful at all, but reflective of reality in some cities such as Norilsk, Nizhny Tagil, Magnitogorsk, the "valley of death" between Donetsk and Dnepropetrovsk in Ukraine, and many others. Chemicals also are a danger to the work force and adjacent populations in the so-called "chemical cities," Sterlitamak and Salavat being among the worst. Some recent reports claim that almost all of the work force in some military chemical plants have died. Many reports can be cited of elevated numbers of birth defects among the children of women who worked in these plants. Some reports about the proportion of cyanotic children (blue babies at birth) cannot be credible and need much verification.

Liquid rocket fuel is another component of the chemical hazards present in the former Soviet Union. Heptyl, or dimethyl hydrazine, is a supertoxic, volatile, nerve-paralyzing, and carcinogenic chemical compound used for missiles. Perhaps 100,000 to 150,000 tons of heptyl are in missiles, in storage, in transport, and in the production process, according to various sources. No known technology can defuse this material and only firing from stationary rockets will get rid of it. But this is very hazardous to the adjacent flora and fauna, let alone any person in the area. Major losses to nature have occurred over a 30,000-square-mile area of the Plesetsk Cosmodrome territory from the heptyl ejected from rockets launched at the northern launch area (Baikonur is the similar facility in the south), as well as from the fuel in parts jettisoned during missile and rocket flights from the site.

*Biological Threats*

So far, not enough is known about former bacteriological warfare facilities such as Vozrozhdeniye Island in the middle of the Aral Sea. With the latter's desiccation, the land exposed may allow any unknown residual hazardous bacteria to traverse the new space to the adjacent populations. In the past, large numbers of fish and animals have died unexpectedly in the coastal region. Has the abandoned site been thoroughly and completely detoxified? This remains unknown. New reports about violation of international agreements (and consequent potential health hazards) may suggest continuing health problems.

*Water Crisis*

Chemicals, radioactivity, and biological issues noted above, while widespread, are not as imminent a danger to the populations of the former Soviet Union as the water problem. Thus, Yablokov, Minister of Environment Viktor Danilov-Danilyan, and the head of the former ecology committee of the former Supreme Soviet, Vladimir Vorfolomeyev, and many others decry the poor quality of drinking water, river water, and water that enters into the food chain.

Some 75 percent of all surface water is polluted, and 50 percent of all water is not potable. But people need water to drink. Portable filters such as those used by campers are not widely available. Bacterial dysentery, hepatitis, diphtheria, cholera, and other diseases are generated and spread from the polluted waters. The Volga, Dnieper, and many other rivers are eutrophied—deprived of oxygen; the fish that manage to live in them become contaminated.

The fish catch in the Sea of Azov, the Caspian Sea, and many other seas and lakes has been markedly reduced due to the environmental degradation. Poor water, combined with excessive use of herbicides and pesticides, as well as mineral fertilizers, have led to a very high percentage of food being contaminated. According to Yablokov and other reports, 30 percent of all food is contaminated, 10 percent of all food is toxic, and 40 percent of all baby food is contaminated.

*Land Denigration*

Land is also poorly treated by nature and by human activities. Thus, 50 percent of all arable land is wind eroded, water eroded, compacted, salinated, swamped, deprived of humus, or otherwise degraded. If these conditions are not ameliorated, much of the effort to improve agriculture will fall far short of its goals.

Part of the underlying cause for the erosion, for example, is the excessive clearcutting and poor management of forests. Current economic conditions have removed constraints for large-scale clearcutting by some foreign countries as the need for hard currency overwhelms sensibilities regarding its impact on the ecosystem. Unofficial estimates, if correct, would indicate more forest cutting each year than in the Amazon rainforest.

Further development of land during the initial privatization of farms may also lead to more denigration of the land. Individual farmers or developers may not heed environmental rules as they seek to increase production and minimize short-term costs. In the long run, other problems will be exacerbated or develop new facets that were previously restrained by the state or by collective farms—that are now in private hands. Ensuring that these new farms will observe environmental rules about pesticides, agricultural waste run-offs, and contaminants in mineral fertilizers so they do not become dispersed without control is a serious issue.

## The Impacts

In 1991, according to the *State Report on the Status of the Environment in the Russian Federation,* jointly issued by the office of the presidential adviser on environment and health and the Ministry of Ecology of the Russian Federation, a major warning was given that 75 percent of all women suffered a pathology such as late toxemia, sepsis, or anemia during pregnancy. Only 40 percent of all children born to such women are healthy. The causes very likely include poor food, water, and air quality in places where women work, such as chemical, metallurgical, and many other industries, as well as women living in adjacent areas to these plants.

Maternal mortality is six to seven times higher than that of the United States (which is not the best in the world). Infant mortality is perhaps three to four times that of the United States, again not the lowest rate in the world. Anemia, rickets, and hypotrophy affect one-quarter of all children in the Russian Federation before the age of five (we do not even collect data on rickets anymore, though isolated cases may appear). Hypotrophy, or underweight, regrettably, is prevalent among children born to women who are poor, malnourished, on drugs, or otherwise unhealthy before giving birth. It is a major contributor to the number of children who die during their first year of life.

Distrust of the diphtheria, pertussis, and tetanus (DPT) vaccine produced by Soviet, now Russian, industry is in part related to an unsubstantiated charge several years ago in the newspapers that the vaccine was contaminated with mercury. Allegations about polluted vaccine are only one cause of the spectacular rise in diphtheria in Russia, Ukraine, and elsewhere in the former Soviet Union. Unconfirmed reports (as of the time of writing) indicate that the number of cases in Russia more than tripled during 1993 compared with 1992 (more than 15,000 compared with fewer than 4,000, respectively), or to a level unheard of in the developed countries since before the vaccine became available. In Leningrad/St. Petersburg, the number of cases increased from twelve cases in 1990 to 1,845 in 1992.

That the medical establishment is not trusted is a major factor in the rise of alternative medicine. The turning toward nonstandard medicine provided by individuals such as Dzhunya, who supposedly makes people well by use of her hands alone, is but one notorious example. Mullahs, shamans, and others whose folk medicine may be efficacious in limited terms but not for all purposes to which the population turns as sources of putative healing also are being utilized by the population in its fear and distrust or even because of the lack of medicines in hospitals and other medical facilities. Thus, the chain from poor environment to poor health and to death becomes all too clear.

Moscow, the capital of the country, is enveloped by poor air, consumes poor water, is subject to radioactivity in many locations, and has an unhealthy population. Perhaps surprisingly to those who have never been to Moscow, but not to those who have been, there are ten thousand or so industrial enterprises, six thousand of which are classified as "active environmental polluters." [2]

Many enterprises had been in the outskirts when first established, but with the extension of the city to include a large agglomeration, these plants are now surrounded by housing facilities, schools, and medical institutions. Most plants do not have filters to capture pollutants, or if they do, these devices tend to be outdated and are not tailored to a specific industry or pollutant. Plant managers know when emissions are monitored (three or four times a day as opposed to the 24-hour surveillance in the United States); many turn off their filters and let unmeasured bursts into the air. Some estimates are that at least 30 percent and perhaps 50 percent more air pollution needs to be added to the official figures.

Combining industrial pollution with the use of leaded fuel—only recently has construction begun on a factory to produce catalytic converters—yields very high levels of lead, carbon monoxide, and other pollutant recordings in the city. It is not surprising, therefore, that Moscow children have respiratory disease rates 1.8 times higher than the average child in Russia; rates for skin problems are 44.3 percent higher; for congenital anomalies 44.2 percent higher; and for urinary and reproductive health problems 3.4 times higher.

More closely related to water problems and poor quality food, Moscow children are recorded as having 1.9 times more diseases of the digestive tract than the average for Russia as a whole. Toxic dump sites, including pesticide dump sites from farms previously outside the city limits, unauthorized household and industrial waste sites, and radioactive toxic waste sites are found frequently. Until 1992, we knew very little of this phenomenon; but thanks to the recent policy of glasnost', much more is known today.

**Prognosis**

Although the knowledge is frightening, priorities for clean-up could be established and carried out. The outlook is cautious, however, given continuous shortfalls in environmental expenditures.

This is all the more worrisome because, clearly, the shift to capitalism provides no quick fix. This is not only true with regard to land use, as already noted, but in industry as well. For example, the amount of air pollutants emitted by industry has not declined in proportion to falls in industrial output due to the ongoing compression of the Russian economy. This is disturbing because an economic recovery and restoration of industry will lead to even larger increases in pollution levels.

Russian enterprises are just seeking to survive at present. They want to produce for the market and make a profit, not spend large sums installing or retrofitting emission-control devices that would reduce air or water pollution. Thus, the dumping of toxic wastes continues apace, and the surrounding lands in urban areas as well as those at farm sites are being utilized without caring for the pollution and damage such unchecked activity is causing.

Russia's military is just beginning to recognize that they are responsible for many pollution-related problems, including in those areas that are designated as closed cities. New units of the armed forces that are assigned to deal with these problems are understaffed and seem overwhelmed by the tasks assigned them.

Russia's attempts to begin to deal with its extensive, grave environmental situation deserve recognition. Internally, besides the new military units mentioned above, there are some new programs, such as the activation of an interagency Ecological Security Commission in Russia's Security Council. Russia's new programs, however, sadly lack sufficient funding.

Realistically, and given Russia's serious economic problems, it is only with outside assistance that something can be accomplished in the short term. Efforts by the outside world to help are just beginning. Whether motivated by humanitarian concerns or by fear of the consequences of any worsening of the situation, the totality of support and programs is still far short of the tasks at hand. The needs are simply enormous.

Foreign aid, grants, and assistance are necessary but not sufficient, especially in the long run. Ultimately, Russia and the rest of the new countries of the former Soviet Union will have to provide for themselves in addressing these problems.

## Notes

1. This work is based on Murray Feshbach and Alfred Friendly, Jr., *Ecocide in the USSR: Health and Nature Under Siege* (New York: Basic Books, 1992); Murray

Feshbach, "Toxic Archipelago," *Washington Post*, July 11, 1993, p. A1; Murray Feshbach, *Ecological Disaster: Cleaning Up the Hidden Legacy of the Soviet Regime* (Twentieth Century Fund, February 1995, forthcoming); and Murray Feshbach, editor-in-chief, *Environment and Health Atlas of Russia* (Moscow: PAIMS, March 1995, forthcoming).

2. Also see David E. Powell, *Environmental Problems in Moscow*, 1994, p. 2. This paragraph is largely based on this source.

# 11 An Agenda for Russian Economic Reform in 1995

John P. Hardt and Phillip J. Kaiser

Economic and political reform in Russia has proceeded by fits and starts since Mikhail Gorbachev became general secretary of the Communist party in 1985. A watershed event occurred in 1991 when the central power of the Soviet Union disintegrated and the republics became new independent states. With this political revolution dissolving the Soviet system, the leadership in Moscow broke with the autocratic command economy and the police-administered past. However, market and democratic institutions in a legal and regulatory framework did not exist to provide the foundation for the new order either within the Russian Federation or among the other former states of the Soviet Union. Most current economic difficulties are the result of this collapse and the burdensome legacy of the old system. The aftermath of the confrontation between Boris Yeltsin and the opposition that culminated on the "bloody Sunday" of October 3, 1993, gives Russian policy makers an opportunity to take the measures required for the necessary economic reform, setting the country resolutely on the course toward democratic and market development under a rule of law—a second, economic, revolution.[1]

The overall outcomes of Russia's December 1993 election, despite the strong showing of the ultranationalists, give some reason for optimism that a sustainable reform effort will ensue. Voters were able to choose in contested democratic elections both houses of a new parliament and local councils. At

The authors' views are their own and should not be taken to represent those of the U.S. Congress, Congressional Research Service of the Library of Congress, or the United States government.

This chapter draws from John P. Hardt and Phillip J. Kaiser, "Russia's Post-Election Reform Prospects: The Economic Factor," *Congressional Research Service Report*, December 3, 1993. See also John P. Hardt, "Russian Reform and G-7 Assistance: The Second Chance," *CRS Report*, May 1993; and "Economic Reform in Russia: Lessons from Experience," a memorandum by World Bank and International Monetary Fund staff dated December 30, 1993, which raises many points reflected in this paper.

the same time they approved a new postcommunist constitution providing the legitimacy necessary to effectively pursue reform. Reform-oriented political parties led by Yeltsin lieutenants formed political alliances with local leaders that could provide more effective support later on for political reform in a federative context.

The strong central leadership established by the constitution could provide an opportunity to establish the necessary institutions for reform such as a strong, independent central bank; an effective revenue system; legal and regulatory systems for dealing with monopolies, crime, and corruption; and viable institutions for facilitating foreign commerce.

The violence of the October 1993 confrontation, with the extraordinary use of military, police, and special forces, is now viewed widely as an undesirable alternative to compromise—providing motivation to make the new system work. Safeguards to preserve the democratic process and establish freedom of the press and human and civil rights in all segments of the federation need to be, and may be, enacted.

On the other hand, there are those who argue that the Russian federation is already too fissured to reintegrate; some posit that Yeltsin is a spent force or that he has made a "deal with the devil" in the form of the army and special forces that saved him on "Bloody Sunday." [2] Some predict renewed Russian imperialism and authoritarian rule based on the strong showing of chauvinists, nationalists, and representatives of the old system in the December 1993 elections.

It is true that the reformers remaining in the new government are not strong enough by themselves to implement a comprehensive new economic strategy to improve economic performance and provide the basis for economic reintegration. The new legislature and government includes gradualists, populists, statists, and local protectionists who oppose the rate or direction of policies for restructuring the economy. Many do not trust the market; they fear massive unemployment and foreign exploitation and may oppose comprehensive reform policies. Many support an exclusive nationalism that favors Russians at home and abroad and blames other ethnic groups and foreigners for poor economic performance.

Indeed, appeals by those who claim to be reformers but who are drawn to policies of continued inflationary subsidies, slower privatization and restructuring, retention of important elements of the command-economy institutions, and local protectionism are attractive to many voters and members of the new parliament. Economic performance in the Yeltsin period has been decidedly negative, with high inflation, steeply falling production, fear of massive unemployment, and uncertainty about the social safety net. Without implementation of the economic strategy those economic indicators are likely to worsen rather than improve.[3] This would feed the opposition to reform.

In the future, reform candidates facing populists, gradualists, statists, and local-first candidates should have something material to offer if they are to gain support in the Federation Council, the State Duma, and local councils for new economic legislation and regulations. The president and reform members of the federal assembly must be able to say to voters and leaders, "Support my program and you will be better off." The arguments for adopting comprehensive market reform must be convincing to local politicians and electorates, not just to professional, Western-oriented economists.

A renewed economic reform strategy that promises coordination of Western and Russian efforts and coordination between the central government and local authorities might finally reverse the economic decline and put Russia on the path of recovery. This strategy would need to include both an effective anti-inflation program integrating the local and federal economies and significant interconnections with the global market and international economic institutions. It would also need to include accelerated privatization and restructuring of enterprises and further development of market-friendly legal and regulatory institutions.

An effective democratic and market reform process requires a combined effort and programs supportable by local reformers like Boris Nemtsov; central reformers like Gregori Yavlinski, Viktor Chernomyrdin, and Boris Fedorov; and Western advocates of providing more support for reform. A concrete, politically saleable economic strategy will need to involve a combination of complementary assets that each of these actors can bring forth to support a coordinated reform strategy.

Failure to reach a sustainable transition in 1995 may have significantly negative consequences, possibly leading to the further disintegration of the federation and enhanced power of confrontational anti-Western leaders in Russia. On the other hand, a successful democratic and market transition would mean credible prospects for a permanently diminished threat of nuclear war, lower defense budgets, vast new markets, and cooperation on the global and regional issues that once divided Russia and the United States.

Assistance from the G-7, focusing on key sectors and institution-building technical support, could reinforce the Russian economic strategy, pursuing the line announced at the Tokyo G-7 summit. Key points include coordination of assistance, leveraging assistance with structural change, and prompt funding of key projects for timely results.

## A Politically Sustainable Economic Reform Policy

A politically sustainable economic reform policy would include an emphasis on quality of life improvements, more focus on privatization and performance in key sectors, the establishment of market-friendly institutions, movement toward a federative market system, international integration, an improved environment for mutually beneficial investments, and a public awareness program for the many Russians unfamiliar with the benefits of a market economy. That such a program is attainable and would show results in politically meaningful economic performance may be supported by historical experience in market transitions in Western industrial economies and in Central-Eastern European economies since 1989.

### Improved Quality of Life

The reform program must provide credible evidence that it will raise living standards, provide economic security through new social safety nets and employment opportunities, and stabilize the currency so that working hard and investing savings will be meaningful. The public must also be convinced that its despoiled environment will be improved and the hoped-for economic miracle will be shared equitably with all citizens. Safety-net support needs to be targeted on the most vulnerable citizens (pensioners and children, for example) and not provided through universal subsidies. Important demonstration programs that address the crises in health, environment, and housing through coordinated action of local, federal, and Western participants could be helpful.

Public works projects such as those undertaken or planned in Central Europe may be significant because they would provide important economic and social benefits through infrastructure projects such as roads and telecommunications.[4] Hungary is planning EC-supported road construction that will absorb unemployed workers and improve the regional distribution network.[5] With foreign support, Poland is extending health and telephone systems from urban to rural areas and building hospitals and special-care facilities.[6] The U.S. contribution to the Polish hospital effort involved conversion of agricultural debt to fund local projects such as the children's hospital at Krakow with domestic currency.[7] Assistance from groups such as the World Health Organization to fight the outbreak of diphtheria in Russia could provide vital tangible support to desperate citizens faced by unprecedented health crises. Outside the region, toll roads are being built in the People's Republic of China by a consortium of foreign investors, local government, and central authorities.[8]

A number of local and regional water quality projects may be candidates for such coordinated efforts. One suggested by a Japanese economist involves the hot-water-supply system of Khabarovsk that badly needs repair and is beyond the ability of local authorities to deal with. Imported pipes funded by Western aid might be installed by local participants to provide a reliable year round hot-water supply.[9]

### Improved Performance, Privatization, and Restructuring in Key Sectors

A greater focus on efficient economic performance and privatization in key sectors such as food, energy, and infrastructure through coordinated action of local, federal, and Western participants would likely show very positive returns. Specifically, major new programs dealing with the quality and quantity of food and energy supplies should be introduced in 1995. Market changes and monetary stabilization alone will not provide sufficient benefits for citizens and workers to be politically effective. Recently announced changes in land ownership providing effective privatization may promote restructuring and increase productivity, provided adequate support for privatized enterprises (for example, technical assistance, marketing plans, and farmer-to-farmer exchanges) is available. The private farming activities within the larger cooperative land units in Hungary during the period of the New Economic Mechanism may be a useful model. Breaking up land holdings to very small individual plots may harken back to the uneconomic changes that followed the end of serfdom.[10]

Improvement of energy output by very selective and modest assistance to independent oil industries may provide a significant multiplier effect. A more systematic approach to output, processing, distribution, and sales could show increasing value in multiple billions judging by Kazakhstan's experience with Western investment.[11] Increased efficiency through conservation of resources is to be expected as consumers are charged more realistic prices for energy. Meters for gas and electricity would promote this efficiency.

### Firmly Established, Market-Friendly Institutions

Market-friendly institutions must be established and made operational in the near term. Among the needed institutions are a strong independent central bank headed by a reform monetarist; a viable private commercial banking system; a working revenue system with collectible returns from value added tax (VAT) and income taxes; a regulatory framework for demonopolization; and institutions for foreign commerce that would facilitate joining the world market. These institutions should be brought into fundamental operation within the year to make an economic strategy viable.

A strong and independent central bank can regulate monetary policy and, together with the private commercial banking system, help provide capital for necessary growth. Price stability and control of the rate of growth of credit need to be established by the central bank. The Polish and Hungarian national banks may be models. The Polish banking law of January 1989 permitted the national bank to transform the financial sector. With strong, independent power, the Polish central bank can manage the banking industry, implement monetary policy, and fulfill foreign-exchange-control functions. A Banking Supervisory Inspectorate was established in 1990 to monitor banking norms and standards (capital adequacy ratios, liquidation ratios, loan classifications and exposure limits, and so on). Rapid licensing of privatized, formerly state-owned banks occurred between 1990 and 1993.[12] In Russia, the new constitution includes a provision for establishment of an independent National Bank of Russia with Western central bank features.[13]

An efficient and equitable public revenue system is important for financing necessary government expenditures and balancing the budget deficit. The old revenue-collection system based on collections by regional state banks is inappropriate and ineffective in the transition period; and even in the current jerry-built system a substantial portion of revenues is not collected.[14] Inadequate local support and insufficient benefits to localities prevent formation of a political consensus to create and support a functioning revenue system.

To establish market-friendly institutions, local support will be required. "State desertion"—or government abdication of responsibility for the economy—implies that the state lacks concern for financing market-friendly state institutions at the federal and local levels. The OECD could help recognize and provide technical assistance and badly needed training to establish a secure revenue base.[15]

Regulatory institutions to control monopolies, limit economic crime and corruption, and oversee the market are necessary. An improved economic statistical base could be obtained by joining the Partners in Transition in the OECD; an economic survey may then be requested. These surveys have led to important improvements in economic data and better informed economic policy debates in Central Europe.[16]

Presently, participants in economic debates in Russia seem to bring their own statistics, so that a factual basis for compromise is often lacking. International sources of information on money flows would be useful to Russian decision makers. For example, international banks can provide information about capital flight and irregular transfers of funds from Western sources. The further development of stock markets would create avenues for domestic and foreign private investment and provide sources of capital for new and privatized enterprises. Western technical assistance in the spirit of the Marshall Plan should offer training in the operation of the new institutions.

### Integration of the Economy within the Russian Federation

A strong federation requires a new basis for economic reintegration that protects local rights while promoting a viable, integrated market economy. The interdependence of enterprises and regions provides a ready market, but long-suppressed ethnic and regional aspirations for control over decisions create obstacles to economic development. Market-friendly institutions need to provide efficiency and equity throughout the federation to ensure implementation of policies and enforcement of laws, and to prevent barriers to trade and investment.

With the political basis for supporting economic reform, key institutions must be established that benefit both the center and the localities. As mentioned above, these include a strong central bank fostering a stable private commercial banking system (perhaps along the lines of the U.S. regional federal reserve banks); an effective tax and fiscal system that clearly defines responsibilities; and effective federal laws that provide protection from monopolistic practices and corruption.

In April 1917, Lenin sought power promising bread, land, and peace. He found that he had struck a deep chord of yearning in the Russian populace. Yeltsin's new revolution may find support in an appeal for jobs, land, and freedom. To be politically credible Yeltsin's economic promises must be based on doable programs designed to improve both efficiency and equity across the country. This type of approach could be fueled by an inclusive type of Russian patriotic nationalism—as contrasted with the exclusive, chauvinistic view of some of the reactionary forces emerging from the December 1993 election.

### Interregional and International Integration

Reforms that would be convincing to the local voter can also be effective bases for attracting and justifying foreign assistance and investment. The same economic criteria, keyed to the generation of more output, employment, and price stability, can meet the needs of foreign participants in the reform process, attracting foreign aid and investment. Other steps toward international integration which could have a positive influence on trade are Russian accession to the GATT and reduced barriers on trade that have been regulated in the past by COCOM (the Western Coordinating Committee on Multilateral Export Controls, which has regulated exports of sensitive technology to Russia).

International integration should now include cooperation with the successor states to the former Soviet republics. Payment clearing mechanisms, customs agreements, and trade promotion initiatives could provide some respite from the problems generated by disintegration of the Soviet Union and Council for Mutual Economic Assistance. The European Energy Charter and the International Committee for Reform and Cooperation may be effective mechanisms.[17]

*Mutually Beneficial Investment Environment*

The foreign-investment environment must be improved if significant foreign investment is to be expected. Such an improvement could generate much broader support for the overall economic reform effort, as the locals come to see the benefits in concrete terms. Key popular investments could be announced in the months ahead using models of mutually beneficial investments in other countries in the Newly Independent States and Central Europe. The new Russian legislature may finally get around to approving the Bilateral Investment Treaty with the United States, which could set the stage for increased trade between us.

Increased foreign investment may be a critical factor in the improvement of the economy. A positive environment for mutually beneficial foreign investments may be created by the following actions:

*At the locality.* Foreign investment coupled with privatization can provide critical local advantages such as job creation with improved average real income, fringe benefits through private social safety nets, and environmental protection. Local authorities and citizens can participate in contract negotiations and help to ensure good relations with foreign management. Privatized joint-stock enterprises with foreign participation may be saved from bankruptcy and given technical assistance to make them competitive. Once they are made viable, such enterprises may provide more external market access. These results—local job creation, saving enterprises from bankruptcy—have been achieved in many areas in Central Europe and other states of the newly independent regions. Focusing on sectors such as energy, agriculture, and forestry may maximize the utility of low labor costs and, with quality control from foreign participation, may make the privatized enterprises more competitive at home and abroad. Labor costs may be low for joint Russian-Western enterprises even with wages and fringe benefits substantially higher than in domestic firms. Stable taxes and strong contract laws will be important to attract businesses. Building "social infrastructure" (clinics, roads, schools) for localities has become a standard requirement of investors and may strengthen local support for reforms.

*At the center.* Oil, gas, and timber could all attract substantial initial investments that would increase output, thereby strengthening the Russian balance of payments in the short run. A European Energy Charter or other interregional legal and regulatory associations would be helpful in encouraging cooperation by providing for a regionwide legal and regulatory framework. The EC-proposed Energy Charter is now supported by the U.S. government.

*At the international level.* A coalition of local, federal, and Western officials and private enterprises should be formed to promote reform. A functioning authority to monitor international agreements and enterprise contracts also would be helpful. The investment law (President Yeltsin's decree of September 19, 1993) is a useful step that could be supported by political agreement at the local level. Once major Western enterprises begin operating in the Russian economy, a lobby for continued political support for investments will grow both in Russia and in the West. One or more major agreements could have an important demonstration effect—for example, a major oil contract in Russia resembling the Chevron deal in Kazakhstan.[18]

Foreign partners and investors can provide loans and equity capital to modernize obsolete plants and upgrade production processes. Russian managers will need technical assistance in preparing financial statistics, business plans, and investment instruments.[19] Examples of beneficial Western investments can be cited throughout Central Europe and other newly independent states.

The reason for citing the oil deals first is that the questions of risk and return on investment are easier to handle in the case of a commodity that can be readily sold in any likely commercial volume. Also, better control over elements of output, processing, and distribution assures effective technology transfer and reasonable returns. Neutral foreign investment advisers can provide objective assessments on market rates of return. Local consumer interests, real income, the environment, and public health should be protected by contract and regulatory provisions. This seems to have been an important basis for the finalization of successful Western energy contracts in Kazakhstan.

An avenue to be explored for increasing foreign investment while alleviating Russia's debt burden may be debt-equity and debt-for-nature swaps. Debt-equity swaps could provide near-term hands-on involvement of foreign firms that could promote improved performance. Debt-for-nature swaps could assist in the expensive chore of environmental clean-up and reduce the debt burden as well.

### Public Awareness of Market Advantages

A media and communications program to educate the public and the political leaders on the positive aspects of comprehensive reform is clearly needed. A series of educational television and radio programs could help provide the necessary public support for the market-reform strategy by fostering a more objective understanding of the process. A World Bank-supported effort in Russia may spearhead such activity. The populace must understand that privatization and restructuring, a functioning legal and regulatory framework, effective monetary stabilization programs, and economic integration within the federation and with the global economy can contribute to rising living standards, increased employment opportunities, improved economic security, and a higher quality of life.

Television and other media, supported by funding from international organizations such as the World Bank, and domestic educational institutions could provide graphic information about the utility of an effective economic reform strategy in popular formats.[20] It should be pointed out, for example, that it takes far fewer hours of work to earn the income to buy high-value consumer goods in countries with moderately successful stabilization programs. A Russian has to work an hour for a liter of milk and thirty hours for a kilo of beef, while his Polish counterpart works just fifteen minutes and two hours, respectively, for the same goods.[21]

The pain from price liberalization and austerity appear to be obvious, judging from Russian election results, but the gains may not be. Also, the successful experience of market transitions in Europe, Asia, and elsewhere may be highlighted. The effectiveness of the public awareness programs during the Marshall Plan period may form an instructive historical model.

*Legislative Agenda*

Boris Yeltsin and the government must present a legislative agenda dealing with economic reform. Basic legislation along this line would include an act regulating the central bank and the commercial banking system, a revenue act to ensure collection of revenue and revenue sharing, legislation for demonopolization, social security legislation, and legislation setting forth statistical reporting requirements.

Other important subjects for legislation include the budget process; definition of the respective powers of the federal government, regions, and localities; judicial review and oversight; foreign commerce (a legal and regulatory framework to harmonize domestic legislation with foreign regulations and international agreements, notably GATT); and equalizing taxes on imports and exports and reducing or eliminating export quotas. Legislation simplifying the licensing and taxing of new businesses, and regulating insurance would be useful, as would the implementation of laws and decrees on privatization of land and on mortgages.

## The Role of Western Assistance: Timely, Coordinated, Sufficient

The economic reform policies discussed above need to be implemented by the Russian government and parliament. Western assistance could provide important support for these measures, and improve prospects for successful transition. While U.S. policy is keyed to the economic reform needs of the center of Russian governance and supports promising local initiatives, success may require larger allocations, more timely dispersal, and better coordination of Western assistance.

Treasury Secretary Lloyd Bentsen named a former World Bank official, Michael Gillette, to lead a task force to coordinate G-7 aid to Russia.[22] While the reform strategy mapped out at the G-7 meeting in Tokyo in July 1993 was innovative, the agenda laid out for future change may not go far enough. The need for further improvements in Western approaches to assistance was summarized for the Senate Foreign Relations Committee by Under Secretary of Treasury Lawrence Summers in these key points:

The G-7 needs to focus on larger, more coordinated allocations that will be adequate to meet Russian needs. Initially, support should not be conditioned upon specific political or economic improvements. Programs must be promptly funded and the funds promptly disbursed if Russian reform programs are to be timely and successful. Russian commercial banks must support restructuring at the local level, thereby leveraging early moves toward privatization and restructuring. The World Bank should support the process of recreating the social safety nets formerly provided by enterprises.

The key points of the Clinton administration's policy do indeed move toward fulfilling the needs for a comprehensive and coordinated economic strategy. However, that policy raises several issues.

Support based on need first, then conditionality, is a risky policy that makes the United States a full partner in the success or failure of Yeltsin's reform. How much assistance is enough is difficult to establish, but the level of assistance must be established and scaled to the fulfillment of appropriate conditions at appropriate points. While disbursement of resources at an early date would seem more likely to have a positive effect, it is based on faith that conditions will be adhered to.[23]

Leveraging step-by-step privatization and restructuring implies fine-tuned, timely allocation of resources. Closely coordinated activity is expected to provide a demonstration effect that will generate support for overall reform, but questions remain about how closely step-by-step privatization and post-privatization restructuring can be leveraged, and how large a demonstration would be necessary to attract widespread support.

The West's backing of Yeltsin over the opposition leaders in the 1993 parliamentary crisis appears more defensible than open-ended support of Yeltsin's future reform policies. Although support for reform is not intended to be unqualified support for Yeltsin, in practice the distinction may be difficult to delineate.

Asserting that timely aid can make a "critical difference" in Russia's future implies that effective Western assistance will play a central role in tipping the balance toward success. This is difficult to prove, but given U.S. policy interests, it may be a reasonable and justifiable act of faith.

Still, because the administration anticipates little increase in appropriated funds, the effective use of available bilateral and multilateral funds is critical. Intuitively we can accept that this is a critical time and the window of opportunity will not be open long; and while more timely disbursement and utilization of funds to support reform programs would be a welcome change from the past and would raise the probability of success, this development is not assured.

### Prospects for Failure and Success

The crucial period that began in December 1993 does appear to offer an opportunity for President Yeltsin and the Russian reformers to make decisive steps to take Russia down the road to a market economy. These steps must be taken vigorously; they must include effective coordination with the West; and they must meet the local needs. Above all, Russian voters must be able to find in them the credible promise of an improvement in the quality of life. Economic performance for the period of Yeltsin's rule has been disappointing to say the least, and substantial unemployment is likely if ambitious privatization leads to restructuring and corporatization as projected.[24] Without a commitment to sustainable economic reform policy the economy may recede into the pattern of 1992-1993, when periods of monetary discipline and programs for full privatization were followed by easy credit, recession, and policies of populism, gradualism, statism, and local protectionism that in turn brought deeper economic malaise and weakened governance. It should be clear that Yeltsin's economic policies have contained little consistent monetary austerity and have been less comprehensive than other successful transitions. Without a resolute commitment to crossing the threshold to sustainable reform, backsliding may again occur in 1995. This downward spiral of economic performance could sink the opportunity for change, possibly ending the best chance for market transition in a democratic system that the Russians have ever had.

However, to quote Secretary of State Warren Christopher:

If the people of Russia succeed in their heroic struggle to build a free society and a market economy, the pay-off for the United States will be transforming: a permanently diminished threat of nuclear war; lower defense budgets; vast new markets; and cooperation on the global and regional issues that once divided us.[25]

Clearly, the stakes in Russian economic reform over the next few years are incredibly high for all parties.

### Notes

1. See the testimony of Strobe Talbott, ambassador-at-large and special adviser to the secretary of state on the Newly Independent States before the House Foreign Affairs Committee, October 6, 1993, and that of Daniel V. Speckhard, deputy for economic affairs to Ambassador Talbott, before the House Committee on Government Operations, November 5, 1993. See also John P. Hardt, "Vision and Program for Russia: An American View" (in French), in *Mutations á l'est: transition vers le marché et intégration est-ouest,* proceedings of the Summer University held at the University of Pau, France,

ed. Marie Lavigne (Pau, France: Economica Press, 1994). An English-language version of the last paper is available from the author upon request.

2. Peter Reddaway, "Dictatorial Drift," *New York Times*, October 10, 1993; William Odom, "Yeltsin's Deal with the Devil," *Washington Post*, October 24, 1993.

3. For economic indicators see OECD, "Short Term Economic Indicators, Transition Economies," April 1993, 60-61; WEFA, *Eurasia Outlook*, October 1993, 224-225; and PlanEcon, *Russian Economic Monitor*, December 19, 1993.

4. John Redding and Quentin Peel, "Next Chapter of the Railway Children, Europe's High-Speed Rail Links Planned for 2010," *Financial Times*, November 18, 1993.

5. Kalman Mizsei, "Hungary: Gradualism Needs a Strategy," in *Economic Transformation in Central Europe*, ed. Richard Portes (London: Centre for Economic Policy Research, 1993), 154.

6. John P. Hardt and Jean F. Boone, "Poland's Renewal and U.S. Options: A Policy Reconnaissance Update," CRS-87-889S, July 1987. See also Murray Feshbach and Alfred Friendly, *Ecocide in the USSR* (New York: Basic Books, 1992), 260-267, for specific examples of Russian needs.

7. Hardt and Boone, "Poland's Renewal," 33.

8. Patrick E. Tyler, "Hong Kong Tycoon's Road to China," *New York Times*, December 31, 1994, D7, D14.

9. Suggested by Kazuo Ogawa, vice director general, Institute for Russian and East European Studies (ROTOBO), Tokyo, based on his discussions with the vice-governor of the region.

10. The Citizens Network for Foreign Affairs provides useful binational agricultural models. See also, Michael Marrese, "Hungarian Economy: Moving in the Right Direction," *East European Economies: Slow Growth in the 1980s*, U.S. Congress, Joint Economic Committee, vol. 3, March 28, 1986, 322-340.

11. "Kazakhstan Emerging as Next Oil Giant," *Journal of Commerce*, June 23, 1993.

12. A statement by Mrs. Hanna Gronkiewicz-Waltz, governor of the National Bank of Poland, to the Congressional Staff Forum on International Development, Washington, D.C., September 24, 1993.

13. For the text of the constitution see *FBIS Daily Report*, November 10, 1993, 18-37, as published in *Rossiyskaya gazeta*, November 10, 1993.

14. According to ITAR-TASS reports, surveys show at least a quarter of tax revenue is not collected. One assumes the tax base is small under the transitional system.

15. OECD, *Multinational Training Network for Tax Officials from Central and Eastern European Countries and the New Independent States* (Paris: Organization for Economic Cooperation and Development, 1993).

16. Hungary received the first economic survey by OECD in 1991. Since then others have been prepared for Poland and Czechoslovakia.

17. John P. Hardt and Richard Kaufman, "Transition and Integration in Newly Independent States," *Introduction to the Former Soviet Union in Transition*, vol. 2, U.S. Congress, Joint Economic Committee, May 1993.

18. The Kazakhstan arrangement included joint ownership and control, an investment fund, government guarantees, and other agreements based on negotiations with American and other Western participants.

19. Statement by Lawrence H. Summers, under secretary for international affairs, U.S. Treasury Department, to the Senate Committee on Foreign Relations, September 7, 1993.

20. At the request of Russian reformers, funding is being arranged by the World Bank for a series of Russian television, radio, and print media programs to improve the understanding of the general public, journalists, and media managers of market economics and reform programs. Several pilot projects have been proposed, including one on the threat of hyperinflation.

21. "Inflation Is Eating up Purchasing Power," *Transition*, July-August 1993, 10. *Transition* is produced by the Socialist Economies Reform Unit, Country Economic Department, The World Bank, Washington, D.C.

22. *The Washington Post*, January 13, 1994, A20.

23. The exchange of letters between Jeffrey Sachs of Harvard and John Odling Smee, director of the European II Department at the International Monetary Fund, *Financial Times*, November 11, 17, and 22, 1993, indicated a difference of view as to what is needed and on what conditions the resources should be made available. The central difference may be captured by the titles of the letters: Smee's "IMF to fund Russia on performance not promises," and Sachs's "IMF rules for loans to Russia a 'cop out.' " See also, "Economic Reform in Russia: Lessons from Experience" (Unpublished memorandum by World Bank and IMF staff, December 30, 1993).

24. OECD, "Short-Term Economic Indicators," passim.; WEFA, *Eurasia Outlook*, passim.; "Russia's Economy in Eight Months," *Moscow News*, no. 42, October 15, 1993. Corporatization is a step in the privatization process in which a state-owned enterprise becomes legally independent of the government and is able to restructure, sell shares, spin off or close unprofitable activities, and so on. Government financial support, subsidies, and bailouts stop, forcing the enterprise to face a "hard budget constraint." This process is likely to result in increased unemployment.

25. Testimony of Warren Christopher before the Senate Foreign Relations Committee, November 3, 1993.

# Part III    Regions and Nationalities

## 12 Regions, Republics, and Russian Reform: Center-Periphery Relations in the Russian Federation

Paul A. Goble

Moscow's kaleidoscopically changing relationships with the Russian Federation's regions and republics will determine the scope and pace of political reform in that country, the foreign policies that Moscow pursues, and the borders as well as the very survival of the Russian state. Thus, it should come as no surprise that an increasing number of scholars and officials both in the Russian Federation and abroad are attending to this critical but much neglected issue. But the mass of rapidly shifting details gathered by and presented in these studies often has obscured the underlying structural elements of these relationships and led to radically divergent predictions about the future.[1]

One way out of this situation is to focus on the structural elements underlying Moscow's relations with the regions, elements that are changing much less quickly than the statements of central and regional leaders. By doing so, we can explore the ways in which those structural underpinnings delimit the possibilities of the various actors and thus define the range of possible outcomes.[2] Although such an approach is not entirely satisfactory—it fails to predict which of the possible outcomes will occur—it nonetheless is perhaps a more useful one over time, providing as it does a map of the arena in which the various political forces of post-Soviet Russia will necessarily have to contend.

### A New Arena

Like the blind men and the elephant, many Russians and Western observers of Russia have fastened on one or another element of the extraordinarily complex situation that is post-Soviet Russia and concluded that it and it alone will define the future. Thus, some have seen the emergence of the Russian Federation as the final formation of a Russian nation-state that will have an easy time making the transition to democracy. Others have insisted that the Russian Federation is simply the Soviet Union writ small and will suffer the same disintegrative fate. Still a third group has drawn an analogy with earlier Russian "times of troubles" and concluded that Russia can be reconstituted only as an authoritarian state.

While there is undoubtedly some truth in each of these conclusions, all of them are incomplete both as descriptions and as predictions. Consequently, it seems more probable that the future of the Russian Federation and its regions—Russian and non-Russian alike—will be defined less by what the federation is than by what it is not.

First and foremost, the Russian Federation is not the Soviet Union. That represents both a plus and a minus for its future development. On the plus side, the Russian Federation is more than 80 percent ethnic Russian, as opposed to the Soviet Union, which was barely 50 percent Russian. Its non-Russian entities have less experience of and desire for complete independence than did the non-Russian republics of the USSR and are in any case less definitively non-Russian: only six of the twenty-two non-Russian entities in the Russian Federation have non-Russian majorities; most are overwhelmingly dominated by ethnic Russians. Perhaps most important, the negative experiences of Russians, many non-Russians, and the increasingly conservative international community of the end of the Soviet Union make secession less appealing and recognition less likely. That in turn gives Moscow more room as it seeks to cope with governmental decay and de facto regionalization.

But on the negative side, the fact that the Russian Federation is not the Soviet Union is perhaps far more important. First, the loss of Communist party control of the country means that the basic sinews that held things together in the past are gone and must be replaced. So far, there is no obvious candidate for such legitimation or control. Second, the trauma of the collapse, the loss of prestige, and the loss of the state as a definer of what it is to be a Russian (ethnic Russians, unlike the fourteen non-Russian nationalities, were never encouraged to think of the Russian Federation as uniquely theirs) have contributed both to a loss of identity on which new state authority could be built and to a decay of the state because of that lack. And third, the new situation has led to a multiplicity of elites—economic, political, and otherwise— who are competing in a situation where the limits remain undefined both at the center and on the periphery and who are thus contributing to the decay of old structures without yet constructing any consistently agreed upon new ones. As will be seen below, all these groups see ethnicity—Russian as much as non-Russian—as one resource among many to be employed in the struggle. In short, Russia remains in a revolutionary situation, even though it and its friends abroad have been unwilling to draw that conclusion aloud.

Second and perhaps equally fateful, the Russian Federation is not Russia. Not only are there the much discussed twenty-five million ethnic Russians outside Russia's Stalin-imposed borders, there are also thirty million ethnic non-Russians inside its borders—nearly one-fifth of the population that in many cases sits on top of key resources. These latter are especially problematic both because their ethnically defined territories occupy far more space—53 percent of the Russian Federation's land area—than their population would seem to justify and because local ethnic Russians may in many cases be exploiting non-Russian identities to pursue their own goals. In addition, Russians do not view the existing borders of the Russian Federation as in any way appropriate and legitimate. Most have not accepted the independence of Ukraine or Belarus, the two East Slavic nations to the West; and many believe that borders will have to be changed in order to create Russia. Such attitudes power much of the imperial revanchism which now is at the center of Russian political life and thus complicate the process of attempting to convert Russia into a democratic nation-state. And finally, the fact that the Russian Federation is not wholly legitimate in the eyes of its own population contributes to the decay of the Russian state and fuels its imperial pretensions towards its neighbors.[3]

This last point is especially important because it is usually neglected. It has three elements. First, unstable, weakened countries like Russia are often a threat to their neighbors. That is because power is relative, not absolute, and Russia remains far stronger than any of her neighbors, and because foreign policy is for the Russian leadership what it is for many other elites, a way of working out domestic problems and of generating the only kind of legitimacy available to a state that is not viewed as genuine or effective by the population under its nominal control. Second, historically, Russia has been a state-nation rather than a nation-state. That is, identity has been centered on the state, which became an empire long before the population consolidated as a nation. As a result, Russian identity and support for the state is directly proportional to how strong the state appears to be. When the state is strong, Russians typically tend to feel more comfortable with themselves as well as with it; when it is weak, their own sense of self-definition becomes more problematic and their identity with the state more uncertain. This too drives much of the politics of this revolutionary period. And finally, the absence of a clearly defined Russian nation in the usual sense puts demands on the central leadership as it seeks to generate support during the difficult transitions it has attempted and gives opportunities to both rightist politicians in the center and regional Russian elites that would not normally exist, opening the way for a redefinition of not only what is Russia but who is a Russian.[4]

And third, the Russian Federation is not a federation. Calling it one does not make it so. One recalls the observation of a Soviet émigré from the 1950s who noted that he objected to calling the Soviet Union an industrial society, not because it was not industrial but because it was not a society. The same thing is true here. Both historically and even now the Russian Federation has been managed more imperially than was the Soviet Union.[5] There is not even a constitutional fiction that the entities within the Russian Federation are self-standing entities having federal rights. They were created by the center to be run from the center. Federalism presupposes both the sharing of power and the rule of law, neither of which is characteristic of the Russian Federation. Instead, all the units—oblasts, krays, and non-Russian autonomies—within the Russian Federation were created to support the centralization of power in Moscow.[6] During the Soviet period, they did not enjoy even the limited privileges and autonomies of the fourteen non-Russian republics.

The regions—Russian as well as non-Russian—typically have gained power not as the result of an agreement to share powers but rather as a result of the decay of central authority. When the center is strong, the regions are weak, this view holds; and when the regions are strong, it is only because the center is weak. Russian and non-Russian regions alike see ethnicity as a resource in what all view as a contest rather than a convention. Here too the problem is that there is no agreement on what constitutes the republic, and hence we remain in a revolutionary situation that can be ended only by the reassertion of central power over the regions, exit of one kind or another of the regions from central control, or the elaboration and acceptance of a new kind of public authority that accepts the limits of the system, supports the rule of law, and agrees that strong regions will contribute to a strong center.

Few Russian or non-Russian players in the political drama now taking place in the Russian Federation accept these ideas—they represent a shift without precedent in Russian history—but for various reasons, some quite unexpected, the number of those who see decentralization as necessary is growing. Consequently, we now need to examine the structural arrangements of the new players on the board just described and the new politics being playing on it.

## New Players and a New Politics

Typically, discussions of center-periphery relations in the Russian Federation treat Moscow and its regions—Russian and non-Russian—as if they were each single players. That might have been true at one time; it is certainly not true now. There are now multiple players in both categories, some old, some new; and importantly there are even new categories of entities, such as the self-proclaimed economic and political regions that have sprung up around the periphery. This very complexity has led to unexpected alliances and unexpected turns in the political struggle.

Before turning to the participants themselves and the politics they are engaged in, three preliminary observations are in order. First, as noted above, decay of central control over the regions is not the same thing as decentralization and federalization. Second, even decentralization of power is not a single thing but rather a range of possibilities: on the one hand, there can be decentralization to regional political elites; on the other, there can be decentralization to industrial plants. The first threatens the integrity of the state unless the rules of the game are universally understood and accepted; the second undermines the power of existing regional elites, may spark the formation of new regional groupings, or may contribute to elaboration of a more participatory political culture precisely by drawing more elements into the process. And third, ethnicity is not a cause or a block; it is a political resource that can be used by Russians and non-Russians at both the center and the periphery, mobilizing people to support either a recentralization or a further decay of the Russian state.[7] The role of non-Russian national identities both for non-Russian and Russian elites ruling over non-Russian regions is clear, but the role of Russian national identity, precisely because it remains up for grabs in many contexts, is far more ambiguous. As the elaboration of regional identities—such as that of "Sibiryak"—shows, Russian nationalism can be used against the center—particularly if the center is viewed as somehow anti-Russian.

Analytically, we can distinguish among three groups of participants, each of which is internally fissured and has allies outside of its group and opponents within its own group. The first of these groups is in Moscow itself. With the collapse of the communist system, the party has disappeared, the army and the KGB are in a totally different position, the mafia has arisen, the ministries have changed their relationship to the economy, and the parliamentary institutions have provided a new power base. Each of these groups has its own agenda with respect to the regions, each can reach out to find supporters, and each must compete with others in Moscow and the regions to advance its agenda. Some benefit from a devolution of power—the parliamentarians at least in the short run—and others lose—the ministries and the military, for example. Precisely because of this complexity, dramatic and unexpected shifts have occurred (chronicled by others[8]), and Moscow has tended to seek to rely on Russian identity as a means to promote unity and reassert control over the regions. Thus the drive by many in Moscow to reassert Russian hegemony over the former Soviet space as a means simultaneously to exploit and generate this sense of Russianness.

The second group comprises the Russian regions. These are far more variegated both among and within than Moscow and the non-Russian regions. As the state has declined in importance, private entrepreneurship and "nomenklatura capitalism" have expanded, and new actors have taken the stage. Each of the new groups has a very different agenda—some seeing central control as essential; others seeing it as an obstacle to their goals. This pattern is complicated by the fact that some Russian regions are rich in resources and can easily export them for hard currency, while others are rich in resources but cannot export them without the assistance of the center as a guardian of interstate commerce. Still others are poor and dependent on subsidies from the center. Moreover, many of the effective regions are not the pre-existing ones, leading to a new overlay of political and economic actors.[9]

The third group, the non-Russian autonomies, is equally diverse. In addition to all of the complexities outlined for the Russian regions, this group is divided among those where non-Russian actors dominate non-Russian areas, those where Russians dominate all or part of the economy in a particular space, those where Russians dominate the political but not the economic sphere, and so on. Each of these units is obviously affected by and can use ethnicity as a resource in a different way.

Surmounting the three groups are the new regional organizations, which cut across all of these entities and seek to exploit entirely different identities and interests, of which ethnicity is only one, one that is often much less important than economic concerns.

From this mass of competing groups, with very different power possibilities and political goals, we can make five general conclusions about the nature of politics:

First, Moscow and the regions are each too fragmented to act as individual actors. Increasing cross-cutting cleavages could lead to gridlock and demands for harsh centralism or regional exit or to the evolution of something like a civil society, depending on economic and political developments largely exogenous to this center-periphery issue.

Second, any attempt to impose a common solution on all of the regions will backfire precisely because the regions are so different. Indeed, the Yeltsin government finds itself increasingly caught in the same dilemma Gorbachev did: a common approach will radicalize the least radical, while a differentiated approach will lead to the politics of reclassification, in which the regions struggle to be placed in one category or another for fiscal or budgetary purposes. That is what happened with the "war of sovereignties" and the declaration of Russian regions as republics in 1992 and 1993. But the danger of this has not passed; indeed, the attractiveness of a single "solution" to the regions is perhaps the greatest threat to the integrity of the country.

Third, the rise and fall in the level of political participation will determine the ability of elites to use ethnicity as a weapon in both directions.

Fourth, new coalitions are developing between some actors in the regions and some in Moscow. Thus, areas that need central protection to be able to export are more inclined to support a stronger center than those that do not have to receive such protection in order to prosper.

Fifth, the regional card is more likely to be played in Moscow than by the regions themselves. Moscow's claims that the regions are threatening secession helps the center, especially given Western attitudes since 1991, and any effort to secede by any region thus strengthens those who want an authoritarian solution in Moscow.

In sum, the politics of center-periphery relations are and will remain messy, with the Russian state becoming increasingly weak and irrelevant to what goes on in the regions. To the extent that the center can still extract enough resources to begin to reform, its only real losing strategy is a direct attack on the regions: that could shatter the fragile Russian Federation; and to the extent that many of the regions still benefit from not being forced to bear the burden of independence, they will benefit from not directly challenging the center, an action that could generate exactly the response they do not want. It is to this unexpected—and largely unappreciated—commonality of interests that we now turn, for it and it alone helps to explain why the most dramatic scenarios of either hyperrecentralization or complete disintegration are unlikely to define the entire future course of the Russian Federation.

## A Kaleidoscope of Outcomes

Both Russians and Western observers of Russia have gone through three stages in attempting to comprehend the dramatic changes that have followed the end of the Soviet Union: denial, then analogy, and only at the end empirical observation of the facts of the case. The conclusions that Russia will inevitably end up either as a unitary state, as a decentralized one, or as a fragmented set of states are all based on analogies rather than observation, analogies that seek to simplify enormous complexity by means of a single rubric or that assume that the complexity can be embraced and dealt with by a single political strategy. Unfortunately for both analysts and the politicians involved, such simplicity cannot be achieved except at costs (in terms of coercion, chaos, or confusion) that no one may be willing or able to pay.

This section focuses on three key issues: first, the nature of the Russian state and why our general approach to it has been defective; second, the extent to which efforts by either central or peripheral elites to achieve their goals directly will necessarily produce the reverse of what they intend; and third, the marginal but not irrelevant role of the West in this calculus.

The major reason that no one in the West seems to be able to make sense of what is going on in Russia is that the notion that Russia is a state is simply wrong. What we are watching is not decolonization, as was the case with the end of the Soviet Union, or radical reformation as has been the case in the former Soviet republics, but rather the difficult process of the death and rebirth of a state. The Russian state is dying and its death is calling into question Russian identity. It is a Western conceit that the most important force on a given territory is the state. While that may be true in many places, it is not true now in Russia. Instead, we have a situation in which many entities are stronger than the one that calls itself a state and hence center-periphery relations are not about devolution and decentralization but rather about decay. No one now active in politics or political analysis has had experience with such a collapse. The last time it happened was in Germany at the end of World War I.

Because of the weakness of all structures—including even the mafia, which is strong only in some areas—the usual politics of the current situation break down. Direct pursuit of any one of the three goals—secession, restoration of a unitary state, or planned decentralization—in each case leads to results very different than those intended. Should regional elites seek secession, they will help fuel central demands for the restoration of a unitary state, and that, in the current context, will lead to more uncontrolled devolution of power. Should central elites seek an immediate restoration of central authority, regional elites will think more and more about secession, leading in some cases to just that and in others to further decay of the state. And should both groups be willing or unable to do anything about the currently uncontrolled devolution of power, both secession and efforts at recentralization are likely to continue.

Is there an immediate way or ways out of this potentially vicious circle? Yes, but only under two conditions—a dramatic increase in coercion justified by foreign policy forays against neighboring countries or a long and slow consolidation of the Russian nation. But this complex calculus means that Russia and her regions are likely to go through a kaleidoscopic set of changes at incredible speed, where the various pieces will remain in play but where their relationships are likely to change dramatically. Moreover, this process is likely to be extremely diverse, with some parts going in one direction and others in a very different one—in short, a future far more complex than anyone heretofore has suggested, but one also far more interesting if not terribly pleasant for all concerned.

What role is reserved for the United States? A marginal but not irrelevant one. Western policy to oppose any secession from secession, or any further fragmentation of the new states—what one might call the "back to Biafra" syndrome—tends to push the system in an authoritarian direction. Moreover, our elevation of economics over politics as a point of concern, while ultimately productive of stability, is almost certainly generating instability in the short run. And our promotion of communications technology within and across borders of the Russian Federation is putting pressures on the system that it cannot easily cope with.

In short, we are part of the calculus as well, albeit unwillingly and without a good understanding of the situation. And we, like the residents of the Russian Federation, thus face a future in Eurasia where there is no prospect of stability within current borders except at levels of coercion that no institution in that region is currently able to impose.

## Notes

1. For continuing monitoring, see especially the articles by Elizabeth Teague and Vera Tolz in the RFE/RL daily and weekly reports, SAIC's *Center & Regional Affairs Monthly: News and Analysis on Russia and its Regions; Russian Far East Update* (Seattle, Washington); *Russian Far East News* (Anchorage, Alaska); *Ethnopolis*, four numbers in 1992 and 1993; and *Russia in Asia* (Honolulu, Hawaii). Among specific studies, see Michael J. Bradshaw, *Siberia at a Time of Change* (Economist Intelligence Unit, no. 2171, 1992); Jessica Eve Stern, *Why Russia is Not a State* (Unpublished paper, Lawrence Livermore Laboratories, 1993); D. V. Olshansky, *Alternative Scenarios of the Disintegration of the Russian Federation* (McLean, Va.: Potomac Foundation, 1993); A.B. Zubov, "Sovetskiy Soyuz: iz imperii—v nichto?" *Polis* (Moscow) no. 1/2 (1992): 56-74; O. B. Glezer, et al., "Sub'ekty federatsii: kakim im byt'?" *Polis* no. 7 (July 1991): 149-159; Christine Wallich, *Fiscal Decentralization: Intergovernmental Relations in Russia* (Monograph, World Bank, Washington, D.C., 1992); Sherman Garnett, "The Sources of Conflict in Eurasia," *Politichna Dauks* (Kiev), 1994; Gerhard Simon, *Regionalismus in der Sowjetunion* (Koln: BOIS, 1987); Marie Mendras, ed., *Un Etat pour la Russie*

(Brussels: Complexes, 1992); Marie Mendras, "Existe-t-il un Etat Russe?" *Politique etrangére* 1 (January 1992): 25-34; Jean Radovanyi, "And What if Russia Breaks Up?" *Post-Soviet Geography* 33 (June 1992): 69-77; Tatiana Yarygina and Grigory Marchenko, "Regional'nyye protsessy v byvshem SSSR i novoy Rossii," *Svobodnaya mysl* (Moscow) 14 (March 1992): 1-4; Paul B. Henze, *Ethnic Dynamics and Dilemmas of the Russian Republic* (Santa Monica: RAND, 1991); Emil Payin, "Russian Federation Facing Fate of USSR?" Meeting Report XI, Kennan Institute for Advanced Russian Studies, Washington, D.C., August 1993, p. 16; Sergei Beliaev, "Federalism: Tendencies in the New Equilibrium," *The Federalism Debate* (Ottawa) 1 (June 1993); Laurance J. Aurbach, "Decentralization in Russia: The Role of Our Section," *Urban, State and Local Law Newsletter* 16, 3 (Spring 1993); Paul Goble, "The Coming Collapse of the Russian Federation," *NEFTE Compass* (London) 2, 2 (January 1993): 5-6; Henry Huttenbach, "Can the Russian Federation Survive?" *Surviving Together* (Fall 1993): 8-10; and Emil Pain, "Dezintigratsionnyye protsessy v Rossiskoy federatsii," *Politike v Post-SSSR* (Moscow) (June 1993): 15-21.

2. For an example of such an approach, see my "Readers, Writers and Republics: The Structural Basis of Non-Russian Literary Politics," in *The Nationalities Factor in Soviet Politics and Society,* ed. Lubomyr Hajda and Mark Beissinger (Boulder, Colo.: Westview, 1990), 131-147.

3. Mendras, "Existe-t-il un Etat Russe?"

4. For studies of Russian statism and nationalism, see Mendras, "Existe-t-il un Etat Russe?" and the well-known works of Frederick Barghoorn, John Dunlop, and Edward Alworth.

5. That is the conclusion of many Russian observers, too. See Georgy Satarov, "Imperiya ili federatsiya," *Nezavisimaya gazeta,* September 8, 1993, among others.

6. It is one of the delightful coincidences of history that the official who described the first Soviet attempts at rearranging the political landscape of the Russian Federation was named B. Yeltsin. Writing in 1919, he acknowledged that all such refederalization was simply part of a strategy for the "ingathering of the Russian lands." See his article in *Vvlast sovetov* no. 6/7 (May 1919): 9-10, cited in Richard Pipes, *The Russian Revolution* (New York: Random House, 1991), 515n.

7. Ethnicity may be a constraint on elites precisely as more and more people enter politics, and it may become less so as people exit from participation in political life. As participation falls over time—and that is what is happening and is likely to continue to happen in the Russian Federation—ethnicity may become a diminishing asset to both Russians and non-Russians who seek to use it. On this possibility, see Crane Brinton, *Anatomy of Revolution* (New York: Random House, 1938), 185-186.

8 Goble, "The Coming Collapse of the Russian Federation," and Mendras, "Existe-t-il un Etat Russe?"

9. For more details about the replacement of pre-existing regions with new ones, see Mendras, "Existe-t-il un Etat Russe?" and Goble, "The Coming Collapse of the Russian Federation."

# Ukraine and Nation Building
## Editor's Note

John W. Blaney

Ukraine has had a difficult passage since the end of the Soviet Union and its independence. Indeed, the challenges to Ukraine appear to be increasing as time passes. The relationship with Russia is choppy. There is real tension over Crimea's future, evident in that region's parliamentary vote in May 1994, which attempts to put in place mechanisms to establish Crimea's sovereignty. Economic relationships between the two countries have been politicized highly, exemplified by Russia's use of gas supplies as leverage over Ukraine. Complicating all aspects of the relationship is the rising tide of Russian nationalism, which is regarded widely in Ukraine as a threat.

Internally, the situation is no better. The economy is in shambles. Politically, the April 1994 parliamentary elections did not serve to unify the country. Nationalists did well in western Ukraine, but Communists and leftists won the largest block of seats. However, the largest group of new deputies consists of independent and unaffiliated legislators. Candidates pressing for economic reform did poorly. Generally, those in western Ukraine seek stronger relationships with the European Union and the West, while eastern Ukraine is focused more on stronger relationships with Russia.

The United States has a range of very important interests in Ukraine. At the top of the list, as discussed earlier, are nuclear issues (including nuclear weapons, proliferation, and ecological security concerns). Also quite important, however, are the dangers that would be posed by the disintegration of Ukraine. In such an event, Russia's conduct would, of course, be critical. The demise of Ukraine probably would destabilize other successor states. Furthermore, the failure of another, and in this case very large multiethnic nation-state would damage the already taxed efforts of the international community to create a reasonably stable international security system in the post-Cold War period.

To all these reasons for a detailed close-up on Ukraine must be added the interest of some in building a geographic security belt—anchored on Ukraine—around a posited neoimperialist Russia. Although this is not the view or policy of the U.S. government, the question of Ukraine's suitability for such a role has appeared in the press from time to time, and a more complete treatment of the underlying situation in Ukraine should help assess the realism of such an option.

In response to all these issues and concerns, we have turned to three top authorities on Ukraine to analyze Ukraine's complex situation and its efforts at nation building. Their works are Roman Szporluk's "Nation Building in Ukraine: Problems and Prospects"; Orest Subtelny's "Imperial Disintegration and Nation-State Formation"; and Ilya Prizel's "Ukraine's Foreign Policy as an Instrument of Nation Building."

Combined, these essays come to grips with several fundamental questions about Ukraine. Some of these are: How enduring are the underlying tenets of Ukraine, as a nation-state so abruptly born amidst the death throes of the Soviet Union? Do the historical roots of Ukraine run deep enough to sustain nationhood? Was the crucible in which Ukraine was forged as a nation-state hot enough for success? Can the highly complex relationship with Russia ever be rationalized? How useful has Ukraine's foreign policy been in nation building, and what are the limits to its utility? Finally, what factors will most influence where Ukraine goes from here?

Particularly valuable in all these essays are the explanations of the psychologies and motivations of different groups in Ukraine. For example, how different were the reasons why key groups and leaders supported independence? What might this imply about the governance of Ukraine now and in the future?

The three essays overlap occasionally in their coverage, but such overlap is the price of a fair comparison of contrasting viewpoints on this vital region.

# 13 Nation Building in Ukraine: Problems and Prospects

Roman Szporluk

Nation building in contemporary Ukraine is taking place in a setting that was created in 1991, when Ukraine attained its independence and the Soviet Union collapsed. Properly speaking, the events of 1991, and those immediately preceding them, form the initial chapter of the Ukrainian nation-building project. Ukraine's most pressing problems today, domestic and external, are defined by the decisions and solutions adopted at that time. They are the source of Ukraine's strengths, and also of its weaknesses, at the present stage of its history.

## The Way to Independence

Ukraine won its independence owing to a combination or coalescence of two factors. First, there were external, "objective" conditions on which the Ukrainians depended, but which they influenced only to a limited degree. In 1991 those conditions, or circumstances, included a major political crisis in Moscow; the rise of other non-Russian nations, especially the Balts; and the establishment of formal Russian-Ukrainian relations before the August 1991 crisis. It was very important, too, that at that particular historical juncture democratic nationalists in Russia were defining the Russian national agenda in opposition to the defenders of the imperial Soviet "center" and also against extreme nationalists of the right.

Second, there was the domestic or internal scene; in other words, that "subjective" factor for which the Ukrainians themselves were primarily responsible. As we shall argue below, the Ukrainians seized the arising opportunities, some of which they did not create themselves. They mobilized their forces and built coalitions between former rivals and in the end attained their goal of national independence without having to fight for it against outside forces, and without experiencing a civil war or unrest.

The August 1991 coup would not have ended so fast, or it might even have succeeded, had there not emerged, earlier, a conflict between the Russian Federation, led by Boris N. Yeltsin, and the government of the Soviet Union, personified by President Mikhail S. Gorbachev. This conflict reflected the Russian nation's rejection of communism and by extension—or so it looked in 1991—its desire to abandon the idea that Russia had to be an empire. But the split between Russia and the USSR—"Russia's secession from the Soviet Union," as some put it—also had a personal dimension, which took the form of a struggle between two leaders for power. Many observers, especially in the West, did not notice that the contenders did not fight for the same job: they represented two different political entities—Russia versus the Soviet Union. Thus it was a triple confrontation: Yeltsin versus Gorbachev; democracy against communism; and the national liberation of Russia against the "center" or empire. There were reasons to believe that the Russians wanted to build their own nation-state, to make Russia a "normal" country, thus breaking once and for all with the old nationalist myth that for the Russian people a multinational empire was the only acceptable home.[1]

But the August coup, although an "external" factor for Ukraine, was connected to what was going on in Ukraine. The plot had been hatched by diehard Communists as a response to what they saw as a gradual subversion of the Soviet Union that had begun in the late 1980s. In their view, Ukraine played a major part in that subversion of the Soviet state. Indeed, the Ukrainian republic played a role in 1991, when, in June, its parliament decided that Ukraine would not sign the Union treaty on August 20, 1991. The coup organizers rightly viewed the Ukrainian decision for what it was: it amounted to Ukraine's de facto withdrawal from the Union. As some plot leaders have since admitted, Ukraine's June decision was on their minds when they decided to act.

But this decision had its antecedents. There is no room in this brief summary for an account of those developments in Ukraine prior to 1991, especially in the Gorbachev era, that made Ukraine capable of doing what it did in August-December 1991. The Chernobyl nuclear accident created that intellectual and psychological climate in which it would be possible to think about a break with Moscow. The rise of Rukh, in 1989, and the fact that Kiev party leaders allowed Rukh's founding congress to be held in Kiev (Rukh's Belorussian counterpart held its first congress in Lithuania) inaugurated the demonopolization of the public discourse. Leonid M. Kravchuk, in his role as party ideology chief, engaged Rukh in public debate, allowing his opponents access to television. That he spoke against Rukh mattered less in the long run than that in this manner he made Rukh a legitimate part of the political scene.

Then there was also the parliamentary election of March 1990, which sent about one hundred noncommunist representatives to Kiev. Very different people met face to face in the halls of the parliament—including former prisoners and their former persecutors. In local elections, the opposition, led by Rukh, won overwhelmingly in west Ukraine, and something resembling a formal and peaceful transfer of power from Communist to national-democratic hands did take place on the provincial level in Lviv and several other western regions.

Following Russia's declaration of sovereignty in June 1990, the Ukrainian parliament adopted its own declaration to the same effect. It envisioned Ukraine's neutrality and spoke about Ukraine's right to have its own military. The declaration publicized the concept of "the people of Ukraine" as an entity embracing all of its citizens, without regard to ethnic or religious affiliation. Early in 1991, the Kiev parliament in fact sabotaged Gorbachev's referendum regarding the Union by adding a specific "Ukrainian" question about Ukraine's sovereignty. For Ukrainian nation building, these were significant actions. For the first time in its history, Ukraine had a parliament in which were represented, however imperfectly, all of its regions. East met west, Communists sat in one hall with anticommunists, and nationalist poets learned to talk politics with party officials and plant managers. Ukraine was getting its first lesson in noncommunist politics and was beginning to create rudiments of a tolerant and pluralistic political culture. For the national self-esteem of the newly independent Ukrainians, it was a source of satisfaction that their independence was also a result of their choices and actions. At the final stage of Ukraine's march to independence, the national-democratic opposition in the parliament managed to reach an accord with important segments of the Soviet Ukrainian establishment on how Ukraine should respond to the events in Moscow on August 19 and after, even though such a decision was not easy to make, considering the Communists' record.

The Ukrainians knew that there was a fundamental difference between the situation in Moscow and that in Kiev. In Moscow, opponents of the coup could and did raise the national flag of Russia against the communist center. They brought that flag with them as they talked to the troops, appealing to their Russian patriotism. But what worked in Moscow would have brought a disaster in Kiev. Those who criticize Leonid M. Kravchuk, or the Kiev establishment in general, for their alleged "wait and see" position at the time when

Yeltsin actively opposed the coup forget one essential thing. If the Ukrainians in Kiev had imitated the Russians in Moscow by appealing to the Soviet army in Ukraine in the name of *Ukraine's* freedom, they would have assured the army's prompt and decisive intervention in favor of the coup. It was one thing to ask the army in Moscow to liberate Russia from communism, and quite another to ask it in Kiev to liberate Ukraine from communism and from Russia: in Ukraine communism and Russia were one and the same thing.

On August 24, 1991, Ukraine's supreme soviet, or Rada, adopted a declaration of independence by an overwhelming vote, even though the parliament had a Communist majority. The forces of national democratic opposition and their Communist opponents proved capable of agreeing on Ukraine's break with Moscow. This called for a willingness to compromise on both sides. One last-minute deal provided that the question of independence would be submitted to a popular vote on December 1. (Also on December 1 Ukraine elected its first president in a contested and free election.) The subsequent popular vote was overwhelmingly for independence. By the end of December, there was no Soviet Union anymore.[2]

But Kravchuk and his friends remembered what it was that had forced them to act differently from Yeltsin during the coup. A decision was made, within days after the coup, to establish a Ukrainian armed force. High-ranking officers serving in the Soviet military in Ukraine agreed to undertake the task of creating a Ukrainian army, navy, and air force. The winning over of the military (and, one may presume, of key elements of the police) was a landmark step, after the accord between the opposition and the proindependence Communists, on Ukraine's march to independence.

### Setting Priorities

The Ukrainian case offers an interesting perspective on what Barry R. Posen calls "a problem of 'emerging anarchy' " that arises, he argues, after the collapse of empires. Posen writes:

The longest standing and most useful school of international relations theory—realism—explicitly addresses the consequences of anarchy—the absence of a sovereign—for political relations among states. In areas such as the former Soviet Union and Yugoslavia, "sovereigns" have disappeared. They leave in their wake a host of groups—ethnic, religious, cultural—of greater or lesser cohesion. These groups must pay attention to the first thing that states have historically addressed—the problem of security—even though many of these groups still lack many of the attributes of statehood.[3]

Posen agrees with the view of "realist theory," according to which "the condition of anarchy makes security the first concern of states. It can be otherwise only if these political organizations do not care about their survival as independent entities. As long as some do care, there will be competition for the key to security—power."[4]

These propositions were understood in Kiev in 1991. Posen's specific comments, however, require modification with reference to Ukraine. First, new sovereigns in the republics preceded the demise of the "sovereign" in Moscow, and by their very rise they directly contributed to that outcome. Second, Ukraine was a political entity, not something being organized by and for an ethnic group. The concept of a "people of Ukraine" was civic and territorial, not linguistic or ethnic. However, Posen's point that "security" must be "the first concern of states" if they want to survive helps us to appreciate properly the centrality—and propriety—of Kiev's decision to create its own army at once.

That decision changed Ukrainian politics, which until then had been the domain of poets and professors on the one side, and of party *apparatchiks*, industrial managers, and bureaucrats on the other. Ukraine's relations with Moscow were transformed as well.

In light of the facts mentioned here it is hard to accept the statement that "Soviet totalitarianism," and with it the USSR, just decayed and collapsed and that Ukraine was practically handed its independence.[5]

There was nothing predetermined in what transpired in Kiev during or after the collapse. Rather, an unprecedented historical situation did emerge, and within it was contained, among many possible outcomes, the theoretical possibility that Ukraine might become an independent state—provided, that is, that people on the spot, in Ukraine, saw that potentiality and were willing and able to make the potential real. It took more than Soviet collapse, for example, to induce active-duty Soviet generals to organize, in open defiance of their military superiors, a Ukrainian army.[6]

In assessing the contributions to nation building in Ukraine stemming from the events of 1991 and those preceding, it must be recalled that post-Soviet Ukraine was not an entirely new entity, one based on an ethnic, religious, or cultural group, but a state that claimed to be the legal continuation of the Ukrainian Soviet Republic. As noted above, it defined "the people of Ukraine" in legal and civic terms.

Ukraine's withdrawal from the USSR was carried out by constitutional bodies of the Soviet republic, thereby securing acceptance of the new state's independence by Soviet loyalists while preventing the rise of rival claimants to power from among opponents of communism. Thus the actions of political actors of all persuasions made it possible to avoid a civil war between "Sovietists" and nationalists, between ethnic groups, or between regions. There was no war with Russia or "the center."

### The Challenge of Nation Building

Ukraine's independence was a most impressive accomplishment, but it created only the foundation for the task of restructuring and reforming Ukraine's economy, creating a modern state machinery, building democratic institutions, and developing extensive relations with the outside world.

At best, Ukraine was and remains a "protodemocracy."[7] Those who knew how to make Ukraine independent were not best qualified to guide it afterwards. Their strengths—as "insiders" in Soviet politics—became handicaps after the end of the Soviet Union. Ukraine's nation building requires the emergence of new leaders and activists, especially from among the young.

Neglect, or rather faulty diagnosis and consequent mishandling, of the critical economic issues, besides being destructive economically, may subvert a key element of the Ukrainian nation-building project. Many of those voting for Ukraine's independence in 1991 did so for economic reasons. To retain their loyalty it was imperative to prove they had been right to vote for Ukraine.

It is a gross oversimplification to speak of the Russians or Russian-speaking people in Ukraine as a single ethnic or national bloc. Many Ukrainian patriots, including some major figures in the events of 1991 and after, have been Russian by ethnic identity or Russian-speaking non-Russians. Ukraine's progress in building a culturally plural civil society depends on its retaining the loyalty of the Russian element, and especially in forestalling that element's politicization as an ethnic minority. This would be an especially dangerous development because it might lead to a territorial breakdown of Ukraine along Yugoslavian lines.

This essay argues that Russia played a crucial role in the collapse of the Soviet Union. One might have expected that after August 1991 the relations between the two large Slavic successor states would be, if not harmonious, then at least good. This did not occur. Virtually overnight, within one week of Ukraine's independence declaration, a spokesman for the Russian president raised the possibility of Russian territorial claims on Ukraine and Kazakhstan.[8]

Among the issues of discord, the nuclear weapons question acquired an extraordinary prominence, largely for symbolic reasons, although the consequences of the dispute, and especially of Ukraine's stand in it, have been much worse than merely symbolic. In a period of growing tensions between Moscow and Kiev, the same author who rather optimistically described Ukraine's "quiet secession" in the summer of 1991 openly worried in March 1992 about "how to keep divorce from leading to war."[9] What went wrong?

Looking for more immediate explanations, one may point to a change in the correlation of forces in Russian politics and the adoption of a nationalist agenda by some democratic politicians. Whether under pressure from the military and other imperially minded circles or out of their own conviction, many politicians in Moscow appear to have adopted imperial restoration as a goal taking precedence over nation building within the Russian Federation. In August 1991 it looked as if nation-builders had defeated the empire-savers in the struggle over the definition of Russia.[10] Boris Yeltsin was their leader. Things have changed since then, and the election of December 12, 1993, made Russian politics even more complicated.

Like Ukraine, Russia is led by the old Soviet-descended elites, even though their democratic credentials enjoy more credence in the West. Those elites, especially in the military, are pursuing the goal of empire-restoration. That course is camouflaged in the meantime by politicians and journalists who invoke the rights of "Russian speakers" in the Near Abroad as a justification for Moscow's pressure or even direct intervention. More candid commentators admit that for some people the only way properly to secure the rights of the Russians outside the Russian Federation is to bring those republics back into the Empire.[11]

If such views become dominant, this will not bode well for the future of Ukrainian-Russian relations and will be especially dangerous for Ukraine's internal stability. (Crimea is on the current agenda.) What is the 14th Army, now stationed in the so-called Dniester Republic, really for? Is it perhaps preparing to engage in a "peacekeeping" mission somewhere in Ukraine, say Odessa, when an opportune moment comes?[12]

## What Is to Be Done?

Obviously Ukraine needs to develop, and then follow resolutely, a comprehensive program of economic, social, cultural, and political development. The country finally may be adopting such a program in the aftermath of the election of Leonid D. Kuchma as president in July 1994. In October, about a hundred days after entering office, Kuchma put forward a radical program of reform that permits private ownership of land. Kuchma's program enjoys the support of the International Monetary Fund. At the G-7 meeting in Winnipeg, Canada, in October 1994, the leading Western democracies pledged support for market-oriented reforms in Ukraine. The meeting was attended by an uninvited participant, Russian foreign minister Andrei Kozyrev, who declared Russia's "solidarity" with Ukraine while pressing "Russia's case for a role in Ukraine's economic reform." [13]

At home, Kuchma's plan was received very favorably by many of those who had opposed him in the presidential election. While remaining faithful to his commitment to seek good and close ties with Russia, Kuchma takes great care to declare himself unequivocally an advocate of Ukraine's independence. He has made it clear there would be no return to an unequal relationship between Russia and Ukraine. Although Western commentators at first viewed Kuchma's victory and Leonid Kravchuk's defeat as a sign of a deepening polarization of Ukraine along ethnic and linguistic lines, just the opposite seems to have happened. The involvement of areas such as Crimea, Donetsk, and Luhansk in the electoral process not only secured Kuchma's victory, but also legitimized Ukrainian statehood where it had been least popular.

The future of Ukrainian reform, and of the survival of the Ukrainian state itself, will depend heavily on the nature and extent of Western aid. It is especially important for Ukraine's security that the country should develop ties with other nations, especially its Western neighbors. Ukraine's nation building will be accelerated by such ties. There are signs that some nations, especially Poland, whose role in Ukrainian history is comparable to that of Russia, are disposed favorably towards such ties.[14]

Russia will obviously remain the central issue. Ukraine cannot influence Russia's domestic agenda, but it can work to promote the idea that an independent Ukraine does not need to be perceived as Russia's loss or defeat. But the Russians will need to give up, finally, some of their cherished myths about the precise nature of their historic relations with Ukraine. Of these the most misleading and politically dangerous is the idea that Ukraine had been attached to Russia for over three hundred years prior to its "secession" in 1991. This idea is encapsulated in the so-called Pereiaslav myth, which views the year 1654 as the date of Ukraine's incorporation into Russia. Needless to say, this myth is factually wrong. Most of present-day Ukraine has been under Russian control only since the late eighteenth century. Some key areas became Soviet, without ever having been under Russia, during or after World War II. Nevertheless, the Pereiaslav idea serves as a justification of current policies directed against Ukraine's status as a sovereign nation.[15]

Moscow needs to accept the legitimacy of Ukrainian independence. The disintegration of the USSR and the rise of new states has transformed the national identities of their peoples. Russian politicians need to understand that even if it proves within their capacity to restore their dominion over the old Soviet republics, they and the Russian people will pay a heavy price for it.

An independent Ukraine, if it survives, will mark one of the most revolutionary changes on the political map of East Europe, comparable in its impact on the whole region to the restoration of an independent Poland in 1918, or to Poland's partitions in the late eighteenth century, or to Russia's conquest of the northern coast of the Black Sea in the same century. If good relations between Ukraine and Russia are established, they will facilitate democratic nation building in both countries. There are signs that the younger generation of Russians is more ready to accept the Russian Federation as its country and no longer considers Ukraine to be a part of Russia. If that view prevails, and if Ukrainians do not develop anti-Russian sentiments, prospects for Ukrainian-Russian cooperation will improve.

Also improved will be the prospects for democracy in Russia. Since 1991 independent Ukraine has become a normal condition for millions of Ukrainians, especially the young. However critical they may be of their situation or of the politics of their government, they do not wish to "return" to Russia. Educated young people appreciate Ukraine's unprecedented opening to the world at large, which they correctly attribute to Kiev's transformation into the capital of an independent country. Any attempt by Russia to bring Kiev, or Ukraine as a whole, back under Moscow's control would meet with fierce resistance; a Russian-Ukrainian war, whatever its outcome, would doom democracy in Russia as well as in Ukraine.[16]

## Notes

1. For an analysis of Russian politics during and after the fall of communism see John B. Dunlop, *The Rise of Russia and the Fall of the Soviet Empire* (Princeton, N.J.: Princeton University Press, 1993).

2. Bohdan Krawchenko, "Ukraine: The Politics of Independence," in *Nation and Politics in the Soviet Successor States*, ed. Ian Bremmer and Ray Taras (Cambridge: Cambridge University Press, 1993), 75-98.

3. Barry R. Posen, "The Security Dilemma and Ethnic Conflict," *Survival* 35, 1 (Spring 1993): 27-47.

4. Posen, "Security Dilemma," 28.

5. Alexander J. Motyl, *Dilemmas of Independence: Ukraine after Totalitarianism* (New York: Council on Foreign Relations, 1993), 23-24.

6. Bohdan Pyskir, "The Silent Coup," *European Security* 2, 1 (Spring 1993): 139-161; Valeriy Izmalkov, "Ukraine and Her Armed Forces," *European Security* 2, 2 (Summer 1993): 279-319. See also Bohdan Pyskir, "Mothers for a Fatherland: Ukrainian Statehood, Motherhood, and National Security," *Journal of Slavic Military Studies* 7, 1 (March 1994): 50-66.

7. Timothy J. Colton, "Politics," in *After the Soviet Union: From Empire to Nations,* ed. Timothy J. Colton and Robert Legvold (New York: W. W. Norton, 1992), 17-48.

8. For a close scrutiny of the complexities of Russo-Ukrainian relations under and after communism see Roman Solchanyk, "Ukraine, The (Former) Center, Russia, and 'Russia,' " *Studies in Comparative Communism* 25, 1 (March 1992): 31-45.

9. Strobe Talbott, "The Quiet Secession of a Large Country," *Time*, July 1, 1991, 45; "How to Keep Divorce from Leading to War," *Time*, March 2, 1992, 34.

10. For an elucidation of these concepts, see Roman Szporluk, "Dilemmas of Russian Nationalism," *Problems of Communism* 38, 4 (July-August 1989): 15-35. Reprinted in Rachel Denber, ed., *The Soviet Nationality Reader: The Disintegration in Context* (Boulder, Colo.: Westview Press, 1992), 509-543.

11. Leonid Mlechen, "Russkii vopros v rossiiskoi politike 1994 goda," *Izvestia*, January 4, 1994.

12. Karen Dawisha and Bruce Parrott, *Russia and the New States of Eurasia: The Politics of Upheaval* (Cambridge: Cambridge University Press, 1994), 42-43, 299-307, and passim; and Daria Fane, "Moldova: Breaking Loose from Moscow," in *Nation and Politics in the Soviet Successor States*, ed. Ian Bremmer and Ray Taras (Cambridge: Cambridge University Press, 1993), 121-153.

13. Margaret Truehart, "Russia Tells International Lenders It Wants Share of Aid to Ukraine: Moscow Foreign Minister Shows Up at Conference Uninvited," *Washington Post*, October 28, 1994, A35. See also Clyde Farnsworth, "Ukraine Wins Pledges of Support at Canadian Summit," *New York Times*, October 28, 1994, A7.

14. Ian J. Brzezinski, "Polish-Ukrainian Relations: Europe's Neglected Strategic Axis," *Survival* 35, 3 (Autumn 1993), 26-37; Stephen R. Burant, "International Relations in a Regional Context: Poland and Its Eastern Neighbors, Lithuania, Belarus, Ukraine," *Europe-Asia Studies* 45, 3 (1993): 395-418; Ilya Prizel, "The Influence of Ethnicity on Foreign Policy: Case of Ukraine," in *National Identity and Ethnicity in Russia and the New States of Eurasia*, ed. Roman Szporluk (Armonk, N.Y.: M. E. Sharpe, 1994), 103-129.

15. John Morrison, "Pereyaslav and After: The Russian-Ukrainian Relationship," *International Affairs* 69, 4 (October 1993): 677-703. The idea that since Ukraine had been a part of Russia for about 350 years it might "return" to Russia now, after having proved incapable of reforming its own economy, was presented by Eugene B. Rumer, "Eurasia Letter: Will Ukraine Return to Russia?" *Foreign Policy*, no. 96 (Fall 1994): 129-144. In fact, only a small part of Ukraine was ruled by the Russian czar after 1654, and it was not until after the partitions of Poland in 1793-1795 that a majority of Ukrainians found themselves under Russian rule. For details, see my letter to the editor of *Foreign Policy*, no. 97 (Winter 1995, forthcoming).

16. For recent assessments of the Ukrainian situation, see Roman Szporluk, "Reflections on Ukraine after 1994: The Dilemmas of Nationhood," *The Harriman Review*

7, 7/9 (March-May 1994): 1-10; Taras Kuzio and Andrew Wilson, *Ukraine: Perestroika to Independence* (Edmonton: Canadian Institute of Ukrainian Studies, 1994); Alexander J. Motyl, "Will Ukraine Survive 1994?" *The Harriman Institute Forum* 7, 5 (January 1994): 3-6; Roman Solchanyk, "The Politics of State Building: Centre-Periphery Relations in Post-Soviet Ukraine," *Europe-Asia Studies* 46, 1 (1994): 47-68; Peter van Ham, *Ukraine, Russia, and European Security: Implications for Western Policy*, Chaillot paper no. 13 (Paris: Institute for Security Studies, Western European Union, 1994); and Frank Umbach, "Russia and the Problems of Ukraine's Cohesion: Results of a Fact-Finding Mission," *Berichte des Bundesinstituts für ostwissentschaftliche und internationale Studien*, no. 13 (Cologne: Bundesinstitut für ostwissentschaftliche und internationale Studien, 1994).

# 14 Imperial Disintegration and Nation-State Formation: The Case of Ukraine

Orest Subtelny

The collapse of empires and the concurrent emergence of nation-states is a familiar phenomenon in the twentieth century. It occurred after World War I when the fall of the Romanov, Hapsburg, and Ottoman empires led to the rise of Poland, Czechoslovakia, the Baltic countries, Finland, and Turkey. Another wave of imperial disintegrations followed World War II as the British, French, and other Europe-centered empires broke up, giving rise to the states that comprise much of the Third World. Finally, as the Cold War ended, the last of the empires, the USSR, passed into oblivion, leaving in its wake fifteen nation-states.

Viewing the USSR in terms of empire, once the height of political incorrectness, is now a generally accepted practice. And one of the reasons for this is that the Soviet Union disintegrated into nation-states, just the way other twentieth-century empires did. Thus, the thinking goes, if it died like an empire, it must have been an empire. The implications of this imperial perspective on the USSR are vast. If the USSR was an empire, then when did it become one? If one concludes that this occurred when the Bolsheviks reassembled, by force, much of the former tsarist empire, then the Bolshevik revolution was—in addition to whatever else it might have been—also a *restoratio imperii.* This would indicate that traditionalist, that is, Russian imperialist, elements in Bolshevik thinking and practice were much more prevalent than has been commonly acknowledged by Sovietologists.[1] Certainly this reconstitution of a collapsed empire was a most uncommon feat. It meant that the Russian-based empire was the only one in the twentieth century that was resurrected, albeit in a radically different form. But in 1991 history caught up with the restored empire and it met the fate that had been postponed for over seventy years.

Obviously the imperial model cannot replace the view of the Soviet state as the great experiment in the radical restructuring of society. It can, however, complement it by accentuating the Soviet Union's Janus-like nature, one which encompassed both innovative (Soviet) and traditionalist (imperial) elements. One might even argue that it was the irreconcilable tensions between the innovative and the traditionalist aspects that were ultimately responsible for the failure of the Soviet experiment. In any case, both in terms of its origin and form the USSR occupied a unique place among twentieth century empires. Such a conclusion invites another question: If the USSR was a unique type of empire, then do not its successor states possess unique features that set them off as a group from the postimperial states formed after World War I and World War II?

To address this question, one can apply the case-study approach. By focusing attention on one of the Soviet successor states, it should be possible to isolate more effectively the distinguishing features of its transformation from imperial province to independent state. And given the many similarities among all the post-Soviet states, it is likely that what applies to one post-Soviet state will also apply, to a greater or lesser degree, to the others. Primarily because it lies within my area of expertise, I have chosen to make Ukraine the object of this exercise.

### The Missing Liberation Struggle

An important feature of the new Ukrainian state is striking due to its absence: the new state arose without a national liberation struggle. In the history of postimperial nation-state formation, this is most unusual. For example, the emergence of the Polish, Estonian, Latvian, Lithuanian, and Czechoslovak states from the ruins of empire was accompanied by military conflicts of varying scope and intensity. The same is true for most of the Third World states that emerged from the British, French, and Portuguese empires. But Ukraine has avoided such conflicts, which means that the "heroic period"—a time of common effort, struggle, and sacrifice (real or perceived) that normally looms large in the history of all nation-states—is missing. As a result, Ukraine will find it difficult to mold an inspiring "founding myth" that is a standard feature of new state formations.

The lack of a heroic period also means the absence of the heroes and martyrs that are invariably associated with the rise of new nation-states. Even the most assiduous manipulators of history will be in a quandary about casting Leonid Kravchuk in a patriarchal, "father of his people" role. A clever and flexible politician, he is best known for his adroit leap from the sinking ship of communism to the bandwagon of nationalism. But this hardly qualifies as a feat of heroism. It is a generally held opinion in Ukraine that altruism, even patriotism, are also very rare characteristics among the Ukrainian leadership.[2]

For a time it seemed that former dissidents, who had spent years in the gulags for the Ukrainian cause and had been prominent in the drive for independence, might attain the status of national heroes. However, most of them chose to cooperate with the refurbished Communist establishment—in order to gain its support for independence, they would argue—and were, to greater or lesser extent, coopted by it. As they obtained positions of power and privilege, the former dissidents lost their claim to hero status. Because more was expected of them, popular disillusionment with the former dissidents was even greater than with the former Communists.

Another gap in the ideological arsenal of the new Ukrainian state is the lack of well-defined enemies. True, relations with Russia are tense.[3] And, in historical terms, Russia is often mentioned as the foremost enemy of Ukrainian statehood. But for a variety of reasons, the Ukrainian government, media, and educational system are loath to identify Russia as a perennial enemy. Such statements would alienate the eleven million Russians in Ukraine. They would also not sit well with the eastern Ukrainians among whom intermarriage with Russians is widespread and whose contacts with Russia are centuries old.[4] Moreover there is no history of bitter Ukrainian-Russian ethnic conflicts. Finally, it is simply not politic to irritate the big northern neighbor who controls Ukraine's energy supplies. Consequently, Ukraine's only potential enemy cannot be identified as such. A reflection of this unusual dilemma is the difficulties that Ukraine's parliament and military planners have had in attempting to discuss potential security problems without specifically mentioning Russia.[5]

This is not to say that Ukraine need bemoan the fact that it has no explicitly defined enemies. If that, in fact, were the case, Ukraine would be fortunate indeed. The point is, however, that most new nation-states have real or perceived enemies and the possibility of a confrontation with these enemies usually helps to develop a sense of solidarity and common purpose among their citizens. But Ukraine must do without this type of negative reinforcement for statehood.

Perhaps the most concrete consequences of the absent "national-liberation struggle" are related to cadres.[6] Usually the builders of new nation-states have been the people who fought for it. From their ranks came the statesmen, military officers, bureaucrats, and teachers who were crucial to the state-building process. Participation in the liberation struggle not only propelled the veterans into positions of leadership but also gave them a moral right to demand sacrifices of their fellow citizens. The role played by the Polish and Czech legionnaires during the interwar period is a case in point. Such a cohort of committed state-builders is also sorely missing in Ukraine.[7]

Lacking these standard accoutrements of emergent statehood, the Ukrainian state has been unable to evoke enthusiasm for independence. This is especially evident in the eastern regions of Ukraine where national consciousness is much weaker than in the west. Although 90 percent of the land's inhabitants voted for independence in 1991, in eastern Ukraine, and especially among its Russian population, this vote reflected primarily pragmatic considerations. Many of eastern Ukraine's inhabitants were led to believe that an independent Ukraine would be a rich Ukraine, one in which their standard of living would rise. Independence, as such, did not excite them. This was underscored in the generally phlegmatic reaction with which crowds in most major Ukrainian cities greeted the overwhelming vote for independence. On this historic occasion the predominant attitude was not one of achievement but of waiting to see what material benefits independence would bring.[8]

When the economic situation turned for the worse, support for independence waned, especially in the east. And the leadership, which provided few examples of sacrifice for or genuine commitment to the new state, was not in a position to place demands on its citizens. In fact, it had practically no recourse to the standard rationalizations that a nation-state normally utilizes to raise the morale of a disgruntled citizenry. Thus, while Ukrainians can be grateful that they have been able to avoid conflicts, they must also realize that their good fortune is not without political and ideological ramifications.

## The Holdover Effect

In terms of institutions and leadership, the new Ukraine has very little that is new about it. Indeed, never has an emergent postimperial state retained so many elements of the previous, imperial regime. To a large extent this can be explained by the pseudo-federal system that existed in the USSR. While it allowed the republics practically no autonomy, it did provide them, as a kind of consolation prize, with the forms and institutions of statehood. Thus, Ukraine had its own parliamentary bodies, state ministries, and even a seat in the United Nations. Therefore, when Ukraine declared independence, it already possessed a ready-made state. Certain elements, such as the army and diplomatic corps, had to be added, but, by and large, Ukraine's leaders had much less state-building to do than one normally expects in a newly emergent state. The problem that confronted Ukraine's leaders was to make what looked like a state function like one. They had to become accustomed to decision making and take responsibility for the welfare of the state's citizens. This required of the former provincial elite a radical political, ideological, and psychological transformation which, to date, it has had great difficulty in making.

Ukraine's inheritance from the Soviet system includes more than state structures. Although nineteenth-century Ukrainian scholars delineated the somewhat vague Ukrainian ethnographic limits, it was the Soviets who established the land's current borders. In 1918, when local anti-Ukrainian Bolsheviks attempted to create a separate Donets-Kryvyi Rih Soviet republic, Lenin, intent on winning over the Ukrainians, insisted that the region remain a part of Soviet Ukraine.[9] As a result of the Soviet victory in World War II, Stalin detached Ukrainian-inhabited lands from Poland, Hungary, and Romania and incorporated them into Soviet Ukraine, thereby uniting all Ukrainians for the first time within the boundaries of a single state. And, for some still unclarified reason, Khrushchev attached the Crimea to Ukraine in 1954. Given their weakness in 1917-1920, it is extremely doubtful whether Ukrainian nationalist forces could have ever been as effective in maintaining and expanding Ukraine's borders as was the Soviet regime.

The retention of Soviet-era structures has meant that many of the people who manned these structures have also remained in place. Therefore the new nation-state emerged from the ruins of an empire with an unprecedentedly small turnover in personnel. For some Ukrainians, this was to be expected. As far back as the early 1920s, Viacheslav Lypynsky, an anti-Soviet émigré and the ideologue of Ukrainian monarchism and conservatism, argued that a Ukrainian state could not be created without including Ukraine's Communist elite in the process.[10] Ukraine simply had no other source of experienced bureaucrats and politicians. Similar views were espoused after World War II by another well-known émigré writer and former communist activist, Ivan Bahriany.[11]

The almost complete holdover of personnel has its ironies. One of them is that the leadership of the Ukrainian state is in the hands of people who only a short time before vehemently opposed the idea of national independence. Self-preservation was certainly a major factor in the Ukrainian political elite's hasty adoption of proindependence positions. With the Soviet system tottering, it had to embrace, or, to be more precise, coopt the concept of a national state or go down with the crumbling empire. Less frequently mentioned but certainly crucial to this transformation was the desire of the Kiev apparat to free itself of the Moscow's overlordship. Indeed, it is quite likely that many members of the

Ukrainian elite were more interested in attaining and maintaining exclusive control of Ukraine rather than achieving national independence as such. Thus, the events of 1991 might be viewed as a liberation of a regional elite from central control as much as, or perhaps more than, the liberation of a nation from an imperial yoke.

The power grab by the Ukrainian regional elite was carried out under the cover of classic nationalist rhetoric and agitation. The Kiev intelligentsia, the Rukh movement, and the largely west Ukrainian activists, motivated largely by traditional nationalist sentiments and principles, created the slogans, the demonstrations, and the organizations that raised the call for independence. The new state that emerged seemed to be the product of a typical mass-based nationalist drive for self-determination. But independence also coincided with the much more pragmatic interests of the Ukrainian apparat, or, more precisely, its more flexible elements. And it was the apparat, utilizing nationalist argumentation, that actually uncoupled Ukraine from the empire and retained control of the newly independent state. Today the people who carried out this successful operation are often referred to as the "party of power."

The Western media delights in noting Leonid Kravchuk's sudden and well-timed conversion from communism to nationalism. Similar comments are frequently made about many of Ukraine's current leaders. However, such statements are misleading: they ascribe to Ukraine's elite a much greater degree of nationalism than it actually possesses. Kravchuk has never called himself a nationalist, and there is reason to believe that this former Communist ideologue does not consider himself to be one.[12] As president, he rarely missed an occasion to emphasize that he was the leader of the people of Ukraine, not only of ethnic Ukrainians. Such a pluralistic, multicultural, and liberal approach is certainly praiseworthy, but it is not nationalism.

Certainly the current Ukrainian leadership does not identify itself with the integral Ukrainian nationalism of Dmytro Dontsov or Stepan Bandera, which was widespread in western Ukraine in the 1930-1940s. Nor do the speeches of Kravchuk, Prime Minister Leonid Kuchma, or parliamentary leader Ivan Pliushch evoke the relatively liberal nationalism of the 1917-1920 era. They rarely mention such nationalist shibboleths as national struggle, national goals, national sacrifice, or national mission. The lack of nationalist slogans is matched by the lack of nationalist policies. Little has been done on the issue of linguistic Ukrainization, a matter of burning concern to all Ukrainian nationalists.[13] Kiev's response to separatism, most notably in Crimea, has been astonishingly lackadaisical. And in the confrontation with Russia over the Black Sea fleet, Kiev has retreated, greatly infuriating the nationalists.

Even Rukh, the popular movement that led the drive for independence and that constituted the national-democratic opposition to the Kravchuk government until the March 1994 elections, has kept its distance from Ukrainian ethno-nationalism. From the outset, it stressed that it was a multiethnic movement that united all those who supported democratic reforms in Ukraine. Especially in early stages, its ranks included a significant number of Russians, Jews, Tatars, and other nationalities. It appears that the Soviet regime's harsh, systematic repression of nationalism, which lasted for generations, has had an effect. Consciously or unconsciously, many Ukrainians, and especially the former *nomenklatura*, are wary of identifying themselves with nationalism.

But the practical absence of nationalist influence among Ukraine's political elite does not mean that it consists of closet communists. On this point the "party of power" was adamant, repeatedly stressing that its break with communism was complete and irreversible. Considering the bitter criticism that the Kravchuk government received from communist loyalists, it appears that one can accept their rejection of communism at face value. The comments of Leonid Kuchma to the effect that "there is no going back to the Soviet Union" indicate that the same holds true for Ukraine's new president.[14]

If Ukraine's leaders are neither nationalists nor communists, what are they? In all probability they are people who have no clear-cut ideological commitments and whose decision making is guided by simple pragmatism. This nonideological stance is hardly surprising. On the one hand, it can be explained as a reaction to the heavy Soviet emphasis on ideology in general. On the other hand, it reflects the generally nonideological climate of our times. Nonetheless, the absence of a guiding ideology is a striking feature of Ukrainian statehood because it stands in sharp contrast to the all-important role that ideology has played in the formation of all nation-states in the previous periods.

The ideological vacuum in Ukraine has a positive aspect. Because of it, political confrontations in the country have been relatively mild. If it were otherwise, if nationalists and communists were as fanatically committed to their causes as they were a generation or two earlier, Ukraine could easily have become a scene of ferocious fratricidal conflicts. But there is also a negative aspect to the situation. Because Ukraine's leaders have no ideological orientation points, they lack a sense of direction. They are unable to explain to themselves and to the people what they are trying to achieve. In short, they lack a vision of the type of state and society they would like to create from the rubble of the

Soviet system. And this raises the question of whether a vast undertaking such as this can be completed successfully without some sort of ideological guidelines.

Obviously, ideologically committed groups do exist in Ukraine. In the western regions, there are vocal organizations of the integral-nationalist type, and nationalist traditions are widespread among the population. In the eastern regions, especially in Donetsk, the Communist party has been resurrected. It even garnered a sizable portion of the protest vote in the March 1994 elections.[15] Nonetheless, both extreme nationalists and communists have not yet had a decisive influence on policy in the new Ukrainian state.[16]

What, then, can serve as the focus of political loyalty in Ukraine? Judging from their speeches, it seemed as if Kravchuk and his associates wanted it to be the state as such, and an ideologically neutral one at that. Indications of this preference were already perceptible in the referendum on independence in December of 1991. As was noted above, the argument for independence that the government-controlled media repeated most often and with greatest effect was that independence would assure "rich Ukraine" of a higher standard of living than it had had under the exploitative rule of Moscow. This was a pragmatic, nonideological argument that was meant to appeal to Ukrainians and non-Ukrainians, leftists and rightists. It goal was to unite a variegated populace, not to divide it. And since attaining independence, the Kiev leadership has continued to stress state interests and state-building, as opposed to national interests and nation-building. Today, on the eve of elections, one repeatedly hears in the media, in electoral campaign speeches, in daily conversations, that candidates for office need not be committed nationalists or communists but that they should be professionals, skilled in running the state. It appears that statism was as close as Ukraine's "party of power" came to having an ideology.

### The Ties That Bind

In socioeconomic terms, the nation-states that arose after the two world wars had a crucial feature in common: they were, to a greater or lesser extent, agrarian societies. Most of their populations lived in self-sufficient villages that produced enough to satisfy their basic needs. The industries that did exist, except, perhaps, for those in the Czech lands, were not large or complex. Nor were they wholly dependent on external resources and markets. And because the economies of the new states were relatively undeveloped, the economic repercussions of imperial collapse in the post-World War I and post-World War II eras were not as traumatic as they have been in the post-Soviet states.

When Ukraine acquired independence, it had a huge, if unbalanced and antiquated, industrial base which employed about two-thirds of its population. Its economy was, and continues to be, linked with other components of the former USSR in basic and countless ways. (By way of analogy, this economic relationship is similar to that of the Great Lakes region of the United States, which is a primary agricultural and industrial producer to the country as a whole.) In fact, the Soviet economic system was purposely designed so that the republics would be economically interdependent. A well-known example of this built-in economic interdependence is Ukraine's dependence on Russia for 90 percent of its energy requirements and its export of about 80 percent of its GNP to its northern neighbor.

Under these circumstances, an attempt by any former republic to alter its relationship with the rest of the former Soviet economic system will obviously have vast economic ramifications.[17] Due to its large size and heavy industrialization, this is especially true in the case of Ukraine. Even allowing for Ukraine's own exceedingly limited, inept, and haphazard attempts at economic restructuring, the chaos that resulted from the Soviet collapse and the shift of decision making to Kiev has produced a monumental economic disaster. Ukraine's industries have been cut off from sources of raw materials, crucial components for its products and traditional markets. Industrial production has plummeted. And inflation and financial disarray are rampant. Clearly the economic aspect of attaining independence in the post-Soviet age involves much greater problems and complexities than ever before.

Perhaps most devastating for the proponents of independence is that their main argument, that "rich" Ukraine would benefit economically from independence, has backfired. Instead of improving the standard of living of Ukraine's inhabitants, independence has been associated, in popular opinion, with its catastrophic decline. For the revitalized opponents of independence there are other economic considerations that appear to buttress their case. They stress that at a time when in Western Europe economic and political integration is well under way, it makes little sense for Ukraine to swim against the current and to seek to loosen its links with its "natural" economic and political partners. Proponents of independence counter that only independence will allow Ukraine to define its specific economic interests. Only after this is achieved can integration into a greater economic unit be considered.

Thus, independence remains a necessity, even in economic terms. Regardless of the merits of these arguments and counterarguments, it is clear that the focus of the discussion on independence is moving increasingly to an economic plane. And this primacy of economics is yet another unique feature of post-Soviet state formation.

Viewed broadly, the context in which Ukraine and the other post-Soviet states appeared—that of a collapsed empire and emergent nation-state—is a familiar one in the twentieth century. However, the fact that these new states arose from a specifically Soviet as well as a generally imperial system accounts for the key features that differentiate them from other postimperial states. None of the other empires were totalitarian. And it is Soviet totalitarianism that explains, to a large extent, the absence of a national liberation struggle in the formation of the new Ukrainian state. The extensive controls that a totalitarian regime can impose on its subjects make open resistance impossible. An essential element of totalitarianism, the one-party system, helps to account for the fact that the leadership of the new states was drawn primarily from former communists: it was they who had a monopoly on politically sophisticated and experienced cadres.

Because the Soviet empire was the only one which adamantly denied that it was an empire, it was constrained to create a pseudo-federal system. But the republics, which Lenin hoped would help the Soviets to finesse the "nationality issue," served instead as an invitingly convenient way of deconstructing the USSR and creating the successor states. Finally, the ideological vacuum. To a certain extent the present ideological vacuum is a reaction to the heavy emphasis on ideology in the Soviet Union. That communism has been discredited, especially among the younger generation, is obvious. Recent communist gains in the elections are seen by many as a transitory protest vote.[18] The relative weakness of nationalism among the leadership of the new states may be explained, at least in part, by seventy years of Soviet indoctrination that represented national sentiments as the most heinous of ideological crimes. Moreover, integrative trends throughout the world hardly encourage old-fashioned nationalism. There are, of course, exceptions, as in the case of the former Yugoslavia. But they are so striking exactly because they stand in contrast to the prevailing global tendencies. In any case, it is clear that compared to other nation-states which arose in twentieth century, the post-Soviet states possess a number of strikingly unusual features. The question is whether their future development will be equally unique.

This paper was completed in fall 1993.

## Notes

1. On the now widespread application of the imperial model to the USSR, see O. Subtelny, "American Sovietology's Greatest Blunder: The Marginalization of the Nationality Issue," *Nationalities Papers* 22, 1 (1994): 152-153.

2. See O. Vyshniak and V. Pylypenko, "Vlada i polityka v dzerkali hromadskoi dumky," *Geneza* 1,1 (1994): 226-230.

3. See R. Solchanyk, "Russia, Ukraine, and the Imperial Legacy," *Post-Soviet Affairs* 9, 4 (1993): 337-365; and C. F. Furtado, Jr., "Nationalism and Foreign Policy in Ukraine," *Political Science Quarterly* 109, 1 (1994): 81-104.

4. For an interesting discussion of how Ukrainians and Russians perceive each other see I. Bremmer, "The Politics of Ethnicity: Russians in the New Ukraine," *Europe-Asia Studies* 46, 2 (1994): 261-283.

5. See J. Jaworsky, "The Military-Strategic Significance of Recent Developments in Ukraine," project report no. 645, Department of National Defense, Ottawa, 1993; and S. Oliynyk, "The Emergence of the Post-Soviet Army: The Ukrainian Variant," *Military Review*, no. 3 (March 1994): 1-10. See also "Ukrainska viiskova doktryna," *Narodna armiia* (Kiev), October 26, 1993, 1.

6. For a discussion of Ukraine's "postcolonial elite" see A. Motyl, *Dilemmas of Independence: Ukraine after Totalitarianism* (New York: Council on Foreign Relations, 1993), 149-174. Also see K. Mihalisko, "Ukrainians and Their Leaders at a Time of Crisis," *RFE/RL Research Report*, no. 31, July 30, 1993, 54-62. Also see "Politychnyi protsesy i politychna elita," *Politychna dumka* 1, 1 (1993): 11-14; and Vyshniak and Pylypenko, "Vlada i polityka."

7. If the Ukrainians had succeeded in gaining independence in 1917-1920, such a cohort of state builders probably would have been formed by the sixty to seventy thousand veterans of the Ukrainian National Republic forces and the Ukrainian Galician army.

8. An analysis of the Ukrainian election and referendum results may be found in P. Potichnyj, "The Referendum and Presidential Elections in Ukraine," *Canadian Slavonic Papers* 35, 1-2 (1992): 123-137.

9. See Y. Bilinsky, "The Communist Takeover of the Ukraine," in *The Ukraine, 1917-1920: A Study in Revolution*, ed. T. Hunczak (Cambridge, Mass.: Harvard University Press, 1977), 113-114.

10. See I. L. Rudnytsky, "V. Lypynskyj's Political Ideas from the Perspective of Our Times," *Harvard Ukrainian Studies* 9, 3-4 (1985): 342-356.

11. See I. Bahriany, *Tak Trymaty* (Neu Ulm, 1972), 29-31.

12. An example of Kravchuk's views in the final days of the Soviet Union is his "Deiaki metodolohichni aspekty vykhovannia v umovakh perebudovy," *Ukrainskyi istorychnyi zhurnal* 12, 333 (December 1988): 5-18.

13. See D. Arel, "Voting Behaviour in the Ukrainian Parliament: The Language Factor," in *Parliaments in Transition*, ed. T. F. Remington (Boulder, Colo.: Westview, 1994), 124-158, and his "Language Politics in Independent Ukraine: Towards One or Two State Languages?" *Nationalities Papers* (forthcoming). Also see R. Solchanyk, "The Politics of Language in Ukraine," *RFE/RL Research Report* 2, 10 (March 1993): 1-4.

14. *Ukrainian Weekly* (Jersey City, N.J.), October 23, 1994, 1.

15. See D. Arel and A. Wilson, "The Ukrainian Elections: The Revenge of the East," unpublished manuscript. Also see V. Khmelko, "Druhi prezydentski vybory," *Ukraina*

*i svit* (Toronto), September 28, 1994, 12.

16. The blockage by Communists of many market-oriented reforms seems to be motivated more by the pragmatic interests of their supporters than by ideological conviction.

17. Estonia has demonstrated that such a relationship can be altered quickly and successfully. In 1991 more than 90 percent of its trade was with the republics of the former USSR. By 1994 more than 60 percent was with the countries of the European Union. *Economist*, November 19, 1994, 60.

18. See the results of polls conducted in Lviv, Kiev, and Odessa, reported in *Post-Postum* (Lviv-Kiev), June 10-16, 1994, 1.

# 15 Ukraine's Foreign Policy as an Instrument of Nation Building

Ilya Prizel

Foreign policy is a vital component of any country's struggle to shape its political identity and mold a national consciousness. Although it is generally assumed that only newly independent countries are dependent on foreign policy as a means of nation building, empirical evidence suggests that elites in well-established as well as emerging countries rely on foreign policy as a means to both build and maintain a national identity. It was the War of 1812 that enabled the United States to enter the "era of good feelings" and to transform itself from a collection of disparate colonies into a genuine national entity. It was General Charles De Gaulle's theatrical manipulation of foreign policy symbols that made it possible for France to regain its sense of confidence as a polity and thus put aside its legacy of defeat and colonial retreat in favor of nation building with a Eurocentric slant. Similarly, it was Margaret Thatcher's success in the Falklands campaign against Argentina that enabled her to recast Britain's self-image, thereby allowing her to launch a profound reorganization of British society.

Among newer countries lacking deeply rooted political traditions and institutions, it is often foreign policy that serves as the key instrument in nation building. Few historians would disagree with Jawaharlal Nehru's assertion that it was the conflict with Britain that created a distinct Indian national identity.

## Square One

Ukraine is by no means a new nation, but rather an entity with a millennium-old history fortified by a distinct language, literature, folklore, and several short-lived bouts of national independence. Nevertheless, because of historic circumstance, Ukraine is starting with few national institutions and little in terms of "usable history" which would ease its process of nation building. Furthermore, powerful regional, linguistic, and religious cleavages along with a fragmented collective memory make foreign policy a vital tool in this torturous process. In order to understand the role of foreign policy in Ukraine it is essential to examine the way by which the country attained independence and the long-term impact of that process.

Because of centuries of partition—first between Russia and Poland, and later Russia and the Hapsburg Empire—Ukraine did not manage to become a unified entity until after World War II when the Soviet Union expanded. World War II, itself, however, had a very divisive impact on Ukraine. While millions of Ukrainians fought against the Nazis and therefore, for the Soviet regime, hundreds of thousands fought against it, and further fractured the polity. Paradoxically, the fact that Ukraine's independence was achieved as a result of the implosion of the Soviet Union rather than a protracted war of independence denied Ukraine the kind of nation-molding experience that has proved to be a useful element of the nation-building efforts of scores of emerging nations.

Although nearly 90 percent of Ukraine's citizens voted in December of 1991 in favor of separation from the Soviet Union, in reality this overwhelming vote reflected a remarkably diverse coalition of interest groups rather than a consensus about the validity of the Ukrainian idea. Although Ukraine has a venerable tradition of nationalist dissent concentrated in, but not limited to, the western part of the country, large parts of eastern and southern Ukraine had been profoundly Russified and "Sovietized." The disaster at Chernobyl did serve to galvanize resentment in Ukraine over the country's status as a junior partner within the Soviet empire and served as a catalyst for political mobilization even in the traditionally conservative parts of the country. A substantial part of the support for independence, however, was generated not by genuine nationalists committed to Ukraine's statehood, but rather by interest groups who hoped by separating Ukraine from the USSR to ensure privileged positions secured during the *ancien regime.* The strikes by coal miners in the Don Basin—which were the harbinger of political unrest in the highly Russified industrial eastern Ukraine, and which ultimately translated into separatism— were initially triggered not by profound aspirations for independence, but rather by the precipitous decline in Ukraine's coal industry and the apprehension that Moscow would endorse the "Kuznetsk Variant" backing the expansion of mining in Siberia while phasing out the exhausted fields in Ukraine.[1]

## A Marriage of Convenience?

Unlike Ukraine's nationalist intellectuals and the clergy of the Uniate church, who consistently supported Ukraine's independence despite fearful odds, Ukraine's political elite, under the leadership of hard-line communist Volodymyr Shcherbytsky, initially attempted to preserve their status by lining up with the opponents of perestroika. Even as late as August 1991 when the failed coup took place, Ukraine's Leonid Kravchuk actually supported the putschists (initially) and blamed Gorbachev for unleashing democratic reforms.[2] The collapse of the coup and the disintegration of the Soviet Union begot a most unusual coalition of players to lead the newly independent Ukraine. The country's nationalists, dominated by the broad coalition known as Rukh, realized that without the support of the communist elite they might not be able to obtain a convincing majority in favor of independence. The communist elite in turn recognized that they would not be able to preserve their position of privilege in Ukraine were the country to remain within a rapidly changing Soviet Union. Given these imperatives, hard-line communist industrial and agricultural managers determined to preserve the political order within Ukraine coalesced with nationalists whose main agenda was securing independence for Ukraine while retaining the country's territorial integrity and avoiding violence.

## Foreign Policy—Key to Nation Building

The breadth of the coalition supporting independence and the contradictory agendas of the coalition partners made the process of nation building a daunting task. The differences between nationalists eager to launch a profound marketization of the economy and communists eager to preserve "soviet power" in post-Soviet Ukraine precluded the use of the domestic agenda as a vehicle for the creation of a national identity. It was the sphere of foreign policy that afforded the new Ukrainian state the opportunity to launch the process of nation building.

A key element of this process, which almost any Ukrainian government would have felt compelled to follow, was to establish a distinct Ukrainian identity in the international consciousness. To overcome its virtual invisibility in the international arena, the result of over three centuries of Russian domination, the first order of business was inevitable—an attempt to create an international identity distinct from that of Russia.

What makes the separation between Ukraine and Russia so very complex is the fact that unlike Ukraine and Poland, where despite centuries of cross-pollination each nationality retained its distinct ethnic identity, in the case of Russia and Ukraine the national ethos of each country, almost by definition, denies the other's national identity. Even the origins of their respective states remain subject to mutual controversy. Eighteenth century Russian historiography, as presented by giants such as Nikolai Karamzin, S. Soloviev, and Vasily Kliuchevsky, took the position that it was Vladimir-Suzdal and later Moscovy that were the successor states to Kievan Rus.

Thus, the possession of Ukraine as a part of the lands of Rus became a vital ingredient in the legitimization of the Russian empire as a whole. In fact, one can make a case that it was the acquisition of Ukraine that transformed Russia from a nation into an empire and made Russian imperial hegemony part of Russia's national myth. The power and acceptance of this myth to the present should not be underestimated. For example, even Andrei Sakharov, a man with no sympathy for Russian imperialism, showed very scant understanding of Ukrainian national aspirations.[3]

Conversely, Ukrainian historians of the late nineteenth century led by Mykhailo Hrushevsky asserted that the true successor of Kievan Rus was Galicia-Volhynia—whereas Moscovy was a product of a different civilization altogether.[4] For Russian nationalists to admit that Ukraine and Belarus are, indeed, separate units entitled to a separate national life would mean that many parts of the contemporary Russian Federation have no lesser right to secede from Russia. The Russian philosopher Aleksandr Tsipko (of Ukrainian ethnic origin) noted that without Ukraine as a part of it "there can be no Russia in the old, real sense of the word." [5] Conversely, for Ukrainian politicians to admit any "special relationship" with Russia is to question Ukraine's status as a separate sovereign nation.

Thus, establishment of a separate international identity and relations with Russia in general have long been key to Ukraine's process of nation building. One of the most difficult legacies of the Pereiaslav agreement (which in 1654 essentially made Ukraine part of the Russian Empire), and later of the various Russification campaigns, was Ukraine's disappearance from the international consciousness as a nation entitled to independence.

Almost constantly during the twentieth century outsiders have confused Ukraine with Russia and rejected Ukraine as a legitimate player within the international system. Ukraine's delegation to Versailles was all but ignored by the Western powers, despite its support for Polish, Czech, Baltic, and other drives for independence. The allied conferences during World War II, aside from agreeing to Stalin's demands to use the Curzon line as the demarcation between Poland and the USSR and promising a seat in the United Nations for Ukraine, hardly raised the issue of Ukraine. Even at the height of the Cold War, when Ukrainian nationalists continued to wage a bitter guerrilla war against the Stalinization of Western Ukraine, the policy planning staff of the National Security Council in an internal memo insisted: "While the Ukrainians have been an important and a specific element of the Russian Empire, they have shown no signs of being a 'nation.' " [6]

Although the OSS did provide the Ukrainian insurgents with some help, the West did not demonstrate, in the face of the Soviet domination of Ukraine, the outrage it showed against the Stalinization of Poland, the Baltics, or Czechoslovakia. This indifference became evident again in the late 1980s and early 1990s, when the international community showed far greater sympathy to Baltic aspirations for independence than to those of Ukraine. In his "Kiev speech" President Bush warned Ukrainians not to push for independence or pursue "suicidal nationalism." Similarly, Chancellor Helmut Kohl of Germany clearly sided with Gorbachev in his efforts to preserve the Soviet Union.

Given this historical experience, it stands to reason that any Ukrainian government would attempt, at the earliest possible moment, to establish a separate identity from Russia. President Kravchuk's efforts to establish separate embassies, or a separate navy or, on a more quixotic plane, to insist on Ukraine having the USSR's seat on the UN Security Council, or Ukrainian deputy prime minister Igor Yukhnovsky's statement that Ukraine "cannot pass up the assets and payments of our own debt if we want to build an independent state," [7] somehow equating indebtedness with independence, may have baffled many Western observers. However, in the context of establishing a distinct identity, this policy has its own logic for Ukraine. While a "rational" approach may dictate the perpetuation of "special relations" with Russia, Ukraine's fragile ethno-national identity at home, as well as its low profile abroad, explain a degree of assertiveness which at times appears to run counter to its national interests.

### Defense Policy and "Standing Tall"

Similarly, Ukraine's defense policy—the insistence on a large army of 400,000 men, a viable blue water fleet, and likely retention of nuclear weapons—may appear to the West to be a short-sighted policy that antagonizes

Russia and isolates Ukraine from the West. Nevertheless, these policies do have a rationale in the context of Ukraine's history.

It was the absence of military power that led to the loss of Ukrainian independence during the last three centuries. Khmelnitsky's Pereiaslav agreement with Tsar Iliac reflected Ukraine's military impotence. Mazepa's attempt to use the international system as a guarantor of Ukraine's independence through an alliance with Sweden failed after the defeat of the Swedes at Poltava in 1709, and the Rada regime's efforts to attain an ideological understanding with Russia immediately following the October revolution likewise failed to secure Ukraine's independence. It would, therefore, be very hard to convince any Ukrainian government that a credible deterrent was not necessary for Ukraine to survive as an independent state.

This situation is further aggravated by the power base of Leonid Kravchuk, a former ideology chief of the Ukrainian Communist party who turned nationalist relatively late (in fact, after the collapse of the coup in Moscow). Kravchuk, who narrowly lost out to Leonid Kuchma in the 1994 presidential elections, represents the complexity of Ukraine's political makeup. The referendum for independence as well as Kravchuk's 1991 electoral campaign was a successful attempt to please two divergent constituencies—the western part of Ukraine, along with the Kiev metropolitan area, where nationalist fervor ran high and separatist feelings were strong, and the Donetsk Basin, or Donbas, along with the southern fringe of Ukraine, where the Russian-speaking population remained keen to preserve the existing economic order.

President Kravchuk managed to build his power base and, perhaps, retain the unity of the country by appealing to both groups. By opposing painful economic reforms he managed to retain the support of the industrial east, while through assertive nationalist policy he undercut Rukh leader Viacheslav Chornovil in the western regions. Ukraine's assertive foreign policy, which would have been inimical to almost any government in Moscow, is exacerbated by the bombastic tone that Ukrainian leaders have been forced to adopt if they are to retain a political hold over Ukraine's nationalist west. In fact, as President Kravchuk's ability to sustain the Soviet-style economy in the industrial east falters, his popularity in the Donbas is rapidly evaporating. Meanwhile in the western part of the country, where his communist past initially made him suspect, his ability to "stand tall" to Moscow made him the region's prodigal son.[8]

The policy of "standing tall" when dealing with Moscow, which prompted President Kravchuk to predict that before long Poland would supplant Russia as Ukraine's main trading partner, was based on several assumptions. Perhaps the most basic assumption was that Ukraine, with its bountiful agriculture and skilled labor, would manage to revive its economy with far greater ease than Russia. In fact, in the heady days after independence, many Ukrainian politicians not only assumed that the Russian economy would be far less adept than that of Ukraine in recovering from the break-up of the USSR, but also expressed strong doubts as to whether the Russian Federation would survive as a coherent political entity. As Oleksander Honcharenko, head of national and international security in the Ukrainian Academy of Sciences and a senior official in the Ukrainian Republican party, told the author: "Divine providence always favors the number three. First we have witnessed the breakdown of the Soviet bloc, then the breakdown of the USSR, and soon we'll see the breakdown of the Russian Federation." [9] This perceived Russian weakness, as well as a belief that Russia would not be able to bring itself to fully sever its economic links from Ukraine, made Kiev fairly confident that assertive dealings with Moscow did not pose a major threat to Ukraine's political or economic security.

### Eyes Westward

A companion assumption to the belief that Russia was on the verge of prolonged political and economic disintegration was a conviction among much of the Ukrainian elite that given the imminent disintegration in the East, the West would adopt Ukraine as the latter day *antemurale christatis*, serving as a bastion separating the West from chaotic Russia. The notion of becoming an important component of the West appealed to Ukraine on several levels. First, a close association with the West was viewed by many Ukrainian politicians as a powerful means to establish an international presence separate from that of Russia. Based on the assumption that Ukraine would be able to procure support and possible integration into the West and "return to Europe," it was willing to renounce readily its nuclear arsenal.

The prospect of reintegration into Central and Western Europe appealed to the Ukrainians on several levels. In economic terms association with the West was perceived as a means to establish a relationship with the wealthiest economic bloc in the world and simultaneously to end a relationship of dependency with Russia. No less important, however, was the psychological aspect of a link to the West. Ukrainian intellectuals from Hrushevsky on had argued that unlike Russia, whose political culture was a product of centuries of Tatar domination, Ukraine's political culture was grounded in the West. Therefore, close association with Central and Western Europe was perceived in Kiev as a vital element in the drive to enshrine a distinct identity.

## Initial Results

Ukraine's foreign policy of distancing itself from Russia served it reasonably well during its first year of independence. Ukraine, the perennial "invisible nation," emerged as a player in the international arena as more than a hundred countries recognized its sovereignty. In domestic terms, President Kravchuk's foreign policy appeared to have gained him the support of many nationalists who were willing to overlook his past and accept his spirited defense of Ukraine's identity. Although Kravchuk's foreign policy might have elicited far less support in the Russified Donbas, Ukraine's ability to continue to procure cheap Russian energy as well as the issuance of massive credits (denominated in Russian rubles) initially allowed Ukrainian industry and the public to avoid the painful dislocation inflicted on the Russian public after Yegor Gaidar freed prices in the Russian Federation on January 1, 1992. Kravchuk's initial ability to continue to rely on cheap Russian energy and ruble-denominated credits enabled the Donbas to avoid dislocation analogous to that occurring in Russia and thus substantially legitimated in the east both Ukraine's president and the country's independence.

The fundamental weakness of Ukraine's foreign policy was not that it was based on a series of flawed assumptions about Russia and Western policy toward the region; far more important was the fact that President Kravchuk's foreign policy was used to a very large degree to obscure the absence of any plausible effort to reform the country's economy so that Ukraine might be a credible partner for the West or the Visegrad group. Furthermore, while many Russian nationalists found it very difficult to reconcile themselves to the "loss" of Ukraine, and repeatedly attempted to rekindle the issue by raising the questions of the ownership of Crimea and dual citizenship for the residents of Donbas, among others, the young reformers clustered around Yeltsin adopted a "Russia First" policy that called for systematically cutting all disadvantageous links to the former republics of the Soviet Union.

Increasingly, the Russian government seems to accept Fedor Shelov-Kovedyaev's thesis that Russia can regain its influence with the Commonwealth of Independent States (CIS) only on the basis of successful reforms at home.[10] Some of Yeltsin's closest advisers, such as Alexandr Shokhin, have taken that notion even a step further, arguing that in order to carry out successful reform at home, Russia must reduce its bonds with the "near abroad" (including the friendly states of Belarus and Kazakhstan) to normal neighborly relations, have separate currencies, and conduct all economic intercourse on a purely commercial basis. Shokhin allegedly complained that any "special relationship" with the former republics of the USSR would force Russia once again to play the role of a "wet nurse," a role which Moscow could not afford.

The impact of Russia's insistence on total separation of the economies had a devastating impact on Ukraine's economy. Russia's ejection of Ukraine from the ruble zone in November 1992 created a situation where Ukraine could go on with its massive subsidization of inefficient industry and state-owned agriculture only at the peril of depreciating its currency, which ultimately led to hyperinflation. Furthermore, Moscow's insistence on energy prices nearly equal to those prevailing in world markets led Ukraine to incur a huge debt to Russia and eventually triggered a curtailment of deliveries in the middle of the coldest winter in fifty years.

### Reevaluation—A Further Course

Russia's economic assertiveness, along with growing imperial rhetoric following the December 1993 elections, sharply divided the Ukrainian polity on several levels. Whereas elites have retreated from acrimonious polemics between Moscow and Kiev, popular attitudes have become more radical.

Unlike former president Kravchuk, who made scrappiness with Moscow a source of personal political legitimacy, Leonid Kuchma, coming from the Eastern part of the country and being well aware of Ukraine's sinking economy, has made the restoration of a good relationship with Russia a priority as prime minister and president. Recognizing that Poland would not become Ukraine's gate to the West, Kuchma stated frankly: "We need an economic union. Ukraine probably needs it more [than Russia does], and Belarus and other republics need it even more. Russian needs it less; however, all need it." [11] If Kravchuk argued that Yeltsin represented the high point of Russian liberalism and that Ukraine must prepare itself for the day when it faced a reactionary irredentist Russia, Kuchma's supporters repeatedly stressed that historically Russia had expanded not into a demographic vacuum but rather into a political vacuum. Kuchma went on to insist that unless Ukraine jump-started its economy (a virtual impossibility without Russian collaboration), the country would degenerate into a political vacuum which would tempt outside forces to inject themselves into Ukraine's internal affairs. This view that Ukraine must go beyond building the trappings of a state and concentrate on building a viable economic structure seems to be shared by the Ukrainian public, as the last presidential elections indicated.

Kravchuk and later Kuchma shifted away from a belligerent posture toward Moscow, arguing that Ukraine's economy could not regain its balance without the reestablishment of close economic links with Russia. Furthermore, Kravchuk reversed himself and argued before the election that Ukraine's long-term security as well as the acceptance of Ukraine as a serious player in the international system was contingent on a normal relationship with Moscow. With that in mind, the Ukrainian government made several conciliatory gestures toward Moscow, ranging from initialing an accord on "joint economic space" with Russia and Belarus to an agreement (later rejected by the Ukrainian parliament) to swap Ukraine's Black Sea Fleet for the debt owed to Russia and, recently, to an agreement by Ukraine's armed forces to establish an institutional relationship with the CIS.

### The Present: Polarization and Gridlock

This shift in foreign policy, along with the deepening economic crisis, profoundly polarized Ukraine's body politic. Rukh, which started out as a broad coalition of opponents of the Soviet domination under the leadership of Chornovil, has increasingly mutated to a predominantly ethnic Ukrainian party with an increasingly strident nationalist tone and growing anti-Russian rhetoric. The Rukh-led coalition of the "Anti-Imperialist Bloc" more and more favors an accelerated transfer to a market economy as well as an end to all remaining links to Russia under the auspices of the CIS. Another problematic factor is that Rukh not only has an increasingly nationalist orientation but also relies increasingly on western Ukraine as its power base. In terms of foreign policy, Chornovil argues that what Ukraine is witnessing in Moscow is the apogee of Russian liberalism, which is bound to rapidly recede and be supplemented again by a historic imperial urge. With that in mind, the nationalist camp in Ukraine views the current period as a short-lived window of opportunity which Ukraine must utilize to fully separate itself from the hegemony of Moscow, relying on its nuclear forces to deter Russian aggression. Conversely, in Russian-speaking east Ukraine, a communist party favoring the resuscitation of many Soviet institutions, including an enhanced CIS and closer links with Russia, is reemerging.

Ukraine's predicament continues to be critical as the country faces economic collapse, ethnic and regional strife, and a Russian Federation in which, in Roman Szporluk's typology, nation builders are in retreat while "empire savers" are showing renewed vigor. Even Boris Yeltsin, who over the last few years had argued that Russia no longer wanted to be anyone's "older brother," reversed his pronouncements, stating that within the CIS, Russia must be "first among equals." [12] Ukraine's ability to respond to these heightened challenges is hindered by a stalemate between the executive and legislative branches of government as well as between the nationalist and communist factions in parliament.

### Crossroads for Ukraine

Ukraine's painful process of nation building is facing a historic crossroads. For Ukraine to guarantee its long-term independence, it must halt its degeneration toward political and economic vacuum, a vacuum which the Kremlin has centuries of experience in manipulating and ultimately dominating. Foreign policy, although a vital tool in the process of nation building, cannot be a substitute for establishing functioning national institutions and a viable economy.

Ukraine will need a government that has both the courage to carry out painful but essential reforms while arriving at a realistic relationship with Russia, taking into full account the fact that Ukraine's economy will remain closely intertwined with that of Russia for a long time to come. The use of disassociation from Russia as a means to build a national identity by Ukraine has probably run its course. As Prime Minister Kuchma, in a meeting with Polish prime minister Hannah Suchodcka, observed, "No one is awaiting us in the West."

Although profound economic reforms are bound to alienate the old party elites and workers in the decrepit industrial east, and a rapprochement with Russia will certainly anger the nationalist element in Ukrainian politics, failure to find a new centrist position in Ukrainian politics may well mean the end of Ukraine as an independent country.

### Notes

1. See David R. Marples, *Ukraine under Perestroika* (New York: St. Martin's Press, 1991), ch. 6.

2. John B. Dunlop, *The Rise of Russia and the Fall of the Soviet Empire* (Princeton: Princeton University Press, 1993), 189.

3. See Yaroslav Bilinsky, "Political Relations between Russians and Ukrainians in the USSR: The 1970s and Beyond," in *Ukraine and Russia in Their Historic Encounter,* ed. Peter J. Potichnyj, Marc Raeff, Jaroslaw Pelenski, Gleb N. Zekulin (Edmonton: Canadian Institute of Ukrainian Studies, 1993).

4. See Mykhailo Hrushevsky, "Traditional Scheme of 'Russian' History and the Problem of Rational Organization of History of Eastern Slavs," reproduced in *From Kievan Rus' to Modern Ukraine: Formation of the Ukrainian Nation*, Ukrainian Millennium Series, Ukrainian Studies Fund, Harvard University, 1984.

5. Quoted in Vera Tolz and Elizabeth Teague, "Russian Intellectuals Adjust to Loss of Empire," *RFE/RL Research Report* 1, 3, February 21, 1992, 38.

6. Internal memo S. W. Soures, Executive Secretary of NSC, 20/1, RG 273, August 18, 1948.

7. *Moscow News*, January 20, 1993.

8. In the December 1991 election President Kravchuk garnered around 60 percent of the votes in the east, but got less than 25 percent of the votes in the Lviv Oblast (see Henry R. Huttenbach, *Analyses of Current Events* (New York), December 1991. In a public opinion poll carried out in late 1992, Kravchuk lost his support in the East; in western Ukraine he was supported by 53 percent of the respondents (*RFE/RL Research Reports* 1, 41, October 20, 1992).

9. See Chrystia Freeland and Julie Corwin, "The Ukraine Votes for Independence," *U.S. News & World Report*, December 2, 1991, 67-69.

10. See John Lough, "Defining Russia's Relations with Neighboring States," *RFE/RL Research Report* 1, 20, May 14, 1993, 53-60.

11. Interview with Leonid Kuchma, Radio Moscow, January 13, 1993.

12. *Rossiskaya gazeta*, January 12, 1994.

# 16 The New Nations of Central Asia

Martha Brill Olcott

O ne of the persistent fallacies that accompanies the breakup of multiethnic empires is that the nations that emerge from the rubble are "new"; in fact, in all but the rarest of instances, the new names that appear on the maps belong to large groups of people who share common languages, common cultures, common histories, and a desire to control their own affairs. In most instances, it is the stubborn persistence of these nations beneath the denying cover of the imperial government which, in the long run, makes multinational empires so difficult to administer that they ultimately collapse.

### Nations without Nationalists

Central Asia differs from many postcolonial geopolitical entities in the very important particular that no separatist or nationalist movements of any consequence helped bring about the independence of the former Soviet republics of Kazakhstan, Kyrgyzstan, Tajikistan, Turkmenistan, and Uzbekistan.[1] Nevertheless, by most generally accepted criteria, the people inhabiting these five countries can be considered to have been "nations" that had been ingested into but never digested by the Russian empire. Even in the case of the Kazakhs and Kyrgyz, peoples whose languages and cultures resemble one another closely enough that imperial Russia had treated them as a single people, seven decades of Soviet division of the two into separate republics created enough sense of national differentiation to justify different countries, and indeed the division of Central Asia into the present configuration. The five republics more or less contain peoples who share a single language, a common culture, and a common history.

That common culture was one reason why the republics were able to act so quickly after the 1991 coup to set up the basic appurtenances of statehood, in

This research was supported by the United States Institute of Peace.

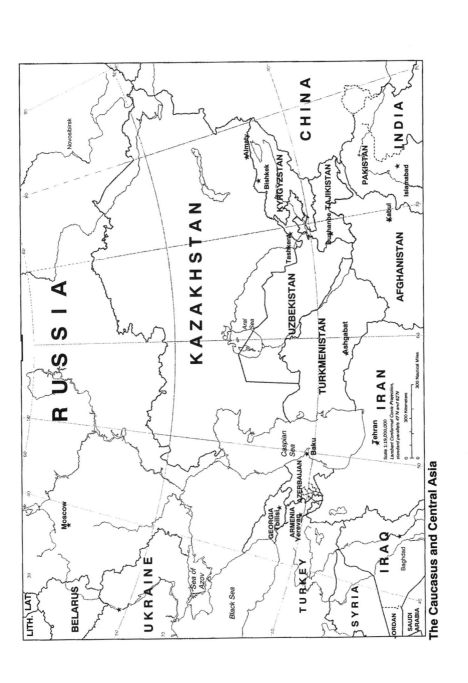

The Caucasus and Central Asia

spite of the fact that the leaders of the republics were not only not heroes of national liberation movements, but were, with the sole exception of Kyrgyzstan's Askar Akaev, Moscow appointees who had been given specific briefs to contain separatist sentiment in their respective republics. Beginning with Kyrgyzstan, in August 1991, and ending with Kazakhstan, in December 1991, each of the republics declared formal independence; soon afterward they also created national symbols like flags and state seals, elected state leaders, and began to form bodies of law, formulating and ratifying them in indigenous political structures specific to each republic.

The world community generally resisted recognizing the movement of the Soviet republics toward independence until December 1991. After the formal dissolution of the USSR and Gorbachev's resignation, however, the world ratified these formal declarations of nationhood, extended formal recognition, admitted them to the United Nations, the CSCE, and other international bodies, and exchanged ambassadors.[2] Since then, these formal markers of nationhood have only increased: the five Central Asian republics have adopted new state constitutions; all five have created national currencies; Uzbekistan has established a national army and set up a national airline; Kyrgyzstan has established a national guard and Kazakhstan has begun plans to create an independent military, including a navy; and customs officials have been put in place on the various borders. Of course, it is the external symbols of sovereignty—flags, anthems, and constitutions—that are the easiest parts of new nations to establish.

### The Economics of Central Asia

Much more critical to the functioning of states, old and new, is the stability and strength of frameworks internal to the nation, such as the existence of a national economy, the elaboration and defense of a national foreign policy, and the creation of what might be called "civic culture," a loose term for the general agreement of the population that the state represents them and their interests, for which reason they are willing to cede some personal interest and autonomy to state authority. Most of the Central Asian nations have addressed the creation of these internal girders, which are so necessary to the viability of nations, but with varying success.

Each of the Central Asian nations has had to face the legacies of the Soviet economic system. One feature of that system—that Soviet central planning attempted to achieve economies of scale by concentrating points of production in enormous factories designed to serve the entire USSR—has affected the economies of all of the newly independent states (NIS), while the other—that Central Asia was viewed as a provider of raw materials, either agricultural (foremost among these was cotton) or natural (ores, coal, oil, hydroelectric power, and others) and as a captive market for the generally low-quality goods produced from those raw materials—has had a particularly strong impact on Central Asia.

At the time of the dissolution of the USSR, the economies of the republics were inextricably intertwined. Factories everywhere shut down in waves because suppliers of crucial components were now in different countries, which made shipment that much more difficult. Equally, the traditional customers of many factories were also either in newly foreign countries, in collapse themselves, or, in many cases, able to find new supplies from abroad. Even in cases where business was still being conducted, the extraordinarily slow interrepublic system of clearing payments and credits, further exacerbated by the hyperinflation of 1992-1993, meant that most factories, at least in Central Asia, essentially ground to a halt. In Kyrgyzstan, for example, the hundred largest factories are all either on a shortened week or a shortened day, surviving on the hoarded remnants of Soviet-era supplies.[3]

For a period after independence, the NIS continued to sell goods and services to one another in rubles at essentially the Soviet prices, which were generally a fraction of world prices. Almost immediately, however, supplier nations began to balk at supplying for cheap rubles goods and commodities which could be sold elsewhere for dollars; this was doubly so in instances where the recipient nations themselves resold those cheaply acquired products—usually oil, natural gas, or metals—abroad at higher, dollar prices.

### The Dividing Line: Marketable Natural Resources

The increasing need to possess hard currency has set up a sharp differentiation among the new nations between those that have natural resources for which world markets exist and those which do not. At one end of the scale is Turkmenistan, which combines a small, very homogeneous population (about four million) with vast reserves of natural gas and oil; at the other end are Tajikistan and Kyrgyzstan, both of which are mountainous, small, and virtually without oil.

President Niyazov, in Turkmenistan, has used the wealth generated by sales of his country's resources to continue, or even to increase, Soviet-style subsidies of the internal economy.[4] This has shielded his citizens from the economic deterioration of the rest of the former Soviet Union. The other side of this coin, however, is that the government maintains an extraordinary level of political control (including a cult of Niyazov's personality so strong that published photos of him must pass through quality-control censorship to prevent inadvertent insult through poor photo reproduction), which has forestalled any development of a nongovernmental economic sector.

At the other end of the scale, the economies of both Kyrgyzstan and Tajikistan have all but collapsed. Tajikistan has been in a state of (intraethnic) civil war ever since independence, kept alive by infusions of cash and supplies from various outside sponsors (Uzbekistan and Russia on one side, Afghanistan on the other), so that it is difficult to speak of that state as even having an economy.

In Kyrgyzstan, which has so far been spared civil war, the difficulties of economic state building are clearer. With almost no oil of its own (it produces only 125,000 tons per year), Kyrgyzstan consumes 1.8 million tons of oil. Similarly, it produces 2.5 million tons of coal, but consumes 4.3 million tons; produces 55 million cubic meters of natural gas, but consumes 2.1 billion cubic meters.

Even before Kyrgyzstan's decision in May 1993 to introduce its own currency, after which supplier states began to require payment in dollars, the effect of energy costs was devastating. In 1991, oil and gas import costs had taken only 10 percent of the total state budget, but in 1992, this had swollen to 50 percent. By the beginning of 1993, the year's projected energy costs were more than 80 percent of the republic's entire budget, even though a large amount of gas will be supplied by Turkmenistan at only 60 percent of the world price. The reluctance of Kyrgyzstan's neighbors to be paid in som has further reduced suppliers' willingness to subsidize the republic's energy costs.

The effect on the republic's economy is stark. An estimated 70 percent of Kyrgyzstan's citizens are below the state-set poverty line, while retail prices in 1993 were fourteen times what they were in 1992. The gross domestic product has been dropping 15-30 percent per year since 1991, so the country's per-capita GNP is now one of the lowest of any of the former Soviet states.[5]

Introduction of the som has put further stress on Kyrgyzstan's economy. Some effects made themselves felt immediately, whereas others will be felt only after the IMF funds that are presently stabilizing the som have been spent. When the new currency was introduced, both Kazakhstan and Uzbekistan closed their borders to the passage of goods and began demanding payment for services in dollars. Although the flow of goods has resumed, Kyrgyzstan is economically isolated, and the internal situation is heading toward catastrophe, particularly since development of the nation's one convertible resource—gold—has become mired in accusations of corruption and political favoritism.

## Viable States: Uzbekistan and Kazakhstan

In many ways, the best indicator of the growth of national economies in the fledgling Central Asian states is provided by Uzbekistan, Central Asia's most populous state, and Kazakhstan, the region's largest state. In both nations, the state of the economy is parlous, but at the same time there are grounds to suggest that a sustainable national economy is forming.

Culturally, the two nations represent the extremes of Central Asia. Uzbekistan has a fairly homogeneous, sedentary culture, with densely settled cities, intensive agriculture (frequently with irrigation), and a system of well-established social controls. On the other hand, Kazakhstan is a Soviet creation, with as many Slavs as Kazakhs. The Kazakhs are the descendants of nomads who raised livestock and controlled pasturage rather than owned land. With their traditional life all but destroyed by the Soviets, the Kazakhs have considerable social problems that can be ascribed, in one way or another, to lack of self-identity.

Both nations remained tied to the ruble until November 1993, which exposed them to the ravages of Russian inflation, greatly lowering the average standard of living. At the same time, however, each nation has had some success in attracting world investment and in marketing its products—mostly raw materials—abroad.

In this regard, Kazakhstan is unquestionably the wealthier, with proven oil reserves in the Tengiz fields alone of about twice those of Alaska's North Slope. Most world oil companies have acquired or are acquiring concessions in the republic, while negotiations are underway with various foreign companies to build refineries and pipelines to move the petroleum to market. Negotiations are presently stalled, however, by Kazakh insistence that Russia should be included as a last-minute partner, at the expense of the foreign partners' share. Nor is oil Kazakhstan's only resource; with some validity the republic can boast of possessing the entire periodic table of elements in exportable quantities. For example, development has begun of the republic's Bakyrchik gold fields, financed by shares sold on the London stock exchange. Although all of this development is being pursued by state-owned companies, there is considerable movement of capital into the private sector, most of it illegal but sufficient to support growth of subsidiary service industries such as the Mercedes Benz dealership and service center in Almaty.

Uzbekistan is less wealthy in oil but has about 25 percent of the gold reserves of the former USSR.[6] It has been refining and depositing gold abroad. The nation also has more developed commercial structures and traditions than does Kazakhstan, so that secondary economic functions such as retail trade are healthier than in Kazakhstan. Uzbek adaptation to the Soviet system also has meant that important clans and families began independence with accumulations of capital, amassed in some cases by controlling state contracts in the Soviet period. This has allowed them to expand and consolidate retail and agricultural monopolies, creating a domestic economy sufficiently robust to support, for example, a national airline which now links London to Pakistan, and the strongest national army in Central Asia.

### Foreign Policy Development

For all the importance of their economies to the citizens of Central Asian nations, in many regards it is the elaboration of differentiated foreign policies which is the best indicator of the progress of nation-building, because a country's leaders and citizens will begin to understand national self-interest only after they have begun to articulate a sense of being a nation. The Central Asian states began independence predisposed to view themselves as a natural geographic unit, the interests of which were very similar. Indeed, most of the presidents of Central Asia were strong proponents not only of a unitary Central Asia, but of a unitary Commonwealth of Independent States (CIS), in large part because of their awareness that they stood to gain much more from a commonwealth than they would lose. Shunned by the Slavs at the initial formation of the CIS, they were forced repeatedly over the next two years to admit the truth which Uzbekistan's president Karimov articulated in April 1993; namely, that Russia was the CIS, for all serious purposes.[7] The Central Asians have, nevertheless, clung longest to concepts of a post-Soviet, multi-state identity. Even after the July and October 1993 currency reforms, which among other things were a muscular demonstration of Russia's claim to sole control of the ruble, Uzbekistan and Kazakhstan announced that they were still resolved to remain tied to the ruble, which they reversed only in November 1993, after Russia further demanded that ruble-zone nations also transfer their gold reserves to Moscow's control.

The foreign policy advantages of a unified CIS looked considerable to Central Asia at independence. A unified defense would minimize or remove entirely the cost of raising and maintaining armies. Central Asia would have been protected against traditional enemies, most notably China. Perhaps most important, placing responsibility for defense in the hands of an outside party would have lessened general apprehensions among the Central Asians that their various states might begin to explore grievances and rivalries among one another, some of which extend back centuries, and all of which were put in abeyance by Soviet control. Although the current configuration of Central Asia is a reasonably logical one, both by nationality and by geography, it is not the only historically and ethnically defensible arrangement of state authority. All Central Asian states are aware that if national borders among themselves begin to be contested, the possibility of enormous and bloody conflicts are immediate.

However, the process of economic differentiation, accelerated by Russia's failure—caused in part by lack of desire, in part by lack of means—to impose control on the territory, has meant that nations increasingly have been forced to realize that their interests do diverge.

Again, Turkmenistan occupies one extreme of the process. Wealthy and geographically remote from Moscow, with a minuscule Russian population, the country has increasingly cleaved away from the CIS, and, indeed, from Central Asia. Although President Niyazov or his representatives continue to attend CIS meetings, their participation has become perfunctory. Niyazov has clamped a lid of tight political control on the populace which exacerbates the sense of separation from the more turbulent changes in other republics (most of which are driven by the deteriorating economies).

Turkmenistan in Soviet times was the most traditional, least Europeanized of the republics. Niyazov's aggressive Islamification of the nation has accentuated this tendency, although Turkmenistan's religious revival is being tightly shaped around traditional conservative Islam and not fundamentalist teachings. Sharing a long border with Iran and Afghanistan, Turkmenistan is increasingly seeking to live in harmony with its immediate neighbors. Although the nation has exchanged ambassadors with most Western nations and is seeking Western investment partners, its evolutionary foreign policy seems increasingly to steer Turkmenistan toward the Muslim world of the Near East.

Kyrgyzstan took an opposite course. Trading on its position as a leader of the democratic transition in the USSR, Kyrgyzstan made an early effort to compensate for its lack of natural wealth by transforming the country into what President Akaev called "an Asian Switzerland," [8] meaning a place of intellectual and financial freedom for the rest of Central Asia. Until September 1994 the political climate in the republic was the most free and most democratic of any in Central Asia, making the first part of this effort a comparative success. However, in spite of aggressive efforts to entice foreign businesses and banks into the country, the financial part of Akaev's vision thus far has been largely unsuccessful.[9]

Even worse, the consequences of Kyrgyzstan's efforts to attract foreign business and resuscitate her failing economy have helped demonstrate to the other Central Asian leaders that in the world arena nations are competitors as well as allies. Akaev's early willingness to permit his nation to be a political soapbox for the region helped remove domestic political pressure from Kazakhstan's Nazarbaev but clearly antagonized Uzbekistan's Karimov, who is trying to maintain very tight political control in his republic. The presence of a huge and restless Uzbek irredentist population in the southern part of the republic (which is separated from Kyrgyzstan's capital by all but impassable mountains), as well as Uzbekistan's army, the largest and most experienced in Central Asia, makes it particularly unwise to irritate Karimov.

However, even Nazarbaev, who has shown considerable indulgence for the Kyrgyz (in part because their cultural and linguistic similarity to the Kazakhs has allowed him to shunt Kazakh nationalist pressures into the neighboring republic and so delay confrontations with the equally nationalist Russians) has been forced to protect his republic against the consequences of Kyrgyzstan's economic actions. The introduction of the som was handled in such a way that only six billion of the fifty-five billion rubles circulating in Kyrgyzstan in May 1993 were exchanged for som. The danger of the unchanged forty-nine billion fleeing to neighboring Kazakhstan and Uzbekistan, and so adding to inflationary pressures that were already explosive (or, the converse, further exacerbating shortages of goods) was so great that both Karimov and Nazarbaev temporarily closed their borders to Kyrgyzstan while mechanisms could be put in place to insure that only "domestic" rubles could be spent. Subsequently, both presidents have secured a promise from Akaev that "dumped" rubles would be redeemed, and both have imposed regulations which require payment in dollars for services, such as purchase of airplane or train tickets. This has served to further isolate Kyrgyzstan. Shortages of jet fuel in Kyrgyzstan have meant that Almaty has been the republic's de facto international airport for more than a year, while Bishkek was never more than a spur on the Soviet rail system.

## The Effects of Tajikistan

The state which has proven the strongest reagent for Central Asian politics is Tajikistan. Already in deep civil conflict when independence was declared, the republic has since illustrated all the dangers which clan-based power struggles can present to Central Asian societies.

Each of the countries, however, has taken the lesson in a different way. Without a common border, and with commercial and religious interests in Iran and Afghanistan, Turkmenistan has kept its distance from the conflict. Kazakhstan has as well, although for somewhat different reasons; Nazarbaev endorsed a plan to send a CIS contingent to Tajikistan in October 1992 but later decided not to override his parliament's refusal to permit use of Kazakhstan's troops in such a force. Balanced as he is between Russian and Kazakh populations of virtually equal size, Nazarbaev cannot afford to provoke civil anger by dispatching Russian boys to fight in what their parents will perceive as Central Asian affairs, any more than he can dispatch Kazakh boys to fight against coreligionists. This is especially true at a time when Kazakh nationalists are pressuring him hard to put a more clearly Kazakh stamp upon the country. Nazarbaev is, however, acutely conscious of the destabilizing effect that a wider Tajik civil war will have on all of Central Asia; accordingly, a small troop of Kazakhstani soldiers joined a CIS deployment in Tajikistan in spring 1993.

Although Kyrgyzstan also backed the October attempt to mount an intervention force and similarly failed to get parliamentary permission, the consequences are much different. The ethnic Kyrgyz irredentist population in Tajikistan was cut off by the civil war from their normal markets in Kyrgyzstan, while Tajik refugees and "freedom fighters" made full use of the porous southern border between the two countries, especially after November 1992, as the Rahmonov government in Tajikistan began to purge its defeated enemies. Accounts of political, financial, or religious kidnappings along the border became frequent, but Kyrgyzstan has been able to do little about the situation. Kyrgyzstan is particularly aware of the longstanding water-usage and land disputes between the two republics and understands only too well the possible implications of Tajikistan's failure to ratify their common border by treaty.

The country for which the Tajik conflict has been most defining is Uzbekistan. The coalition that brought President Nabiev to power in Tajikistan is too uncomfortably reminiscent of President Karimov's own power base for the Uzbekistan president to ignore the forces that drove Nabiev from office. Karimov has chosen to classify Nabiev's opposition as Islamic fundamentalists, the threat of which he uses to justify the growing militarization of his own republic, in turn encouraging his neighbors to become military powers as well.[10] An all-Uzbek army was instrumental in helping the Rahmonov government establish and maintain control in Tajikistan, which has given Karimov's armed forces invaluable training and experience.

However, the continued disintegration of Tajikistan, and the increasing degree to which Afghanistan and Russia are being drawn into the conflict, has also forced Uzbekistan into a more independent foreign policy than she had in the beginning of the Tajik conflict. In the beginning, Karimov had been content to mask his own ends in Tajikistan as a post-Soviet version of "fraternal assistance" and as assistance to the Russians, who had maintained a large force in the republic. Once Russia began to warn of retaliatory strikes within Afghanistan itself, however, Karimov felt it necessary to stipulate that his troops would take no part in such exercises because of the danger that forces in Afghanistan could begin to strike directly at Uzbekistan across their common border, rather than through Tajikistan.

### The Elusive Goal: A Civil Society

There is another lesson in the disintegration of Tajikistan, which the societies of Central Asia have taken in different ways. The conduct of politics at the point of a gun led by fall 1992 to a nearly complete disintegration of the social fabric in Tajikistan, a situation which has been remedied, however incompletely, only by the use of still greater force. To at least two republics, Turkmenistan and Uzbekistan, the lesson of Tajikistan is the threat which democracy and diversity of opinion present to society. Thus, both presidents have expended considerable resources to create one-man political rule in their respective republics. Both have repeatedly detained and prosecuted leaders and activists of democratic political movements.[11] Both states have adopted postindependence constitutions, but political reality in both republics is that all decisions are taken by the president, then ratified, if need be, by a rubber-stamp parliament.[12] For example, the twelfth session of Uzbekistan's parliament took two days to consider and pass thirty laws, as well as to ratify a number of treaties, including the charter of the CIS.

In both Turkmenistan and Uzbekistan, the political climate has prevented the development of even the most fragile roots of a civil society. They both exhibit all the characteristics of despotic states, including a classic inherent weakness, that political stability becomes invested in a person, rather than in an institution or institutions. Turkmenistan's wealth may insulate the republic from difficulties of succession, if Niyazov's potential rivals feel that they would have more to lose from civil strife than they would gain, but Uzbekistan, which is comparatively much poorer, will probably face a crisis of political leadership that could well be resolved in part by force.

As noted, Kyrgyzstan has made much more genuine attempts to create a society based upon rule of law. The drafting of the state constitution was very public, with considerable access for the expression of dissent and the incorporation of alternate views. The major functions of government have been invested in the offices of president and parliamentary leaders, without reference to the persons currently occupying them. Although less independent than its American counterpart, a judiciary with considerable autonomy was formed. Judicial guarantees for freedom of person, property, belief, and speech have been established, although the growing independence of presidentially appointed *akims*, or regional administrators, and the general disregard for law in the republic mean that such guarantees are only fitfully observed.

At the same time, however, there is a growing cynicism in the republic, perhaps best expressed by a journalist's observation that "in Kyrgyzstan you can write and say whatever you want, because nobody pays the slightest attention to any of it." [13] There has been a serious outflow of non-Kyrgyz citizens from the republic, including the particularly public defection of former vice president E. Kuznetsov who in July 1993 immediately took up a senior position in Moscow. This out-migration has decimated industry, medicine, and other important fields, and experts now warn that the next wave of émigrés is likely to be the Kyrgyz intelligentsia, further accelerating the republic's decline. The fabric of life in the republic has worn exceedingly thin; public transportation is grinding to a halt, cities are having trouble heating, water is not being chlorinated, medicine is difficult to come by, and crime is growing. In short, for an urban population, Kyrgyzstan's freedom must be a bitter prize; for the republic's rural population, however (still 60 percent of the country), the chance to return to the clan-based pastoral life of the past may be more welcome.

Ironically, the republic which seems to be making the greatest strides toward creation of a civil society is also the one which would seem to be facing the greatest challenge. Kazakhstan is inherently riven, because of the delicate balance between the Slavic (especially Russian) population and the Kazakh population. The competing desires, expectations, and fears of the two populations make the political situation in the republic virtually a zero-sum game so that, for example, Nazarbaev can support the growth of Kazakh nationalism only at the risk of stimulating an answering Russian nationalism.

Perhaps as a consequence, the emerging civic culture of the republic is showing signs of being more encompassing and less restrictive than those of Kazakhstan's neighbors. Unlike Uzbekistan and Turkmenistan, Kazakhstan has given Islam no special status in the republic and has controlled the activities of religious parties.[14] On the other hand, unlike Kyrgyzstan, Kazakhstan has provided constitutional status for the Russian language, making a legal (but not entirely comprehensible) distinction between the "state language" (Kazakh) and the "language of interethnic communication" (Russian).[15] Political control in the republic is much more stringent than in Kyrgyzstan, with strict constitutional penalties for "insults to presidential dignity" (which were invoked in one case that drew the attention of international human rights monitors), but it is nothing like that in Uzbekistan, Tajikistan, or Turkmenistan.

Nazarbaev seems by nature to be a manager, so that he is content to permit diversity of opinion and expression as long as it does not interfere with the state's ability to fulfill its basic functions. Although Nazarbaev was elected president with a Soviet-style 98.9 percent of the vote, he shows no signs of attempting to create a personal cult. His timetable for the republic's development implies that he intends to honor the provisions of the new constitution, which will restrict him (and any subsequent president) to two five-year terms. Indeed, after initially rejecting the creation of political parties, Nazarbaev seems to be moving toward forming a party-like civic movement, known as SNEK—the People's Union for Unity of Kazakhstan. SNEK would further institutionalize the development strategy which Nazarbaev has begun, while also providing a mechanism to discipline the abuses of position which have been flourishing.[16]

### The Acid Test

The political situation in Kazakhstan remains volatile. Economic recovery has been slow, with evidence of malfeasance at every turn, while the uncertainty of Russia's future, both political and economic, has exerted a strong distorting tug on the republic's development. Nazarbaev remains convinced that his nation must find an accommodation with its giant neighbor to the north. He would prefer that the relationship be one between equal partners, but he seems able to accept the likelihood that Russia's imperial habits will inevitably make it more like the "big brother-little brother" relationship of the past, rather like former ties between the USSR and the other Warsaw Pact nations. What is equally clear, however, is that even Nazarbaev is not willing to return to a relationship with Russia that is one of owner and owned, as was essentially the case in the Soviet Union. He has stated unequivocally that any attempt to modify the existing borders of his state will be a cause for war.

The military inferiority of Kazakhstan to Russia, and indeed of all the Central Asian republics, even Uzbekistan, to Russia, makes the effective value of such sentiments of dubious importance. Nonetheless, the fact that such sentiments now exist may be the truest measure of whether or not the new nations of Central Asia are "real."

Before independence was forced upon them, what most Central Asians wanted was cultural autonomy, not self-rule. Now that independence has come, it is likely to be fiercely defended, no matter how small the likelihood that the defense might be successful. The appearance of independence has the effect of creating real independence, as the increasing differentiation of the five Central Asian republics over the past two years demonstrates. The economic survival of at least two of the five, Tajikistan and Kyrgyzstan, is a great question mark; the political evolution of three of them, Turkmenistan, Tajikistan, and Uzbekistan, is another. None of the five is likely to become as prosperous or as civilized (by which is really meant "Western") as the Baltic states, Poland, or the Czech Republic, but there is no question that Kyrgyzstan, Kazakhstan, Uzbekistan, Tajikistan, and Turkmenistan are nations. Whether these nations continue to enjoy a separate existence, or are swallowed again into other states (as could happen, either from the north or from the east), they will remain real and of account to the world community.

## Notes

1. Until January 1993 standard terminology made a distinction between Kazakhstan and "middle Asia," which encompassed the other four nations of the region (Tajikistan, Kyrgyzstan, Turkmenistan, and Uzbekistan). After a meeting in Tashkent, it was agreed by signatories from all five nations that henceforward the region would be known by the collective name of "Central Asia."

2. As an example, Kyrgyzstan's newly appointed foreign minister, E. Karabaev, said in January 1993 that 120 countries had recognized his nation, and 51 had established diplomatic relations. *Erkin Too* (Bishkek), January 13, 1993, 1.

3. K. Baialinov, "Stometrovka prezidenta," *Komsomolskaya pravda*, August 4, 1993, 3.

4. As of January 1, 1993, charges for domestic water, gas, and electricity were elim-

inated. *Turkmenskaya iskra* (Ashkabad), October 27, 1992, 1.

5. *Financial Times*, November 11, 1994, 15.

6. Uzbekistan's gold reserves are the reason the country is the first of the Central Asian nations to receive funds from the European Bank for Recovery and Development. *FBIS Daily Report—Central Eurasia*, FBIS-SOV 93-017, January 28, 1993, 47.

7. *Nezavisimaya gazeta*, February 2, 1993, 3.

8. *FBIS Daily Report—Central Eurasia*, FBIS-USR 93-003, January 8, 1993, 105.

9. See for example *Svobodne gory*, January 18, 1993, 2.

10. See the interview with A. Pulatov in *Nezavisimaya gazeta*, May 16, 1992, 3.

11. For some examples, see *Nezavisimaya gazeta*, March 2, 1993.

12. *FBIS Daily Report—Central Eurasia*, FBIS-USR 93-071, June 9, 1993, 83.

13. Baialinov, "Stometrovka prezidenta," 3.

14. *FBIS Daily Report—Central Eurasia*, FBIS-SOV 93-030, February 13, 1993.

15. *Kazakhstanskaya pravda*, November 11, 1992.

16. *Nezavisimaya gazeta*, February 9, 1993.

# 17 Chaos in Post-Soviet Caucasia, Crossroads of Empires: In Search of a U.S. Foreign Policy

Henry R. Huttenbach

Throughout post-Soviet Caucasia, turmoil and bloody upheaval are a daily affair. Just some of the most publicized recent events include the shooting death in Georgia of Fred Woodworth, a U.S. diplomat and alleged CIA officer; the assassination of former KGB head Marius Yuzbanion in Armenia; the ouster of Azerbaijani president Elchibey by Heyda Aliyev; the killing of Viktor Polyanicko, provincial administrator in North Ossetia and Ingushetia; the continuing violence in Nagorno-Karabakh; and the death of Georgia's former president Zviad Gamsakhurdia in Chechnya.

Of what interest is all this violence to U.S. policy makers? Are these isolated events, or are they in some manner significantly interconnected? How are they to be analyzed and assessed? What, if any, response should the United States make? Are the events to be seen as relatively benign, mere aftershocks of the collapse of the Soviet Union; or are they omens of a chronically unstable future? Should the United States be a primary player in the region's developments; should it act indirectly through surrogates; should it remain neutral but interested or aloof and unconcerned? All these questions as well as others need to be confronted knowledgeably if the country's post-Soviet regional policies are to rest on a bedrock of reliable guidelines.

## Origins of the Problem

One thing is certain: of the myriad events exploding throughout the Caucasus these days (as in the former Yugoslavia), the majority have their roots in the pre-Soviet past; only a few can be traced exclusively and directly to the seven-and-a-half decades of Soviet rule. What we are now witnessing is not only the repercussions of the *bolshoi raspad*—the collapse of the Soviet empire—but also the dismantling of a century of imperial Tsarist rule, a process fitfully begun in the wake of the 1917 Russian Revolution but forcefully interrupted in 1921 by Bolshevik reimposition of Russian domination.

223

One of the dynamics taking place—one which serves as a useful common denominator for much of the turmoil presently ravaging the territory between the Black and Caspian seas—is the effort to dismantle the artificial ethnopolitical units imposed by Soviet imperial architects upon this richly multiethnic region, once described by Trotsky as "a Babel of ethnicities." Fundamental to this process is the elimination of the colonial-style dichotomy that divides the region of the three Transcaucasian post-Soviet republics (Armenia, Azerbaijan, and Georgia) in the south, from the region constituting the Northern Caucasus, consisting from west to east of Adygeyskaya (in Krasnodarsk), Karachayevo-Cherkesskaya, Kabardino-Balkarskaya, Northern Ossetia, Checheno-Ingushetiya, Daghestan, and, possibly, Kalmytskaya.

The three Transcaucasian republics and the six autonomous units are presently separated by an international border, that of the Russian Federation, itself a by-product of the *bolshoi raspad*. In fact, the two tiers north and south of the Caucasian Mountains overlap inextricably—religiously, linguistically, and historically. Thus, for example, the Abkhazians in northwest Georgia seek to secede and then possibly join the recently formed anti-Moscow North Caucasus Federation (so far a federation only in name, one marred by serious internal rifts); Ossetians in northern Georgia seek to form a country with their brothers in Russia; the Lezgin minority in northern Azerbaijan have asked to join Daghestan; and Kalmytskaya has declared its independence from the Russian Federation.

The reasons for all these ethnic events are formidably complex: for example, the Abkhazians, Orthodox Christian like the Georgians, desire separation in part for language reasons; the two Ossetian regions, speaking two distinct dialects, nevertheless wish unification along religious lines; the Lezgins prefer to be with their Sunni Moslem kin than with the overwhelmingly Shiite Azeris. Yet even these explanations oversimplify the dynamics of the dozens of ethnic separatisms and mergings threatening the post-Soviet borders in the Caucasus. Unless one assumes an all-Caucasian perspective can a modicum of sense be made of this smoldering multiethnic region. That is to say, one should not count automatically on the continuity of the borders between and within the three Transcaucasian republics nor on those in the north, presently technically still inside the Russian Federation. These northern territories are straining either to leave the federation or to achieve constitutional recognition of their requests for regional autonomy, requests bordering on quasi-independence. In short, what is taking place, as a result of long-suppressed ethnic interests, is a dramatic resurgence of a highly complex ethnic politics within the Caucasus.

From without, the Caucasus is rimmed, as it has been for centuries, by three states with varying geopolitical interests in this strategic region between the Black and Caspian seas: Iran, Russia, and Turkey. For the moment, since the recent retreat of Russian/Soviet rule, none of the three rivals has the capacity to dictate events throughout the Caucasus and claim hegemonic control. This has permitted local conflicts to come to the fore in both Transcaucasia and North Caucasia. To date, the sum total of these conflicts has brought about far greater division than cohesion to the Caucasus, providing more opportunities for outside intervention, whether Iranian, Russian, or Turkish. Because these powers presently lack the means—military, economic, and ideological—to gain a monopoly of influence, their presence and rivalry merely compound the already complex situations prevailing in the Caucasus, situations that need to be understood in both local as well as regional terms.

## The Republic of Georgia

The Georgians' history reaches back well before their early conversion to Christianity, which they received from Constantinople when it was the capital of the Byzantine Empire in the late fifth century. Despite repeated conquests by Muslim powers—Turkish and Persian—Georgians managed to survive culturally intact over the centuries. Tsarist Russian rule since the early nineteenth century, while not offering any territorial provisions for the Georgian people per se, nevertheless did not seriously disturb communal-territorial identities.

The break-up of the Russian Empire in 1917 set in motion a dynamic Georgian independence movement that was brutally suppressed by the Bolshevik army, in part because of the Menshevik leadership that had established itself in the capital, Tbilisi. After a short period of Soviet experimentation with the idea of an all-Transcaucasian administrative arrangement, the architects of the USSR, prompted by Lenin, gave in to the principle of ethno-territoriality. This gave rise to the borders of the Soviet Georgian Republic. However, what the Soviets devised was a republic with a complex multiethnic population capable of exerting centrifugal tendencies, despite the presence of a Georgian majority.

A large measure of the troubles plaguing newly independent Georgia stems from unassimilated ethnic minorities and their geographic distribution. According to the last census, ethnic Georgians numbered approximately 3,750,000, constituting less than 70 percent of the population. The geographic distribution of the 30 percent non-Georgians is crucial to a basic understanding of ethnic political issues. In this respect, the ethnographic map of Georgia can be roughly divided into three strips, the central east-west band being largely inhabited by ethnic Georgians. In the southern strip, from west to east, are (1) Adzhars (Sunni and semi-turkified Georgian Moslems), with their own autonomous republic; (2) Armenians (Monophysite Christians of the Eastern rite), who make up close to 10 percent of the population and who, until very recently, were a major part of the elite in Tbilisi; and (3) Shiite Azeris, who not only make up more than 5 percent of the population but have strong ties with the Ingiloi, Shiite Moslem Georgians. In the northern band—again from west to east—reside (1) Abkhazians, closely knit despite mixed religion (Sunni Moslem and Christian), residing in their own autonomous republic; (2) a medley of Sunni Cherkessians; (3) the Christian Tuallag Ossetians in their separate autonomous oblast, who make up more than 3 percent of the republic's population; and (4) Sunni Daghestanis. Psychologically, ethnic Georgians feel surrounded within their own borders by significant numbers of non-Georgians, most of them Muslim and many non-Orthodox Christians.

### Georgian Nationalism's Rocky Road

These potential interethnic conflicts all surfaced with the rise of ethnic Georgian nationalism during the Gorbachev years (1985-1991). Led by the anti-Soviet dissident, Zviad Gamsakhurdia, Georgia soon emerged as one of the most eager of the Soviet secessionist republics. Shortly before the 1991 break-up of the USSR, Gamsakhurdia was elected president (in May); he was elected largely by an ethnic Georgian electorate.

Despite his dissident anti-Russian background, Gamsakhurdia evinced an ethno-nationalist authoritarian quality that quickly proved his undoing. He mishandled in a violent manner South Ossetia's political aspirations to affiliate with North Ossetia, by displaying an inflexible monoethnic and Georgian-centered view and by promoting a centrist irredentism that caused anxieties among all non-Georgians. At the same time, he highhandedly mistreated his political opponents and critics in the parliament, in the opposition parties, and in the media.

The result was a grassroots rebellion composed of intellectuals and key units of the army. After a few days of destructive fighting, largely in the capital, Gamsakhurdia was forced to flee, first to west Georgia (the center of his political support) and then to Chechnya, where he conducted a campaign in exile to regain his presidency until his death. In the meantime, the republic's leadership was conferred on Eduard Shevardnadze, Gorbachev's former foreign minister. It was believed that Shevardnadze's personal prestige and world stature would be sufficient to stem the forces of post-Soviet national disintegration: economic decline, rising non-Georgian ethnic separatism, and political fragmentation.

Unfortunately, despite a few initial successes, there was little Shevardnadze could do to consolidate the post-Soviet Georgian republic into a viable nation-state. He did manage to buy a partial peace in South Ossetia, but only through a politically dangerous agreement with Russia: units of Russian and Georgian troops are now stationed in the autonomous oblast keeping a very shaky peace that, in the long run, may likely be a cure worse than the disease. At present Ossetians on both sides of the border see themselves divided not just by a Soviet colonial legacy, but by a nefarious neocolonialism in the form of a Russian-Georgian collaboration that is denying them ethnoterritorial unification and political self-determination. In this case, neither Russians nor Georgians seek to unleash the genie of separatism. Nevertheless, this view of a Russo-Georgian entente has spread throughout the Caucasian mountain peoples, the majority of whom are Muslim. Many also see this as a Christian-inspired alliance aimed specifically at Muslims. (The long Armenian-Azeri war over Nagorno-Karabakh has helped to fortify this perception, as have events in Bosnia.)

The quasi-pacification of South Ossetia has given Shevardnadze's government little comfort. From his mountain hideout in Chechnya, deposed President Gamsakhurdia managed a guerrilla campaign to destabilize the government of Shevardnadze. Despite his death, the Ossetian cauldron is still boiling. At the same time, Abkhazian separatism evolved into an open war of secession. Numerous attempts, both military and diplomatic, failed to resolve or to contain this conflict. Instead, Abkhazians have been actively helped by the newly formed North Caucasian Federation, as they had been earlier by contingents of Russian troops stationed in Abkhazia during Soviet days.

At first, the Russian presence was openly prosecessionist. As far as can be ascertained, Moscow's purpose was to expand Russia's presence along the Black Sea littoral. Despite Shevardnadze's much vaunted connections with Moscow, new Russian troops arrived in Abkhazia on June 2, 1993, this time from the Dniester splinter republic in eastern Moldova, ostensibly in response to a January 1993 treaty of cooperation between the Dniester Republic and Abkhazia, an obvious ruse for deeper Russian involvement that made a mockery of Russian foreign minister Kozyrev's mission to "mediate" a ceasefire. By June 25 bitter fighting had resumed.

Poor military leadership on the part of the demoralized Georgian national guard—largely symptomatic of the bungled politics of Shevardnadze—split open his government, leaving him the loser in Abkhazia and at home. Only after Shevardnadze bowed to major demands from Moscow—for Russian basing rights in Georgia, and later that Georgia join the Commonwealth of Independent States (CIS)—did Russia assist him against the separatist groups.

## Shevardnadze's Many Woes

From the outset of his tenure as president of the parliament, Shevardnadze has had to face the solid and persistent regional opposition of Gamsakhurdia's supporters in western Georgia. (The legitimacy of the present government in Tbilisi is still in question because the westerners boycotted elections.) Continued economic decline, the situation in Abkhazia, the after-effects of the smoldering civil war with Gamsakhurdia, and growing unrest in the southern ethnic enclaves combined to create a less than loyal parliamentary opposition, with more and more voices calling on Shevardnadze to resign. As early as mid-June 1993, Iraklii Tsereteli, the head of the Georgian National Independence Party, held Shevardnadze responsible for failing to resolve the Abkhazian problem, pointing in particular to a feeble foreign policy on all fronts, supposedly Shevardnadze's forte. Shevardnadze's patriotism is also questioned, and he is seen by some as Russia's stalking horse because he gave into Russian pressure to bring Georgia into the CIS.

Meanwhile, along Georgia's southern tier, the spillover of the Nagorno-Karabakh war entered the Azeri-populated areas of Georgia. For months, terrorist acts have managed to obstruct the flow of supplies through Georgia to Armenia. The Tbilisi-Yerevan rail link which transports oil to Armenia has been repeatedly blown up, on occasion with Armenian and Georgian fatalities. Most serious have been repeated attacks on gas pipelines. With each attack, the inability of the Shevardnadze government to exercise control over its own territory has been underscored. For all practical purposes, just as the northern tier of Georgia has been drawn into the feuding clan world in the Caucasus mountains, so has the southern tier, in particular the Azeri and Armenian enclaves, been absorbed into the raging conflict over Nagorno-Karabakh.

## Georgia's Challenge—Survival

In sum, over the years, the loyalties of ethnic minorities of Georgia have been effectively siphoned away from Tbilisi towards external ethnic poles of power. Whether a future government can recapture their loyalty, short of force, and prevent the ethno-regional fragmentation of Georgia is at issue. The apparent trade-off for unity, greater obeisance to Russia, is one that deeply troubles almost all peoples of Georgia.

### The Republic of Azerbaijan

In many respects, post-Soviet Azerbaijan resembles Georgia. It, too, is multiethnic, though statistically the Azeri (Shiite Muslim) titular majority enjoys a stronger (83 percent) advantage. But that is deceptive due to significant clan differentiations that account for local loyalties overriding those to any central government. (Similar rifts lie at the heart of the civil war presently tearing Tajikistan apart.) Initially, however, during Gorbachev's years of perestroika, during which the Azeri Popular Front emerged to lead Azerbaijan's republican separatism, these intraethnic fissures were less visible to the unschooled observer, in part because they were purposely papered over. The common enemy—the Soviet Russian—encouraged a strong Azeri alliance of all the rival factions, each of which during the decades of Soviet rule had forged accommodating arrangements with the Tsarist and, later, Soviet overlords.

Shortly after the aborted August 1991 putsch in Moscow, the presidential election in Azerbaijan was won by Ayaz Mutalibov, former Communist party secretary. The election was conducted in a somewhat highhanded Soviet manner by Mutalibov's cohorts, who crowded out any other candidate. This included the Popular Front which, after the election, still found itself a frustrated but popular opposition attempting to operate under autocratic political circumstances.

On the one hand, Mutalibov's government openly backed those seeking the ouster of the reformers in Moscow, thereby hoping to neutralize a potential pro-union intervention from Moscow, as had been the case under Gorbachev. On the other, the new Azerbaijani government unleashed an ethnocentric policy of repression against Nagorno-Karabakh, the Armenian enclave in the west, thereby assuring Azeri popular support but further polarizing Armenian opposition to Baku. This left little room for compromise, but the Mutalibov government thought compromise unnecessary because it presumed it could gain a quick victory. Instead, the war dragged on inconclusively, generating a steady flow of Azeri refugees and seriously draining the already weak economy.

Little wonder that social discontent rapidly came to the fore, giving the Popular Front its opportunity. In the wake of repeated defeats in Nagorno-Karabakh, the Popular Front forced Mutalibov from power in the spring of 1992. In May, it pushed through parliament the acceptance of a temporary president, Yakub Marmedov, in a blatant and unconstitutional maneuver.

By early June, the Popular Front held carefully prepared and controlled elections to assure victory of their own candidate, Abulfez Elchibey. He ran on a platform promising decisive victory in Nagorno-Karabakh, a shortsighted but effective demagogic use of rhetoric, especially in the wake of the much publicized Khodzhaly massacre. Moreover, the Popular Front election victory defeated the old Azeri Communist elite and their followers. In their stead now ruled the "anticommunists," a motley cluster of Azeri factions with little in common but a desire for the spoils of victory. Most lucrative was the power to negotiate with a foreign oil consortium prepared to pay tens of millions of dollars in "seed money," or old-fashioned palm-greasing to get the wheels of government bureaucracy to turn favorably.

*From Bad to Worse*

The Elchibey government fared little better than its predecessor. In fact, within a year it reaped the harvest of its own follies as well as the mistakes of those whom it deposed. Elchibey's rule began with the loss of Lachin, a strategic city that broke the siege of Nagorno-Karabakh and gave the enclave a safe land corridor to Armenia. No less significant was pro-Armenian cooperation from the Kurds, a small but disaffected minority living in the Lachin region. Repeated Azeri efforts to recapture the territory ended not only in failure but in further Armenian territorial victories, expanding the corridor northward (to Kelbajar) and southward (to Fizuli), making Nagorno-Karabakh contiguous with Armenia and extending the capture of Azeri territory eastward beyond Nagorno-Karabakh. This caused a tidal wave of thousands of refugees for whom the government had no accommodations. No wonder that the Popular Front government felt the need for military vindication in order to retain its credibility. By then it had lost 10 percent of its territory to Armenian forces; the figure is now closer to 25 percent.

One means to attempt strategic improvement was to increase the draft, but to do so the government foolishly sought to press non-Azeris into uniform. This was done to ease, partially, the burden on Azeris, many of whom resisted the draft (revealing symptoms of political alienation and social demoralization).

In response, the Lezgins, a sizable minority of Sunni Muslims historically closer to the mountain peoples of Daghestan and Chechnya, collectively opposed serving in a war they felt was strictly ethnic. Quite correctly, they pointed to the Azeri-centric policies of the Elchibey government, an issue at the heart of the Nagorno-Karabakh autonomy struggle and a factor that goes back to the Brezhnev period when Moscow granted Baku considerable leeway in ethnic policy. Recently, some Lezgins have called for a self-governing territory of their own; others have called for complete independence from Azerbaijan; and still others have gone so far as to demand full incorporation into Daghestan. (The latter group has recently declared sovereignty within the Russian Federation, a step short of actual secession).

Accompanying the ethnoterritorial rumblings in northern and western Azerbaijan by Lezgins, Kurds, and Armenians, separatist noises have begun to be heard in the south from the Talysh. When the city of Lenkoran fell into the hands of rebel forces, the Talysh declared their intention to set up a separate state of Mughan-Talysh on the Azeri-Iranian border. Their first formal act was to apply for membership in the CIS.

*Another Succession*

The anti-Elchibey rebellion broke into the open in western Armenia at the beginning of June 1993. Discontent with the government's failure to deal with Nagorno-Karabakh once again sparked civil war. Colonel Surat Guseinov, a former regional military commander, hoisted the flag of rebellion. He was backed by contingents of the army and local villages whose inhabitants were afraid of becoming refugees in the event of further territorial losses to Armenia, for it must not be forgotten that this was also a merciless war of ethnic cleansing.

The explicit goal was to force the president and his cabinet to resign. Implicitly it was understood by all that a new Azeri faction sought a share of central power in Baku, where lay the promise of access to large sums of oil money that could be used to distribute largesse to political supporters of various factions in the Azeri political ranks.

The rebellion spread exceedingly quickly, catching the complacent Popular Front government by surprise and rendering it militarily unable to reimpose its authority. Too many units had shifted their loyalties or decided to remain neutral. Within a few days, key towns in the west (Gyandza) and in the south (Lenkoran) were under rebel control. Hundreds of local progovernment officials were arrested and a march on Baku began. No amount of maneuvering helped Elchibey, who, on June 18, fled the capital for his home province of Ordubad, in Nakhichevan.

Elchibey's powers were immediately given to Geydar Aliyev, the parliamentary chairman. Significantly, as soon as Aliyev reestablished a measure of order, with Guseinov's conspicuous help, the government was promised (on June 22) $70 million in "good faith" money from the Western oil consortium of British Petroleum, Amoco, and Pennzoil. This had a momentary stabilizing effect and allowed the shaky parliament to demand Elchibey's resignation on June 23 in the face of strong, but not unanimous, reservations on the part of the international community. The European Community, Turkey, and the United States all had issued statements supporting Elchibey. In contrast, Iran and Russia withheld any public comment to what they both described as an "internal power struggle." Much to the new government's shock, negotiations with the oil consortium were postponed indefinitely and payments held up, probably due to pressures exerted on the oil companies by their respective governments.

In this uncertain domestic and international climate, the post-Elchibey government resumed major military and diplomatic offensives in order to bring the Nagorno-Karabakh affair to an end. The results, however, were much worse than before, with Armenians overrunning huge hunks of Azerbaijani territory. In fact, Azerbaijani forces fell into disarray, offering little resistance to advancing Armenians. This happened in part because Azerbaijani military forces are poorly coordinated and lack coherent strategy, despite some training from retired Turkish officers and improved supplies of weapons. One problem is the "regionalization" of the army. It consists of many units loyal to local commanders.

With each day, Azerbaijan's political crisis deepened by the draining demands of a war, rising urban unemployment, the precipitous fall of the local currency (the *manat*), and the growing militance of non-Azeri minorities. The potential social dynamite of increasing numbers of refugees, and the maneuverings of external powers—notably Russia—who have found a footing in Azerbaijan through military and economic aid and diplomatic support further compound the political crisis. In sum, Azerbaijan's inability to find a *modus vivendi* with Nagorno-Karabakh has forced it into the quagmire of an undeclared war with Armenia and made it more subject to Moscow's influence.

## The Republic of Armenia

Like the Georgians, but unlike the Azeris, the Armenians look back onto centuries of a well-defined national identity and an ancient tradition of statehood. An Armenian empire once dominated the east Anatolian plain before it was broken up by larger imperial powers from the west (Rome) and from the east (Persia). Buffeted by imperial conquerors and swept back and forth by invaders, large and small pockets of Armenians could be found by the turn of the century from the eastern Mediterranean coast to the western shores of the Caspian.

For centuries most Armenians lived under Ottoman rule. The majority of these were in east Anatolia, but a sizable minority lived across the border in the Russian empire as well as in its major cities such as Baku, Tbilisi, and Moscow. The genocidal massacres of 1915-1921 at the hands of the Turks virtually ended Armenian life in eastern Turkey and the Russian province of Nakhiche-van. Thereafter, the demographic center of the Armenian population shifted to Transcaucasia. Since then, burning historical memories have stimulated dreams of resettling in some distant day those depopulated, historically Arme-nian lands, very much as Zionists responded to the Roman dispersal of Jews from Judea.

After the collapse of Tsarist Russia, a brief but tumultuous moment of Ar-menian political independence ended abruptly, as it had in the case of Georgia and Azerbaijan, with Armenia's incorporation into the Soviet Union. The for-mation of a Soviet Armenian republic was a bittersweet pill. It provided a national territorial base but a truncated one—without Nakhichevan in the west and Nagorno-Karabakh in the east. Both of these areas were attached administratively to Azerbaijan. Furthermore, in the north, across the border in Georgia, lived large clusters of Armenians who made up majorities in two or three Georgian districts.

In the light of the very recent past with Turkey, Armenians found a measure of collective security inside the new USSR, but the price—the loss of large Armenian tracts of historic lands and populations to other republics—was also seen as a national calamity, an injustice inflicted by foreign rulers, no matter how benign their policies in other matters. Over the course of the next seven-and-a-half decades, Armenians occasionally protested or appealed to Moscow to reconsider the borders of Armenia, though to no avail. The commissars in the capital knew the consequences of setting the precedent of redrawing ad-ministrative lines in response to grassroots initiatives, especially with regard to Nagorno-Karabakh. The last thing Moscow wanted was to open this Pandora's box and risk destabilizing its sensitive southern border in Transcaucasia.

### The War
Thus, with the coming of Gorbachev and his call for an honest airing of disputes (glasnost), the issue of Nagorno-Karabakh sprang back to life. The

initiative, however, did not originate within Armenia but within Nagorno-Karabakh itself, where, in the fall of 1987, a petition was sent to Moscow that Nagorno-Karabakh be returned to Armenia. The request was turned down by Gorbachev's government in February 1988. Since then, the dispute has intensified and become a full-fledged war that remains independent Armenia's primary engagement. Armenia emerged out of the Soviet Union in December 1991 entirely enmeshed in this undeclared war with Azerbaijan over Nagorno-Karabakh. Little about Armenia since 1991 can be understood outside the context of the Nagorno-Karabakh matter and its consequences.

More than 500,000 people have been uprooted by the conflict. Anti-Armenian riots in Baku and Sumgait and anti-Azerbaijani reactions in Armenia brought more than a quarter of a million refugees pouring into the young republic. The best the Armenian government could do was to offer them housing in villages abandoned by Azeris who had fled to Azerbaijan. But this by no means resolved the problem of assimilation and integration. The Armenians from Azerbaijan are mostly urban, professional, and largely Russified, linguistically and culturally. Their urban background and differing Armenian dialects make them strangers in their own country.

The stagnating Armenian economy also has little capacity to absorb them. Furthermore, the government of President Ter Petrosian is unable to stimulate the economy as long as Armenia is virtually cut off from vital supplies: Azerbaijan has imposed an effective rail blockade that even denies Armenians construction materials to rebuild the areas devastated by the 1989 earthquake; and Georgia's rail and fuel pipelines are under constant attack by Azeris living in Georgia. In this regard, a new development has been the repeated sabotage of gas lines running from the Russian Federation through northern Caucasia to Georgia and Armenia by terrorist groups in Northern Ossetia. Thus Armenia has become adversely affected by Caucasian disputes in which it is not a direct party. Finally, Turkey refuses air transportation except for limited humanitarian aid until Armenia ceases to lend its support to the enclave of Nagorno-Karabakh. And herein lies the next problem.

*Thinly Veiled Involvement*

Nagorno-Karabakh has received assistance from unofficial Armenian sources for its war with Azerbaijan. Officially, the government in Yerevan claims noninvolvement and openly encourages diplomatic measures to reach a negotiated settlement. In fact, the reality is far more complex. Acknowledged financial and material help has been sent by the Armenian diaspora in France and the United States for Nagorno-Karabakh's war effort. All of this took place with the consent of the Armenian government, which has allowed money and supplies to enter Yerevan and from there to be shipped to or used for Nagorno-Karabakh.

Furthermore, foreign Armenians have been permitted to join the Nagorno-Karabakh Self-Defense Force (SDF). The ranks of the SDF also contain more than a few ex-Armenian officers and men who had been part of the Soviet army. And, ever since the capture of the land corridor to Nagorno-Karabakh, the regular supply line now in operation makes any distinction between the SDF and the regular Armenian army a mockery. Ter Petrosian's denials notwithstanding, the porous border has hopelessly blurred the distinction between the two. Azeris believe they are fighting a single enemy.

### Through Executive Eyes

Ter Petrosian's problem is one of a president who has lost control of his armed forces and of the nationalist political elements that favor direct participation in the Nagorno-Karabakh war. He no longer enjoys majority support in the unicameral Armenian parliament. Though in office by direct popular election, Ter Petrosian is torn between his own desire to find a quick end to the war (in order to rebuild the shattered economy of his potentially rich country) and the equally fervent desires of others to win the war over Nagorno-Karabakh and annex the enclave. Battlefield victories, especially significant territorial gains, have not enhanced chances for peace.

The psychological backdrop for governance is important. Even though Armenia has a very homogeneous population (93.5 percent Armenian), its population of 3.6 million is deeply divided between those whose priorities are national economic reconstruction and those favoring national reconstruction via the liberation of historical lands and unification with Armenian minorities in Nagorno-Karabakh. For the latter, land and people are a key factor in the redemption of Armenia as a viable state and Armenians as a viable nation. In their eyes, the present struggle is the last opportunity to reverse the tragic trend of Armenian history in the twentieth century. The collapse of the USSR left Armenia landlocked and virtually surrounded by Muslim states perceived by Armenians to be aggressive. One of those states is Turkey and the other Turkic (Azerbaijan). The deep mistrust of anything Turkish has paralyzed most Armenian moves for a peaceful resolution.

So far, Ter Petrosian has been unable to forge a consistent policy for reliable negotiations, constantly having to appease his critics on the right who accuse him of harboring a willingness to leave Nagorno-Karabakh inside Azerbaijan. But Nagorno-Karabakh refuses to accept such a solution. Its minimum goal is independence, a goal that is totally unacceptable to Azerbaijan, which correctly sees independence as a step leading to annexation. Hence the stand-off. Inside Armenia, more and more parliamentarians call for a recognition of Nagorno-Karabakh's independence, while Ter Petrosian knows this would ruin all chances for peace.

As opposition mounts against him in Armenia's 260-seat parliament, calls for new elections increase. In February 1993, the president dismissed his entire cabinet, but the new one continues to reflect the fissures in parliament and debates over economic and political reform that have helped bring effective government to a standstill. Food and fuel shortages have left the population stoic but very vulnerable to winter. Periodic talk of reopening a nuclear power plant raises new concerns, especially with the memory of Chernobyl and the 1989 earthquake in Armenia fresh in everyone's mind, despite the critical shortage of electricity. The dispute has already caused numerous public outbursts and demonstrations.

Meanwhile the intractable Nagorno-Karabakh issue erodes any hope for a more stable future. A corrosive siege mentality has hardened everyone's position, leaving the president with his hands tied as he tries to assemble majority support for any position on any issue. Armenia is now in the grip of political paralysis; unceasing activity at home and abroad brings few measurable results. At present, Armenia suffers from a kind of anarchy (of which political assassinations are symptomatic) that does not allow for effective decision making. Uncoordinated government agencies issue official statements by the dozen, creating more confusion than clarity both in the public mind and in foreign chancelleries.

The war and its outcome underlie all political discussions. Deep distrust of Azerbaijani intentions, gnawing fears of Turkey, reflexive suspicions about Iran (Iran has offered to build a pipeline to the Armenian border, even while issuing public statements condemning Armenia), anxieties over the ineffectiveness of European diplomacy, growing concern over Russia's involvement with Baku, and overall confusion regarding U.S. policy have all added to the sense of malaise and international isolation. A large and steady flow of emigrants further darkens the national mood.

## Limits on External Intervention

And so one returns to the original question: What can and should U.S. policy be in a region emerging from the colonial grips of the Soviet empire, a region now faced with an agenda filled with contentious issues, most of which have centuries-old roots? Ideally, of course, the United States would have cordial relations with all three Transcaucasian states. But given all this feuding— Georgia over Abkhazia and Armenia and Azerbaijan over Nagorno-Karabakh are but two obvious examples—universal cordiality is unrealistic. Polarized conditions make it next to impossible for a third party to remain neutral.

Furthermore, for the United States to act as mediator would require it to come to Transcaucasia with a better record than it presently enjoys. The agonizing delay of direct involvement in Bosnia is symptomatic of a government loath to enter multiethnic settings—a prudent policy. All the more so with respect to far-away Transcaucasia.

For a time, U.S. diplomacy in the region deferred to Turkey as an acceptable post-Soviet surrogate for the United States, especially as a deterrent to Iranian (read: militant Islamic) penetration. But pan-Turkic ambitions notwithstanding, Turkey simply lacks the reach to do more than it already has in Azerbaijan. Burdened with its past vis-à-vis the Armenians, Turkey in Transcaucasia is more a liability than a positive agent. Its primary geopolitical interest in the post-Cold War era lies in forging a Black Sea regional arrangement among the littoral states and not a harmonious fusion of state interests in Transcaucasia. Internal security considerations (for example, the Kurds in southeastern Turkey) force the Turkish government to refrain from engaging in foreign involvements too far from home.

That leaves only the Russians to try and act as the regional superpower but, despite Russia's recent muscle flexing in the region, it remains highly debatable whether the present Russian Federation can act effectively. So far, its ad hoc handling of each crisis in northern Caucasia and its direct and indirect interventions in the Abkhazian dispute have poured oil onto the fire. The presence of Russian troops has predictably turned guns against Russian soldiers and exacerbated the problem. Indeed, given the contradictory role of Russian troops throughout the Caucasus—in Abkhazia, in Georgia, in Azerbaijan and Armenia, in the Ossetias, and so on—one wonders at times whether Moscow has any more control of its military units than does Baku or Yerevan. Worse, it is difficult to identify a coherent foreign policy emanating from a Moscow when conflicting orders are sent simultaneously to military commanders by the executive, by the legislature, by the military, and by the ministry of internal security. Increasingly, local Russian commanders seem to be taking matters into their own hands and negotiating private policies, some resembling those of mercenaries.

Any U.S. policy that depended on a Russian surrogate to act as a regional gendarme would be very dubious. At present, U.S. policy for post-Soviet Transcaucasia strikes one as improvisational and ad hoc; there is, for example, confused support "in principle" for deposed President Elchibey, but U.S. oil companies meanwhile negotiate with the "rebel" Aliyev government for rights to a four-billion-barrel off-shore oil reserve.

In Georgia, the State Department or the CIA, or both, have decided to back a besieged President Shevardnadze by providing him with a U.S.-trained security guard. Shevardnadze's trip to the United States in early 1994 reaffirmed those ties, and strengthened U.S. support levels. But why?

In Armenia, the United States has sporadically called for the withdrawal of Armenian troops from Azerbaijani territory outside Nagorno-Karabakh. But it has done so without enunciating a clear stand on how and why it wishes the issue to be resolved, thereby stiffening the resolve to resist on the part of Nagorno-Karabakh and its irredentist allies in Yerevan, who are seeing their struggle both in terms of Israeli history and in the light of Bosnia's experience.

What kind of policy or policies do U.S. "initiatives" in the three Transcaucasian capitals add up to? Do they rest on a regional policy? Are they more than ad hoc reactions? Is anyone coordinating these separate decisions? Further, are there contingency plans to meet the rising crisis in Russian Caucasia? Is the United States promoting a policy favoring the territorial integrity of the Russian Federation? Or is it interested in promoting contacts with elements of the separatist movements (for example with those in Chechnya), in the event of their exit from the Russian Federation? What signals are being sent? Does the United States regard the Abkhazian war as an "internal" struggle, even though it has been internationalized by the participation of Russian troops? What is the proper role of international organizations such as the United Nations and the Committee on Security and Cooperation in Europe, especially in light of the CSCE proposal to send an international peacekeeping force to Georgia? Is the United States, in the case of Abkhazia, tacitly condoning Russian military intervention in a regional war of secession and propping up a Shevardnadze government committed to keeping Abkhazia an integral part of Georgia? Are U.S. policy makers prepared to fine-tune these contradictions or suffer the consequences?

It is of some urgency that the United States adopt some meaningful policy guidelines for this troubled post-Soviet region. Otherwise, history will be written there in part as a result of poor U.S. diplomacy or missed opportunities for constructive U.S. action. Is the Caucasus a region "far away," beyond U.S. strategic interests, or does it fall within the range of national security? This question must be answered immediately by those familiar with multiethnic Caucasia. Above all the respondents must provide a coherent picture of the region upon which U.S. policy makers can base their decisions.

Above all, events in the Caucasus must be understood in terms of the dynamics of the *bolshoi raspad*, the great collapse of the multiethnic Soviet empire. Ethnic factors—language, religion, social structure, history, and territory—are the key to an understanding of much of the region's past, present, and future. The process of break-up—the dismantling of the colonial past—will go on.

At the same time, as traditional rivalries emerge, the region is returning to a pre-imperial stage; that is, to a condition following the retreat of one dominant power and preceding the arrival of another, which may be Turkey, Iran, or, as was the case in the 1920s, the postrevolutionary Russians. The return of imperial hegemony is not a certainty, of course, but the dynamics of imperial rivalry for control of the Caucasus are unquestionably present. That rivalry is already in progress. Whether and how the United States wishes to play is the question policy makers must answer.

This paper was completed in May 1993.


### Sources

This essay has relied on data drawn from the following sources. The interpretation of the information is strictly that of the author.

*The Armenian Weekly* (Armenian Revolutionary Federation, Watertown, Mass.); *Bakinskii Rabochii* (Baku); *The California Courier* (Glendale); *Chronicle Express* (Moscow); *The Current Digest of the Post-Soviet Press*; *Digest* (Commission on Security and Cooperation in Europe); *Die Zeit*; Embassy of the Republic of Armenia press releases; *The Economist* (London); *Frankfurter Allgemeine*; *Golos Armenii* (Erevan); Karabakh News Agency; *Monitor: Digest of News and Analysis from the Soviet Successor States* (Union of Councils for Soviet Jews, Washington, D.C.); *Monthly Digest of News* (Office of Research Analysis, Armenian Assembly of Armenia, Washington, D.C.); *Moscow News*; *New York Times*; *News Digest* (Zohrab Information Center, New York); *Nezavissimaya Gazeta* (Moscow); *Research Bulletin* (Radio Free Europe/Radio Liberty, Washington, D.C.); *RFE/RL News Briefs* (Munich); *RFE/RL Research Report* (Munich); *Russkoe Slovo* (New York); *Transcaucasus: A Chronology* (Armenian National Committee of America, Washington, D.C.); United Nations press releases; U.S. State Department press releases; *Washington Post*; Zoryan Institute archives (Cambridge, Mass.).

# 18 The Baltic Countries: Between a Rock and a Hard Place

Tönu Parming

Estonia, Latvia, and Lithuania have been lumped together as the Baltic countries with such persistence that their unique features tend to be overshadowed.[1] It is, nevertheless, useful to keep in mind a point made by the Royal Institute of International Affairs more than fifty years ago:

> The grouping together of the three Baltic States is to some extent arbitrary, since, although they share much in common, and although for geographical, historical, and social reasons many of their problems are the same, they form what are essentially three separate and distinct national groups. Their differences are at least as striking as their similarities.[2]

To be sure, the problems and needs of de-Sovietization have certain commonalities in all postcommunist societies: for example, the reestablishment of sovereign political institutions (idealized as democratic), recreation of civil society (idealized as "open" or "free"), and the decentralization of the economy (idealized as market based). But whatever the similarities might be at an abstract level, the concrete developments in Estonia, Latvia, and Lithuania are today quite divergent. It may be argued, as the Royal Institute argued fifty years ago, that the differences are at least as important as the similarities.

The sharp contrast is between Estonia and Lithuania, with Latvia falling in between in regard to most issues. In the present essay the main emphasis is on an explication of political distinctions. Although political and economic processes are surely interrelated, it would appear that the desired economic transformation in de-Sovietization cannot readily be accomplished without antecedent, or at least concurrent, political change.[3]

In contrasting Estonia and Lithuania, we might at the outset consider the following. In the parliamentary elections of September 1992 in Estonia, and in the government which ensued, former top leaders and even ordinary members of the Communist party were largely unsuccessful. Indeed, not a single candidate on the list of the Party of Democratic Labor, as the Communist party was renamed in each of the Baltic countries, was elected to parliament. But in the parliamentary elections in Lithuania in October-November 1992, former top leaders of the Communist party were returned to power, with the Party of Democratic Labor receiving a strong 46 percent of the vote. In the ensuing presidential elections in February 1993, the winner, Algirdas Brazauskas, had earlier been a Communist party first secretary in the Lithuanian SSR.

In Estonia, a new constitution was prepared by a constitutional assembly that had a wide political base, and it was submitted to referendum vote about three months prior to parliamentary elections. In Lithuania, a new constitution was drafted by those in power and submitted to referendum concurrently with the holding of parliamentary elections. The Lithuanian constitution continues a strong presidential system, the precedent for which dates back to the 1920s and which was continued even during the Sajudis period of rule from 1990 to 1993. The Estonian constitutional assembly rejected the idea of a presidential system of governance, which had upheld an authoritarian regime in the second half of the 1930s, and instead offered a parliamentary system with a weak president.

Estonia readopted its own currency in mid-1992. The result has been a stable monetary climate and a shift in foreign trade away from Russia, which now constitutes about 20 percent of exports and imports. Lithuania is still struggling to implement a genuine currency; inflation remains high and foreign trade remains disproportionately with Russia. Estonia has in essence free-trade agreements with its two closest Western neighbors, Finland (Estonia's principal trade partner) and Sweden, while the Lithuanian-Polish border is an obstacle to the free movement of people and goods. The estimate of the International Monetary Fund is that in 1994 Estonia's economy will show among the strongest growth rates in Europe.[4] There is no equivalent optimism for Lithuania.

In all key political and economic developments, Latvia falls, as noted, between Estonia and Lithuania, except that it was the last to carry out parliamentary elections, which did not take place until June 1993. Latvia retained, with some changes, its prewar constitution, which continues a political tradition of a strong president. Its monetary reforms are further along than in Lithuania but hardly as advanced as in Estonia. Its patterns of foreign trade are more Western-oriented than those of Lithuania but not as extensively so as those of Estonia.

**The Baltic states**

### Roots of Difference

In grappling with the question of why Estonia's transition is so far more advanced than Lithuania's, we need to focus on political developments during the years 1987-1992. Gorbachev's policies of perestroika and glasnost expanded the arena of allowable political discourse and the boundaries of tolerated political activity to an unprecedented degree in Soviet history. The new thaw in the Soviet system reached the Baltic region quickly. Only a few years ago the predominant tendency in Western commentary was to attribute the political dynamics in the Baltic countries on the road to reindependence to the three respective People's Fronts (named Sajudis in Lithuania). As E. Eugene

Pell, president of Radio Free Europe/Radio Liberty, put it in 1991: "Political developments in the Baltic states continue to move toward independence. These developments are guided by the three popular movements (i.e., the three People's Fronts)." [5]

The first of the three People's Fronts was founded in the Estonian SSR. Promulgated in April 1988 and formally founded that October, it appears to have influenced developments elsewhere in the Soviet Union as well, including the Latvian and Lithuanian SSRs. The distinctions among the three fronts in the Baltics, including their relative political influence during the years 1988-1991, have been regrettably ignored or underrated in Western analysis. Yet these distinctions are of major analytic significance. Indeed, the greater advances made by Estonia and the lesser advances by Lithuania cannot be adequately explained without consideration of the distinctions in question.

The main point is that Estonia's advances may be attributed largely to the fact that alternatives to Soviet-era political institutions were created almost immediately after alternatives became possible in the climate of the nascent Gorbachev era. The People's Fronts were formally launched to advance perestroika, and while they indeed came to power, what they achieved was the control of Soviet-era political institutions, of which they themselves became victims.

Be that as it may, in the Estonian parliamentary elections of September 1992, the People's Front received only 15 percent of the popular vote. The People's Front government, headed by its founder, Edgar Savisaar, had fallen from power eight months earlier. Lithuania's Sajudis, headed by Vytautas Landsbergis, held on to power until the parliamentary elections of October-November 1992, when Sajudis won only 14 percent of the seats. In Latvia, too, the People's Front held power until the parliamentary elections, in June 1993, winning no seats in parliament and receiving less than 3 percent of the vote.

Lithuania had a much stronger guerrilla resistance to Soviet rule after the Second World War than did either Estonia or Latvia.[6] And during the 1970s, the degree of explicit national resistance to Soviet rule in Lithuania through organized dissidence was also much more extensive than among its northern neighbors.[7] Yet the emergence of Sajudis in 1988 pushed this earlier resistance, individually as well as organizationally, largely out of the political picture. Sajudis claimed in essence to represent the national will, portraying itself as the sole possible political alternative to the Soviet system. Ironically, many of its successful candidates in the elections for the Supreme Soviet of the Lithuanian SSR in February 1990 were former or even current members of the Communist party of the Soviet Union (CPSU). Although Landsbergis had reportedly not been a member of the CPSU, the prime minister of the first Sajudis cabinet, Kazimiera Prunskiene, had been a rising political star in the old Soviet system.

The People's Fronts from the outset faced an internally irreconcilable dilemma, that of acting as the Pope and Luther at the same time.[8] On the one hand, the Fronts claimed to be reformers with national interests in mind; on the other they came to hold political power in a decaying Soviet system. The Fronts all included individuals in leading positions whose main stated objective was reform of the Soviet system, and others whose goals were genuinely nationalist. Thus these were irreconcilable contradictions in setting the goals of the Fronts: a redefined Soviet system with greater regional autonomy versus the reestablishment of genuine independence.

The political discourse of the period from 1988 to 1991 was wrought with dialectics. If someone spoke of "sovereignty" or "independence," it was persistently unclear as to whether this meant sovereignty or independence within the Soviet system or outside it. In the absence of alternative political institutions and clearly expressed goals, genuine domestic reform became impossible. This helps explain the quick demise of the People's Fronts, which in the end satisfied neither democratic nationalists nor reform Communists. In Lithuania, the Gorbachevian Communists returned to power, but in Estonia, it was the democratic nationalists who gained power.

The contrast in political outcomes is so profound as to require further explanation. Two sharp distinctions are evident between Estonia and Lithuania. First, in Estonia the political dissidents of the pre-Gorbachev period organized themselves anew several months prior to the creation of the People's Front and beat the Front to the political punch in defining goals that later reflected the preference of the large majority of Estonians. And second, the Estonian exile community, unlike Latvian and Lithuanian exiles, never significantly embraced the People's Front.

From all accounts the decision to hold the Chautauga Conference meeting between the Soviet Union and the United States in the Latvian SSR in 1986 had significant consequences. As an AP dispatch from Riga put it: "An entourage of Americans visiting Soviet-ruled Latvia stirred up enough nationalism in five days to trigger a clash between Latvian nationalists and the KGB, despite almost a half-century of Russian domination."[9]

In June 1987 Latvian dissidents organized the first major nongovernmental political rally in Riga since the end of the Second World War. Tiit Madisson, an Estonian friend of one of the Latvian organizers from the time of their incarceration as political prisoners, was so inspired by the events in Riga that he spearheaded an unofficial political rally in Tallinn on August 23, 1987, the anniversary of the Molotov-Ribbentrop Pact of 1939, the secret protocols of which had placed the Baltic countries in the Soviet sphere of influence, with the consequence of their occupation and annexation less than a year later. The demonstration in Tallinn's Hirve Park, organized by recently released prisoners of conscience, attracted several thousand people, and it is widely considered a political watershed.

There is a direct path from Hirve Park in August 1987 to the announcement of the creation of the Estonian National Independence Party in January 1988. This party of Estonian dissidents was the first overtly operating opposition party to the Communist party in the Soviet Union. The People's Front was still several months away. The Estonian National Independence Party was denounced by officialdom, its organizational efforts were widely harassed, and the CPSU undertook a number of efforts to offer its own alternatives. Whether the People's Front, announced in Tallinn in April 1988, was one such alternative is now moot. Tiit Madisson, prime mover of the Hirve Park rally, was expelled from the Soviet Union in the early fall of 1987.

Another organization created in late 1987, "from below" rather than "from above," was the Estonian Heritage Society. Similar organizations were already legally active elsewhere in the Soviet Union, including the Russian SFSR, which may account for the ease with which it received official permission from the Estonian SSR authorities. Heritage societies had already existed at the local level in Estonia for a few years; now there was a national body as well, and membership grew very rapidly. The primary contribution of the society was the reconstruction of national history in all of its many forms, including the restoration of patriotic monuments that had been destroyed during fifty years of Soviet occupation.

Two of the key founders in both the Estonian National Independence Party (Tunne Kelam and Lagle Parek) and the Estonian Heritage Society (Trivimi Velliste and Mart Laar) have played a leading role in recent Estonian politics. Laar became prime minister after the September 1992 elections; Velliste, foreign minister; Parek, minister of the interior (until December 1993); and Kelam, deputy speaker of parliament and head of the Estonian delegation at the European parliament in Strasbourg.

The formation of the People's Front of Estonia was announced, as noted, in April 1988 by Edgar Savisaar, a rising young star in the old Soviet order. A member of the CPSU, he was the head of the Estonian SSR division of the State Economic Planning Committee (GOSPLAN) and soon became deputy chairman of the Council of Ministers. He was also one of the delegates chosen from the Estonian SSR in 1989 to Gorbachev's new Congress of People's Deputies in Moscow. A number of other key leaders in the Front were also CPSU members. From the outset, the political tension between the Front and the democratic nationalists was pronounced.

### The Congress of Estonia

At a commemorative assembly on Estonian Independence Day on February 24, 1989, the Estonian National Independence Party, the Estonian Heritage Society, and the Estonian Christian-Democratic League, one of several new political groupings founded in mid- and late-1988, launched a new movement based on the citizens of the Republic of Estonia. Their objective was to register all the citizens of that Republic of Estonia which had been occupied by the Soviet Union in mid-1940 and on this basis to convene a Congress of Estonia. Their instrument was to be newly created citizens' committees. Here, then, was the practical seed for alternative political mobilization and the pursuit of alternative goals. If there is an historical analogy to be made, it would be to the Committees of Correspondence and their role with the Continental Congress in the American Revolution.

Put simply, those who advocated the citizens' committees had as their goal the factual reestablishment of the Republic of Estonia, which was still recognized *de jure* by almost all Western countries. Those who led the People's Front proposed at first greater autonomy in a Soviet Union redefined by a new Treaty of the Union, and later a "Third Republic," derived not from the prewar Republic of Estonia (the first republic), but from the Estonian Soviet Socialist Republic (the second republic).

Related to this debate over goals was inevitably the question of citizenship. Because the Third Republic would be derived from the Estonian SSR, its advocates urged the more-or-less automatic transfer of citizenship in the USSR to citizenship in the new Estonian state (the so-called "zero option" in citizenship). The opposition insisted on the continuity of citizenship based on the continuity of statehood. In the constitutional referendum of June 1992, the idea of a carryover of citizenship from the USSR was rejected in principle.

In any case, throughout 1989 the debate over citizenship and the goals of statehood galvanized public opinion in the direction of full independence. The leadership of the People's Front was opposed until very late in the game to the citizens' committees and the convening thereby of a congress of Estonia. In April 1989, 56 percent of Estonians supported the idea of full independence; by February 1990 this had risen to 84 percent and by May 1990 to 96 percent.[10] In early February 1990, the idea of full independence found overwhelming affirmation at the convention of all elected representatives at all levels of government.

The registration of citizens proved highly successful, and more ballots were cast in the elections for the Congress of Estonia at the end of February 1990 than in any of the prewar Estonian parliamentary elections. The Congress convened on March 11, 1990, and steered a steady and principled course for the restoration of independence on the basis of the historical continuity of statehood. In the election of the Council of Estonia, the executive arm of the Congress, the former dissidents and other supporters of restoration received not only a majority but also a clear mandate.

The political competition with the People's Front did not end here. The Front became the dominant force in the Supreme Soviet of the Estonian SSR, elected in late March 1990. Some of the democratic nationalists ran in these elections as well, and they formed an effective and growing opposition to the new Front government in the Supreme Soviet. But Estonia now had two competing authorities: a new body representing the citizens of the Republic of Estonia versus a Soviet-era institution representing Soviet citizens residing in Soviet-occupied Estonia. These two constituencies did not fully overlap and therefore neither did the political tendencies in the two institutions.

To be sure, neither the Supreme Soviet of the Estonian SSR nor the Congress of Estonia directly achieved independence for the country in August 1991. Independence in a practical sense fell in place in the circumstances and context of the events in Moscow that month. But the Estonian state which was reestablished on August 21, 1991, reflected a clear victory for the Congress of Estonia. Arguments in Tallinn about the format of statehood ran deep into the night of August 20. The leader of the People's Front and the chairman of the Council of Ministers, Edgar Savisaar, did not play a key role in these deliberations, having been in Stockholm when the events in Moscow began to unfold. In the end, what was issued was not a declaration of new independence, but a decision on the reestablishment of the Republic of Estonia on the principle of the continuity of statehood. Leaders of the Congress participated in formulating the compromise wording of the decision.

A compromise was also reached on another point: a constitutional assembly would be convened on the basis of parity between the Supreme Soviet and the Congress of Estonia. The assembly convened in the fall of 1991. It rejected a proposal from within Savisaar's Council of Ministers for a constitution embodying a strong executive. Instead, the working draft that ultimately was adopted had been offered by those in the leadership of the Congress, more specifically, a working group from within the Estonian National Independence Party. The result was, in any case, a parliamentary rather than a presidential system of governance. Diehards who wanted to resuscitate the strong-executive constitution of 1938 lost out as well in the affirmation vote in the Congress in early 1992.

The Savisaar government fell in January 1992, and was replaced by one headed by Tiit Vähi. Although himself a former member of the Communist party and a minister in both the Savisaar cabinet and the one which preceded it, Vähi from the outset announced that his was to be an interim cabinet. The new constitution was endorsed by 91 percent of the voters, with about 65 percent of those eligible voting on June 28, 1992. Parliamentary elections followed in September. A number of factions had split from the People's Front during 1990-1991 to form new groups. Some of these, such as the Liberal-Democrats and Social-Democrats, are part of the current governing coalition, which includes the Christian-Democrats and the National Independence Party as well.

The democratic nationalists clearly had thus won on all key points, and with their allies they achieved the controlling majority in the new parliament. The primary partner in the current coalition government is the conservative National Coalition Party "Pro Patria" headed by Mart Laar, who became prime minister. The constitution specifies that the president be elected by the parliament rather than directly by the citizenry. An exception was made for 1992, the first post-Soviet election. None of the four candidates received a majority in the first, popular round of voting in September 1992. The People's Front candidate, Rein Taagepera of California, received 24 percent of the vote; a prominent former dissident, Lagle Parek, received 4 percent; one of the former top Communists, Arnold Rüütel, received 43 percent; and the candidate of the present governing coalition, writer Lennart Meri, 29 percent. The question was decided in a second round of voting in the parliament between the two top vote getters, Rüütel and Meri. The latter, not surprisingly, won.

Most members of the new cabinet, as well as the president, had been delegates to the Congress of Estonia, many of them members of its executive arm, the Council of Estonia. Indeed, the majority of those elected to parliament in 1992 had been elected to the Congress in 1990.

A citizens' movement emerged in Latvia as well, modeled after Estonia's, and a Congress of Latvia was convened, but it never enjoyed the prestige and influence of its Estonian counterpart. One major reason for this is that the Latvian National Independence Party itself became affiliated with the People's Front of Latvia, which was thus an umbrella political group, unlike in Estonia. In addition, members of the Latvian National Independence Party ran for the Supreme Soviet of the Latvian SSR in 1990, while in Estonia members of their sister-party did not. In Lithuania, as noted, Sajudis effectively shut out the earlier dissidents, assuming for itself a monolithic political role, ironically functionally equivalent to that of the earlier CPSU. In the end, Sajudis lost the ability to act as an effective agent of reform because it could not challenge power, which it itself had achieved.

To summarize this point: the Congress of Estonia provided the democratic nationalists an alternative institutional basis for activism, for honing organizational skills, and for advancing their goals. Those in the main current of the Congress could thus act as a genuine political opposition to both the traditional Communists as well as the reform-minded Gorbachev communists who controlled the People's Front. Furthermore, the Social-Democrats, Liberal-Democrats, and Christian-Democrats were all active in the Congress, and after September 1992 in the governing coalition. They also became members in 1991 of their respective international bodies. This provided a superb new channel for meaningful political contacts in the West, whereas the People's Fronts had no institutional counterparts.

Although the Fronts officially claimed to be movements, in practical terms they were organizations. They were centralized, almost to the extent of operating on a leader principle, but had no formal membership. Thus it was unclear whom the Fronts represented. They were indeed effective in organizing events at home, gaining the upper hand in Soviet-style legislative bodies, and attracting extensive media-attention in the West. But they were ineffective in forming useful liaisons with democratic parties in the West. The political parties of the democratic nationalists in Estonia, operating outside Soviet-type bodies, were much more effective in pursuing substantive foreign contacts.

The events in Estonia suggest that the differences among Estonia, Latvia, and Lithuania after August 1991 derived in large part from the competition for influence and power in the few years preceding re-independence and from the outcome of those key struggles.

## The Balts in Exile

The pattern of support by the exile communities was the other key factor that helps to explain the uniqueness of the political outcome in Estonia.[11] All three exile communities had for decades demanded an end to the Soviet occupation and supported their respective dissidents. Yet the Latvian and Lithuanian communities came quickly and extensively to support the People's Fronts while the Estonian community did not. The Estonians had strongly supported the dissidents who organized the aforementioned Hirve Park demonstration in August 1987 and the announcement of the formation of the Estonian National Independence Party the following January. The Estonian exile community remained by and large cool to the People's Front in 1988, instead supporting the citizens' movement and the Congress of Estonia during 1989-1992.

Why the People's Front of Estonia did not receive noteworthy support from the Estonians in the West remains unclear. A perusal of the Estonian-language press in the West would suggest that two developments in 1988 clearly worked to the Front's disadvantage. First, in February 1988 the presidium of the Supreme Soviet of the Estonian SSR, headed by Arnold Rüütel, replied publicly to members of the U.S. Congress who had urged Gorbachev not to crack down again on dissidents in the Baltic. This particular communication praised the Estonians' "voluntary and irrevocable" choice in 1940 to pursue a socialist future as part of the Soviet Union.[12] Second, in October of that year, a secret directive issued by the Communist party's Central Committee and the Council of Ministers of the Estonian SSR stated explicitly that greater contacts were to be pursued with the émigré community in order to convince it that Estonia's future lay irrevocably within the Soviet Union.[13]

It is questionable whether the course and outcome of the competition for political influence and power in Estonia would have been what it was if the exile community had thrown its weight behind the People's Front in 1988, as occurred in Latvia and Lithuania. In the Estonian parliamentary elections of September 1992 the votes from abroad were crucial to the outcome. Almost ten thousand citizens voted from abroad, nearly 90 percent of them for candidates who represented the victorious coalition.[14] In the complex proportional voting system in effect in Estonia, this vote translated into about one-and-a-half parliamentary seats, which is not insignificant given the very narrow margin of victory: the coalition that formed the Estonian cabinet in October 1992 had at first but 51 seats of 101 in the parliament. The voters from abroad also gave 85 percent of their votes to the Estonian National Independence Party and "Pro Patria" presidential candidates. Although this made no difference in the first round of voting for president, it certainly did in the second round, the outcome of which depended on who was in the majority in parliament. The People's Front presidential candidate received a mere 4 percent of the vote outside Estonia.

There had been debate in all three Baltic countries as to whether or not citizens living abroad should be able to vote or not. In Estonia, the Savisaar faction of the original leadership of the People's Front was opposed to voting from abroad, while those representing the Congress of Estonia supported the possibility. At the heart of the debate was a more fundamental question, namely, whether or not those who constituted the exile community, in other words those who had fled the Soviet occupation primarily in 1944, should even be considered citizens of contemporary Estonia. Savisaar, as chairman of the Council of Ministers, had gone so far as to send a letter to a U.S. senator in February 1991 stating that the Estonian exile community in the United States did not represent the interests of Estonia.[15] But the position of the Congress of Estonia prevailed on the questions of continued citizenship and voting rights just as it had on other key points of debate.[16]

Estonians, Latvians and Lithuanians from exile around the world participated in the elections of 1992 and 1993 in other ways as well. Financial support for the contending parties was a less significant factor than the fielding of candidates. In Estonia, the top vote-getter in the parliamentary elections and an extreme right-winger, Jüri Toomepuu, was from the United States. In Latvia, the most successful party, "Latvia's Way," was a peculiar alliance that included political leaders from exile and former Communists. Its top figures included Latvian-American Gunars Meierovics, president of the World Federation of Free Latvians. Meierovics was one of the initial candidates for president, but he bowed out in favor of the eventual winner, Guntis Ulmanis. A relative of Latvia's prewar president, Ulmanis (like President Meri of Estonia) had spent part of his youth as a deportee in Siberia, but unlike Meri he later joined the CPSU. In Lithuania the main challenge to Brazauskas came from Stasys Lozoraitis, a long-time Lithuanian diplomat in exile. At the time Lozoraitis was Lithuania's ambassador in Washington. Rein Taagepera, the losing presidential candidate of the People's Front of Estonia, was from California.

Estonian and Latvian citizens from the West also came to serve as ministers in the new governments. Furthermore, a number of former military officers in Western countries serve in various capacities in Estonia, Latvia, and Lithuania. The first minister of defense in Laar's cabinet, Dr. Hain Rebas, was a reserve captain in Sweden; his brother, also a Swedish reserve officer, became the inspector general of Estonia's defense forces. The commander of Estonia's defense forces, Major General Alexander Einseln, is a retired American colonel. The number of Estonians, Latvians, and Lithuanians from exile who have returned to work in their ancestral homelands in one capacity or another is noteworthy. Their presence is felt even in the diplomatic corps: for example, the ambassadors of both Estonia and Latvia in Washington were born in exile and are former naturalized American citizens.

In closing this political overview, we might note that the People's Front of Estonia ended its existence in late 1993. Some in the former leadership still support the so-called centrist faction in parliament, which is headed by Savisaar, while others abandoned him in the fall of 1993 to form a new political group. For practical purposes Lithuania's Sajudis transferred its political functions to the new Fatherland Union, of which Landsbergis became chairman in May 1993. The People's Front of Latvia has decided to muddle on.

### Key Domestic Issues

With regard to fundamental economic problems, nothing distinguishes one Baltic country from another, at least on the surface. Yet if we are to accept the views offered in the reports of the World Bank and International Monetary Fund, and in leading financial newspapers , then Estonia clearly leads the transition pack. There are several reasons for this. First and foremost is the outcome of the political struggle for power during 1987-1992, as discussed above. The Estonian cabinet that came to power in the fall of 1992, as well as its successor cabinet in November 1994, have been more effectively dedicated to substantive change than has been the case in Latvia or Lithuania. This commitment to market economics and private enterprise has affected monetary policy, property rights, land reform, taxation, the export of profits by foreign firms, privatization, and trade.

It is not insignificant that Estonia is the least dependent of the three Baltic countries on Russian energy sources. Electricity is produced mainly by the domestic oil-shale industry. In addition to this, Estonia has had a special historical relationship with both Finland and Sweden. As a result, patterns of business investments, formal foreign aid, people-to-people assistance, and so forth, have appeared to be more favorable in Estonia than in Latvia and Lithuania. The reference here is to a broad spectrum of foreign economic relations above and beyond that which has been offered by G-7/G-24 countries and international organizations. If Jeffrey Sachs and his shock therapy approach to economic de-Sovietization are proven correct anywhere, it most likely will be in Estonia, where one of his Harvard protégés, Dr. Ardo Hansson, a Canadian citizen, has been economic adviser to the Laar government. He also serves on the governing council of the Bank of Estonia.

Other problems, such as the legacy of pollution, training a civil service and police force, the decentralization of government, the establishment of an independent judiciary, restructuring education, and so on, are not unique to the Baltic countries and will not be discussed here. The most crucial domestic problem at first was the legacy of Soviet colonial demographic policy. Before the Second World War, Estonia had the most ethnically homogeneous population of the three countries: 88 percent of the inhabitants were ethnic Estonian. By 1989 this had changed; only about 60 percent were Estonian. Latvia was the most heterogeneous before the war (75 percent) and remains so today (52 percent in 1989). But Lithuania's population has remained unchanged in relative terms: it is still about 80 percent Lithuanian.[17]

The fundamental question deriving from the demographic changes of the Soviet period is that of the rights—including the citizenship status—of the former colonial subpopulation, the bulk of which is Russian. Moscow chose in the late 1980s to make this both a bilateral and international issue, claiming as late as the end of 1993 an inherent right to "protect the interests," however undefined this remains, of all Russians and even all Russian-speakers within the boundaries of the former Soviet Union. Shades of Hitler's *anschluss* into Austria and Sudetenland color this issue, but, historical analogies aside, the political problem for Estonia, Latvia, and Lithuania has been quite real.

The demographic issue became very sensitive within the Baltic countries because Russians residing there after the war identified less with the republic in which they lived or with Russia than with the Soviet Union.[18] It is probably for this reason that the pro-Soviet "intermovements," which were critical of the national movements for independence and democracy, gained such strength in the Baltics during the late 1980s and that the support for independence among Russians living in the Baltics was far weaker than it was among native Estonians, Latvians, and Lithuanians during the 1991 referendums. Substantial numbers of Russians in Latvia and Estonia supported the coup against Gorbachev in August 1991. In the Russian parliamentary elections of 1993 there was relatively far more support for Vladimir Zhirinovsky among Baltic Russians than there was among Russians living in Russia.[19]

Lithuania basically granted citizenship to all Soviet citizens residing permanently on its territory. Estonia and Latvia did not, insisting strictly on the continuity of citizenship along with the continuity of statehood. The more accommodating stance by Vilnius did not yield significant dividends during 1991 and 1992, but it may have been a factor in Moscow's decision to pull out its last troops from Lithuania in mid-1993 but not from Latvia and Estonia. In the case of the latter two, troop withdrawal remained linked to the issue of the "treatment of Russians" through the end of the year. Even though Russia finally withdrew its remaining troops from Latvia and Estonia in 1994, Moscow continued to link troop withdrawal to other issues until the very end.

Much of the discussion of citizenship has ignored three key points. First, while Moscow has blustered about the fact that Soviet citizenship was not transferred into Estonian and Latvian citizenship, Moscow itself has not granted automatic citizenship in Russia, the formal successor to the USSR, to Soviet citizens living outside Russia proper. Second, Moscow does not appear to acknowledge the historical continuity of Estonian, Latvian, and Lithuanian statehood, but rather sees the independence achieved in August 1991 as derived from the three countries' status as Soviet Socialist Republics. This interpretation not only irritates the Baltic leadership but also makes the resolution of the citizenship issue much more complex politically. And third, Moscow has attempted in its international actions and statements to link the citizenship status of Russians, especially in Estonia and Latvia, not only with charges of human rights violations and ethnic discrimination but also with the withdrawal of its remaining military forces.[20]

Ethnic tensions in Estonia, Latvia, and Lithuania are not very high, and for practical purposes there is no ethnic conflict. The demographic legacy is a domestic issue which is important foremost because of its impact on relations with Russia and the Baltic countries' image in the West. Prime Minister Mart Laar stated in an interview at the end of 1993 that in his view the most serious domestic problem Estonia faces is crime.[21] Similar views have been expressed in Latvia and Lithuania, but an analysis of this complex problem is beyond the present essay.

### Foreign Relations

The Baltic countries, unlike other areas of the Soviet Union, enjoyed a special status in international law: in spite of more than fifty years of occupation, their legal existence was still recognized by virtually every Western country. Nevertheless, from the spring of 1990 onward the quest for "recognition" became a major concern of Baltic foreign policy, most pronouncedly by Landsbergis in Lithuania. Western insistence that countries, not governments, were recognized; that the recognition of Lithuania, Latvia, and Estonia dated to the early 1920s and remained in effect; and that diplomatic relations could not be normalized until the governments had effective control over their territory often fell on deaf ears. Foreign Minister Lennart Meri of Estonia went so far as to question the essence of America's nonrecognition policy in an opinion piece in the *New York Times* on July 13, 1991.

Nevertheless, the events of August 1991 in Moscow proved favorable to Estonia, Latvia, and Lithuania. The statement issued by the NATO ministerial meeting in Brussels on August 21, 1991, provided support for Baltic aspirations.[22] The Nordic countries and then the European Community quickly acknowledged Baltic reindependence by announcing the reestablishment of normal diplomatic relations. Boris Yeltsin, as president of the Russian SFSR, issued decrees recognizing the independence of Estonia, Latvia, and Lithuania within a few days, and the Soviet Council of State confirmed this within days after the United States announced the normalization of diplomatic relations with the Baltic countries on September 2, 1991. The diplomatic notes of the Western countries emphasized that recognition of statehood had occurred in the early 1920s, thus affirming the restoration of Estonian, Latvian, and Lithuanian statehood on the basis of the principle of historical continuity. Within a few weeks recognition was received also from the multitude of countries that had not existed before the Second World War or had not then recognized the Baltic countries.

For Baltic leaders the period from March 1990 to August 1991 was a difficult one in foreign affairs. Although the leaders were received by some Western governments, they were excluded from the CSCE meeting in Paris in November 1990 as a result of pressure from Moscow. The three former members of the League of Nations were admitted to the United Nations on September 17, 1991. They also became regular members of the Conference on Security and Cooperation in Europe and other international bodies, and they participate actively in the North Atlantic Cooperation Council (NACC). Lithuania and Estonia were admitted to the Council of Europe in May 1993. The question of Latvia could not come up until after its parliamentary elections in June of that year. Thus, within a short period after having regained independence, Estonia, Latvia, and Lithuania acted and were treated by the international community as normal countries.

The normalization of diplomatic relations and the establishment of an international presence were substantially easier than finding an effective basis for the guarantee of national security. Although the domestic differences in the Baltic countries are so extensive as to preclude meaningful joint analysis, in international affairs the three are often perceived and present themselves as a regional unit. The leaders of Estonia, Latvia, and Lithuania clearly see the existence of a regional security vacuum that needs to be filled quickly. While relying at present on international organizations, including the new Council of Baltic Sea States, which also includes Russia, government statements from Tallinn, Riga, and Vilnius evidence a strong desire to join NATO. Perhaps fortunately for the three Baltic countries, their security concerns have been viewed as a regional issue by their Nordic neighbors, as evidenced by government statements, the cohosting of regional security conferences, and even the provision of military equipment and support for military training. In late 1993, Estonia created a regional strategic studies institute. Baltic cooperation in military affairs has led to plans to create a joint Baltic battalion for participation in UN peacekeeping operations.

### The Russian Bear

The leaders of the Baltic countries perceive a single external threat to their national security: Russia. Nevertheless, they have repeatedly emphasized that the advancement of democracy and the success of economic reform in Russia are crucial to Baltic security. In other words, the Russian threat is related to the risk of "imperial regression." Between mid-1991 and mid-1994 the principal worry in Estonian, Latvian, and Lithuanian foreign policy was the continued presence of former Soviet military forces on their territories. As a key concern in foreign relations, this was closely followed by the ominous tone of statements made by some Moscow leaders concerning "the near abroad," an area contiguous to the Russian Federation in which Moscow claimed a special role.

Baltic representatives at the UN raised the issue of the Russian troops in joint presentations in December 1991. The point was strongly emphasized in the joint appeal by the Baltic heads of state to the CSCE countries and in the joint statement to all countries participating in the Rio de Janeiro world environmental conference. In mid-1992, Estonia, Latvia, and Lithuania found support for their demand that Russian forces be withdrawn in the CSCE declaration in Helsinki in July 1992 and in the UN General Assembly resolution of November 25, 1992. The U.S. Congress had made some assistance to Russia contingent on troop withdrawals from the Baltic countries. Several Western countries offered to help Russia build housing for the withdrawn troops, and diplomatic support was also received to deflect Moscow's aim of linking the troop withdrawal issue with other questions, such as the alleged discrimination against ethnic Russians, and "social guarantees" for retired military officers.

Bilateral talks with Russia had not proven fruitful through mid-1993. On June 18 the Estonian ambassador in Moscow was given a very sharply worded note at the Russian foreign ministry. A week later Yeltsin's statement threatened economic sanctions and military intervention if necessary "to protect" the Russians in Estonia. The Baltic presidents jointly appealed to the G-7 countries on July 5. The CSCE parliamentary assembly, meeting in Helsinki, provided diplomatic support to Estonia, Latvia, and Lithuania. The sharpest rebuke to Russia came from Sweden's prime minister, Carl Bildt.[23] The U.S. Department of State, in a statement dated August 23, also supported the Baltic countries. Nevertheless, Moscow announced the suspension of previously negotiated troop withdrawals from Lithuania.

The presidents and prime ministers of Estonia, Latvia, and Lithuania issued a new joint statement on regional security on September 13. The question of Russian troops was once more raised by the three presidents in their speeches at the United Nations later in September. They also met jointly with President Bill Clinton in New York on September 27, and the White House press release of the same day made it very clear that Washington expected Moscow to get its troops out of the Baltic countries. By this time Moscow had again changed its mind with regard to Lithuania, and its last units had left by the time of the New York meeting. This may have been a tactic to split the united Baltic position in foreign affairs, but such a split did not occur. Baltic representatives again addressed the issue of Russian troops during the CSCE ministerial meeting in Rome at the end of November and at the NATO meeting in Brussels a few days later.

In spite of Moscow's blustering over the past few years, the number of troops in Estonia and Latvia nevertheless decreased dramatically. According to Estonian estimates late in 1993 there were then about 2,500 Russian troops in Estonia and 12,500 in Latvia. It might be added that the past two years have presented the Estonian, Latvian, and Lithuanian governments with prestigious new forums in the West to address various issues of interest to them, particularly with regard to security. An excellent example of this is Prime Minister Laar's speech to the German Foreign Affairs Association on June 28, 1993.

All three Baltic countries have pursued bilateral negotiations with Moscow. The issue of the military units has not been the only item on the agenda in these talks. A number of routine matters have been settled bilaterally. In the case of Estonia and Latvia the question of the border with Russia remains unresolved, and Lithuania's initial demands for reparations for the fifty years of occupation represented a serious stumbling block. Baltic lobbying in Moscow goes back to 1988 and especially to the period of the Soviet Congress of People's Deputies during 1989 and 1990, when the Estonians, Latvians, and Lithuanians managed to embarrass Moscow over the substance of the secret protocols of the Molotov-Ribbentrop Pact of 1939.

When Gorbachev cracked down in the Baltic in January 1991, Boris Yeltsin provided significant political support for the governments in power there. At least into early 1992, relations with Yeltsin appear to have been positive. Russian Foreign Minister Andrei Kozyrev was in Tallinn in mid-January 1992 and the Baltic foreign ministers met with him again in Moscow that August. During the past few years, however, it has not been clear to the Estonian, Latvian, and Lithuanian governments who in Moscow represents the "true" Russian position in foreign affairs. In fact, there might be no such true position, which makes negotiations difficult.

The summer of 1993 was the most difficult period in Russian-Baltic relations since January 1991. Nevertheless, support for Estonia, Latvia, and Lithuania from the West and from international organizations had become much stronger. The number of foreign dignitaries—including the Dalai Lama, the Pope, monarchs and presidents from Western Europe, and government ministers—who have visited the Baltic countries in the past few years is remarkable, and this provides Tallinn, Riga, and Vilnius with a diplomatic shield which earlier did not exist.

President Bill Clinton made a brief but historic visit to Riga in early July 1994 and pledged continuing American support for the removal of Russian troops from Latvia and Estonia. A few days later, following the meeting of the leaders of the G-7 countries in Naples, Russian president Boris Yeltsin stood beside Clinton at a press conference and stated that Russian troops would be removed from Latvia—but not from Estonia—by the end of August. This was the date to which Moscow had earlier committed itself for the withdrawal of its troops from all three Baltic countries. Under Western diplomatic pressure, the deadline was nevertheless met with regard to Latvia as well as Estonia.

The mediating role of President Clinton was clearly crucial. Without Clinton's intervention, it is doubtful that the Estonian and Russian presidents would have met in Moscow in late July 1994. As it was, Lennart Meri and Boris Yeltsin concluded agreements in the Kremlin on July 26. In the case of Estonia, Tallinn agreed to certain "social guarantees" with respect to retired Russian officers residing in Estonia; in return, Moscow agreed to remove its remaining military units and equipment forthwith. In the case of Latvia, Riga had to accept the continued presence of Russian military technicians at a radar site in Skrunda for five-and-a-half years. In spite of the withdrawal of Russian military forces from the Baltic countries, the Russian card in Baltic affairs remains an uncertain one.

## Conclusions

As late as 1989 everyone knew with certainty that the Soviet Union would never allow Eastern Europe "to be free," and predictions about the imminent collapse of the USSR were judged to be pure lunacy. Another certainty was that Moscow would never disengage from the Baltic countries, which it had occupied and annexed in 1940. To be sure, Estonia, Latvia, and Lithuania still remain between a rock and a hard place, where they have often been before, but the rock and the hard place both appear much softer than they did only a few years ago. There is no reason to expect that the three countries cannot succeed in the transformation from dependence to independence, but much remains to be seen.

Domestic political legitimacy is no longer in question in Estonia, Latvia, and Lithuania. To be sure, the extreme right wing of Estonian politicians has hammered away at the theme that President Meri and former prime minister Laar do not represent the true interests of the Estonian people. President Meri has even been accused of having collaborated with the KGB. In Lithuania the opposition sought to embarrass President Brazauskas by sending a derogatory letter to the British parliament. During the presidential campaign Brazauskas had been forced to deny plans to steer Lithuania back into the Commonwealth of Independent States. In all three countries minor military insurrections occurred during 1993 and 1994.

However, such developments do not appear to threaten the domestic political order. More worrisome for domestic political stability are the frequent cabinet turnovers. Between August 1991 and the end of 1994 Lithuania had six prime ministers, Latvia had three, and Estonia four. In Estonia, Prime Minister Laar strongly beat back a motion of no confidence in November 1993, about a year after taking office. But in September 1994, the parliament revived, and this time passed, a motion of no confidence. Laar was voted out of office by defectors from his own ruling coalition.[24]

The success of reindependence will depend on both domestic and foreign considerations. Russia remains unpredictable, as does the West's commitment to extend the NATO umbrella eastward to fill the security void there. It is helpful to the Baltic countries that the German government considers itself to have "a special historical obligation to guarantee the security of the Baltic states." And Sweden's prime minister has noted that the Baltic countries should be considered to be the West's "near abroad," to use the new political terminology of 1992-1994.

One of the noteworthy achievements of Estonia, Latvia, and Lithuania is effective cooperation in foreign affairs. This is a vast improvement over the situation that existed in the 1930s. But parallel cooperation to create a Baltic region internally may prove to be as futile today as it was before the Second World War, despite joint statements by the three presidents about the necessity of "Baltic integration" as a step toward the countries' reintegration into Europe. Lithuania and Estonia have gained entry into the Council of Europe, and Latvia is expected to follow in early 1995. The three Baltic countries will also soon become associate members of the European Union. Estonia, Latvia, and Lithuania have indeed returned to Europe.

## Notes

1. The debate over Baltic regionalization is best covered in Dietrich A. Loeber, V. Stanley Vardys, and Laurence P. A. Kitching, eds., *Regional Identity under Soviet Rule: The Case of the Baltic States* (Hackettstown, N.J.: Association for the Advancement of Baltic Studies, 1990). Composite volumes on the three Baltic countries include: Walter C. Clemens Jr., *Baltic Independence and Russian Empire* (New York: St. Martin's Press, 1991); Romuald J. Misiunas and Rein Taagepera, *The Baltic States: Years of Dependence*, 2d ed. (Berkeley: University of California Press, 1992); and Anatol Lieven, *The Baltic Revolution: Estonia, Latvia, Lithuania and the Path to Independence* (New Haven, Conn.: Yale University Press, 1993). Recent monographs include Toivo U. Raun, *Estonia and the Estonians*, 2d ed. (Stanford, Calif.: Hoover Institution Press, 1991); Rein Taagepera, *Estonia* (Boulder, Colo.: Westview, 1994); and V. Stanley Vardys, *Lithuania* (Boulder, Colo.: Westview, 1993). The best source for current information remains the various reports of Radio Free Europe/Radio Liberty in Munich.

2. Royal Institute of International Affairs, *The Baltic States* (London: Royal Institute of International Affairs, 1938), 3.

3. The point of departure in such a choice reflects, among other considerations, the recent suggestion by Zbiegniew Brzezinski that political change may be more important than economic change. Zbiegniew Brzezinski, "The Great Transformation," *The National Interest*, no. 33 (Fall 1993): 3-13.

4. Information received from the Estonian prime minister by telephone, December 29, 1993.

5. E. Eugene Pell, "Preface," in *Toward Independence: The Baltic Popular Movements*, ed. Jan A. Trapans (Boulder, Colo.: Westview, 1991).

6. V. Stanley Vardys. "The Partisan Movement in Postwar Lithuania," *Slavic Review* 23 (1963): 499-522; Mart Laar, *War in the Woods: Estonia's Struggle for Survival 1944-1956* (Washington: Compass Press, 1992).

7. V. Stanley Vardys, *The Catholic Church, Dissent, and Nationality in Lithuania* (Boulder, Colo.: Westview, 1978); Thomas Remeikis, *Opposition to Soviet Rule in Lithuania, 1945-1980* (Chicago: Lithuanian Institute, 1980). The best overview of pre-Gorbachev dissent in the Baltic may be found in Ludmilla Alexyeva, *Soviet Dissent: Contemporary Movements for National, Religious and Human Rights* (Middletown, Conn: Wesleyan University Press, 1985).

8. Tõnu Parming, "Neither Luther nor Pope: The Estonian People's Front" (Unpublished paper presented at RFE/RL conference on the Baltic popular movements, Munich, September 1989).

9. Ojars Kalnins, ed., *Chautauga/Jurmala 1986: A Latvian-American Perspective* (Rockville, Md.: American Latvian Association, 1987).

10. Estonian survey data as published in Toronto's Estonian-language weekly *Meie Elu*, July 26, 1990; also, *Päevaleht* (Tallinn), July 14, 1990.

11. A case study of this is offered in my paper "The Estonian-Canadian Community and Politics in Estonia 1987-1993," delivered as a guest lecture at the University of Tartu in November 1994. See also, Janis J. Penikis, "Soviet Views of the Baltic Emigration: From Reactionaries to Fellow Countrymen," in *Toward Independence*, ed. Trapans; and "Notes" in *Baltic Forum* 6, 1 (Spring 1989): 63-66, and *Baltic Forum* 6, 2 (Fall 1989): 88-91, 95-99, 110-113.

12. The communiqué was published in *Kodumaa*, the weekly publication of a KGB front organization in the Estonian SSR on February 24, 1988.

13. Reprinted in *Eesti iseseisvumise teel. I osa. Kroonika 1987-1990* (Toronto: Estonian Central Council, 1990). Also reprinted in most Estonian-language newspapers in the West.

14. See voting returns reported in *Meie Elu* (Toronto), September 24, 1992.

15. As reported in *Meie Elu* February 14, 1991; copy of letter in author's files.

16. Although it was possible for Lithuanian citizens residing abroad to vote, this was much more strictly regulated than was the case with Estonia. Latvia again fell in between its two Baltic neighbors. The important point is that the vote from abroad did not decisively influence the outcome of parliamentary elections in Latvia and Lithuania.

17. Data from Soviet and prewar census publications.

18. See, for example, Toomas Hendrik Ilves, "Reaction: The Intermovement in Estonia," in *Toward Independence*, ed. Trapans.

19. Information received from the Estonian Embassy, Washington, D.C.

20. As evidenced in the many Russian official statements and the official reaction of the Baltic governments to these.

21. Interview given to Toronto's *Meie Elu*, December 29, 1993.

22. The references in this section of the essay are to official documents issued by various international organizations and by the Baltic and other governments; copies in the writer's research files. Almost all of the documents have been reproduced or trans-

lated in Toronto's *Meie Elu*.

23. *International Herald Tribune* (Paris), July 27, 1993. See also Carl Bildt, "The Baltic Litmus Test," *Foreign Affairs* 73, 5 (September/October 1994): 72-85.

24. The broad coalition behind the Laar cabinet began to unravel in the first months of 1994. The underlying crisis was within the principal partner in the coalition, the Pro Patria party, which Laar himself heads. The party splintered in the summer of 1994. If Pro Patria defectors had not voted against Laar in September 1994, the motion of no confidence would have failed. However, the coalition behind Laar's successor as prime minister, Andres Tarand, is in essence the same one that brought Laar to power in 1992. Tarand himself belongs to no political party. He was elected to Parliament on the slate of the left-of-center Moderates, an electoral alliance of the Social-Democratic party and the Rural Centrist party that was one of the junior partners in the Laar coalition. Tarand had been minister of the environment in the Laar cabinet.

# Part IV   Key International Relations

# 19 United States Policy and National Development in the Post-Soviet States

S. Frederick Starr

Under both Republican and Democratic administrations, the policy of the United States toward the Soviet successor states has sought to foster democracy, strengthen free markets, and enhance security by containing and shrinking the stockpile of nuclear weapons. To this end, Washington has extended recognition to all fifteen of the new states, worked with three of the four nuclear powers among them to dismantle nuclear arms, encouraged Boris Yeltsin's political and economic reforms and called for analogous transformations elsewhere, backed the International Monetary Fund's (IMF) fiscal and monetary programs, and offered aid to several of the countries.

All these efforts have gone forward amidst deep anxiety over the future. The persistence of communist-dominated regimes in several Central Asian countries, the return of former communist leaders to the presidencies of Lithuania, Georgia, and Azerbaijan, and resistance to economic reform by an ex-communist president in Ukraine have all heightened the general sense of peril. Open warfare between Armenia and Azerbaijan, fighting in Moldova involving rogue forces nominally under Moscow's control, territorial conflicts in Kyrgyzstan, and virtual civil war in Tajikistan and Georgia only further deepen the aura of gloom.

Looming over these various pitfalls is the specter of nationalism. At a time when transnational solutions to problems seem ascendant in both Europe and North America, the newly independent states appear to be veering in the opposite direction. Narrow-minded nationalism seemed everywhere to be clouding internationalist vistas, whether by fanning interethnic hostilities in all the countries of the Caucasus and in several of the Central Asian countries, or by opposing the new order in Russia. With memories of fascist Germany and

---

This chapter was extracted from a longer study prepared for the Aspen Strategy Group in the summer of 1993. It appears here as written in 1993 and does not attempt to account for events that have taken place since that time.

Japan still fresh after fifty years, and with the evidence of the Milosevic regime in Serbia starkly before their eyes, policy makers and publicists have identified nationalism as a dangerous voice from the past and the single greatest barrier to democracy, free markets, and nuclear security.

America's initial response to the emergence of the fifteen successor states was to support integrative policies, whether in the form of the Commonwealth of Independent States, an extensive ruble zone, or the transnational programs of the IMF. Having conceived economic development as an alternative to nationalism and not a product of it, United States policy attempted to work around nationalist sentiment rather than through it or with it.

This chapter accepts the obvious fact that national feeling in our century has often been in conflict with free markets, pluralistic democracy, and the demands of international security. Recognizing the very real danger posed by extreme forms of nationalism today, the chapter nevertheless attempts to address the issue of nationalism and patriotic sentiment in their broader historical context. It affirms that the rise of democracy was linked closely with the emergence of nation states beginning with England in the sixteenth and seventeenth centuries and with France after the Revolution of 1789. It notes that patriotism and private enterprise have often gone hand in hand, especially in the centuries following the demise of mercantilist theory. And it appreciates the truth that the most successful transnational links have been built on the foundation of secure national states rather than on their suppression. Above all, it sees the situation within Russia and between Russia and the other newly independent states as part of a continuum of postcolonial national development that began when the American colonies declared their independence in 1776.

Current American policy favors new forms of economic (but not political) integration within the former Soviet Union and looks toward the gradual assimilation of Russia and its neighbors into global political and economic life. American critics of this policy, impressed by the ominous longing of many Russians for their lost empire, oppose any Russian-sponsored regional reintegration and argue the need for a new policy of containment vis-à-vis Russia. The approach adopted here differs from both of these alternatives while drawing on each of them. It recognizes that imperial longings exist within the Russian public and government, just as anti-imperial antipathy toward Russians thrives elsewhere in the former empire. It seeks to impose strict constraints and limits on both sentiments, and considers such bounds to be essential if existing sovereignties and borders are to be confirmed. Once the diverse national strivings of the newly independent states are both affirmed and bounded, they can be mobilized in support of regionally integrated free markets, democracy, and true mutual security in its various dimensions.

## The Constructive Currents of Nation Building

Viewed in retrospect, it is clear that nation building has for years been one of the most powerful concerns of peoples and governments in the former Soviet lands. National movements were functioning in most of the fifteen republics by the 1970s and made inexorable if invisible progress during the last decade of Soviet rule.

The dynamics of this process were nearly identical in all republics. Soviet educational policies had created or rebuilt a large cadre of local intelligentsia. While a few of these educated men and women built successful careers in the larger Soviet system, most found their upward progress blocked by Russians and had to settle for careers within their own republic. Seeking to expand their sphere of activity locally, they advocated greater autonomy for their region, direct contact with the outside world, and the creation of a multipolar USSR in place of the "one hub" system that then existed.

For the nonelite, the USSR's economic progress in the past thirty years meant urbanization. Local ethnics from the countryside poured into cities like Baku, Tashkent, Alma-Ata, and Dnepropetrovsk. In the cities they encountered Russian street signs and the Russian language enshrined as the medium of business and government—this in spite of the fact that in the USSR as a whole only 25 to 60 percent of non-Russians could speak Russian and even fewer "colonial" Russians in non-Russian republics had bothered to learn the local language. During the late nineteenth century Prague was transformed from a German to a Czech-speaking city within a generation, thanks to rapid urbanization and ethnicization. Precisely the same process took place in cities throughout the non-Russian parts of the Soviet empire beginning in the 1970s.

As this occurred, a reverse migration by Russian settlers began to gain momentum. Between 1970 and 1980, more Russians returned to Russia than settled in the non-Russian territories, thus signaling the start of decolonization. High birth rates by non-Russians in the Caucasus and in Central Asia hastened this demographic shift. Even in Latvia and Estonia, where Russian in-migration continued and where local birth rates were low, up to a third of Russian settlers declared their intention to leave.

As the re-ethnicization of non-Russian republics progressed, tensions between titular and subtitular nationalities grew in many places. Long before the fall of the USSR, conflicts had arisen between Georgians and Abkhazians in Georgia, Azeris and Armenians in Azerbaijan, and Uzbeks and several competing nationalities in Uzbekistan.

The Soviet state's reaction to these processes was a powerful new wave of forced Russification. Far from accommodating diversity, the Brezhnev constitution of 1978 (Article 75) declared the USSR to be a unitary state. Reflecting this goal, official policy throughout the 1970s promoted the "merging of peoples" (*sliianie narodov*) by compelling the entire population to learn Russian, by artificially promoting interrepublic mobility of labor, and by requiring that all dissertations for advanced degrees be written in Russian. These "integrative" policies of the 1970s led directly to the breakup of the 1990s.

With regard to his policy toward the non-Russian nationalities, Gorbachev was indistinguishable from Brezhnev. Born a Ukrainian but raised in a Russian environment in the recently Russified Stavropol district, Gorbachev did not distinguish between his own Soviet and Russian nationalism and was incapable of appreciating the strength of national consciousness among other peoples.

In a process of literal "dis-integration," in 1989-90 the various popular fronts transformed themselves into national political parties opposed to Soviet policies of assimilation. In the Baltic republics and the Caucasus a strong and general sense of nationhood existed prior to the attainment of independence. In Ukraine, Belarus, and Moldova national consciousness was strong in parts of the population but had to be generalized in the postindependence period. In most of Central Asia, with the possible exception of Uzbekistan, statehood was achieved before a full-blown national identity had formed. The realization by the old ethnic elites of Central Asia that Soviet policies had actually subsidized their region, even as they exploited it, muted official support for the growth of national identities there. This delayed the rise of national consciousness in these Muslim regions but did not prevent it. "Kazakhization" is now making rapid progress in oil-rich Kazakhstan, just as "Turkmenization" is now discernible in gas-rich Turkmenistan.

Although numerous qualifications must be entered, there is a correlation between the pace of nation-building in the waning USSR and the vigor of democratic currents. Where national identities were already consolidated, as in the Baltic countries and Armenia, democratic and promarket forces were also strong; indeed, a consolidated national identity enabled democratic governments in Estonia and Latvia to move briskly to introduce new currencies, reduce shortages, and control inflation. By contrast, in those countries of Central Asia where national forces have yet to break the control of the old communist elites, democratization is nonexistent and marketization lags. Ukraine, large and potentially powerful, presents a middle course. Here, national consciousness was strong but not generalized, and so the mixed communist and democratic government established after secession felt compelled to devote a full year to building sovereignty, in the process severely retarding the process of economic reform.

### A New Geopolitical Map

As the Soviet empire broke up, the geopolitical map of Eurasia changed dramatically. The Scandinavian area expanded with the addition of the three Baltic countries, all of which worked closely with the Nordic Investment Bank and other regional institutions. Moldova has held off reunification with Romania for the time being, but now looks westward rather than northward in both foreign and domestic policy. Ukraine, eager to reassert its traditional links with Central Europe, seeks to participate actively in a new Carpathian economic zone embracing Poland, Slovakia, Hungary, and Romania. The Caucasus have returned to the ambiguous status between Iran, Turkey, and Russia that existed prior to their union with Russia in the late eighteenth and early nineteenth centuries.

The five Central Asian countries, along with Russia, were for long the staunchest supporters of the Commonwealth of Independent States. Four of them still remain within the ruble zone. In spite of this, they have moved to reclaim the distinctive geopolitical identity between China, Iran, Afghanistan, and Turkey that they enjoyed for the millennium before the Russian conquest. Filling the vacuum created by Moscow's crisis, Turkey, Saudi Arabia, and Iran have begun subsidizing these countries. South Korea has also invested heavily in Uzbekistan and Kazakhstan, while China has moved briskly to become the principal trading partner of Uzbekistan and Kyrgyzstan and the second trading partner (after Russia) of Kazakhstan. When recently the Kazakh government appealed to hundreds of thousands of ethnic Kazakhs in China to cross the border to the new nation-state, it further reinforced its East Asian orientation.

Simultaneously, a new economic geography is emerging. Regional differentials in wealth long suppressed by Moscow are now asserting themselves. No longer drained by central taxes and in spite of high energy costs, the Baltic states are surging forward. Turkmenistan and Kazakhstan are also fated to make solid economic progress, as is gold-rich Uzbekistan. The other two central Asian states—Tajikistan and Kyrgyzstan—have little or no chance of economic viability. Ukraine, not long ago identified by the Deutsche Bank as especially rich in economic potential, is being dragged into economic chaos by the high prices Russia is charging for oil and by its own unreformed economy. All three states of the Caucasus, and especially oil-producing Azerbaijan, are potentially viable, but are for the time being impoverished by conflict.

### National Revival in Russia

In the history of colonial breakdowns, Russia is the only instance of a metropolitan country seceding from its own empire. This occurred because Russia itself suffered from Soviet imperial policy and because it experienced the same kind of national revival that occurred in the non-Russian republics. True, Russia did not feel the impact of the USSR's pro-Russian language and cultural policies. However, Russia alone among the republics lacked its own complement of national institutions, as its structures had been merged with those of the Soviet state as a whole. During the 1970's and 1980's many Russians revolted against their country's authoritarian state structure, much as Portuguese and Spaniards did during the same years. They accused the imperial regime of impoverishing the country, ruining it ecologically, and destroying its national traditions. As with the criticisms of the British Empire launched by English writers, many Russian arguments against Soviet authoritarianism were subsequently taken up by non-Russians.

Under the impact of the seven-year war in Afghanistan, the Russian public lost its "imperial will." The majority of Russians supported their republic's eventual secession from the USSR, and also that of the Baltic countries. The strength of Russian support for secession by the other republics was mixed, but anti-imperial feeling was high as Yeltsin came to power. Only later did Russians come fully to appreciate the full measure of their country's lowered status caused by the loss of empire.

The Austrian writer Peter Handke once explained his mother's adherence to fascism in the 1930s by her feeling of "being at home" throughout the Reich. With the breakup of the USSR, Russians ceased to be supercitizens of a superpower, and could no longer feel themselves at home beyond the borders of their own republic. Instead, they became citizens of a geopolitically diminished country that was in deep crisis. The once vaunted Red Army had all but collapsed, their new government had become a supplicant for international aid, their language no longer ranked as a major lingua franca, and once familiar vacation spots in other republics now lay beyond their country's borders. Worse, more than twenty million Russian residents in other republics found themselves in foreign countries. Few peoples in the twentieth century have undergone so sudden or humiliating a loss of status as did the Russians between 1984 and 1991.

As in the case of France when that country lost Algeria, many Russians responded with a deep nostalgia for their lost empire. A rising tide of reverse Russian migration from the newly independent states back to Russia has fanned this sentiment, just as the arrival of *pieds noirs* from Algeria stimulated French chauvinists. Such sentiment will only grow if the reverse tide reaches six million persons in the coming years, as foreseen by Russia's new Federal Migration Service.

On the opposite side of the political spectrum are many Russian democrats and champions of civil society in Russia who also pine for Russia's lost global and regional role. Even though they dream of a "common democratic space" rather than a new authoritarian empire and use the civil rights of Russians abroad as their weapon, such democrats often end up supporting the revanchist cause as vigorously as the state nationalists. Also, among Russia's new entrepreneurial and banking class are many people of strong patriotic sentiment.

Such postcolonial nostalgia in other countries has often led to dangerous consequences. It caused Great Britain to resist American independence by arms, Spain to invade Peru and Chile in the 1860's, Portugal to fight its seceding West African dependencies, and France to plunge into the Algerian War in the 1950s, to cite but four examples. The distinctive feature of Russia's situation is that it has lost all its imperial dependencies at once, thus rendering postcolonial nostalgia there more potent than in any of these other countries.

Russia's official reaction to these losses differs greatly, depending on which newly independent state is being assessed. In the Caucasus, Central Asia, and Moldova Moscow has already become involved in conflicts.

Russians' support for Baltic independence was initially strong, but the fate of ethnic Russians in the three Baltic countries has become a special cause even for Russian liberals. Forgetting the circumstances that led to the settlement of millions of Russians in Latvia and Estonia, and ignoring the fact that the citizenship laws of those countries are no less restrictive than those of Switzerland, Russian reformers have backed policies of economic pressure and military intimidation in the region. Illegal flyovers are frequent, and local Russian army commanders in Latvia were permitted to carry out an exercise on retaking that country in March 1993 without rebuke from the central command in Moscow. Energy embargoes and nonpayment of debts to Baltic countries by Russian firms and banks also became common in the first year of independence. Such actions need not lead to reconquest, of course, but they all imply that Russia has adopted its own kind of Monroe Doctrine vis-à-vis the former republics, which are often euphemistically called their country's "near abroad."

Extreme chauvinists in Russia view Central Asia with particular concern, seeing it as natural that their county should reestablish its control there. Vladimir Zhirinovsky, the leader of this group, is a specialist in Turkic languages who keeps alive the nineteenth century dream of Russian hegemony extending from Karachi to Constantinople. If the growth of national movements in Central Asia follows its predictable course, one might expect the view that Moscow has a special role there to grow stronger. Enthusiasm in parts of the Russian press for the Russian bloc in the parliament of Kazakhstan reflects this perspective, as does the speed with which the Russian army is moving to establish bilateral security agreements in the area to replace the now abandoned CIS joint command. Russia's commitment to maintain its Central Asian bases also serve this policy.

Far the most urgent focus of Russia's imperial nostalgia is Ukraine. Three hundred years of tsarist and communist rhetoric about the "unity of all the Russias" and the Ukrainian language's supposed status as a "dialect" left Russians ill-prepared to deal with Ukrainian independence and the passions behind it. At the time Ukraine seceded, nearly all Ukrainians and even a strong majority of Russian residents in Ukraine believed independence would foster their republic's development, which had been thwarted by tsarist suppression of Ukrainian culture, by Stalin's genocide against Ukrainians, and by the republic's subsequent subordination to Russia.

Russians, by contrast, view Kiev as the seat of their own Orthodox Church, southern Ukraine as the "New Russia" settled by Catherine II in the eighteenth century, and western Ukraine as the well-earned booty of war. Offended by Ukraine's apostasy, even prominent Russian reformers tend to treat Ukrainian sovereignty as a mere passing phase. Yeltsin's foreign minister, Andrei Kozyrev, has even spoken casually of the "mythical state" of Ukraine.

The Russian government has used oil pricing and other economic weapons to pressure Ukraine to sign the START I treaty and pursue other policies desired by Moscow. Ukraine, feeling itself to be faced with blackmail, has countered by claiming full control of nuclear weapons on its territory and by seeking Western guarantees of its sovereignty.

Tension among the newly independent states thwarts the political reform and radical economic programs that are essential to the reestablishment of stability and equilibrium in the region. Indeed, Russia's difficulty in accepting the new realities threatens to bring to a close the reform era that began in 1988-1989.

The present danger is that a crisis with Ukraine or with others of the newly independent states could lead to a cessation of reform in Russia and hence in many other new countries of the former Soviet Union. Such a crisis would not only weaken stability and equilibrium throughout the region but would destroy the foundations on which true stability and equilibrium might be built.

## American Policy and the Newly Independent States

It would be hard to fault the United States' objectives with regard to the newly independent states. Free markets, democracy, and control over nuclear weapons are worthy goals anywhere. Their shortcomings are not philosophical but operational, in that none of them is achievable unless another strategic goal is met, namely, the establishment of stability within the region. Such stability could be based either on some new form of hegemony exercised by Russia over its neighbors or on some other more equitable arrangement based on the mutual security of all of the new states and on equilibrium among them.

Is the first alternative feasible? One will search in vain for an instance in which a former colonial power established and sustained some new form of control over its former subjects. The closest approach to this is France's economic control over some of its former colonies in Africa, but this has by no means fostered development or domestic peace in the latter. Assuming that Russia will be no exception to this pattern, it must be concluded that the regional security upon which the achievement of other objectives depends can only be established with the full consent of all the independent states involved.

This in turn implies that the United States' policy must be directed toward all the newly independent states and not just toward Russia. To date, American policy has focused overwhelmingly on Russia, with the other states treated virtually as afterthoughts. Given Russia's size, this is understandable, but such an approach will not suffice to create the equitable security framework through which the United States' main goals can be advanced. All the United States' recent experience in the region underscores this point.

It is doubtful, however, that the United States has the political will to expend the economic resources to carry out such a task. Given this, it is imperative that American policy confirm at least one other center of political and economic power in the region, in order to provide some degree of balance to Russia. The obvious candidate for this is Ukraine. By supporting simultaneously the political and economic development of both Russia and Ukraine, the United States (along with other countries) can do its best to assure that all sovereignties in the region will be respected, and hence that economic development can be pursued on an equitable basis.

The United States cannot alone create conditions of security among the former Soviet lands. However, the United States' activity or passivity will be as important as any force outside the region in shaping the outcome. On one point in particular the United States government must speak directly and without the slightest ambiguity, namely, that it fully acknowledges the sovereignty of each of the fifteen new states and believes that existing borders can be changed only through normal processes of international law.

The United States has not always made known to other countries the true depth of its concerns over such issues. Ambiguous American signals to the Soviet government on the eve of the Afghan war and to the Iraqi government on the eve of its seizure of Kuwait helped shape undesirable outcomes in both cases. There should be no such ambiguity about sovereignty and borders among the newly independent states of the former USSR.

The recent fate of the Maastricht agreement has shown that sovereignty and national identity cannot be treated casually even in highly integrated Western Europe. Still less should their importance be minimized in the former Soviet Union. It is no paradox to say that only by affirming the sovereignty of the newly independent states can one expect serious movement toward regional security and economic development based on free markets and integration. This in turn requires at least ten separate steps:

- In extending diplomatic recognition, the United States must appoint qualified ambassadors and establish adequately staffed embassies throughout the region. Consulates should be opened in the larger states at roughly the same ratio to population as in Russia.
- Henceforth, the United States must not only deal with each of the new states directly but also it must use its preponderant influence over the IMF and World Bank to assure that those bodies, too, proceed on the principle

that economic integration will come about only after the national sovereignty of each state is fully established.

- The United States should acknowledge the legitimacy of each newly independent state's concerns regarding security and defense. Now that joint control over CIS forces has been abandoned by the participants themselves, the United States must not allow Russia to be the sole patron and protector of what General Saposhnikov called a "common security space" in the region.

- American policy with respect to Ukraine has been a failure because it has, until recently, sought to punish that country for what are in fact its legitimate concerns over security. The United States must accept Ukraine's moves in the security area as arising from legitimate concerns, however unwelcome the moves themselves. We must be prepared to offer a genuine quid quo pro to Ukraine in order to win that country's agreement with U.S. objectives.

- As part of its acknowledgment of the new sovereignties, the United States must make absolutely clear that it would acquiesce in adjustments of existing national boundaries only if they are negotiated and approved through normal international processes rather than by unilateral action by any one country. This matter is particularly acute with respect to small territories like the Narva district of Estonia, the Abkhazian territories of Georgia, and Ukraine's jurisdiction in Crimea. On a larger scale, there is serious potential for discord over the eastern districts of Ukraine and the northern region of Kazakhstan, both of which have large Russian populations.

  Within the next two years, one can expect that Russian policy will promote plebiscites in such regions (e.g., Crimea) and use an endorsement by the local Russian population as a means of advancing the cause of border revisions. The United States should anticipate this move by fostering to the greatest extent possible the principle of federalism in each of these countries, and especially in Georgia, Ukraine, Estonia, and Kazakhstan. Foreign Minister Kozyrev has given every reason to believe that the present government in Moscow would accept federal solutions in each of these cases except Crimea.

- In the same spirit, the United States should accept as reasonable Russia's demand that new states with large Russian populations adopt fair laws on citizenship. Recognizing the wide range of citizenship laws even within the European Community, however, the United States must not seek to impose its own standard in this area. Rather, it should support the practice, pioneered by Estonia, of submitting laws on citizenship to the Conference on Cooperation and Security in Europe (CSCE) or other international bodies for review. Only in this way can the legitimate concerns of Russian "colonials" abroad be protected, while at the same time protecting the new states from Russian revanchism cloaked under the banner of human rights.

- The United States must adopt a policy on Russian forces abroad that is compatible with the sovereignty of the new states and at the same time respects both Russia's legitimate security concerns and the fact that Russia has grounded its policy on what it understands to be the United States' long-established practice regarding its own foreign bases. Specifically, the United States was right to expect Russia to honor its commitments to withdraw troops from the Baltic countries and to facilitate that process. The presence of Russia's 14th Army in the Dniester area of Moldova is a threat to peace in the region and is already the subject of negotiations. The United States should encourage its Western partners to take a direct interest in the outcome of those talks. Similar concerns regarding Russian troops in Georgia should be addressed in the same way.

- United States policy already acknowledges the danger posed by the fifteen Chernobyl-type nuclear generating plants still functioning in the former Soviet Union. However, in proposing their closure, the United States has failed to appreciate the extent to which that step could jeopardize the security and even the sovereignty of several countries involved, notably Ukraine and Lithuania. To correct this, the United States should strongly support the inclusion of all the newly independent states in the ongoing negotiations in Geneva to create a European Energy Charter. Without such a continental energy agreement either the reactors will continue to operate or their closure will bring dire consequences to the economies of several of the countries.

    Similarly, the United States should offer all possible support for the development of gas and oil reserves in Kazakhstan, Turkmenistan, and Azerbaijan, and also the opening of alternative channels for transmitting gas and oil over routes separate from the old Russia-based Soviet grid. Ukraine is particularly exposed in this area, and its efforts to date to develop a direct pipeline from Central Asia to the port of Odessa have been unsuccessful.

- The State Department and other United States agencies continue to treat the "former Soviet Union" too much as a single unit, often rechristening it "Eurasia." Instead, it should accept the tectonic geopolitical changes that have occurred since the collapse of the Soviet empire. Specifically, it should, where possible, be prepared to include the Baltic countries under the Scandinavian rubric and to facilitate the entry of Ukraine and Belarus into the councils of Central Europe.

Abrupt shifts with respect to Central Asia would be inappropriate, given the desire on the part of several countries in the region to maintain their close links with Russia. At the same time, the United States should honor Kyrgyzstan's effort to define itself independently as the "Switzerland of Central Asia." China's growing economic involvement in the region will doubtless be followed by heightened political influence. When Georgian president Shevardnadze on June 30, 1993, reported in Beijing on his concept of a "Eurasian corridor" linking China, Kazakhstan, Turkmenistan, Uzbekistan, Azerbaijan, Ukraine, and the countries of the Caucasus he was playing out a scenario of development that warrants attention. The United States should anticipate the possible competition of world powers in Central Asia and help the countries involved to preserve stability.

A particular concern must be the role of Iran. This issue embraces Iran's ethnically related neighbor, Tajikistan, as well as Azerbaijan, with which Iran has both ethnic links (thanks to its own large Azeri population) and Shiite Muslim religious ties, and Armenia, which Iran has traditionally supported in its conflicts with Turkey. American policy at present excludes Iran from any role in the region. As Iran's radical Muslim ardor cools, however, the United States should cautiously welcome the establishment of normal Iranian ties with these countries.

While these larger relations are being worked out, the United States should be supportive of lesser efforts toward regional integration in the former Soviet Union. The Baltic Council and recent discussions concerning a possible Central Asian common market fall into this category, as does the embryonic Carpathian union involving Ukraine. Such movements toward subregional cooperation foster the kind of multipolarity that enhances security throughout the region.

• Inevitably, the most successful antidote to aggressive chauvinism in Russia is the successful development of a market economy there. Economic change will generate social change by bringing to the fore younger Russian men and women who are more comfortable with their country's new status. Conversely, the failure of economic transformation will multiply crises like the recent U.S.-Russian conflict over the export of rocket engines to India.

Proposals for Western governments to create a social fund and stabilization fund are probably useful, but these pale by comparison with the potential size and impact of private investment in Russia. Given budgetary realities in the United States, moreover, private investment can go far towards meeting expectations of U.S. support that the government itself has created. The task of government policy should therefore be to facilitate such investments by creating risk insurance through OPIC, offering investment loans, and providing other incentives to American businesses and banks. Direct assistance to Russia in planning tax policies would also be useful, as is clear from the fact that Kazakhstan's new tax law has already led to a trebling of foreign investment there since January 1993.

Various reciprocal measures would also foster Russian economic growth. Rapidly developing Russian regions like Sakhalin and Tyumen should be encouraged to open trade offices in the United States, and help should be provided to U.S. governors interested in expanding Russian trade on a regional basis. Further, U.S. tariffs should be reviewed immediately to determine which, if any, are unfairly biased against Russian imports (for example, potash and uranium) and necessary changes should then be carried out.

- A high U.S. priority must be to prod Ukraine toward economic reform. To its credit, the Kiev government now permits citizens to buy and sell private plots on freehold. Yet the government of Ukraine has twice rejected large-scale privatization, in December 1992 and March 1993, and seems disinclined still to move in this direction. Runaway inflation has already set in and threatens to jeopardize Ukraine's very sovereignty. Ukraine's economic instability made it an easy matter for Moscow to engineer a pro-Russian majority in the Crimean referendum in Crimea and even threatened a similar outcome in parts of Eastern Ukraine.

The steps needed include the completion of currency reform, the introduction of a voucher scheme similar to that employed in Russia, and a sharp focus on energy conversion. The U.S. Department of Energy's $100 million fund for energy conversion in Russia should be matched by a proportionate fund for Ukraine. These measures are of the utmost urgency.

- Even though problems in Central Asia do not currently threaten regional stability to the extent of those in Ukraine, Moldova, and the Caucasus, no region of the former Soviet Union poses greater long-term dangers than Central Asia. Kyrgyzstan's and Tajikistan's economic prospects are dismal, while the first signs of national awakening are already evident in communist-ruled Uzbekistan and Kazakhstan. The designation of Uzbek and Kazakh (along with Russian) as governmental languages and affirmative action hiring in both countries have already generated a significant outflow of Russians to Russia.

The United States' objectives in the region should be to develop Kazakh and Turkmen energy resources, to promote federalization in Kazakhstan, to foster intraregional cooperation and integration without enhancing Uzbekistan's hegemonic pretensions vis-à-vis its neighbors, and to diversify the region's trade and international contacts. In pursuing these, the United States should act bilaterally with the countries involved and also in concert with other developed countries, including Russia, Turkey, Korea, China, Pakistan, and India. Moreover, it must do so in a way that recognizes the particular security concerns of Russia. The purpose of such policy is not to negate Russia's legitimate interests in the region but to create a healthy equilibrium between these and the national interests of the other countries involved.

## Conclusion

It may be objected that these proposals reflect an excessive concern for the sovereignty of the newly independent states as opposed to their integration into larger units, and for national sentiment as opposed to more global thinking. It may be objected, further, that the concern for sovereignty and national identity that underlies these proposals will not long remain merely a means to the end of democratization, marketization, and nuclear security but will become an end to be pursued for its own sake.

It cannot be denied that this danger exists, yet if the claims of sovereignty and national identity are ignored, the risks are greater than if they are accepted as legitimate and addressed frontally. This is the lesson of decolonization in Great Britain, Spain, Portugal, and France. National feeling and sovereignty have been the building blocks of modern political and economic institutions in most countries; they have also provided the secure fundament on which equitable international and integrative arrangements have been based. This being the case, the United States should seek to work with, not around, patriotic feeling and sovereignty in Russia and the other post-Soviet states.

# 20 The Overburdened Partner: Germany and the Successor States

Angela E. Stent

The unification of Germany, the collapse of communism, and the disintegration of the Soviet Union destroyed the postwar European security system. That system was a product of the Cold War and was based on a permanent standoff between two antagonistic blocs. Nevertheless, it provided stability for forty years, although for half of Europe it was the stability of repression. Now, repression has greatly diminished and instability has replaced Cold War certainties. Newly independent countries, struggling to become viable, democratic nation-states, fill the geopolitical space between the Oder-Neisse and the Pacific. Reunified Germany, as a new state with new borders, faces the task of integrating its communist and democratic parts.

Russia and Germany confront similar challenges—major domestic reorganization coupled with redefinition of national interest and foreign policy—only they embark on their respective paths from radically different situations. Germany, although facing temporary domestic political and economic problems, is destined to become Europe's leading power, one that will eventually pursue a more independent and active foreign policy. Russia, on the other hand, faces domestic problems that will last for the foreseeable future and weaken its ability to pursue an active foreign policy. Between Russia and Germany lie a group of nations that have traditionally been dominated by one of the two great powers and who question whether they will be able to escape the same fate in the twenty-first century. These nations are trying to create new alliances that will spare them that future.

The historical ties between Russia and Germany are long and complex. Germany and Russia have for centuries been both rivals and partners in Europe. They fought on opposite sides of two world wars, but also formed alliances against other European powers in the nineteenth and twentieth centuries. The Rapallo Treaty of 1922 and the 1939 Nazi-Soviet Pact remind us that German-Russian cooperation has also had detrimental effects on European security. These patterns of rivalry and partnership could reassert themselves once Russia regains its ability to project influence abroad. But they need not necessarily have a negative impact on the rest of Europe if neither Russia nor Germany aspire to become imperial powers.

This chapter will discuss the evolution of Russo-German relations since the collapse of the Soviet Union in the context of both countries' search for a new national and international identity. It will also discuss the emerging German-Ukrainian relationship and its role in German *Ostpolitik*. It will conclude with an examination of possible future directions in German ties with the two most important successor states.

## The Russian Agenda

Russia faces the unprecedented challenge of fundamentally reorienting its foreign policy. A decade ago, what would have been inconceivable is today a basic fact: Russia's most important and complex foreign relations are now with countries that did not exist a decade ago. Some have distant histories of nationhood but have not existed as independent states for centuries. Some scarcely have a sense of nationhood. Ukraine, for instance, has only existed as an independent state from 1648 to 1654 and from 1918 to 1920. The Central Asian states were a creation of Stalin's nationality policy. These are the countries of the "near abroad," as the Russians call the successor states. Russia's triple transition—from totalitarianism to democracy, from centrally planned to market economy, and from imperial to postimperial state—is a daunting challenge in all of its dimensions. However, the dimension in which the lag between perception and reality will be the greatest is the third—the area of foreign policy.

Most Russians have rejected the premises behind the political and economic aspects of communism. Yet they still retain an imperial consciousness that antedates the communist era, even if Russia no longer possesses the necessary capabilities for an imperial foreign policy. After four hundred years of dominating their neighbors, most Russians cannot accept that Kiev and Sevastopol are foreign cities. Russians are embarking on the traumatic process of redefining what it means to be Russian, just as their neighbors are defining themselves as separate from the Russians. The most difficult aspect of redefining national identity for most Russian citizens is to reconcile themselves to the loss of their internal empire. It is easier to reconstruct relations with the world outside the former Soviet Union because there is continuity with the Soviet period in these ties, whereas those with the successor states are quite new.

Russia will remain preoccupied with domestic problems for the foreseeable future; much of its foreign policy will be driven by internal considerations. Yet Russia will remain a great power because of its size, its rich and abundant natural resources, its permanent seat on the United Nations Security Council, its vast arsenal of nuclear and conventional weapons, and its ability to cause instability in Europe. As Boris Yeltsin expressed it, "Russia is rightfully a great power by virtue of its history, its place in the world and of its material and spiritual potential."

There is no consensus within the Russian political elite about how relations with the West, including Germany, should evolve. The "Atlanticists," those who argue that Russia should emulate the West and become a democratic, capitalist country, urge greater economic and political cooperation with the West. The "Eurasianists" argue that Russia is unique and should not seek to be "another European country." It cannot and should not, in their view, aspire to develop a Western market economy. They call for a Russian Monroe Doctrine that proclaims the entire space of the former Soviet Union as a sphere of vital interest against potential Western or Eastern incursions. They are neoimperialist and wary of excessive cooperation with the West, including Germany.[1] Indeed, some in both camps have had second thoughts about German unification. They question whether the Soviet Union could have received more than it did from Germany in exchange for the concessions Gorbachev made on the internal and external aspects of German unification. After all, the argument goes, the Soviet Union helped create what had always been officially depicted as its worst postwar nightmare—the reunification of a capitalist Germany in NATO. The debate between the various camps will continue for some time; but for now, both President Yeltsin and his foreign minister are "Atlanticist" and are seeking closer ties with Germany.

A major Russian interest in Germany is economic. Ever since Catherine the Great brought Germans to settle in Russia to build its cities and farm its land in the eighteenth century, Russians have admired German industriousness and technical prowess. Russian proverbs such as "Whenever you see a machine, there must be a German nearby" or "The Germans discovered the ape" reflect this respect. Germany was Russia's most important trading partner before the Bolshevik revolution and East and West Germany together also comprised the Soviet Union's largest trading partner before German unification. Russian-German trade has traditionally been complementary, with Germany exporting manufactured goods in return for Russian primary products, mainly oil and gas.

So far, Germany has been the single largest donor to Russia, providing DM 80 billion to Russia (about $50 billion, compared to the United States' $9 billion and Japan's $3 billion), more than half of all the Western assistance. This sum includes money for resettling Soviet troops and their dependents departing from East Germany, constructing housing for them in Russia and Ukraine, credit and export guarantees, grants, humanitarian and technical aid projects, and investment projects.[2] In addition, Germany is Russia's largest creditor. It thus has borne the brunt of the Paris Club's rescheduling arrangements, meaning that it had DM 8 billion added to its budget deficit in 1993.[3] Chancellor Helmut Kohl made it clear before the July 1993 G-7 summit in Tokyo that Germany could no longer continue to provide aid to Russia in such amounts because of the enormous cost of unification. Bonn is putting an annual DM 100 billion into reconstructing East Germany and will have to continue this for some years. Unification has cost much more than the Germans initially expected.

German-Russian trade has also encountered difficulties because of Russia's economic problems. Although there are a variety of German firms active in Russia and German centers where Russian managers are trained, German exports to Russia fell from DM 28 billion in 1990, to DM 18 billion in 1991, to DM 13 billion in 1992.[4] Russian problems with payments are the major reason for this decline; but German firms also report the same difficulties in dealing with the Russian economy in transition as do all other Western firms—no clear legal framework, no clear chain of command, inadequate financial institutions, and would-be entrepreneurs who lack a basic understanding of how a market economy functions. Germany is actively involved in rewriting the Russian legal system, including its commercial law, in an attempt to make the Russian system more compatible with German law and so ease some of the difficulties firms encounter. A long-term goal of this effort is to make the Russian market more compatible with the German.

When President Mikhail Gorbachev and Foreign Minister Eduard Shevardnadze negotiated the terms for German unification with Chancellor Kohl and Foreign Minister Hans-Dietrich Genscher, an implicit bargain was struck. In return for the Soviets renouncing their control over East Germany and agreeing to the incorporation of a united Germany in NATO, Germany would compensate the USSR both economically and politically. The economic compensation included credits, the construction of housing for returning soldiers, and a variety of other incentives. Politically, it was understood that Germany would take the lead in persuading its allies to become more committed to helping the USSR, just as Genscher had done in February 1987 with the famous speech—"Let's take Gorbachev at his word"—that encouraged other NATO allies to support Gorbachev more forcefully and match rhetoric with action.[5] Beyond this commitment, however, lay the understanding that Germany would take the lead in championing the creation of a new security system in Europe, one that would replace the moribund Warsaw Treaty Alliance and give the USSR an important role in future European affairs.

After the collapse of the Soviet Union, the nature of the bargain was, of course, open to reevaluation. But inasmuch as Russia has declared itself the legal heir to the Soviet Union, it has inherited the German-Soviet agreements, particularly the Friendship Treaty signed in November 1990. Germany has, to some extent, carried out its promises. Chancellor Kohl has repeatedly called for Western support for the democratization process in Russia and has explicitly backed Yeltsin in his struggles with the Russian parliament, while exhorting Germany's allies to follow suit. During his July 1993 visit to Irkutsk following the G-7 Tokyo summit, Kohl said, "We want to support Russia within the limits of our capabilities," stressing that "if (Yeltsin) doesn't succeed, it will be more expensive for us."[6] Germany is involved with Russia in a multitude of ways, at both the federal and state levels, with individual Laender playing an important role. Sister city projects have sprung up all over Germany and Russia; the German and Russian foreign intelligence services have agreed to cooperate in combating terrorism and drug traffic; and the Russian security ministry is in dialogue with the German Group GSG-9, the elite forces that exclusively fight terrorism.[7]

The second aspect of the bargain—creating a new security system in Europe—is far more complicated. If there is a feeling in some quarters in Moscow that Germany has not done enough on this score, then there is also a recognition that Russia's own problems in reaching a consensus on a new foreign policy have delayed the process. Germans themselves are divided about what a future security system would look like. For now, the German government has explicitly ruled out future NATO membership for any of the members of the Commonwealth of Independent States (CIS), stressing that the North Atlantic Cooperation Council—a body that includes almost all of the former communist countries and meets regularly with NATO for consultations—is sufficient. The German government has also supported the Partnership For Peace, a NATO program of expanded cooperation with the states of the former Warsaw Pact. Russia joined the partnership in June 1994. The Germans' basic commitment to Russian democracy is there; it is too early, however, for any viable new security system to emerge in Europe.

### The German Agenda

German unification has thrust onto Germany new international responsibilities. Germany was unprepared for these responsibilities and has been reluctant to accept them. From 1949 to 1989, West Germany had limited sovereignty, was closely integrated into NATO, and never systematically developed an autonomous concept of national interest or national security. Since the fall of the Berlin Wall, Germans, like Russians, have been engaged in a debate about their national identity and how the incorporation of East into West Germany will affect their role in the outside world. Nevertheless, events in Europe following the collapse of communism have forced Germany to become more active internationally in ways that have caused its allies some concern.

Germany has gone from a refusal to send troops to fight in the Gulf War (although it gave $11 billion to the Gulf Coalition effort) to pressuring its reluctant European Community partners to recognize Croatia and Slovenia in December 1991. After an acrimonious public debate, Germany's Constitutional Court ruled in July 1994 that the Bundeswehr may participate in multinational military operations within the framework of the United Nations and outside of NATO territory. But Germany, because of its recent past, remains wary of accepting the international responsibilities that would normally accompany a country of its size, economic strength and political clout in the European Union.

For now, officials cite the economic, political, and psychological difficulties of integrating eastern into western Germany in addition to Germany's twentieth-century history as the main reasons for their ambivalence about assuming a more active international role, especially a military one. Foreign Minister Klaus Kirkel has said, "We will not move away from the 'culture of restraint.' There will be no militarization of German foreign policy." [8]

Germany's major concern about Russia involves fear of the impact of instability within Russia on Eastern and Central Europe and on Germany itself. For Germany, as for the rest of the West, the Soviet Union under Gorbachev was predictable, relatively stable, and pro-West. The price of liberation from communism has been the collapse of the Soviet Union and the end of stability and predictability. Germany has the largest stake in the outcome of the transition process in Russia because it is more directly affected by the consequences of instability than its European Union partners. Instability in Russia and other former communist states means migrants and refugees; because of Germany's liberal asylum laws (which have recently been tightened), more refugees have come to Germany than any other country since 1989—nearly half a million sought political asylum in 1992 alone.

Moreover, Russia and Eastern and Central Europe are important export markets for Germany as well as sources of energy supplies; instability there means loss of export markets and access to raw materials. Germany, as the front-line state facing an unstable group of countries to its east, has a major and long-term interest in doing all it can to prevent further economic and political deterioration in Russia.

Despite these concerns, German-Russian relations have not been as dynamic as either side initially envisioned, largely because of both countries' domestic problems. The first high-level visit after the breakup of the Soviet Union was by Foreign Minister Klaus Kinkel in October 1992. Then, as subsequently, the Russian side expressed disappointment about Germany's reluctance to commit more financial resources. Chancellor Kohl visited Moscow in December 1992, in the midst of Yeltsin's crisis with the Russian parliament and shortly after Viktor Chernomyrdin replaced Yegor Gaidar as prime minister. During this visit, progress was made on a number of bilateral problems. Throughout the period between December 1992 and the April 1993 referendum on whether Yeltsin's program should continue, Germany explicitly supported the reform process and Yeltsin himself. After Yeltsin won the referendum in April 1993, Bonn was instrumental in securing greater G-7 assistance for Russia. German-Russian contacts increased and there were more high-level meetings. Chancellor Kohl explicitly supported Yeltsin in his struggle with—and eventual assault on—the Russian parliament in October 1993. In May 1994, Yeltsin's visit to Germany was hailed as an example of a "normal" summit, and the personal relationship between the two leaders seemed strong. But the sense, both in Russia and Germany, is that each side's domestic problems will for some time act as a brake on the development of more dynamic bilateral relations.

Two major issues dominate Bonn's bilateral agenda. The first was the withdrawal of Soviet forces from eastern Germany. The Germans wanted this process to continue as smoothly as possible, so as to remove the last major vestige of the Cold War from their territory. As part of the Two Plus Four Treaty on German unification, the Soviet Union agreed on October 12, 1990, to the complete withdrawal of all troops on German soil by the end of 1994. In exchange, Germany committed itself to finance the redeployment of these troops and to construct 36,000 homes for officers and their families, mostly in Ukraine and Belarus.

After the collapse of the Soviet Union, there was concern that the troop withdrawals would encounter major problems. After all, not all the soldiers were Russian, and they had to decide to which country they would return. The bulk of the new housing was to be built in Ukraine, but most officers were returning to Russia. Moreover, some of the troops had tried to stay behind in Germany rather than go back to their disintegrating homelands. Despite all these problems, the withdrawal proceeded uneventfully. The German government maintained a low profile about any problems it had with the process. In addition, it made payments to the Russians over and above what was originally negotiated, in part to cover increased transport costs and in part because it wanted to ensure that the Russians adhered to the withdrawal schedule. From time to time, the Russians requested more money and Germany met their demands.

During Kohl's December 1992 visit to Moscow, both sides agreed to accelerate the timetable for withdrawal of all troops to August 31, 1994, in return for a German commitment of an additional DM 550 million extra to finance more housing for the returning soldiers. The last Soviet soldier left Germany on August 31, 1994. Despite all the political upheavals in Russia, the process went remarkably smoothly. There is, however, a troubling aspect to the troop withdrawals—the environmental damage left by the troops at their bases. The German government estimates that the cleanup will cost DM 25 billion.

What stake will Germany have in Russia now that the troops have withdrawn? Some argue that Germany may be less concerned about developments in Russian domestic and foreign policy now that Russia has lost this source of leverage. Others, however, point to a second area of German concern that will ensure a longer-term German commitment to Russia.

The future of the two million ethnic Germans in Russia, Kazakhstan, and Ukraine is the second main issue on the German agenda. These descendants of eighteenth-century settlers (some of whom still speak in an archaic German dialect), have a constitutional right to acquire German citizenship immediately, unlike non-German immigrants. In the 1970s and 1980s, the West German government offered the Soviets financial incentives to persuade them to let these ethnic Germans emigrate. The irony is that, now that the ethnic Germans are free to go, the German government no longer wants them. It cannot cope with hundreds of thousands of emigres and asylum-seekers because of increasing popular resentment in both parts of Germany against foreigners, as well as outbreaks of anti-foreigner violence. As a result, Germany has offered Russia and Ukraine financial incentives to keep the ethnic Germans in the former Soviet Union. However, progress on this issue has been far less clear than on the troop withdrawal issue.

Between 1924 and 1941, about four hundred thousand Germans lived in the Volga German Autonomous Soviet Socialist Republic (ASSR), a creation of Stalin's nationalities policy. Others lived in autonomous districts all over the Soviet Union. After the Nazis invaded the USSR in 1941, however, the Volga ASSR was dissolved and many ethnic Germans were deported and resettled in Siberia and Central Asia. Although Khrushchev rehabilitated them in 1964, they were never able to move back to their homes on the Volga. Under Gorbachev, the ethnic Germans began to organize themselves into lobbying groups to demand that their republic be restored. The ethnic Germans are, however, divided among themselves. Some want to emigrate, while others are prepared to stay provided they can live in the Volga area or some other autonomous region.

In the past two years, the German government has become increasingly active in influencing Russia's policy toward ethnic Germans. Russia has to some extent ceded to Germany its own policy-making role vis-à-vis its Germans. The German interior ministry has tried to persuade Russia to restore the Volga Republic and Yeltsin has agreed in principle to recreate it piecemeal; but Yeltsin has run into opposition from local Russian groups who do not want the Volga republic restored. The regional Soviet in Saratov, where many Germans are resettling, has rejected several times the plan to restore an autonomous German region. Yeltsin himself remains committed to it—after some initial German prodding—but whether any kind of autonomous region will be restored and rebuilt remains a function of domestic Russian politics and the difficult relations between Moscow and the provinces as well as between Russians and non-Russians.

Meanwhile, the German government and German private organizations are involved in cultural, language, and religious training in magnet areas such as the Saratov region, Omsk, and Altai. They hope to attract to these places ethnic Germans returning from Kazakhstan and other areas. The interior ministry has earmarked more than DM 200 million for housing construction, development of small- and medium-sized firms, and agricultural and medical facilities in these areas, and German companies are building factories and creating modern infrastructure to improve the quality of life. Germany stresses that these amenities are for all the inhabitants of the magnet regions, not just ethnic Germans. To some Russians, however, German government activities raise the specter of the creation of a privileged ethnic German minority at a time when other nationalities are suffering economically. The ethnic Germans are the only non-Russian nationality in the Russian Federation enjoying money, training, and other support from a Western power.

Many ethnic Germans want to emigrate rather than fight with their envious neighbors. They prefer prosperous, stable Germany to unstable Russia. The German government has said that it will not take more than 225,000 ethnic German immigrants per year; twice as many applied to emigrate in the first six months of 1993. The German government and the private sector will do everything they can to encourage ethnic Germans to stay in Russia—but it will be an uphill battle. The issue may well cause major strains between Russia and Germany in the future.

Some enterprising ethnic Germans have resettled in Kaliningrad, the former Koenigsberg, and have urged that an ethnic German republic be established there. This raises a number of unwelcome issues for both Russia and Germany. Since the fall of the Soviet Union, the Kaliningrad district has been physically separated from Russia by Lithuania and Poland, although it remains part of the Russian Federation. A highly militarized area, it had attracted a considerable amount of German investment, which Yeltsin has continued to encourage. The idea of an ethnic German enclave in the former East Prussia, taken from Germany in 1945, poses difficult questions. Germany has unequivocally stated that it is not interested in reopening old territorial disputes or changing borders and is not encouraging ethnic Germans to settle in Kaliningrad. However, the city's anomalous situation will continue to be a potential source of conflict for Russia, Germany, Poland, and Lithuania.

There are other longer-term issues that will continue to preoccupy Germany in its relations with Russia. The Germans, like other Europeans, are concerned about environmental problems in the former Soviet Union and their effects on Europe as a whole. The experience of the Chernobyl disaster and its long-term effects on Europe have influenced the Germans to place environmental issues high on the bilateral agenda. Germany has given money for environmental clean-up in Russia and German firms have also been involved in refurbishing some nuclear reactors. Nuclear proliferation is another German concern, particularly since nuclear materials have been illegally shipped from Russia through Germany to third countries. Russian organized crime is also very active in Germany. Therefore, there has been significant cooperation between the Russian and German intelligence services. These problems directly affect Germany's security and will remain a focus of bilateral relations.

## Ukrainian-German Relations

Germany has focused on relations with Russia, as have its NATO allies. However, it has become more actively involved in Ukraine since 1992, partly because Ukraine represents a strong potential market and partly because, as the second largest post-Soviet state, it occupies a strategic geopolitical position. Initially, the German government was cautious in its dealings with this unknown new state, but in 1993 relations were intensified and Chancellor Kohl visited Kiev. However, German-Ukrainian relations remain very much a function of German-Russian relations.

From the Ukrainian point of view, Germany is a major focus for both economic and political reasons. Ukraine recognizes that it must compete with Russia for German assistance and German business, and it is seeking out German partners. Moreover, since Ukraine has defined itself unequivocally as a European state, thereby differentiating itself from Russia, it is pursuing an active diplomacy toward the European Union, in hopes of one day joining. Ukraine and Russia have similar agendas in their dealings with Germany— economic assistance and political recognition—but Ukraine's bargaining leverage is less than that of Russia at the moment. However, Ukraine's prevarication over the transfer of nuclear weapons to Russia, its own internal political divisions, and its reluctance to introduce far-reaching reforms have made the Germans more concerned about its potential to destabilize Europe.

Ukraine has tried to use ethnic Germans in Ukraine as a bargaining chip with Germany, but the issue has backfired. In January 1992, just before President Leonid Kravchuk made his state visit to Germany, he tried to outdo Yeltsin by offering to resettle four hundred thousand ethnic Germans around Odessa, in southern Ukraine; the same number were deported from Ukraine in 1941. Kravchuk offered visions of fertile farmland that Germans could cultivate. This promise has, however, not been fulfilled. During Kohl's June 1993 visit to Kiev, Kravchuk made it clear that he would only resettle ethnic Germans who had actually been deported; Germany had expected that ethnic Germans from Russia, Kazakhstan, and other areas could also be resettled there.[9] As a result, the agreement on resettling ethnic Germans was not signed at the summit.

Beyond economic and scientific cooperation, Kohl and others have reiterated their support for the reform process in Ukraine and have urged Ukraine to ratify START I, to sign the Nonproliferation Treaty and the Lisbon Protocol, and to commit itself to becoming a non-nuclear state, issues on which the Ukrainian leadership has expressed considerable ambivalence. Germany welcomed Ukraine's signature of the tripartite Russian-American-Ukrainian agreement in January 1994, under which Ukraine agreed to transfer nuclear weapons to Russia. Environmental and proliferation issues are also on the German-Ukrainian agenda. Under Leonid Kuchma, elected Ukraine's president in June 1994, the prospects for improved German-Ukrainian ties are good.

So far, however, those relations have developed slowly. But Ukraine is clearly the second most important successor state after Russia for the Germans. Some observers have argued that, now that the Soviet troops have withdrawn from Germany, and if conditions in Russia continue to deteriorate, Germany might decide to retreat from involvement in Russia. Ukraine would then become the outlying state in a cordon sanitaire protecting Europe from Russian instability, and the Russian-Ukrainian border would be the eastern border of Europe. However, this scenario is unlikely, in part because it is not clear that a cordon sanitaire would have any real meaning in postcommunist Europe.

### Will the Ghosts of Alliances Past Haunt the Twenty-First Century?

Despite the national introversion in both Russia and Germany and the instability of Russian politics, the low profile of German-Russian relations will not last forever. Immediate concerns—migrants, ethnic Germans, Kaliningrad—will ensure a bilateral engagement for some years. But there are historical, geographic, political, and economic incentives for a strong Russo-German relationship that will continue into the next century. United Germany has emerged as the predominant power east of the Oder-Neisse river. It is the largest investor in the region and the one with the most immediate stake in the outcome of the postcommunist transitions because it is the front-line state for migrants and refugees. Germany feels that it has been thrust into this predominant role because it is the only European country willing to take on the burden of dealing with postcommunist turmoil. Germany perceives itself as being weaker than the outside world believes it is, and it has assumed these obligations with reluctance.

As we witness the rebirth of history, with all its negative and violent aspects as well as its more benign ones, the specter of historical ghosts inevitably haunts the German-Russian relationship. Will an economically strong, politically united Germany achieve through economic means in the twenty-first century what it was unable to achieve through military means in the twentieth century, namely the domination of Europe? Will a new *Drang nach Osten* (urge toward the east) inevitably ensue from the power vacuum created by a weak Central Europe, a disintegrating Russia, and a retreating United States? After all, a united (although non-nuclear) Germany is a strong European power facing weakened, disunited Russia (albeit with a vast nuclear arsenal) and other even weaker successor states.

It is extremely difficult to imagine how or why such a scenario could occur. Germany's historical *Drang nach Osten* has become a *Zwang nach Osten*, or an obligation to support needy would-be partners. It would take an enormous leap of imagination to picture a resurgent Germany in the next century exchanging its European Union and transatlantic identity for a primarily East European orientation. It is much more difficult to predict what Russia will look like in the twenty-first century; but, for a few decades at least, Russia is unlikely to be able to affect decisively the reshaping of European security. Nevertheless, the facts of geographic life, if nothing else, will ensure that, in the longer run, Germany and Russia, the two great European land powers, will be instrumental in affecting Europe's future.

Ultimately, the way to prevent the reemergence of historical ghosts is to continue the United States' engagement in Europe, if at a diminished military level. A coordinated Western effort, led by Germany and the United States, to support democracy and free markets in Russia and other successor states is the best insurance against undesirable outcomes. But this will have to include a willingness on the part of the European Union and the United States to open their markets to Russian goods. Germany is not interested in resurrecting the spirit of Rapallo, when Russia and Germany, as international outcasts, concluded an agreement against the interests of the other European powers. It prefers a multilateral program (sponsored by the European Union or the G-7) to promote successful reform in the former Soviet Union. Germany, however reluctant it is to assume new international responsibilities, will remain one of Russia's most important interlocutors and supporters because of the logic of history and geography.

## Notes

1. Sergei A. Karaganov, *Russia: The New Foreign Policy and Security Agenda: A View From Moscow* (London: Brasseys, 1992).

2. *The Week in Germany* (German Information Center, New York), May 7, 1993, 5.

3. *Frankfurter Allgemeine Zeitung*, April 5, 1993.

4. Deutsche Presse-Agentur (DPA, in German), Foreign Broadcast Information Service (FBIS), WEU-93-055, March 19, 1993, 9.

5. Hans Dietrich Genscher, "Let's Take Gorbachev at His Word," (Speech to the World Economic Forum, Davos, February 1, 1987).

6. Cited in *Deutschland Nachrichten*, July 16, 1993.

7. DPA (in German), FBIS-WEU-93-029, February 16, 1993, 134; ITAR-Tass, in FBIS-WEU-93-102, May 28, 1993, 7.

8. Quoted in "The Ruling of the Federal Constitutional Court on the Deployment of the German Armed Forces," German Information Center press release, New York, July 1994.

9. *Frankfurter Allgemeine Zeitung*, June 11, 1993, 2.

# 21  A Watchful China

Thomas W. Robinson

## Introduction

For China as well as the states of the former Soviet Union, the period 1989-1991 was formative of a new direction in domestic developments and in foreign relations. In particular, Beijing's relations with Moscow and with the capitals of the newly independent Central Asian nations stemmed as much from the events of those years as from the entirety of the post-World War II Cold War era. Accordingly, Chinese purposes and policies changed greatly in the areas of economics, security, diplomacy, and ideology. These changes were reflected in Beijing's foreign relations during and after the 1989-1991 transition from the Cold War, both in general and as concerns relations with the states that had made up the internal Soviet empire. When an appreciation of China's foreign relations are integrated with a proper understanding of the equally revolutionary domestic changes in China and with the influence on both Russia and China of external events and the policies of the relevant states, a composite understanding emerges of how ties have altered between Beijing, Moscow, and the Central Asian capitals. And when longer-term regional and global trends are added, it becomes possible to essay on the future of these important relations down to the turn of the millennium, if not beyond.

## Interactive Influences of the 1989-1991 Revolutionary Period

Four interactive events define the intersystemic transitional period. The first was the Tiananmen Incident of June 3-4, 1989.[1] When the Beijing rulers authorized the indiscriminate use of force on the demonstrating citizenry of the capital and some one hundred other Chinese cities, they admitted their failure to govern their country through appeal to the economic interests of the people alone and tacitly acknowledged the necessity to rule mostly by force. By such large-scale, brutal, and unnecessary repression, witnessed by the whole world, they also admitted that the Mao Zedong-Deng Xiaoping revolutionary-reformist leadership had failed, over four decades, to convince the Chinese people of the alleged verities of Marxism-Leninism in both political and economic senses, and that their days in power as the natural leaders of the country were growing short. Moreover, modern communications guaranteed that these lessons would be learned in the other Eurasian states ruled by communist parties. There too, both rulers and commoners concluded that the long period of political-ideological deception was now over and that only direct use of force would prevent overthrow or collapse. It was too late to reform.

The second event was the series of revolutions, in late 1989 and into 1990, in East Europe.[2] Reform was, of course, the watchword of the Gorbachev-led Soviet Union as well as at least some of the East European states. Had the Chinese events not occurred and had Gorbachev himself not decided to cast adrift the East European parties by declaring that Moscow would no longer intervene by force to keep them in power, it is possible that evolution would have been successful in both areas and that the non-reformist East European parties could have continued to rule purely by repression for a while longer. But with long-term political and economic decay becoming more apparent daily, the capability to make vast changes from above gradually disappeared. It might have taken a while longer for these Soviet-style regimes to have fallen of their own weight, but Tiananmen and Gorbachev in combination guaranteed their early demise. The Chinese repression assisted in the rapid demise of the East German regime and the spread of the anticommunist revolution to the other East European states and then back to the Soviet Union itself because it set an example for the East German military, which refused to shoot down the demonstrators in Berlin: they refused, in so many words, to allow the same blood to despoil their hands as had sullied those of the Chinese military. With that, and with Russian troops confined to their barracks, communism in East Europe quickly fell. Even in Romania, where security forces at first remained loyal to Ceausescu, the military was divided, and much bloodshed occurred, the citizens were emboldened to revolt against their oppressors. Needless to say, the violent manner of the Romanian ruler's demise was a great shock to the Beijing rulers.

The third event, or group of events, was the breakup of the Soviet Union itself, the demise of the Soviet Communist party, the attempted reactionary coup in August 1991, the beginning of the long and difficult transition to democracy and a market economy in the members of the Commonwealth of Independent States (CIS), and the establishment of separate foreign relations by fourteen new states.[3] If the East European revolution was thus partly the consequence of Tiananmen, surely that revolution in turn fed the already great insecurity of the Chinese regime, which responded by imposing a severe political repression, an equally strong economic retrenchment from the 1978-1989 liberal reforms, and a circle-the-wagons foreign policy. The worst fears of Deng and his henchmen were confirmed when, in 1990, the Soviet Union progressively came apart, the Communist party leadership was challenged from all sides, a multiparty system emerged and the Communists lost millions of members, and competition for power between liberals and reactionaries took on direct, military form. And when, in 1991, the Russian situation proceeded to direct confrontation between the Yeltsin-led nationalist reformers and the Gorbachev-managed Politburo, and then on to an attempted but aborted right-wing coup, Deng and his followers were reduced to pious hopes that things would somehow correct themselves. Indeed, the Chinese leadership initially overreached itself by recognizing the coup directorate too quickly, only to have to reverse itself almost immediately when the putsch collapsed. The specter of Tiananmen Square clearly showed itself in the military confrontation at the Russian White House in mid-August, when it became clear to all that troops and tanks would not fire on their own people.

In that sense, as in the East German and Romanian instances, mass martyrdom in China was a direct cause of the overthrow of communism in all of East Europe and the Soviet Union itself, and all that followed in the sphere of China's diplomatic, security, and economic relations with the nations of the former Soviet Union. Although the Chinese leaders could pride themselves, for the while, that disorderly democracy had been forcibly kept out of their own land, they henceforth knew that they would have to reform politically as well as economically if they wished to remain in power.

They also began to perceive the outlines of their worst nightmare: a world of flourishing market democracies, including those of East Europe and Central Eurasia, united by similar domestic institutions and foreign policies, isolating by their very existence and their overwhelming command of the globe's resources China and the pitiful leftover rulers in Pyongyang and Havana. The events of 1990 and 1991 demonstrated to Beijing that time was not on their side and that they would have to move very fast just to prevent slipping into the situation in which the East European and Russian communists found themselves, a situation in which no amount of reform from above could avoid popular revolution and overthrow from below. There is no direct evidence that Deng decided to restart the Chinese economic reform machine in early 1991 specifically in fearful reaction to those events, but surely they supported the idea that there was no alternative to market-oriented economic reforms, that the Chinese leaders would have to proceed rapidly, and that the political consequences of the changes in Chinese society would have to be faced eventually.[4]

The fourth defining event was the overwhelming and demonstrative nature of the American military victory in the Gulf War.[5] This provided a further shock to Beijing. Not only did the convincing end of the conflict put an end to the Cold War, but the display of American high-technology military systems informed the Chinese military that they had a much longer path to full military modernization than they had presumed. Further, the Gulf War ratified for China the state of extreme isolation that Tiananmen and the East European and Russian events had placed it in. Accordingly, it had no choice but to reintegrate itself, as best it could, with the international community as the latter went about the business of constructing, slowly and fitfully, a post-Cold War international order centered on the United Nations, its charter-based security mechanism, and the panoply of regional and global security and economic institutions. That explains much of Beijing's post-1991 foreign policy of international cooperation, a policy that can be expected to last at least until China becomes powerful enough, late in the decade, to have a decisive say in Asian developments and a voice in global affairs equal to those of the other emerging power centers.

In combination, these domestic and international changes drove the Chinese leadership to redouble its efforts in the only manner remaining to it: the salvation of rapid economic growth. Once the decision was made (in mid-1991) to resume economic reforms and hence to promote such growth, China's approach to other nations, including those of the CIS, followed.[6] Peace, security, and development were to be Beijing's watchwords. China would keep out of international conflicts and would look the other way if domestic disorders in foreign states threatened international peace. It would try to protect its own borders from influences of various kinds emanating from surrounding states and regions. It would make itself as attractive as possible to Asian and other wealthy countries for the investments necessary for rapid economic development, even if this meant opening itself to international economic influences and making China economically interdependent. It would, at least for the while, put on ice disputes with its neighbors or settle them entirely so long as Chinese interests—as defined by the communist rulers in Beijing—were satisfied. And it would seek to participate, on an equal footing, with the other major power centers around the globe—America, Europe, Japan, and Russia—in the search for a stable and productive new international order.

On the other hand, Beijing began to discover that its rapidly growing economic power had useful political and security consequences. Obedient, as are all states, to the Iron Law of International Relations—that interests change or can be pursued in direct relation to the amount of power available—China more and more began to assert itself in various substantive and geographic spheres. It redefined its boundaries as political and not just physical, became much more difficult to negotiate with, increasingly asserted itself in Asian regional affairs, and moved more of its rapidly increasing economic resources into the military sphere. There thus emerged a contradiction in Chinese foreign policy. In capitals and boardrooms abroad, decision-makers divided between those who perceived the Chinese future with enthusiasm and those who dreaded what might come.[7]

### China, Russia, and Central Asia

Chinese relations with Russia and the Central Asian successor states provided a textbook example of the application of Beijing's new foreign policy direction. During the post-Tiananmen period, the Chinese authorities pursued four goals vis-à-vis the former Soviet Union.[8] Politically, they attempted to prevent Moscow, Tashkent, and the other capitals from establishing inextricably close ties with America, Europe, and Japan. Nothing would be more disastrous for China than an institutionalized league of global market democracies, for Beijing would then be isolated from its sources of technology and capital, as well as from the natural markets for its goods. It would also risk such a group, however informal it might be at first, converting itself into a security community directed potentially at Beijing. Indeed, Deng and his associates watched nervously as the one extant Western grouping of just that sort, the Group of Seven, deliberately opened its door to Russia and, as first Gorbachev and then Yeltsin began to attend their annual meetings, to convert itself into a de facto Group of Eight.

Beijing's response was to bite the bullet, establish as good diplomatic relations with the successor states as possible, and then to develop reasonable political relations on the basis of resolving existing disputes and developing new economic ties. That was, of course, a temporary rear-guard action. The longer-term political goal was to tie the relevant states to China so as to make it difficult or impossible for them to integrate themselves politically with the market democracies. That goal posed a dilemma for Beijing, since in a system-less post-Cold War world, global and Asian regional political arrangement favored marketization and democratization. A careful balance had to be struck between China's own traditional dependence on political balances of power (which no longer existed) and learning how to use new levers of international influence—interdependence, trade, technology, participation in international institutions, and the like.

In the security realm, China's policy toward the Central Eurasian successor states was equally cautious. It would obviously be beneficial if existing security disputes (border issues, for instance) were settled or put aside. It would also be useful if China and the relevant successor states could agree on a set of security arrangements wherein the parties would agree to mutual noninterference, pledge not to direct each other's security assets against the other, and (if at all possible) join together to oppose the emergence of military arrangements elsewhere that could be construed as threatening.

Finally, Beijing perceived an opportunity to obtain high-technology Russian military systems, at least in sample form and perhaps in quantity, at much-reduced prices. Such acquisitions could greatly assist China in shortening the period of great danger from American post-Gulf War military domination and, if Russian-assisted emplacements of military hardware assembly lines could be arranged, China might even draw close to American levels of military sophistication. The trick, throughout, was to strengthen China militarily while warding off security threats as the country grew economically. On the one hand, China had to stay out of harm's way, at least temporarily; on the other hand, it wished to begin to prepare for its own Asian military preponderance without frightening its neighbors into a grand anti-Chinese alliance.[9]

Economically, China adopted a three-pronged economic policy toward the successor states. First, Beijing sought to maintain, and then to enhance, trade relations with Russia, and to establish, and then expand, trade with the Central Asian states.[10] Because of the economic turmoil surrounding desocialization and marketization in Russia and the successor states, this could only mean exchange of Chinese consumer goods for Russian (and FSU) producer goods and primary products and, in the absence of meaningful exchange rates, barter and border trade. Second, China wished to establish more permanent economic relations with the successor states through trade treaties and most-favored-nation-tariff treatment. And third, Beijing attempted to take advantage of the Russian economic situation by availing itself of Russian technology (if not, for the moment, capital) on very favorable terms, and by offering hard currency in exchange for know-how, assembly lines, plans, and technicians.

Finally, China worked out an ideological approach to the successor states. This was not easy, given the postcommunist orientation of those regimes and the confusing mixture of nationalism, religion, modernism, and anticommunism of which they were the expression. Beijing could only try to minimize the differences between these orientations and its own still-communist, incipiently authoritarian, and increasingly chauvinistic orientation. The policy had to be complex, for now China faced a series of nations whose orientations ranged from Catholic to Orthodox to Islamic in the religious sense, from fully democratic to confusedly authoritarian to potentially military in the political sense, and from a simple social class structure to a highly differentiated society in the sociological sense. Such complexity called for sophistication, patience, innovation, and understanding on the part of Deng and his group, qualities which they had not always possessed in sufficient quantity.

## A Sketch of Chinese-Central Eurasian Relations after the Cold War

For obvious reasons, Beijing had to center its attention on relations with Russia as earlier it had on the USSR. The most interesting and commanding fact is the continuity of Beijing's policy toward Moscow throughout the turbulent early post-Cold War period, a continuity reciprocated, with some short exceptions, during both the Gorbachev and the Yeltsin periods. Mikhail Gorbachev had, in his well-known Vladivostok and Krasnoyarsk speeches (respectively in 1986 and 1988), fundamentally altered Soviet policy toward China, from opposition on every front to accommodation, compromise, and renewed friendship. The Chinese leadership, having for nearly thirty years resisted Soviet encroachments, threats, and war preparations, also on all fronts, having competed for leadership of the communist-led group of states (the "camp"), and having cooperated closely with the United States against Moscow, now gradually warmed to Gorbachev's advances. By 1989, the process of Russian bending to Chinese demands for proof of their good intent (the so-called "three obstacles" —withdrawal of Russian forces from Afghanistan, Mongolia, and Vietnam) and the negotiations on the Sino-Soviet border question had both proceeded far enough to schedule a breakthrough summit meeting. This was accomplished in mid-May 1989, when Gorbachev visited Beijing and signed a joint communiqué with the Chinese leadership.[11]

The accident of the timing of the visit, in the midst of the massive Beijing demonstrations leading two weeks later to the Tiananmen repressions, should not detract from the importance of the results. Essentially, the two sides agreed to put aside their ideological and security disputes of the previous three decades and to start anew. Equally important, however, is that their agreement was not a mere clearing of the decks but a significant step toward building a new, positive, and (in many ways) anti-American relationship that resembled an alliance. The wording of the communiqué read much like a nineteenth-century agreement of alignment if not an outright treaty of alliance. Not only did the two sides pledge not to use or threaten force against each other and agree to solve the border question peaceably; they also agreed to resist "actions and attempts by any state to foist their will on others and to seek hegemony in any form anywhere." [12] This clause could only have been directed against the United States. The 1989 pact was augmented two year later when Jiang Zemin, the Chinese Communist party head, went to Moscow and signed another wide-ranging joint communiqué. Although international conditions had changed drastically by that time (East Europe was lost to communism, Germany reunified, the Cold War long over, the Gulf War fought and won, China still isolated as a result of Tiananmen, and the Soviet Communist party about to lose power), this further development of bilateral ties was startling. Now the Soviet Union and China reduced the forces they deployed against each other, stepped up military contacts even further, reiterated their opposition to "hegemonism," and agreed to take similar approaches to most issues in global affairs. [13]

This was followed, early in 1992, by the settlement of most of the border issue (i.e., the Eastern, riverine portion) and then, late that year, by a further joint declaration signed during Boris Yeltsin's visit to Beijing. In contrast to the first two joint statements, this one was not merely a party-to-party announcement (by then the Soviet party had been outlawed as a result of the failed August 1991 coup in Moscow) but a state-to-state declaration, making it all the more authoritative. Aside from repeating the pledges made previously, this declaration stated that "neither party should join any military or political alliance against the other party, [or] sign any treaty or agreement with a third country prejudicing the sovereignty and security interests of the other party." It further provided that both parties would constantly consult each other at all levels on all international issues, that they would continue border-force reductions, and that they would "maintain military contact." [14]

These were not just words. There quickly developed a material base to the new security tie that saw transfer of much Soviet military equipment and technology—symbolized by but hardly limited to the sale of seventy-two SU-27 fighter aircraft —and the setting up of assembly lines for (nearly) the latest

Russian tanks, fighters, computers, and other relevant equipment.[15] Similarly strong ties were established and quickly developed in a host of other fields as normalization was achieved. Trade blossomed, particularly barter trade directly across the border, science and technology delegations were exchanged, tourism arose where there had been practically none before, students studied in each other's universities, cultural troupes regularly came and went, and Russian and Chinese were taught in the other country's schools.[16] Indeed, it is no exaggeration to say that there occurred a second renaissance of Russian and Chinese relations (the first having been the "golden era" of Sino-Soviet relations in the early 1950s).

Why did the two countries, particularly China, feel it necessary to go to such lengths? What were the practical results? Why did China's leaders not feel unduly threatened by the events in Russia after 1989, and why did not other affected states (particularly the United States) react in a highly justified negative manner?

The answers are several. First, both Russia and China worried that the United States, as the "only remaining superpower" after the Gulf War, would dominate the post-Cold War world. This was no less important for China, which increasingly regarded Washington as its security opponent, than it was for the Soviet Union and then Russia, which greatly needed some buttressing of its international position as it weakened internally.

Second, China did not like the fact that the Soviet Union had given away its East European empire, allowed the market democracies to supplant communist rule, and then lost control of its own internal order. But Beijing's isolation drove it to an accommodation with Moscow. Indeed, the parallel with the German-Soviet Rapallo Treaty of 1922 was explicitly drawn in at least the Russian capital: both were arrangements of convenience between Eurasian continental have-nots and temporary international pariahs.[17]

Third, there was the economic argument. Russia had a lot of excess first-class military equipment that would only rust and go out of date sitting on Russian soil. It also lacked many of the economic goods that production of these martial toys had prohibited—consumer goods, an up-to-date infrastructure, a hard currency, and in general a workable economic system. China lacked the kind of modern military systems that had just been put on display in the Gulf War and perceived no near-term opportunity to obtain them (at least without first ruining its economy as the Soviet Union had just done), but it did have the consumer goods, an increasingly large trade surplus, and a semi-convertible currency. The exchange made economic sense.[18]

Finally, the arrangement with Russia fit in with the larger needs of Chinese foreign policy: that is, making the world safe for Chinese economic development and expansion of Beijing's influence, first throughout Asia and later in other regions.[19] Best to arrange matters with most of the rest of Eurasia so that China would be uninhibited in that quest. To which should be added the feeling in Beijing that it would be America and Japan (Europe, possibly, later) that would pose challenges and provide competition for China's ultimate primacy, and perhaps even hegemony, in Asia. Better to have Russia on one's own side, even if it was temporarily down and out.

As for Moscow, dependence on the West for its very livelihood was not looked on with favor in many (particularly conservative) Russian policy circles. Although China and its rulers were hardly admired in the Kremlin, the Russians at least had to begrudge the Chinese their near-term success in reformist economic development while holding political change to zero. With instability the rule in many nations, Beijing's relative political calm and economic success appealed. And Russia and China could think along similar, although hardly identical, lines in their respective relations with Japan, on various components of the Korean question, in Southeast Asian matters, and on the structure of South Asian international relations.[20]

Russian-Chinese rapprochement might not have gone so far, however, had not two further developments taken place. On the one hand, the Russian domestic situation deteriorated even further, and at a seemingly accelerating pace, after the failed August 1991 coup. (A sign of how far political and economic life had deteriorated in Moscow was the bloody struggle at the Russian White House in late 1993 between pro- and anti-Yeltsin forces and the concomitant near-collapse of the Russian economy.)[21] Deng Xiaoping and his associates might have much to fear from a Russia that was successfully democratizing and marketizing; but after 1991 Russia was doing neither. And so long as the Chinese economy continued its rapid upward movement and the political situation at home remained under control, China had little to fear from Russia. The only worry was that the Russian decline should not go so far as to generate disorders that might spill over the Russian-Chinese borders. But they had not, and, since the Russian border was (except for the Maritime Provinces) largely unpopulated, probably would not. (A greater problem, at least potentially, was similar disorders along China's borders with the newly independent successor states of Central Asia, discussed below.)

On the other hand, the United States, Japan, West Europe, and their Asian associates did not become overly exercised by the new, close Chinese-Russian ties. In the American case, a concatenation of reasons explain why Washington more or less ignored these matters. Encouraging East European decommunization, keeping Russia afloat economically, worrying about where Soviet and then Russian politics would take Moscow, fixating security policy on the 1990-1991 Gulf War, and—most importantly—dealing with domestic concerns (the recession and the run-up to the 1992 presidential election) combined to draw American attention away from faraway places like the Russian-Chinese border and tiresome replays of Cold War strategic triangles.[22] Japan, South Korea, Taiwan, and other leading Asian nations took an economics-and-trade first attitude toward China and had other fish to fry with Russia (the Northern Islands question in Japan's case, establishment of diplomatic relations as regards South Korea, and the opportunity to leap out of diplomatic isolation for Taiwan).[23] A rapidly weakening Russia renewing its ties with a rapidly marketizing China seemed to threaten no one in Asia. Only when China, having disposed of the threat from its Eurasian continental hinterland, became so powerful as to direct its energies eastward and southward to threaten its Asian neighbors, and only when Russia recovered its strength sufficiently to add its resources to those of China, would the world begin to worry about the details of the new Chinese-Russian combine.

As for the Europeans, they were still too far away from Asia and had too many problems at home (recession, reunification, redrawing of national boundaries) to worry about China's relations with Russia. They did, of course, greatly concern themselves with the events in Moscow and the other Soviet successor states in Europe. But they had little affection for post-Tiananmen China, which many thought would in any case go the way of the former communist states in their corner of Eurasia. They thought that if Russia wanted to get some use of its excessively large military arsenal, better to let Moscow sell it to China and to other Asian nations than to continue to deploy it west of the Urals for possible use in Europe.[24]

So China and Russia ended up with a much-strengthened relationship, accepted or hardly noticed by others. There remained, for China, the question of what (if anything) to do about the Central Asian successor states: Kazakhstan, Uzbekistan, Turkmenistan, Tajikistan, and Kyrgyzstan. If in the short- to medium-terms these presented no major threat to China, they did pose some dangers and opportunities, while in the long run Beijing would have to decide what general approach to take to them. General unfamiliarity with these regions at first hindered the Chinese rulers, since contacts had previously been channeled through Moscow.

After some initial hesitation after August 1991, caused by post-coup confusion in the now-disintegrating Soviet Union and Beijing's embarrassment at having recognized the coup government too quickly (only to have to withdraw that recognition just as quickly), China found it had little choice but to follow the rest of the diplomatic community in offering recognition to Alma Alta, Tashkent, Ashgabat, Dushanbe, and Bishkek. Until embassies and their staffs were in place and experience in dealing with these new states was gained, China could not take an active role in their regard. That would take time. Moreover, civil strife in many Central Asian areas between various ethnic groups and between local inhabitants and Great Russians confused the internal situation greatly. China, like most other external states, had little influence on or knowledge about these conflicts. Better to stay out for the time being. Further, Beijing's rational interest was first to look with favor on a region both divided against itself and standing in opposition to Russia. That would keep most potential trouble away from their borders with China. Better, therefore, to let well enough alone. Finally, the last thing Beijing wished for, as regards the five successor states, was for them to adopt—together or separately—an Islamic fundamentalist ideology and form of government. With their own restive Kazakh, Uzbek, and other Islamic minority populations in Sinkiang, Tibet, and Inner Mongolia, and with Islamic fundamentalism sweeping the Middle East, Southwest Asia, Iran, Afghanistan, and even Pakistan, the Deng group in Beijing chose to watch, but not participate in, Central Asian volatility.[25]

For all these reasons, Beijing adopted a Central Asian policy of playing it straight. Trade, diplomatic, and cultural ties could gradually be developed, and these were initiated in 1992. But until the Central Asian picture became clearer, until China's own domestic political situation (that is, the succession of Deng and the changing distribution of political power between center and region) was also stabilized, and until China's post-Tiananmen international image improved, it was better to take a low profile. Perhaps by the late 1990s China could think of a more involved policy in Central Asia. Meanwhile, it was best to invest only modestly in the region. The action, for China, would continue to be located elsewhere—in Northeast Asia, Russia, Europe, and North America, and most importantly, in the domestic economic and political arenas.

### The Influence of Broader Global and Regional Trends

Given the already confusing nature of the post-Cold War era, an examination of trends and forces exerting a longer-term influence on China's policies toward Russia and Central Asia might only exacerbate matters. It is true that the range of possibilities in China and the Asian-located Soviet successor states is so vast as to make most forecasts problematic at best. One need only note the changes that the Deng Xiaoping succession will bring to China, the wide range of political and economic possibilities in Russia, and the completely open situations of the Central Asian republics. Together, these beget permutations of possibilities too numerous to count. Reality contains only one actual outcome, however, and that outcome is bounded by external forces even now evident. Let us at least list these forces and offer some preliminary indication of how they might influence the actual train of events.

There are five global trends at work: political multipolarity among five power centers—North America, Europe, Russia, China, and Japan; the triple revolution of democratization, marketization, and interdependence; the universal primacy of domestic problems; the rise of technology as the major force propelling economic and military developments; and the emergence of global issues, especially environmental questions. In Asia, these forces translate into relative equality among the major regional powers (America, China, Japan, and Russia); the further spread and deepening of the drives toward democracy, market economics, and breakdown of national boundaries, engulfing remaining socialist states and stimulating modernization even in the least developed nations; the likelihood of continued peace among the major Asian powers as none can afford to divert significant resources from domestic economic construction or political reordering; revision of the regional "pecking order" according to technology-induced rates of growth; and the need to invent international institutions to grapple with increasingly serious cross-border problems, especially environmental issues.

The trend toward relative equality of the major powers, together with the current absence of any systemic expression of security concerns, implies the need to organize Asian security institutionally. The triple revolution, together with domestic primacy, gives nations sufficient time to work together, if they are wise enough, to construct such a security system, as well as associated regional economic institutions. Technology will be an essential element in solving the many problems that will emerge during the search for international economic and security institutions acceptable to all. And environmental questions challenge the relevant parties to work together for common ends. If, therefore, Asian and trans-Pacific politicians, including those in China and the former Soviet Union, can seize the opportunities thus presented by these positive indications of the future, the manifold problems in East and Central Eurasia may become manageable.

Although specific long-term scenarios are obviously impossible to spell out, the influence of these domestic trends do impel Chinese-Central Eurasian developments in certain general directions. There are five alternatives, all of which depend on how domestic groups (for example, governments, classes, nationalities) in the three great geographic areas—China, Russia, and Central Asia—cope with the combination of their own challenges and the influence of the outside forces just outlined. The first is *prolonged and extended breakdown* of economic, political, and social life, not just in Russia and Central Asia but extending to China as well. There would be little or no agreement on who is to rule; economies would fail to grow sufficiently to deal with international, population, and environmental pressures; social groups (both legacies from history and products of rapid modernization) would face off against each other; and the states in question would tend to fall apart. Chaos could ensue and, to a greater or lesser extent, the peoples of the three geographic areas would become increasingly dependent on the largess offered, or withheld, by the external world. In that case, China could have no positive policy toward Russia or Central Asia, as all would have to fend for themselves.

The second, by contrast, is a settling down to *positively oriented stability*. Russia would progressively recover and move steadily toward democracy and a market-oriented economic system. China would move through the succession period without undue power struggle, begin the process of limiting communist party power and transitioning (over a longer period) to democracy, and stabilize its economic growth at about 6 percent per annum. Central Asia, as well as Russia and China, would progressively integrate itself into the interdependent global economy and discover the benefits of export-led growth. The foreign policy orientation of China would be generally benign and participatory, so that it would be as friendly to Russia and Central Asia as it would be to America and Japan.

The third possibility, somewhere between the first two extremes, is *fascist-authoritarian stabilization* in all three areas. A military regime would take over in Moscow, a party-military combine would emerge in Beijing, and similar nationalist-militarist groups would come to power in Central Asia. Economic growth would be slow but steady, and there would be little room for autonomy of expression by newly emergent social groups. China would link itself closely with Russia in an anti-Western alliance and, together with Moscow, dictate the external orientation of the Central Asian states.

The fourth scenario involves *dynamic, disjointed change* in Russia and China, and probably in Central Asia as well. Political experimentation would be the order of the day, with different kinds of regimes and power groups succeeding each other regularly. Economic growth rates would fluctuate widely, depending on global economic conditions, and there would be massive social transitions of all kinds, as stop-and-start modernization made life alternately less and more difficult for all. China's policy toward the other two areas would vary accordingly, from relatively close ties to comparative distance, and would change rapidly according to the relative fit between its own domestic situation and those in the other two areas.

The final possibility is an *imperialist China*. Here, Russia would continue to disintegrate, the Central Asian states would feud among themselves, and China would maintain authoritarian political stability at home and high rates of economic growth. An increasingly powerful China would seek to exert its influence wherever it could and, finding itself blocked by strong states to the east (and not wishing to enmesh itself in the morasses of South and Southeast Asia), would attempt to subvert large areas of Central Eurasia—both Russian and Central Asian. Such an anti-Russian policy would drive Moscow into the hands of Europe, North America, and Japan, which would form a global anti-Chinese alliance.

With the exception of the second, none of these possibilities is desirable, for they imply conflict, opposition, tension, and breakdown. Fortunately, the five global and regional trends and forces militate against the emergence—or at any rate the severity and durability—of these four unpalatable outcomes. Perhaps, if one or another of them does occur, its time-span might be relatively short, and the general tendency toward the more felicitous outcomes outlined at the beginning would reassert itself. Whatever happens, however, it is likely that the 1990s as a whole, in terms of China's policy toward Russia and Central Asia (as well, possibly, in the more general sense) will be seen, in retrospect, as a decade of transition in China's policy toward Russia and Central Asia.

## Notes

1. Some useful representatives of the increasingly large literature on this subject are Wang Shien et al., eds., *The Truth of Fire and Blood: A Document on the Pro-Democracy Movement in Mainland China in 1989* (Taipei: Institute of the Study of Chinese Communist Problems, 1989) [in Chinese]; George Hicks, ed., *The Broken Mirror: China After Tiananmen* (London: St. James Press, 1990); and Amnesty International, "People's Republic of China: Preliminary Findings on Killings of Unarmed Civilians,

Arbitrary Arrests and Summary Executions Since June 3, 1989" (Washington, D.C.: Amnesty International, August 1989).

2. The fall of communism in East Europe has not, at this writing, received definitive treatment. But see Elie Abel, *The Shattered Bloc: Behind the Upheaval in Eastern Europe* (Boston: Houghton Mifflin, 1990); Charles Gati, *The Bloc That Failed: Soviet-East European Relations in Transition* (Bloomington: Indiana University Press, 1990); Ivo Banac, ed., *Eastern Europe in Revolution* (Ithaca, N.Y.: Cornell University Press, 1992); John Feffer, *Shock Waves: Eastern Europe after the Revolutions* (Boston: South End Press, 1992); and Anatol Lieven, *The Baltic Revolution* (New Haven: Yale University Press, 1993).

3. Supposedly the "best" book to emerge so far is *Lenin's Tomb: The Last Days of the Soviet Empire* (New York: Random House, 1993). But see also James Billington, *Russia Transformed: Breakthrough to Hope* (New York: Free Press, 1992); Helene Carrère d'Encausse, *The End of the Soviet Empire* (New York: Basic Books, 1993); Robert Kaiser, *Why Gorbachev Happened* (New York: Simon and Schuster, revised edition, 1993); Yegor Ligachev, *Inside Gorbachev's Kremlin* (New York: Pantheon, 1993); Peter Reddaway, ed., *Uncensored Russia: Protest and Dissent in the Soviet Union* (New York: American Heritage Press, 1992); and Aleksandr Yakovel, *Preface. Collapse. Afterword* (Moscow: Novosti, 1992) [in Russian].

4. Samuel S. Kim, ed., *China and the World*, 3d ed. (Boulder, Colo.: Westview Press, 1993); Thomas W. Robinson and David Shambaugh, eds., *Chinese Foreign Policy: Ideas and Interpretations* (New York: Oxford University Press, 1993); John W. Garver, *Foreign Relations of the People's Republic of China* (Englewood-Cliffs, N.J.: Prentice-Hall, 1993); and Allen S. Whiting, ed., "China's Foreign Relations," *The Annals* (January 1992).

5. Jeffrey McCausland, *The Gulf Conflict: A Military Analysis*, Adelphi Paper 282 (London: International Institute for Strategic Studies, November 1993); Lawrence Freedman and Efraim Karsh, *The Gulf Conflict, 1990-1991* (London: Faber and Faber, 1993); Department of Defense, *Conduct of the Persian Gulf War*, chaps. 1-7, appendixes A-T (Washington, D.C.: Government Printing Office, 1992); James Blackwell, Michael Maser, and Don Snider, *The Gulf War—Military Lessons Learned* (Washington, D.C.: Center for Strategic and International Studies, 1991); Benjamin Lambeth, *Desert Storm and Its Meaning* (Santa Monica, Calif.: Rand, 1992); and Hwo Hwei-ling, "Patterns of Behavior in China's Foreign Policy: The Gulf Crisis and Beyond," *Asian Survey* (March 1992): 263-276.

6. Chen Qimao, "New Approaches in China's Foreign Policy: The Post Cold War Era," *Asian Survey* (March 1993): 237-251. Chinese views are found in *Guoji Wenti Yanjiu* (International Studies), *Guoji Zhangwang* (World Outlook), *Foreign Affairs Journal*, *Guiji Zhanlue Yanjiu* (International Strategic Studies), and *Xiandai Guoji Guanxi* (Contemporary International Relations), as well as in the official press. A survey of these journals from 1990 to 1993 reveals not only a diversity of outlooks, reflecting the views of the ministries that these journals and their respective institutes serve, but also full knowledge and sophisticated analysis of the factors that influence post-Cold War international relations. See, in particular, Sa Banwang, "Impact of the Gulf War on the World Military Situation and Military Strategy," *Guoji Zhanlue Yanjiu*, no. 1 (1991): 11-21.

7. Compare, for instance, David Shambaugh, "China's Security Policy in the Post-Cold War Era," *Survival* (Summer 1992): 88-106, with Samuel S. Kim, "China as a

Regional Power," *Current History* (September 1992): 247-252. For a statement of the Iron Law of International Relations as it applies to China, see the author's "Chinese Foreign Policy: From the Forties to the Nineties," in *Chinese Foreign Policy*, ed. Robinson and Shambaugh, 561-608.

8. Lowell Dittmer, *Sino-Soviet Normalization and Its International Implications, 1945-1990* (Seattle: University of Washington Press, 1992); Huan Guocang, "The New [Chinese] Relationship with the Former Soviet Union," *Current History* (September 1992): 247-252; and J. Richard Walsh, "China and the New Geopolitics of Central Asia," *Asian Survey* (March 1993): 272-281. Representative English-language Chinese comments on evolving Sino-Soviet [Russian] relations include Liu Jiangyong, "On the Current Changes in the Asia-Pacific Political Scene," Shen Qurong, "Security Environment in Northeast Asia: Its Characteristics and Sensitivities," and Yan Xuetong, "China's Security After the Cold War," in *Contemporary International Relations* (March 1992, December 1992, and May 1993, respectively); and Xu Zhixin, "The Trend of Change in the Former Soviet Union and Its World Impact," *Foreign Affairs Journal* (March 1992): 45-55.

9. John W. Garver, "Chinese Foreign Policy: The Diplomacy of Damage Control," *Current History* (September 1991): 241-246; Roxane D.C. Sismanidis, "China's International Security Policy," *Problems of Communism* (July-August 1991): 49-62; David Shambaugh, *Beautiful Imperialist: China Perceives America, 1972-1990* (Princeton, N.J.: Princeton University Press, 1991); and Robert Sutter, "China as a Security Concern in Asia," unpublished manuscript (Washington, D.C.: Library of Congress, Congressional Research Service).

10. Steven I. Levine, "Second Chance in China: Sino-Soviet Relations in the 1990s," in *China's Foreign Relations*, ed. Whiting, 26-38; Sharon E. Ruwart, "Expanding Sino-Soviet Trade," *The China Business Review* (March-April 1991): 42-50; Huan Guocang, "The New Relationship with the Former Soviet Union," *Current History* (September 1992): 253-256, Sharon E. Ruwart, "Sino-Soviet Trade in the 1980s and 1990s: Politics, Pragmatism, and Profits," in Joint Economic Committee, *China's Economic Dilemmas in the 1990s: The Problems of Reforms, Modernization, and Interdependence* (Washington, D.C.: Government Printing Office, 1991): 912-931; and Yang Shouzheng, "Development of Sino-Soviet Economic and Trade Relations and Its Impact on Northeast Asian and Asia-Pacific Region," *Foreign Affairs Journal* (December 1990): 26-34.

11. Soviet Embassy, Washington, D.C., "Soviet-Chinese Joint Communiqué," *News and Views From the USSR*, May 19, 1989, which also translates "Gorbachev's Speech to Chinese Public."

12. Paragraphs 4 and 13. The next stage was reached when the Chinese Premier, Li Peng, visited Moscow in April 1990. The two foreign ministers, Eduard Shevardnadze and Qian Qichen, signed an agreement to further reduce military forces along the Sino-Soviet boundary, while Li and the then Soviet prime minister, Nikolai Ryzhkov, signed a broad economic, technological, and scientific agreement that formed the basis of much of the improvement in relations during the following years. See the *New York Times* and *Washington Post* editions of April 25 and 26, 1990. In March 1991, China loaned the Soviet Union $720 million for Russian purchase of Chinese consumer goods, the first Chinese loan to a Russian entity in history.

13. "Sino-Soviet Joint Communiqué," Chinese embassy (Washington, D.C.) press release, May 19, 1991. For a Chinese analysis, see Xiao Fan, "Sino-Soviet Relations on the Occasion of General Secretary Jiang Zemin's Visit to the Soviet Union," *Foreign*

*Affairs Journal,* 1-6.

14. The Russian-language text is in Tass of December 18, 1992. The English-language translation, along with associated materials, is in Foreign Broadcasting Information Service, *Daily Report-China,* December 18, 1992, 7-12. For analysis, see *Far Eastern Economic Review,* December 3, 17, and 24/31, 1992.

15. A competent exposition is Bin Yu, "Sino-Russian Military Relations: Implications for Asian-Pacific Security," *Asian Survey* (March 1993): 302-316. See also *Far Eastern Economic Relations,* April 11, 1991; January 23, March 19, and November 12 and 26, 1992; and April 8, July 8, and October 7, 1993.

16. This statement is made on the basis of many reports in FBIS, *Daily Report-China* and *Daily Report-Central Eurasia* (formerly *Soviet Union*) for 1991-1993, *Problemiy Dan'nego Vostoka* (Problems of the Far East, Moscow), and *Sino-Soviet Affairs* (Seoul, in Korean), for the same period, as well as conversations with Russian and Chinese specialists on each other's countries.

17. Hung P. Nguyen, "Russia and China: The Genesis of an Eastern Rapallo," *Asian Survey* (March 1993): 285-301, which cites many Russian sources.

18. Recent Chinese-Russian trade figures are difficult to obtain. But clearly trade and exchanges tilted sharply upwards, as consistent reports of increased trade, establishment of many new border trade outposts, tourism (in the Russian case, mostly for purposes of bringing back Chinese goods for resale domestically at much higher prices), and barter appeared to indicate. For such reports, see *Far Eastern Economic Review,* March 28 and May 30, 1991, and January 7, 1993. For an excellent Russian-language analysis of the relationship of the Chinese and the Russian Far Eastern economies, see the doctoral dissertation, defended in 1993 at the Russian Academy of Sciences, of Aleksandr Nemets, "The Growth of Chinese Economic Potential and the Role of Russia," which analyzes the situation province by province on both sides of the Chinese and Russian borders.

19. The economic argument is at the base of every Chinese foreign policy statement since the Deng-era reforms began in late 1978. For an analysis, see Thomas W. Robinson, "Interdependence in China's Foreign Relations," in *China and the World,* ed. Kim, 187-202. The military argument was initially made by Chinese analysts in distinguishing between China's political and its "strategic" boundaries, wherein the latter would be set at increasing distances from the former as China's military power increased. This is the same argument made by every nation entering the international system as a new military power, and as such is a confirmation of the Iron Law of International Relations set forth above. For recent analyses of Chinese military strategy, see Paul H. B. Godwin, "Chinese Defense Policy and Military Strategy in the 1990s," in *China's Economic Dilemmas in the 1990s,* 648-662, and Godwin, "Chinese Military Strategy Revised: Local and Limited War," in *China's Foreign Relations,* ed. Whiting, 191-201, both of which contain numerous Chinese references.

20. Representative analyses of Chinese Asian regional policy are to be found in "The China Challenge: American Policies in East Asia, China in the Emerging World Order," *Proceedings of the Academy of Political Science* 38, 2 (1991); A. James Gregor, "China's Shadow over Southeast Asian Waters," *Global Affairs* (Summer 1992): 1-13; Stephen Uhalley, Jr., "Sino-Soviet Relations: Continuous Improvement Amidst Tumultuous Change," *Journal of East Asian Affairs* (Winter-Spring, 1992): 101-114; Ming Lee, "The Impact of Peking-Seoul Ties on Northeast Asia," *Issues and Studies* (September 1992): 122-124; Jia Hao and Zhuang Qubing, "China's Policy Toward the Korean

Peninsula," *Asian Survey* (December 1992): 1137-1156; Andrew Brick, "The Asian Giants: Neighborly Ambivalence," *Global Affairs* (Fall 1991): 70-87; Fred Hershede, "Trade Between China and ASEAN," *Pacific Affairs* (Summer 1991): 179-193; entries by Allen S. Whiting, Robert Ross, and John Garver on, respectively, China and Japan, China and Southeast Asia, and China and South Asia, in *China's Foreign Relations*, ed. Whiting, 39-66; Peter J. Opita, "Changing Alliances: China and Soviet Policy Toward the Korean Peninsula," *Aussenpolitik*, no. 3 (1991): 247-257; Mutahir Ahmed, "Sino-Soviet Rapprochement: Its Impact on South Asia," *Pakistan Horizon* (January 1990): 79-88; "China and Japan: History, Trends, Prospects," special issue of *The China Quarterly* (December 1990); Allen S. Whiting and Xin Jianfei, "Sino-Japanese Relations: Pragmatism and Passion," *World Policy Journal* (Winter 1990-1991): 107-136; and Uldis Kruze, "Sino-Japanese Relations," *Current History* (April 1991): 156-169.

Soviet [Russian] Asian regional policy can be followed in Stephen R. Bowers, "Pragmatism and Soviet Foreign Policy: USSR-South Korean Relations," *Asian Affairs* (Spring 1992): 19-34; Peggy Falkenheim Meyer, "Gorbachev and Post-Gorbachev Policy Toward the Korean Peninsula: The Impact of Changing Russian Perceptions," *Asian Survey* (August 1992): 757-772; Kim Yu-nam, "Changes in Soviet-Korean Relations and Their Impact on the Balance of Power System in Northeast Asia," *Journal of East Asian Affairs* (Winter-Spring, 1992): 22-50; Mette Skak, "Post Soviet Foreign Policy: The Emerging Relationship Between Russia and Northeast Asia," *Journal of East Asian Affairs* (Winter-Spring 1993): 137-186; John W. Garver, "The Indian Factor in Recent Sino-Soviet Relations," *The China Quarterly* (March 1991): 55-85; Hiroshi Kimura, "Gorbachev's Japan Policy: The Northern Territories Issue," *Asian Survey* (September 1991): 795-815; Ramesh Thakur, "India and the Soviet Union: Conjunctions and Disjunctions of Interests," *Asian Survey* (September 1991): 847-861; Ahn Byung-joon, "South Korean-Soviet Relations: Contemporary Issues and Prospects," *Asian Survey* (September 1991): 816-826; Wolf Mendel, "Japan and the Soviet Union: Towards a New Deal?" *World Today* (November 1991): 196-200; Eugene and Natasha Bazhanov, "Soviet Views on North Korea: The Domestic Scene and Foreign Policy," *Asian Survey* (December 1991): 1123-1138; Shrikant Paranjpe, "Gorbachev's Asia-Pacific Security and the Regional State System of South Asia," *India Quarterly* (April-September 1990): 113-126; Muthiah Alagappa, "Soviet Policy in Southeast Asia: Towards Constructive Engagement," *Pacific Affairs* (Fall 1990): 321-350; Matthew J. Simeone and Vladimir Wozniak, "Selling Perestroika and New Thinking to Southeast Asia: Gorbachev at His Persuasive Best," *Political Communication and Persuasion* (July-September 1990): 129-146; Robert Legvold, "Soviet Policy in East Asia," *Washington Quarterly* (September 1991): 129-142; Peggy Levine Falkenheim, "Moscow and Tokyo: Slow Thaw in Northeast Asia," *World Policy Journal* (Winter 1990-1991): 159-180; and Michael C. Williams, "New Soviet Policy Toward Southeast Asia: Reorientation and Change," *Asian Survey* (April 1991): 364-377.

21. The events of early October are best accessed in *Current Digest of the Post-Soviet Press*, October 27, November 3, and November 10, 1993, and *Daily Report-Central Eurasia*, October 1-6, 1993, all of which contain many first-hand accounts.

22. The United States engaged in a polite debate concerning the nature and structure of the post-Cold War era. Representative contributions include: Zbigniew Brzezinski, *Out of Control: Global Turmoil on the Eve of the 21st Century* (New York: Scribner's, 1993); Samuel P. Huntington, *The Third Wave: Democratization in the Late Twentieth Century* (Norman: University of Oklahoma Press, 1991); Frances Fukuyama, *The End*

*of History and the Last Man* (New York: Free Press, 1992); Graham E. Fuller, *The Democracy Trap: Perils of the Post-Cold War World* (Portsmouth, N.H.: Heinemann, 1990); and Paul M. Kennedy, ed., *Grand Strategy in War and Peace* (New Haven: Yale University Press, 1991). The pages of *Foreign Affairs* and *Foreign Policy*, among others, were filled with articles on the subject.

23. Thomas W. Robinson, "Trends in the Post-Cold War Balance of the Asia-Pacific Region: Implications for Regional Security and Stability," in *The Chinese and Their Future: Beijing, Hong Kong, and Taipei*, ed. Zhiling Lin and Thomas W. Robinson (Lanham, Md.: University Press of America, 1994), chap. 15, has many references to Japanese, Korean, Taiwanese, Southeast Asian, and South Asian policies toward China and Russia.

24. Michael Yahuda, "China and Europe: The Significance of a Secondary Relationship," in *Chinese Foreign Policy: Theory and Practice*, ed. Thomas W. Robinson and David Shambaugh (Oxford: Oxford University Press, 1993), chap. 10; Geoffrey Howe, "Japan and the United States: A European Perspective," *World Today* (July 1992): 126-128; Brian Bridges, "Europe and Korea: Time for a Relationship," *Journal of East Asian Affairs* (Summer-Fall, 1992): 314-333; Brian Bridges, "Japan and Europe: Rebalancing the Relationship," *Asian Survey* (March 1992): 230-245; David Shambaugh, "China and Europe," in *China's Foreign Relations*, ed. Whiting, 101-114; and Roland Frendenstein, "Japan and the New Europe," *World Today* (January 1991): 11-18.

25. Central Asian developments, as concerns Russia, China, and Asia, can be followed conveniently in the *Far Eastern Economic Review*, June 3 and 17, July 15, September 16, and December 20, 1993; May 14 and 21, September 24, October 15, and November 19, 1992; and March 7, June 13, July 25, and August 1, 1991.

# 22 Conclusion

John W. Blaney

It would be difficult to read these essays and not be impressed by the sheer number of unresolved and dangerous problems that exist in the successor states. Those problems cannot be ignored. The Cold War is over, but the region remains important for the United States and others, for both old and new reasons.

### Security Issues: The Nuclear Hydra

As several of our authors assert, the region's strategic threat to the West has diminished, but it could be revived. Moreover, the traditional, self-contained way of handling East-West strategic arms control matters, across nice green negotiating tables in Geneva or Vienna, seems less suited to successor states motivated or influenced by nonstrategic considerations.

For example, the intrinsic logic of Ukraine seeking an independent ICBM force is very weak. Analysis of strategic forces in the successor states suggests that the fragment of the old Soviet Union's strategic rocket forces remaining in Ukraine would be vulnerable to a first-strike from the West or Russia (due mainly to the MIRVing of ICBMs in Ukraine and the lack of launcher mobility and superhardened silos). Why then, would any government even toy with the idea of creating an unstable strategic situation?

The answer, from our essays on Ukraine, would seem to be that for some, Ukraine's concern for strategic stability takes a back seat to broader security worries about Russia. It also follows from our essays that Ukraine may be bluffing with this dangerous "nuclear card" to further its own nation building—in the absence of more normal historical building blocks—and to prompt greater Western economic assistance.

Steven Miller's essay on the expanding dangers of nuclear proliferation shows that the nuclear hydra has grown still other heads in this region of continuing instability. Some of those heads, as Murray Feshbach's chilling observations on nuclear environmental threats make plain, pose health hazards so enormous as to constitute global security issues that the West cannot afford to neglect.

## In Search of Governance

To this worrisome agenda must be added a host of other very serious problems. Internally, political and economic stability problems haunt almost all the successor states, as many of the foregoing essays have made clear. Indeed, the sovereignty of some states, most seriously Ukraine, is under siege. The reasons for instability vary, but one common denominator appears to be poor progress on establishing viable political and economic systems to replace those of the old communist regime. In fact, some successor states, driven by violence or desperation, have attempted to return to authoritarian ways. In this regard, however, it is interesting that none of our authors sees reconstruction of the Soviet system as a viable option. The pieces of the broken-down Rube Goldberg machine that composed the Soviet economy have already started to evolve autonomously. That machine will never fit together again as it did.

Politically, the sense of many of these essays is similar. Even the communists of the region are starting to understand that there can be no going back to the past and no restoration of the Soviet Union or of its hegemonic Communist party. This does not mean, however, that other historically strong forces, especially unbridled Russian nationalism, cannot prevail against nascent democratic movements and bring on new forms of authoritarian rule. Certainly, communists and ultranationalists share the acute sense of loss felt by many Russians at the demise of the Soviet empire; many advocate reclaiming at least some pieces of it, *de facto* if not *de jure*.

## A Pivotal Point

It would also be hard not to recognize in these works the repeated emphasis placed on Russia's basic attitude toward the other successor states as a key determinant of the future of the region. The essays by Starr, Szporluk, Olcott, and Parming stress the importance of Russia accepting the full sovereignty of the other successor states. They also insist that the United States and other countries have an interest in discouraging Russian efforts to reestablish full-blown hegemony throughout the former Soviet Union. Whether those efforts are viewed as Russia's Monroe Doctrine or in Russia's own terms—the country's new neighbors are known in Russia as the "near abroad"—this issue undoubtedly will be sensitive for the foreseeable future. In this regard, it will be interesting to assess the relationship between continuing centrifugal pressures in Russia and sops offered by Moscow's government to Russian nationalism as a means to check Russia's own disintegration. Here, and in analyzing other issues, the insights provided by John Lepingwell and Michael Waller on the attitudes and possible roles of Russia's military and security forces will be useful to recall.

### Shifting International Equilibriums

Looking exogenously, Olcott, Laird, Huttenbach, Stent, Robinson, and others have reminded us that the aftermath of the end of the Soviet Union and ongoing events in the successor states are causing disruptions in the relationships of other powers that will in turn feed back upon the successor states. The effects of Kazakhstan's success or failure at nation building, for example, will ripple throughout that region. Turkey, Iran, and other outside powers are jockeying for position in the Caucasus. The way Germany sees and develops its relationships with the successor states will affect the nature of its relationships with other Western countries. Which path China chooses, in part a response to events in the successor states, will have a profound effect on Asia and the rest of the globe.

In fact, continuing instability in the successor states may be delaying and making more difficult the establishment of a new post-Cold War international order. Such an order presumably would require a clearer multipolar division of influence than is currently the case. Achieving such a clarification seems doubtful, however, until certain issues come closer to resolution. Most important of these is whether Russia will recover from, or even endure, its continuing decline. The potential for new power vacuums—such as the disintegration of Ukraine or other successor states would create—also mitigates against the establishment of stable international equilibriums.

### The Human Factor

Of all the many dynamics examined in this volume, the repeated importance to political change of movements "from below" is one of the most intriguing. It is hoped that the essays by Starr, Parming, and Gfoeller and Blaney illuminated this neglected area of study. Movements of workers, professionals, students, and other citizens have made history in the former Soviet Union; they are worthy of our close attention.

During the Cold War summitry focused largely on improving superpower and regional stability in a bipolar world. Meanwhile, however, many political amateurs and volunteers, working "from below," helped upend that world forever. But how far can political voluntarism carry the people of the successor states?

Hardly an essay in this book does not, in one way or another, point to the human factor as critical to solving the problems facing the successor states. Whether it is Michael Waller's portrait of Russia's thus far unsuccessful attempt to establish a security establishment controlled by civil law, Eugene Lawson's account of certain aspects of Western civilization not shared by the successor states, John Tedstrom's descriptions of a region trying to join the global economy, or any of several treatments of contrasting nation-building efforts—the importance of the people of the successor states developing new ways of thinking and acting is difficult to exaggerate.

Such progress is also very uncertain and frequently opposed. It is a struggle that intensified greatly during Gorbachev's perestroika and continues into the present, involving millions of people. More importantly than any summit, the outcome of this "war" to engage and open minds will largely determine whether the tremendous opportunity of this twentieth-century "window to the West" will be realized or squandered.

Not that the West has all the answers; it does not. But the West can and should work together with the successor states to help replace the institutions of the Soviet command system with more democratic and market-oriented forms that are intrinsically more peaceful. It is clear from these readings that such a partnership will require great patience and open-mindedness on both sides. For the West, this will mean avoiding dealing too exclusively with only the most Westernized individuals of the region and refraining from habitually dividing up interlocutors into "white hats" and "black hats." The "grey hats," like Viktor Chernomyrdin, will play major roles in determining the outcomes of potential partnerships with the West. They must be engaged.

### The Opportunity

With regard to the future, Hardt and Kaiser's economic analysis and the commercial appraisal provided by Eugene Lawson provide some cautious notes of hope upon which to conclude. Both essays are founded on experienced and realistic views about reform and commerce and on the need to relate carefully the design of reform programs and business ventures to political realities. They also recognize that the impacted structural problems of these economies make them sharply different (and harder to diagnose) than either the West's more cyclical economic problems or those faced by developing countries.

Unlike the generally ineffective assistance the West provided in 1992, present efforts appear to be more likely to help forge genuine partnerships with the successor states. In particular, there is growing understanding that reform of macroeconomic policies must be supported by aggressive sectoral and commercial efforts, especially in the energy sector. A partnership here offers the West an alternative to excessive dependency on Middle Eastern energy and the prospect of greater global prosperity in the twenty-first century.

Nevertheless, the way will be fraught with difficulties and dangers. Instead of partnership, many in the successor states and in the West will advocate xenophobia, a return to confrontation, or isolationism. Demigods will continue to proclaim themselves in these troubled lands of the East. They will assign wholesale to outsiders their own shortcomings. They will call hotly for the return of Russia's "rightful" empire. They will readily sacrifice their countrymen to achieve their own ends.

In the West, unbending skeptics will urge a modified containment policy aimed at Russia. They will denounce as naive possibilities for partnership and greater global cooperation, contending that perpetual balance-of-power maneuvering is the best that can be achieved among countries and by mankind. They will warn against assisting the successor states, for fear of aiding potential future enemies, replaying sternly such empty tautologies as "reform in Russia is a Russian problem."

In our increasingly interdependent world, however, reform and nation building in the successor states are our problems as well. Constructive partnerships with these countries can be built without sacrificing our interests or compromising our principles. Indeed, a deepening of relationships with all the successor states presents a singular opportunity, one that will enhance prospects for a twenty-first century less destructive and violent than this one.

# Index

Abkhazia. *See* Georgia
Achalov, Vladislav, 91*n*5
Adygeyskaya. *See* Caucasian states
Aeroflot airline, 41
Afghanistan
  airborne military forces, 78
  Central Asian countries and, 269
  invasion of, 45
  Russia and, 270, 274
  Tajikistan and, 212, 218
Agricultural issues
  land denigration, 138
  privatization of farms, 138
  in Russia, 102-103
Akaev, Askar, 210, 216
Alfa. *See* Committee for State Security
Aliyev, Geydar, 231-232
All-Russian Extraordinary Commission
  for Combating Counterrevolution and Sab-
  otage (VChK or Cheka), 39, 43, 50. *See*
  *also* Committee for State Security (KGB)
American Federation of Labor-Congress
  of International Organizations (AFL-CIO),
  128
Ames, Aldrich, 48
Amoco, 232
Anarchy, 176-177
Andropov, Yuri, 39
Argentina, 196
Armenia. *See also* Caucasian states; Nagorno-Karabakh; Soviet Union
  Azerbaijan and, 20, 67, 230, 231, 232,
  234-236, 265, 268
  earthquake in (1989), 127, 234
  economic issues in, 234, 235
  ethnic issues, 277
  Georgia and, 233
  history of, 232-233
  military in, 58, 65, 67, 69, 75-76*n*28
  Nagorno-Karabakh Self-Defense
    Committee, 69
  nuclear power in, 21
  political issues in, 234, 235-236
  public sphere in, 12
  Russia and, 67
  security and intelligence issues, 50, 51
  Soviet Union and, 233-234
  Turkey and, 20, 233, 236

United States and, 238
Arms. *See* Weaponry
Asia. *See also* individual countries
  political issues, 306
  possible political and economic sce-
    narios, 307-308
  security issues, 306
Asia, Central. *See also* Kazakhstan;
  Kyrgyzstan; Tajikistan; Turkmenistan; Uzbekistan
  Commonwealth of Independent States
    and, 214-215, 218, 269
  cultural aspects of, 208, 209
  economic issues, 210-214, 215, 269,
    277, 278-279
  ethnic issues in, 267, 268, 288
  foreign policies of, 214-218, 269
  human rights issues, 220
  independence of, 208, 209, 214, 221,
    221*n*1, 268
  map of, 209
  military in, 62-63, 64-65, 70-71, 72, 73,
    215, 221
  nation building by, 214
  nationalism in, 208, 209, 265
  natural resources in, 211-214
  People's Republic of China, 294, 303,
    304-305
  political issues in, 217-221, 265, 277
  Russia and, 269, 271, 272, 277
  Soviet Union and, 210-211, 268, 281
Azerbaijan. *See also* Caucasian states; Nagorno-Karabakh; Soviet Union
  Armenia and, 20, 67, 230, 231, 232,
  234-235, 265, 268
  economic issues in, 232
  ethnic issues in, 224, 229, 230-231,
    232, 277
  Islam in, 224, 229
  military in, 58, 64, 67-68, 69, 76*n*31,
    230-231, 232
  Nagorno-Karabakh, 67, 69
  oil industry in, 10, 230, 231, 232, 270,
    276
  political issues in, 229, 230-232, 277
  press gangs, 64, 75*n*18
  Russia and, 232
  security and intelligence issues, 59

separatist movements in, 231-232
Soviet Union and, 229

Bacterial warfare, 137
Bahriany, Ivan, 188
Bakatin, Vadim, 39, 40, 44, 50, 52-53
Baku, 234, 236. *See also* Azerbaijan
Balance of power. *See* Power, balance of
Baltic Sea States, Council of, 256, 277
Baltic states. *See also* Estonia; Latvia;
Lithuania; Soviet Union
Committee for State Security (KGB),
40
definition of, 240
de-Sovietization, 240
economic issues, 240, 241, 269, 272
exiles, 250-252, 261*n*16
foreign relations, 254, 260
Germany and, 260
independence movement in, 70, 253,
259, 260, 268
map of, 242
military in, 59-60, 62, 65, 67, 70, 73,
256, 276
Molotov-Ribbentrop Pact of 1939,
245, 258
public sphere in, 11, 12
Russia and, 59, 74*n*4, 253, 256-259,
260, 271-272, 276
security and intelligence issues, 50
Soviet Union and, 253, 256
Stalinization of, 200
violence in (1991), 131
Western countries and, 254
Bandera, Stepan, 189
Banking issues, 147-148, 149, 153, 154
Belarus. *See also* Soviet Union
Chernobyl nuclear accident, 135
ethnic issues of, 163
labor issues in, 125, 128-129, 130, 132
military in, 61, 62, 64, 65, 71-72, 73,
75*n*21
nationalism in, 268
nuclear power in, 4, 18, 19, 21, 24, 33-
34
Russia, 71
security and intelligence issues, 50, 51,
59
Belgium, 47
Bentsen, Lloyd, 153
BfV. *See* Federal Office for the Protection
of the Constitution
Bilateral Investment Treaty (United
States-Russia), 150
Black Sea Fleet (Ukraine), 71, 75*n*21, 190,
205
Bolshevik revolution, 184, 188
Bosnia, 237

Brazauskas, Algirdas, 241, 251, 259. *See
also* Lithuania
Brezhnev, Leonid, 38
British Petroleum, 232
Bulgaria, 43
Burlakov, Matvei, 85
Bush, George, 200
Business issues. *See also* Trade
corporatization, 157*n*24
employment, 118
espionage and, 47-48, 50-51
ideal environment, 115-116
in Russia, 101-102, 113-122, 123*n*18

Carpathian union, 277
Caucasian states. *See also* Armenia; Azer-
baijan; Georgia
control of, 239
ethnic issues, 224-226, 267
military in, 68-70, 73, 87
nationalism in, 265, 268
political issues, 277
Russia and, 237-238, 269, 271
Soviet Union and, 223-225
United States and, 223, 237-239
Ceausescu, Nicolae, 295
Central Asia. *See* Asia, Central
Chautauga Conference, 244
Checheno-Ingushetiya. *See* Caucasian
states
Chechnya
military conflict in, 81, 87-88, 89, 91,
93*n*46
Russian attitudes toward, 81
Cheka. *See* All-Russian Extraordinary
Commission for Combating Counterrevo-
lution and Sabotage
Chekism. *See* Repression
Chelyabinsk nuclear accidents, 136
Chemicals. *See* Pollution
Cherkesov, Viktor, 41
Chernobyl nuclear accident, 135-136,
174, 197, 289
Chernomyrdin, Viktor, 83, 119, 145, 286,
317
Chevron, 151
Chile, 271
China. *See* People's Republic of China
Chitiny, 87
Chornovil, Viacheslav, 201, 205. *See also*
Rukh movement
Christopher, Warren, 155
CIS. *See* Commonwealth of Independent
States
Clinton, Bill, 257, 258-259
Coal industry, 136, 212
Cold War. *See also* Containment policies
Eastern expansion during, 32
end of, 31-32, 36-37, 78, 184

Dudayev, Dzhokar, 87. *See also* Chechnya
Dzerzhinsky, Feliks, 39, 40

Economic issues. *See also* Trade; individual countries
  communism and, 8-9, 13
  debt swaps, 152, 205
  global trends, 305-308
  nationalism and, 266
  post-World Wars I and II, 191-192
  ruble and, 203, 204, 213, 214, 266
Einseln, Alexander, 252
Elchibey, Abulfez, 69, 230-231, 238. *See also* Azerbaijan
Engels, Friedrich, 8
Environmental issues. *See also* Pollution
  debt-for-nature swaps, 152
  end of Soviet Union and, 3, 14
  Germany and, 287, 289
  global, 306, 315
  Soviet Union successor states and, 134-141
  World environmental conference, 256
Espionage
  Committee for State Security (KGB), 44
  External Intelligence Service (SVR), 45-46, 47, 48
  Federal Counterintelligence Service (FSK), 48
  GRU, 47, 48
  Russia, 47-49
  technical and industrial, 48-49
Estonia. *See also* Soviet Union
  boundary issues, 275
  Congress of Estonia, 246-249
  economic issues, 195$n$17, 240, 241, 252-253, 268-269
  ethnic issues in, 253, 254, 267
  exiles and international assistance to, 250, 252-253
  foreign policy of, 255-259, 260
  Hirve Park (Tallinn) demonstration, 245, 250
  independence of, 246-249, 254-256
  military in, 58, 65, 67, 74$n$11, 254, 256-257
  as a nation-state, 185
  nuclear power in, 21
  oil industry in, 252
  political issues, 240-241, 243, 244, 245, 252, 253, 259-260
  Russia and, 241, 253, 254, 256-257, 258-259, 271
  security and intelligence issues, 43, 50
  Soviet Union and, 254
  Western nations and, 246, 249
Ethnic issues. *See also* individual countries

Caucasian states, 69, 224, 231, 253
Central Asia, 70-71, 212
  end of Cold War and, 32
  end of Soviet Union and, 2, 4, 69
  in Germany, 287-289
  labor unions and, 133
  military and, 62, 69, 87
Eurasia. *See* Soviet Union successor states
Europe
  People's Republic of China and, 304
  security environment of, 31, 280, 284-285, 292
  United States and, 292
  widening of, 32
Europe, Central, 31-32, 146, 150, 151
Europe, Council of. *See* Council of Europe
Europe, Eastern
  economy of, 3, 32
  espionage in, 45-46
  ethnic conflicts in, 32
  North Atlantic Treaty Organization and, 82
  political systems of, 31-32
  revolutions in 1989-1990, 295
  Soviet Union and, 259
  Ukraine and, 181
Europe, Western. *See also* Western countries
  economy of, 3, 31
  espionage in, 46
  political systems of, 31, 32-33, 37
  unification of, 1, 192
European Community
  Baltic states and, 255
  citizenship laws of, 275
  end of Soviet Union and, 1-2
  Energy Charter, 151
  Germany and, 285
  support of Abulfez Elchibey, 232
  support of Eastern Europe, 146
European Energy Charter, 150, 151, 276
European Union, 292
Exiles, 250-252
Exim. *See* Export-Import Bank
Export-Import Bank (Exim), 122
External Intelligence Service (SVR; Russia), 43, 44-46, 47, 48, 49, 51

FAPSI (Federalnoye agentsvo pravitelstvennoy sviazi i informatsiy). *See* Federal Agency for Government Communications and Information
Fascism, 307
Federal Agency for Government Communications and Information (FAPSI; Russia), 41-42
Federal Border Service (Russia), 42

Federal Counterintelligence Service
(FSK; Russia), 41, 43, 47, 48, 51, 87-88
Federalnaya sluzhba kontrrazvedki
(FSK). *See* Federal Counterintelligence
Service
Federalnoye agentsvo pravitelstvennoy
sviazi i informatsiy (FAPSI). *See* Federal
Agency for Government Communications and Information
Federal Office for the Protection of the
Constitution (BfV; Germany), 46-47
Federation of Independent Trade Unions
of Russia, 132
Fedorov, Boris, 145
Felgengauer, Pavel, 89-90
Finland, 47, 184, 241, 252
Fisheries, 138
Food contamination, 138
Forestry, 138
France, 47, 196, 271
Friendship Treaty (Germany-Soviet
Union-Russia), 284
FSK (Federalnaya sluzhba
kontrrazvedki). *See* Federal Counterintelligence Service
FSU, 299

G-7. *See* Group of Seven
Gaidar, Yegor, 45, 119, 203, 286
Galicia-Volhynia, 199
Gamsakhurdia, Zviad, 68, 226, 227, 228
Gas. *See* Oil and gas industry
GATT. *See* General Agreement on Tariffs
and Trade
Gauck, Joachim, 46
General Agreement on Tariffs and Trade
(GATT), 3, 4, 150, 153
Genscher, Hans-Dietrich, 283-284
Georgia. *See also* Caucasian states;
Shevardnadze, Eduard; Soviet Union
Abkhazian territories, 66, 68, 275
Commonwealth of Independent States
and, 67
economic issues in, 228
ethnic issues in, 224, 225-229, 265, 268
foreign policies of, 227-228
history of, 225
independence movement in, 69, 225
Islam in, 225, 226
military in, 58, 65, 66, 67-68, 69, 227,
276
nationalism in, 226-227, 234
nuclear power in, 21
political issues in, 228-229
public sphere in, 12
Russia and, 276
security and intelligence issues, 50, 51,
59
separatism in, 227

United States and, 238
Germany
Baltic states and, 260
economic issues, 286, 291-292
espionage in, 47
ethnic issues in, 287-290
foreign policy of, 280, 285
military in, 58, 85, 285, 287
nuclear proliferation and, 289-290
political issues in, 292
refugees into, 286, 287-288, 289, 291
Russia and, 280-292
security and intelligence issues, 46-47
Soviet Union and, 285
Soviet Union successor states and,
280-292
troop withdrawals from, 286-287
Ukraine and, 290-291
unification of, 282, 283, 285, 286-287
Germany, East, 46, 47, 286, 287, 295
Germany, West, 285
Gerold, Yuri, 128
Gillette, Michael, 153
Glasnost, 9, 38, 233, 242
Glavnoye upravleniye okhrany (GUO).
*See* Main Guard Administration
Golikov, Vyacheslav, 128
Golushko, Nikolai, 41
Gorbachev, Mikhail. *See also* Glasnost;
Perestroika; Soviet Union
1991 coup, 173-174, 198
Baltic states and, 250, 258
coal strike of 1989, 126, 127
Committee for State Security (KGB)
and, 38
Eastern Europe and, 295
German unification and, 283
glasnost and, 9
military and, 78
mistakes of, 7, 30, 129, 268
People's Republic of China and, 300
perestroika and, 7-8, 10-11
preservation of union, 30, 200
reforms of, 8, 13, 97, 98, 126
Russian regions and, 166-167, 268
support of, 58
Grachev, Pavel, 42, 78-80, 81, 82-83, 84-
86, 88, 89
Great Britain, 196, 271
Gromov, Boris, 88
Group of Seven countries (G-7)
Baltic states and, 252-253, 257, 258
Germany and, 284, 286, 292
Russia and, 117, 145-146, 153-154,
258, 284, 286, 298
Soviet Union successor states and, 292
Ukraine and, 180
GRU, 46, 47, 48

GUO (Glavnoye upravleniye okhrany).
See Main Guard Administration
Guseinov, Surat, 231, 232
Gustafson, Thane, 113, 115

Handke, Peter, 270
Hansson, Ardo, 253
Hapsburg Empire, 184
Hauptverwaltung Aufklarung (Germany), 47
Health issues, 134-141, 146-147
Heritage Societies (Estonia), 245
Honcharenko, Oleksander, 202
Hrushevsky, Mykhailo, 199, 202
Hungary, 146, 148, 188, 269

IAEA. See International Atomic Energy Agency
Iliac (Tsar), 201
IMF. See International Monetary Fund
Independent Miners' Union (IMU; Soviet Union), 128, 129-131, 132
India, 196, 278
Ingushetia, 87
Interlinked System for Recognizing Enemies (SOUD; Soviet Union), 46
International Atomic Energy Agency (IAEA), 21, 22
International Committee for Reform and Cooperation, 150
International Monetary Fund (IMF), 265, 266, 274
Investment in Russia, 114-115, 122, 150-152, 278
Iran, 26, 225, 232, 236, 269, 277
Islam. See Muslims

Japan, 303, 304
Jiang Zemin, 301

Kabardino-Balkarskaya. See Caucasian states
Kalashnikov (Russia), 117
Kaliningrad (Russia), 289
Kalmytskaya. See Caucasian states
Karachayevo-Cherkesskaya. See Caucasian states
Karamzin, Nikolai, 199
Karimov, Islam, 214, 216, 217-218
Karkarashvili, Giorgy, 68
Kazakhstan. See also Asia, Central; Soviet Union
    boundary issues in, 275
    economic issues in, 147, 151, 212-214, 216, 220-221, 269-270, 278, 279
    ethnic issues in, 269, 275, 279, 287
    gold fields in, 213-214
    independence of, 210
    Islam in, 220

labor issues in, 125, 130, 132
military in, 64, 65, 75n21, 210, 221
nuclear power in, 4, 18, 19, 21, 24, 25, 26, 33-34, 136
oil industry in, 151, 152, 156n18, 213, 276
political issues in, 216, 217, 219-220, 277, 316
Russia and, 178, 213, 214, 220-221, 272
security and intelligence issues, 50-51
Soviet Union and, 213
United States and, 279
Kelam, Tunne, 245
KGB. See Committee for State Security
Khasbulatov, Ruslan, 81
Khmelnitsky, Bogdan, 201
Khodzhaly massacre, 230
Kholodov, Dmitry, 85
Khrushchev, Nikita, 82-83, 188
Kiev. See Ukraine
Kievan Rus, 199. See also Russia; Ukraine
Kinkel, Klaus, 286
Kirkland, Lane, 128
Kirpichenko, Vadim, 45
Kitovani, Tengiz, 68
Kliuchevsky, Vasily, 199
Kohl, Helmut
    German unification, 283
    Russia and, 284, 286
    Soviet Union and, 47, 200
    Ukraine and, 290, 291
Kokoshin, Andrei, 83
Korea, South, 269, 304
Kozyrev, Andrei, 180, 227, 258, 275. See also Russia
Kravchuk, Leonid M. See also Ukraine
    coup of August 1991, 176
    defeat of, 180
    foreign policy of, 203, 205
    Germany and, 290
    nationalism of, 185-186, 189, 191, 201-202, 203
    popularity of, 207n8
    Rukh and, 174-175, 190
    Russia and, 200
Kryuchkov, Vladimir, 45, 52
Kuchma, Leonid. See also Ukraine
    German-Ukrainian ties, 291
    nationalism of, 189
    Russia and, 204, 205, 206
    Ukrainian reforms of, 71, 179-180, 190, 201
Kurile Islands. See Japan
Kuznetsov, E., 219
Kyrgyzstan. See also Asia, Central; Soviet Union
    economic issues in, 211, 212-213, 216, 221, 269, 270, 279
    emigration from, 219

324    Index

aid for, 234-235
as Christian-Muslim conflict, 227
effects of, 232
Georgia and, 228
political issues and, 229-231, 233-234, 236
United States and, 234-235, 238
Nation building
in Central Asia, 214, 316
democracy and, 268
economic issues and, 266
ethnicity and, 163
foreign policy and, 196, 214
in Georgia, 226-227
in Russia, 163-164, 174, 179, 181, 206
security and, 176-177
in the Soviet Union successor states, 267-269, 273-279
in Ukraine, 173-181, 196-206
Nation-states
builders of, 186-187
collapse of empires and, 184-185, 193
enemies of, 186
heroic period and founding myth of, 185-186
ideology and, 190, 193, 195n16
post-World Wars I and II, 191-192
Ukraine, 185-193
National Security Council, 200
Nationalism
democracy in, 268
in Estonia, 247, 249
in Georgia, 226
in Russia, 119, 143, 144, 149, 165, 171, 173, 179, 253, 270-272, 281, 315, 316
in the Soviet Union, 50, 190, 244
in the Soviet Union successor states, 265-267, 268
in Ukraine, 188, 189-190, 191, 193, 198, 201, 205, 206
NATO. *See* North Atlantic Treaty Organization
Nazarbaev, Nursultan, 216, 217, 220-221
Nazis, 197, 288. *See also* World Wars I and II
Nazi-Soviet Pact of 1939, 280
Nehru, Jawaharlal, 196
Nemtsov, Boris, 145
Netherlands, 47
*New York Times,* 255
Newly independent states (NIS). *See* Soviet Union successor states
NIS (newly independent states). *See* Soviet Union successor states
Niyazov, Saparmurad, 211, 215, 219
Nizhny Novgorod, 108
Nonproliferation Treaty (NPT), 19, 21, 35, 291
Nordic Investment Bank, 269

North American Free Trade Agreement (NAFTA), 3-4
North Atlantic Cooperation Council (NACC), 255, 284
North Atlantic Treaty Organization (NATO)
Baltic states and, 255, 256, 257, 260
collapse of Soviet Union and, 1
Commonwealth of Independent States and, 284
Germany and, 282, 283, 285
Gorbachev, Mikhail and, 284
membership in, 1, 59-60, 74n5, 82
mission of, 1
partnership of peace, 284-285
Russia and, 33, 101, 284-285
North Ossetia, 87
Northern Islands. *See* Japan
Norway, 47
NPT. *See* Nonproliferation Treaty
Nuclear issues. *See also* individual countries
Chernobyl nuclear accident, 135
custodial systems for, 18-20, 23-24, 25-26, 28n12, 28-29n13, 31, 34
export controls, 21
former Soviet Union, 4, 17-27, 33-34
illegal usage and terrorism, 24, 25, 28n9, 34
proliferation and nonproliferation, 25-27, 30, 35
reactor fuel and fissile material, 18-19, 21-22, 28n8
safeguards, 21, 22, 34
Strategic Rocket Forces, 75n21
unsafeguarded reactors, 21-22
Western countries' objectives, 31

Oil and gas industry
in Baltic states, 252
in Caucasian states, 10, 230, 231, 232, 270
in Central Asia, 151, 211, 212, 270, 276
investment in, 151-152
in Russia, 10, 120-121, 151, 204
in Ukraine, 204, 270
United States and, 238, 276
Western consortium, 232
Operation Desert Storm. *See* Persian Gulf War
Overseas Private Investment Corporation (OPIC), 278
Ossetia, 226, 227. *See also* Caucasian states
Ottoman Empire, 184

Parek, Lagle, 245, 248
Paris Club, 117, 283